EX LIB

VINTAGE **CLASSICS**

LOU SULLIVAN

Louis Graydon Sullivan (1951-91) was a writer, activist, typesetter, trans historian, and queer revolutionary. The Gay People's Union featured Sullivan's earliest writings in their newsletter including the now widely-quoted 'A Transvestite Answers a Feminist'. Though through his transition, many medical professionals he met had never heard of a female-to-gay-male, Sullivan resisted lying about his sexuality, a commitment which became a major aspect of his activism and legacy. Sullivan published *Information for the FTM* (a practical guidebook) and organized the first peer-support group for trans men. When Sullivan was diagnosed with HIV, he decided two main goals: to publish a biography of Jack Bee Garland and to publish his own diaries. He was only able to complete the former in his lifetime. Sullivan left 8.4 cubic feet of archival material from his life and studies to the GLBT Historical Society, of which he was a founding member.

Ellis Martin works with digital derivatives in the interstice of art and archive. He holds a BA in Visual and Critical Studies from Mills College. His short films have screened at *San Francisco Transgender Film Festival* and *Trans Stellar Film Festival*.

Zach Ozma is a poet, potter, and social practice artist. Ozma received a BFA in Community Arts from California College of the Arts in Oakland. He lives and works in Philadelphia and is the author of *BLACK DOG DRINKING FROM AN OUTDOOR POOL* (Sibling Rivalry Press, 2019).

LOU SULLIVAN

Youngman

Selected Diaries 1961-91

EDITED AND SELECTED BY
Ellis Martin and Zach Ozma

VINTAGE

1 3 5 7 9 10 8 6 4 2

Vintage is part of the Penguin Random House group of companies whose addresses can be found at global.penguinrandomhouse.com

Penguin
Random House
UK

First published in Great Britain by Vintage Classics in 2021
First published by Nightboat Books in New York, NY 2019
Nightboat edition edited and designed by Timeless,
Infinite Light in Oakland, CA 2019

The editors would like to thank the following individuals who supported the publication of this book: Kazim Ali, Anonymous, Jean C. Ballantyne, Photios Giovanis, Amanda Greenberger, Anne Marie Macari, Elizabeth Motika, Benjamin Taylor, Jerrie Whitfield, Richard Motika. They gratefully acknowledge the Topanga Fund, which is dedicated to promoting the arts and literature of California.

penguin.co.uk/vintage

A CIP catalogue record for this book
is available from the British Library

ISBN 9781784877347

Printed and bound in Great Britain by Clays Ltd, Elcograf S.p.A.

The authorised representative in the EEA is Penguin Random House
Ireland, Morrison Chambers, 32 Nassau Street, Dublin D02 YH68

Contents

'My Own Interpretation of Happiness'
An Introduction to the Journals of Lou Sullivan

by Susan Stryker

Words cannot adequately express how excited (excited!) I am that Lou Sullivan's journals are finally being published.

I never met Lou in the flesh, but for nearly 30 years he's occupied a huge place in my life, both as a fellow trans person as well as an historian of LGBTQ+ experience and a theorist of gender. I have been gratified to see how many other people have been similarly inspired by the life Lou led and the legacy he left. I'm over the moon that Ellis Martin and Zach Ozma have finally brought his words—in all their vitality, humor, earnestness, heartache, sexiness, fierceness, and unflinching honesty—to an audience that is sure to appreciate them as much as I (and they) clearly do.

I'd seen Lou's book, *Information for the Female-to-Male Crossdresser and Transsexual*, back in the day, circa 1990, on the same bookstore shelves in San Francisco's Castro and Mission neighborhoods where I was cruising for less-medical, more-community-based 411 on what was then called male-to-female transsexualism. Lou's book wasn't the one I was personally looking for as I plotted my own social gender transition, but I was glad it was out there for all the former-butches-becoming-guys I had met through the Bay Area's leather community. There was a groundswell of attention to "FTM" and transmasculine issues in the circles I was moving in around that time—some of it gorgeously documented in the photographer Catherine Opie's still-magnificent *Being and Having* portrait series—but a real dearth of information about how the trans experience was "different for guys" at the dawn of the contemporary transgender scene. Lou was ahead of that curve, by more than a decade, in pulling together informational resources for what was then a tiny community of self-identified trans men.

I remember chatting with a guy named Shane at a play party in a dungeon on 14th Street who told me how a bunch of trans men were taking care of Lou, who was "pretty sick"—common code words for being in the terminal stages of AIDS—and me saying that I'd like to meet him if there was a chance. Shane said Lou wasn't meeting new people anymore, that it was just too much for him to deal with. I shrugged. Oh, well. So it goes.

It's hard to convey to those who have come of age since the retroviral cocktails appeared in the mid-90s just how devastating the AIDS epidemic was before that, how shell-shocked we were, how inured we had become to the steady drumbeat of premature death as people dropped, seemingly daily, around those of us who would survive. To get some sense of scale, read the obituaries for these years in the *Bay Area Reporter*, which are available online. Back then, if you wanted to mourn somebody you needed to take a number and get in line. Losing Lou so early was a tragedy, but a routine one. It's appalling what one can get used to and come to consider normal.

Not too long after that dungeon conversation, sometime in 1991, I showed up at what was then still called the Gay and Lesbian Historical Society—the B and T wouldn't be appended for another half-decade. I announced to the regulars at the then-five-year-old organization that I was in the process of both gender-transition and finishing my Ph.D. in U.S. History at UC Berkeley, and that as a soon-to-be-public trans woman I had somewhat less than a snowball's chance in hell of getting an academic job, and wanted to immerse myself in community-based history, focusing on transgender history. The first words out of the mouth of archivist Willie Walker, the organization's principal co-founder, were "Great! One of our founding members, Lou Sullivan, died recently, and you can learn to be an archivist by processing his personal papers and preparing them for public use." And so I did.

Lou's papers are a historically significant body of materials that documents the emergence of a national transmasculine community, and I'm forever honored to have been the one to put them in order and to write the finding aid that still provides guidance for researchers seeking to access their content. His journals are the crown jewels of that treasure trove—they intimately chronicle his 30-year evolution from ten-year-old Catholic schoolgirl in Milwaukee's suburbs to gay man dying of AIDS in San Francisco, and offer one of the most complete, and most compelling, records of a trans life ever to have been produced.

In 1991, as I was winding down my public life as a young man and starting a more authentic one as a woman, Lou was my posthumous boon companion. Reading his journals was an ongoing compare-and-contrast exercise as I measured my self-perceptions and experiences as a trans lesbian against his as a gay trans man. Reading Lou's words again now, for the first time in many years, takes me back to when I first fell in love with him, watching him grow up and discover himself—his childhood Beatlemania, his boy craziness, his sex fantasies and teenage guilt, his countercultural tendencies and political awakening, his passion for drag queens and rock and roll, his growing sense of being kinky and trans and having no language for it. Lou, writing in isolation but reaching boldly for the deep truth of his own self-knowledge, forged a unique language for his transness that still speaks profoundly to me today.

At age 13, Lou wrote "I wanna look like what I am but don't know what someone like me looks like. I mean, when people look at me I want them to think—there's one of those people…that has their own interpretation of happiness. That's what I am." Those words have stayed with me for decades, and in the intervening years I have still found no better way of expressing what it means to be trans. I see in them the suggestion that we are primarily our own "interpretation of happiness" and only secondarily the "men" or "women" we were assigned to be, or the people we became.

Sullivan, I would go so far as to say, offers essentially the same insight into being trans as that offered by the psychoanalytic theorist Jacques Lacan. Lacan considered transsexuality to represent what he called a *sinthome:* a uniquely personal, idiosyncratic manner of braiding together the psychical registers of the Imaginary (the inner realm of images and the identifications we attach to them), the Symbolic (the social realm of language and representation), and the Real (that which is, whether one wishes it to be or not). For Lacan, every "I" is the symptom—or in Old French, the *sinthome,* which Lacan turns into a pun to suggest that our symptomatic subjectivities are a "synthesis" that becomes our "home"—of a successful attempt to weave those three rings of reality together into a stable pattern and thereby to become a non-psychotic subject. This, for Lacan, is what it means to be a person. The transgender subject is a kind of person who, for Lacan (and, I would argue, for Lou Sullivan) similarly succeeds at the task of becoming a viable, non-psychotic subject by entwining the Imaginary, Symbolic, and Real—but with a twist. Because our Imaginary identifications are different from what the Symbolic says our bodies are supposed to mean, we trans folks bring our identities into alignment with the Real by (re)writing them into our flesh; in doing so we come to appear to others as what might be called an "interpretation of our own happiness" that makes our living feel worthwhile. Lou intuited all that without ever having read a lick of Lacan or of poststructuralist gender theory; he died, in fact, just as Judith Butler's *Gender Trouble* was shifting the paradigm to conceptualize gender as something we do, rather than something we are.

Lou had an amazing career. He never went to college, and worked most of his adult life as an administrative assistant, though toward the end he'd gone into business for himself as a freelance digital editor and publisher. The amazing part was not what he did for money, but what he did with the rest of his time. He networked ceaselessly among trans folks, corresponded with hundreds of people around the world, and played a significant role in forging a broader trans community. He founded organizations. He researched and wrote about trans history, including the book-length biography *From Female to Male: The Life of Jack Bee Garland.* He advocated on behalf of trans people with health-care providers, and, after having been denied medical services because he was open about identifying as a gay rather than heterosexual man, persuaded the doctors and psychiatrists that one could in fact be both gay and trans, as he was. He volunteered for clinical trials for AIDS drugs, and took a perverse pride in saying that he was proud to die as a gay man, even though authorities had said he couldn't live as one. And he journaled, beautifully and purposefully, with a growing sense that he wanted his journals to be published.

I first tried to posthumously publish Lou's journals in the early 1990s, but that was sadly not to be. A small press was indeed interested back then, but wanted to publish only excerpts, and the advance they offered me simply wasn't enough to cover my costs for transcribing and editing hundreds of pages of handwritten script down into something publishable. I was perpetually un- or under-employed in those days—job discrimination rooted in transphobia is no joke—so I settled for writing a quick little article about Lou, "Portrait of a Transfag Drag Hag as a Young Man," and moved on to find other ways of making a living.

Publishing Lou's journals was still a back burner project for me years later, when a young trans history grad student named Brice D. Smith came along, eager to work on Sullivan, and I was only too eager to pass the torch I'd long been carrying. It felt good and right to step back and let go so that others could carry Lou's legacy forward. It's warmed my heart to see Lou's story find its way to audiences hungry to hear it. Brice's dissertation became a biography, *Daring to Be a Man Among Men,* and soon, perhaps, will become a feature film. Sean Dorsey Dance Company produced a beautiful original work called *Uncovered: The Diary Project,* based on Lou's journals. The filmmaker Rhys Ernst has made an experimental short about Lou, as well as a mini documentary about him for the web series *We've Been Around.* And now, at last, a significant portion of the journals are finally seeing print.

Those who knew Lou or knew of his public career will undoubtedly appreciate the intimate portrait that emerges here, painted in his own words, that shows sides of him most people never had a chance to see. And those who are new to Lou? Get ready to meet a great soul.

Editors' Note

by Ellis Martin and Zach Ozma

Toward the end of his life, Lou Sullivan began editing his journals for publication, a task he was unable to complete, writing, "I fear it will never be done after I am dead. Stiff enough task for me, let alone one unfamiliar with a phenomenon such as myself." As editors, guided by Sullivan's own impulse to make his writing public, we steeped ourselves in his diaries and archive.

Our goal was to become fluent in Sullivan's desires and voice, in order to shape an edited volume that approaches the choices we imagine he might have made. We traced Sullivan's early archival impulses, his childhood literary aspirations, and the process of writing the biography of Jack Bee Garland, who lived as a man in San Francisco at the turn of the century.

We began with 24 journals, each densely packed with Sullivan's slanting cursive, some with additional sheets, newspaper clippings, and photographs glued, taped, or stapled-in. We sat in the History Center at the San Francisco Public Library, where his diaries were on loan for a time. Some of the journals literally overflowed. We opened his file folders with a careful, nervous touch; slow as with a new lover. We were finding Sullivan just as—when looking for proof of a man like himself in library archives—he found Jack Garland.

Afterwards, we would emerge from the archive, to touch ground in San Francisco in 2017, acutely aware of all the San Franciscos layered between Sullivan and ourselves, between Sullivan and Garland.

Considering the depth of Sullivan's informal, autobiographical writings, focusing the scope of our work was a formidable task. Sullivan's life as an activist and a publicly gay trans man has been well-documented. We chose instead to prioritize the intangibles of Sullivan's San Francisco, tracing his worldly pleasures and ephemeral expressions of identity formed alongside his queer community of family, friends, and lovers. We intend these narratives to counter flattened portrayals of trans experience and to illuminate the personal, lascivious, quotidian, poetic, and romantic aspects of his archive.

As editors, our own visual art practices shaped our approach to this project. One of us brought a social practice informed by embodiment theory and neoclassical gay imagery. The other offered archival work (digitization projects) steeped in homoeroticism. Cross-genre editors for a cross-genre writer. We worked as Sullivan did, bringing historical materials into our living spaces. Photographing each page of each diary for transcription, we began to understand the diaries as a story as well as an archive—a record of a full and complex life.

We uncovered what kind of book we were assembling together from the passages that made each of us spark. Our views, priorities, and fantasies inevitably shaped this iteration of Lou's story: our contemporary breath touched pages that have lived in the archives for nearly 30 years. During this process, we experienced a tension between our dedication to the particulars of Sullivan's writing and our impulse to shape an elegant, readable representation of his life. As the diaries become more available, we hope this collection stands up as a gesture to a moment in time, to us, to our understandings of Lou Sullivan, to our youth and editorial jouissance, to the future. From the raw material of Sullivan's diaries we have added another tangible object to his archive, a touchstone.

The text begins with Sullivan's very first diary entry. His earliest journals both give perspective on his lifelong themes, as well as his development as a writer and thinker. However, his writings as an adult are our primary focus for this book.

Throughout the diaries, Sullivan most frequently organized the periods of his life by his domestic spaces, usually referring to his homes by their street names. We borrowed this approach as a structuring principle for our chapters.

The diaries are presented in chronological order. We removed the dates of individual entries to improve readability and resonance of the text as an ongoing narrative.

We were compelled by the ways in which Sullivan's language evolved throughout his life, from his Dylan-inspired shortening of words (e.g., singin) to his evolving use of transvestite and transsexual, to the glyph ✦, his plus sign-ampersand hybrid. We have attempted to preserve Sullivan's particular (and at times peculiar) modes of language and punctuation. In part to honor him, and in part because some of his phrasing feels strikingly contemporary (e.g., "I'll prob'ly end up in COLLEGE. Ugh").

The diaries follow Sullivan as he worked to refine and articulate his views of gender and sexuality throughout his life, actualizing an identity as a gay trans man for which he found few models. Sullivan wrote frequently about his sexual encounters, in these moments recalling not only the form and actions of the scene but reliving it in luscious texture. He reveled in male beauty, equally favoring the soft tufts of hair on a man's cheek and the charged atmosphere of a jerk-off club. We wanted to preserve Sullivan's radical openness about his intimate life, while respecting the privacy of his three long-term romantic partners. For this reason, we abbreviated the names of these three by using their first initials.

We chose to illuminate the key people, places, organizations, and personal idiosyncrasies, such as pet-naming conventions that are central to Sullivan's life, in a glossary at the end of the volume. We envision this glossary as working to establish more context around Sullivan's diaries and the evolving queer world he lived in and co-created.

Dedicated to preserving and sharing knowledge, Sullivan frequently gave interviews regarding his experiences as an HIV+ gay trans man. Sullivan also journaled about his health and transition, reflecting the private side of his activism. As such, there are instances of medically-inaccurate information in the diaries. For example, when Sullivan writes, "I have AIDS," he was using the available terminology at a moment when HIV and AIDS had not been fully distinguished from one another. Similarly, Sullivan describes the effects of testosterone in ways no longer considered accurate. Please reference contemporary sources for up-to-date information.

Sullivan's longing for—and lack of—role models repeatedly manifests throughout his diaries. As such, this text can be challenging and at times painful. Responding to the problem of examining archival work in the present day, we shaped the text to position Sullivan in his sociopolitical context while avoiding needlessly recapitulating violent language. We chose to preserve excerpts that include instances of classism, misgendering, misogyny, racism, and stigmatized views of substance use when they were vital to understanding Sullivan's worldview, including his self-understanding. We wish to extend Sullivan's role as a welcoming mentor into the 21ˢᵗ Century while acknowledging his dimensionality and his flaws.

This book encompasses only a small fraction of the writing that Sullivan left in his archive. Our desire is that someday soon the diaries will be scanned and made more fully accessible in a digital archive. In the meantime, we hope this volume feels like a posthumous collaboration with Sullivan.

Much like Sullivan's, our text developed in a series of interior spaces. We worked in bedrooms and in studio apartments; at residencies and on airplanes. We worked long distance, leaving notes for each other in shared spreadsheets: "sexual revery," "Catholic overtones," "Bob Dylan," and "we have to allow him space to breathe in his own story."

This book is an offering. It is a call to experience one person's queer history as a way to ground yourself in the present, as much as it calls to Lou's ashes in the Pacific Ocean. It is proof that queer histories aren't isolated in the past, but instead touch the current moment. It is the surprise you feel when, reaching out for a lover's chest in the dark, you find a thin gold chain around their neck.

Several people have been critical in shaping this work: thank you to Zoe Tuck (for the glowing impetus), Rebekah Edwards (for connecting us to each other via Lou), Julian Carter (a friend in Lou scholarship), Julian Shendelman (for transcription and your quiet help framing this work), Jamie Di Nicola (a fellow son of Lou),

Mars Hobrecker (for wrapping Lou in the most beautiful bow),
Susan Stryker (for cracking open the archive and introducing us all
to Lou), Brice D. Smith (for your comprehensive Sullivan biography),
Julian Talamantez Brolaski and Meg Pendoley (for the proof),
The Painted Bride Art Center (for our first time putting Lou on a
pedestal), William Way LGBT Community Center (for our first
time taking Lou out on the town), GLBT Historical Society (for
your continued support of, and care for, the Lou Sullivan Papers, in
regard to this project and beyond). An exuberant thank you to Andrea
Abi-Karam, Lindsey Boldt, and Stephen Motika of Nightboat Books
for bringing our butt book into this world. Finally, thank you to Joel
Gregory, Lauren Levin, and Emji Saint Spero, our West Coast angels.

E + Z

January 1961 –
June 1969

"See what's in you and don't try
to put anything else in it."

West Bluemound Road
Wauwatosa, Wisconsin

Your saintlike face and your ghostlike soul.

Bob Dylan, "Sad Eyed Lady of the Lowlands"

I made a mistake and ate some Sugar Smacks. And I couldn't go to communion in church. After church I went to Karen's house for a while. When I came home Grandmother was here, Grampa came for supper too. Before I went to bed I laid in Mommy's bed and snacked on raisins and crackers. I went to bed at 9:00. For Christmas I got an accordion, an ice creamer, china, a holster, a missal and this diary.

When you are sick stay up *late*.

Dear Diary,[1]

Today I had to get up and sing 10:30 am. Mass. I wore my red jumper I got for Christmas. Us kids went skating at Washington Park and tobogganing at Currie. I went to bed at about 11:30 or so. I wish I had a boy to take me skating and to talk to. But I'm too young. I wish I'd grow up. This year I'm counting on my period. Well good night! I hope we become good friends.

---

1   Most of Sullivan's earliest entries began "Dear Diary." To improve readability of the text, we have removed many of these instances.

I set my hair tonight now I'm going to bed at 10:00 or so. I'm gonna try to be beautiful in soul, too. I love Jesus.

Sick all day and stayed in bed most of the time. But didn't mind too much. Didn't do anything great except saw "The Beatles" on *The Ed Sullivan Show* and Kathy practically had a bird. They are sorta cute but I think Ringo is swingin, George is cute, Paul is a good singer and John is icky. Too!

Mom thinks it's the beginning of my period or I just hope so. Men are digging up the mountains, Mom says they're gonna build a house. How horrid!!

I feel like a rose knowing that a weed to choke me is near. I got a whole mess of homework that Bridget brought home but I don't have to do it. Well, don't know what else to say. So I'll see ya tomorrow in the next page of my first lasting diary.

Still digging in the mountains darn it.

Today I spent over at Grandmother's and we went downtown. I got a silver ring with a "B" on it for Beatles. I really flip for those excellent guys. I was acting real big with my transistor in hand while shopping.

Did my homework and could *not* wait for The Beatles at 7–8 on *Ed Sullivan*. Went home to see them. Kathy ✦ I ✦ John[2] went in den and screamed! After their last song I started to cry, I guess because they wouldn't be on any more. Mom got mad but Kathy joined me. I guess we feel the same about *them*.

Dear Diary:

Today was Mamma's and Daddy's first fight over how bad I am. I'm a terrible daughter because I like The Beatles and wanted to hear their record on the radio in the car. Dad stormed around and yelled. Mom stuck up for me. I was very mad at Dad, the worst ever. Maryellen sat in the back seat saying, "Shut your sassy mouth" to me as if she were older and I should obey her. Also it is Maryellen's 9th birthday, turning out crummy.

Corpus Christi and a mess of Masses. Today joys:

(1)I'm invited to a party June 12 with 4 other girls (pj)

(2)Mom said I could maybe have a Beatles haircut before the last day of school.

Paul-Ringo-Paul-Ringo they keep bouncing around my head. They're so perfect. Model yourself on them ✦ you'll have no worries. *Paul!* I love the name. Such a beautiful sound to the ear. *Ringo!* Such an adorable boy. So sweet and modest. So bouncy. Know that I love you and I'm not crazy. This is a love so strong and real. Oh, love me, too, anyone.

2   John Sullivan, Lou's brother

My second day of menstruation. I love it! Yesterday, after school, I noticed in the bathroom and practically *ran* home. Mom + I fixed everything up, so now I'm a young lady. The pad sometimes gets in the way, but I manage. Now I'll have to take a shower every day and through summer *UGH*!! I really feel like a different person. All grown up. I should be growing, now, in the bust, too. I love being a girl. So delicate. Someday I'll get myself a boy like *Paul* and we'll get married and have some little kids. Mom and Kathy both are acting nicer to me. *I love it.*

Dear Diary:

Menstruation isn't such a big, hairy thrill to me anymore. At Martha Lake, I can't go swimming + everyone else is. I'm reading "The True Story of The Beatles." So sad—I even cried I felt so sorry for those poor boys. They hardly could get anything to eat. They went without food for 36 hours once. Poor darlings. Today is Sunday. The Beatles mean so much to me. I could never say I didn't like (or even love) The Beatles. I hope God is good to them when they die. I pray for them every day. Ringo, John, George, Paul. These names do something to me. Put me in a *trance.*

ST. ANTHONY'S CARNIVAL!

Today a man was flirting with me. I gave him my ticket for a ride and he wouldn't let go of my hand. I pulled and looked at him. He smiled and went on.

Day went so fast! Kathy found some new Beatles books. A book on each Beatle separately. We got "George" and "John." We need "Ringo" and "Paul" now. I want all! Mostly "Paul" and "Ringo." My diet is OK. I like motorcycles; they're neat. Pat got a 'play' motor on his bike.

It makes a sound like a real motor. I rode it around and decided a motorcycle'd be neat. I wish I had a leather coat, too. Like a car coat. I'd like to be English with an *accent*.

So hot today I sweated like mad. Feel like dashing around naked. Yesterday, John broke a string on his guitar at lessons. I love the guitar and wish I had one. I'm gonna start saying "y'know" for a while. It's fun.

Dear Diary:

I think I'd like a husband under the zodiac sign Libra. John Lennon's from that sign and he seems to be a very wonderful husband. I'd like to be a famous writer of romance and love. I bet I could do it! All I need is the atmosphere and mood and I could write a heart-touching story. I love to think at night, with beautiful music playing, of young lovers and love. Of how they feel, cuz I know, I felt that way about Paul and still do, a little I guess.

Today was my first guitar lessons. [The teacher] said I'm doing good and should remember to practice. Next week! Next Friday, I will see my Beatles. Those creeps want me to sing 8:00 funeral Saturday *morning*. DARN. I hate that. School, ugh-ugh-ugh, is near and I'll just have to listen to stupid old Virgiline screaming in my ear. DARN. I love to wear boy's clothes. To lessons I wore a white shirt, tie, and black slacks. I love it!

John sure must trust me or something. He tells me all his secrets. That he'd never tell anyone. Like he and some guys were shooting rabbits, etc, with BB guns and arrows. And he doesn't think an occasional cigarette will hurt anyone. I'm thinking about another story to write. I haven't come up with anything definite. I want to try to persuade John not to smoke or get in trouble in a way that he doesn't think I'm queer.

Dear Diary:

I'll probably never forget this day. My babies on the stage, alive, in front of me. Pauly! Pauly! Oh, I love you with all my heart, so much. At the end, when outside, kids screamed and ran. I followed, losing the others. I touched it with my hands—their car to take them to the hotel. I cried, lovingly, as I walked to our meeting place, people looked at me, but I didn't care. My darlings were there and I had to leave them. I saw my Pauly! And George, John, Ringo.

When Mom said I couldn't continue guitar and I couldn't wear boots, I went to my room and cried and repeated this to myself many times:

I'll never be happy until I find him and he will touch me and look int my eyes and kiss me.

"He" is my love. He will have long, jet-black hair, twinkling blue eyes. He will be very thin and irresponsible, but he will love me deeply, and I him. We will look into each others' eyes and never leave each other. Our hands will meet and we will cling to each other and forever be protected.

John and I took a walk from about 9:00–9:30 pm. It was dark and he told me his very secret things. Like about dances and how he slugged a guy, butted in for a dance. He told me what he looks for in a girl. Friendliness. He said I should dye my hair blonde and not wear my glasses, only when I *have* to. I told him he could tell me *anything* and I wouldn't tell *anyone*. We have fun together, I'm glad he's like that. We can talk openly and easily.

Soon I'll find a boy that I'll need *just as* much as a radio.

Tonight I saw a real darling boy. Mom sold our old car to his family. They're very poor and needed a car and dad's a mechanic so he could fix it. Dad was talking to his dad and he was leaning against the wall. He had brown, long hair, a green jacket. Very sad eyes. I sat in the other room watching him. He glanced at me a few times and when I was watching him, he looked up and our eyes met. I was going to turn away, but I couldn't. We looked into each other's eyes for a while and then parted. He looked so wonderful. I could have really fell for him. He was so sad and sweet.

I am carrying a picture of Keith Richards with me now. He's one of The Rolling Stones, a bunch of terribly ugly English boys. He's not a trace of ugliness. *So* darling! He's 19 and plays the lead guitar for the Stones. I'd like to know him better—really. St. Jude's, that military camp of a grade school is splitting boys and girls into different classrooms. Don't care. Those boys are just freckle-faced crew-cutted creeps and big loud show-offs.

Dear Diary:

I have reasons to believe that Mom or Kathy have been reading you.
I want a choice of high schools—I want Pius. Mom wants Holy
Angels—ISH! I cried she hurt me so. Oh—I hate it here. Mom said
she knows I just can't wait to get my arms around a boy. How does
she know! You're the only one that I ever told. I have no free will
anywhere—school, home. If I had a cigarette and could get alone—I'd
smoke it, just for kicks. I have to. I'm going to go to every CYO[3]
dance so I can get boys. I'm not aiming to be an old maid like Kathy.
HAH! I don't trust anyone but John—*NO ONE*.

I got a black leather "John Hat." It's called that cuz John Lennon wears
one like it. John said when I get my CYO card he'll fix me up with
some boys and that I wouldn't have any trouble. I'm glad I'm cute. I like
myself!! (HAHA)

I'm sure social working is what I want. Yes—the excitement of getting
a gun away from a teenage boy. Having to talk to him. I'd love that.
Well—my guitar teach (he's 18) asked me if I'm going out with
someone or going steady. I said I was only 13. He said so what. I said
my mother'd kill me. He said well tell her now listen here. He shook
his finger. I want to do that.

I'm not shy anymore! I don't care if people think I'm crazy, I'm gonna
be myself. And guess who helped me to this. The Beatles. The Beatles.

3   Catholic Youth Organization

Grandmother bought me a $20 pair of boots. I donated $7. They're genuine black leather and go up to my knees. They have a 1" stacked heel. A zipper down the side.

A dream come true! Jane Asher[4] has a pair. Excellent. Now I'm broke. Ha-ha!

Wore my boots to school but had to change during class. God, If I don't get to England! I swear I will. I must! I've been swearing a lot— "hell" and "damn" mostly. I wish I could stop!

I've been wearing apricot nail polish. Excellent!

All the kids at school say I'm the most Beatled kid. Everyday they say, "Hey, Sheila, what's new with The Beatles?" I love it. And nearly 98% of the time I have something new! I feel better now that the boys are separated from the girls. I feel more relaxed and I get a chance of becoming class clown. I'd like that a lot!

4   English actor who dated Paul McCartney

John said that Friday night he got "steeved" meaning drunk by some brandy his friend got. He says it's "a lot of fun." How can I stop him? There *must* be a way! There *must* be. He does it for kicks—smokes and drinks (usually his friend, Ralph, who lives on the west side, gets it).

I had a long talk with John since he and I walked to Mass. I tried to work on him but he's as hard as stone. He says getting drunk and smoking was a lot of fun. He nearly got me to smoke a cigarette. He put it down in front of me but I wouldn't touch it. I cried cuz I'm in such a mess, but now I feel better. I'm gonna enter a story contest in a magazine. It's another one of those "poor boy" stories. I hope I get something for it. Some of the stories that win on that deal could use a big fat eraser!

I love my bangs *real* long. Down to the crook of my nose, over my glasses when I got them on. Excellent! I'm working hard on guitar. I can't get chords good.

I really don't know what I'd have done without Paul, George, John, Ringo. I'd probably be real queer. You know, when I was around 7–11 years old, my favorite play would be "boys." One of us, Bridget, Maryellen, or I, would say "Let's play boys." We all had boy names, set up the pretend surroundings, and acted like boys. I remember a few names I had, Bobby Cordail and Chris Roman. Others were Joseph, Dave. It was real fun. Ya! That was the fun days. Dad always called me "the ringleader." Whatever I wanted to do, B and Maryellen and Patrick would do. I could even get them to clean their rooms without fuss, we'd make fun of it.

Dear Diary: I love you. I love you. You are a wonderful thing. When I'm 20 yrs old I'll read you with great fondness and you won't cheat me out of my memories. I want to keep a diary as long as I live.

(1) Black leather ¾ length coat
(2) Black patent leather heels
(3) Half slip
(4) Bubble bath
(5) compact
(6) 50 stamps
(7) black nylons
(8) Beatle book
(9) black skirt
(10) a new diary
(11) black dickie

Grandmother gave me a $6 Beatle album
Grandpa $10
Aunt Joan ✦ Uncle Bud $5 and 12 pencils with my name and holder

Dear Diary:

I had about 4 glasses, no. 5, of pink champagne. It tasted like beer but I'm used to it. We shot off 5 firecrackers at midnight. Whistles blew and everything. I'm kinda dizzy. I loved this last year. Wonderful! It's past one o'clock. Bridget had Coleen over. That's all the guests. My ears are ringing cuz Johnney blew the firecrackers in my ear. By accident I kissed him and he kissed me. He seldom does, you know. I better get to bed. Wow! Kathy cried cuz she wanted Danny at midnight. She's sweet.

Diary, you've been so good to me. I could tell you everything. Things I couldn't even tell mom. You are wonderful. Tomorrow night I start a new diary for 1965. You know everything and when I'm 21 I'll read you with love. I'll think of how I wrote in you every night. Of how I put my love for Paul into you, my tears, my feelings, my words. Thank you for living these feelings with me, for listening without yelling and for lovingly helping me shed my worries into your lap without objecting or getting mad. I'll save you forever, diary, and I'll read you.

I feel so sorry for boys who are in taverns at night, billiard halls, or just walking around. I wish Mom'd let me do that for one week and I would know how it is and try to help those that have to take it all the time.

If I saw a drunk boy at a dance, I'd have to help him. I couldn't let him.

Diary I just want to let it be known to you that whatever I write in any of my diaries is the honest truth and my real feelings, okay

Finished an absolutely *fabulous* story. I got so worked up writing it that I had to take an aspirin to stop trembling after I finished.

To mass I wore boots, leather coat, black skirt and turtle-neck and a white boy's shirt. My John hat, shoulder bag and *sun* glasses.

Saw a movie. After we went to Ace Foods where a table full of boys were. They all looked at me, I had the whole leather bit on. I must admit I tried to lure them upstairs, but I didn't.

Trying to think up a secret way to carry cigarettes in my purse. Just one maybe. I didn't think I should but tough.

I wonder what Virgiline means when she says, "Don't let a boy 'touch' you." Like his arm around you, or holding hands? Darn! Wish they'd get to the point.

Finished the *San Quentin Story*. It ended ...*but I'd rather break a rule than break a heart*. Oh. Now I'm starting the *Stone Walls* one. The other one is bad for me to read. Read part of it about whipping. It arises something I feel is bad in me. Sounds dumb, but when I read about severe whippings and have it thoroughly described to me, I get a sensation of tingling. Bad.

Mom said to me that it's "improper" to wave at motorcycles. I'm sure I care ! !

Long brown fluffy hair, slightly curled on the ends, black coat, gold buttons, belt around the middle, bare legs, no socks, granny heels, also black, shoulder bag, black, transistor radio.

I like black leather and big black motorcycles.

Some *night* I'm gonna dress like a boy and walk down some cool streets—being thought of as a boy.

He smoked. He asked if our piano worked. Yes. He played real great— songs he made up. Real, real good.

At 9:45 he had to go so we walked to the back door. He put his hand on my hair and pulled me over. I kissed him, he kissed me. Real soft and gentle. Bye.

We went to the lakeshore. We went holding hands. We kissed 4 times. The cold winds blew our hair and we sat embracing. I kept saying inside me: Larrie, Larrie.

Went to the basement, turned out all the lights and played Bob Dylan. I cried and understood his songs.

My problem is that I can't accept life for what it is…like it is presented to me. I feel there is something deep and wonderful underneath it that no one has found.

This is me becoming a human being.

I CONTINUE MY LIFE

Dear Diary:

Well, hello! I realize you're a 5 yr diary, but now yer 1 yr. OK? You can hold a lot more than my other diaries. Well, went to church and sat around the house all day practically going insane with restlessness. Today I'm in a horrid depressed mood and I've felt very sexually stimulated. Maybe it was better I didn't see Lar. Lately I've been feeling Lar is growing cold towards me. I don't know why, I just do. And I wish

I could grow up physically. I'm sick of looking like such a baby.

He'd said many times that if he didn't like me, he wouldn't call me. He didn't call me. He didn't call me.

I have a horrible temptation for sex acts. I'd never do these with anyone, though. I do play with myself, which is supposed to be wrong. But I can't see it as wrong. I don't want it to be wrong, cuz I can't help it. I'm afraid what could become of me—the way I'm going. And I don't want to be left without my Larrie. He's still mine, I have his necklace.

I want love. I need it. Please give it to me, Lar. I want it from you. I wished it was all right for us to undress and embrace. Maybe that's a horrible thing to say. But I want it. And I'm glad I can be strong and not do it. I want to run my hand over his back. I hope saying and wanting this is not wrong. Why should it be?

I rather think ugly boys are more interesting inside than cute ones.

Sheila—look at yourself ✦ face yourself. See what's in you and don't try to put anything else in it. Because then you destroy what you are and you tamper with God's work.

My goal: To save money from my job and get enough to spend about a month in a slum of Chicago or some place. To go to a Cafe Espresso (beatnik hangout). To write. These are my destinies.

He asks me if I ever got the urge to have intercourse. I said a lot. He asks what do I do when I have the urge. Then I said to him, "I play with myself." It was so silent. And he said, "Show me one person that doesn't." I was so relieved. I was waiting for him to think horribly of me. He said he played with himself and told his father. I was happy & glad I told him. He said he was proud of me and felt good cuz I trusted him enough to tell him. He seemed to become more understanding and sweet to me. I want something new—I'm uneasy and unsatisfied with what I already have experienced. But if I do, I'll turn into something I hate. A girl who does bad and knows it's wrong.

Wore my fur, bell-bottoms and vest & felt 1,000,000 ft tall. I got cuts and compliments. I luv both. Stayin overnight at Grandmother's. Played Bobby Dylan and talked to Pattie all night. And I wish I could go away from here so bad. I want to roam off on my own just me and I'll have a love or two. But I'll move on…move on. And my mind dwells on sex and I am stimulated by its words and I crave for the actions I cannot perform or have performed.

I wish I was a boy! God, do I want so bad to roam.

Shit, damn, hell.

That's about it. I know more, that's fer sure, but those are the only common every-day ones. I don't like to swear cuz it sounds horrible but it makes me feel big and masculine and tough.

All I wanna do is write 'n write. But I'll prob'ly end up in COLLEGE. Ugh.

Brought paper out 'n sat on the porch suddenly 'n Bluemound was quiet. I got such an urge. I ran out into the vacant road 'n got a spring of delight. The only sound was my heels on the cement 'n the only lights were the dim streetlight. I luv streetlights. I walked down the middle of the little street in front of our house. Then I swung around a parking sign and back to Bluemound.

I picked up two stones and threw 'm in the air, heard 'm drop. A car was comin so I ran back to the porch. I've always wanted to do something like that. Life was worth livin 'n life was so mean. Truth seemed to be everywhere. Truth seemed to be everywhere. I luv the night 'n the street lights shinin dimly on the tree trunks and the street. The night, the night.

Avant Garde—*We* (John, Kath ⊹ I) went about 8:30 we got there. It was upstairs a real dirty hole. NEAT. It was so crowded John, Kath ⊹ I had to stand. We stood on the ledge over the stairway. Bob Dylan records played. It was *very* dark. John gave me a cigarette. There was an assortment of people—very college—very beatnik. Average age was 17 but there were some around 35 and some 14.

A guy next to me (about 24 yrs old) started talkin ta me. We joked around. There was a post next to me on the ledge

 It was as tall as me with a ball on top over the light bulb. He took it off, offered me a cig and we put our ashes in the ball.

On the phone with Pattie and we got pretty deep. She's felt that there's somethin bout me she don't know bout. She ain't kiddin. Yeah—it's my "Bob Dylan Side." It's the side that gives me a thrill when I see a mother tryin ta control 5 little kids walkin down the street ⊹ some are pullin toys. It's the side that makes me pour out my "Bob Dylan style"

writins. It's the side in Avant Garde and it's the me lookin for a look
from anyone. I really can't tell her bout this part of me cuz I don't know
bout it yet. All I know is that it's what I want, what I feel is important.

I yearn so badly to go to Avant Garde. I want it so bad. I love the
atmosphere (friendly) an the music an the people. I love it. I feel like
cryin now. The radio is playin a folk song. An I want this so badly.
It is far. Someday maybe I'll be free, free enough to take this…this
life I desire. An Mom'll say go on Sheila I'll be here if ya need me an
remember I'll always love you. Oh, please let this be.

Avant Garde. Avant Garde.

I wanna look like what I am but don't know what someone like me
looks like. I mean, when people look at me I want them to think—
there's one of those people that reasons, that is a philosopher, that has
their own interpretation of happiness. That's what I am.

After supper Ma & I went to Penney's Outlet ta see about the $10 folk
guitar she saw there. We bought a $16 one an I asked her if they sold
those "unmentionables" meanin the cowboy boots. We went by where
they were an just outa curiosity I slipped a pair on. I walked up an back
with 'm an luved 'm so much. Pulled 'm off, ma grabbed 'm an asked
the sales lady the price…. $5.88! She looked at me an I said come on
let's put 'm back—but inside I said please mama *please*! She looked 'm
an said come on. I couldn't believe it—I went into a complete state of
shock. I said yer kiddin, 'r yu sure??? She said I better quick buy 'm for
she changes her mind. We did an when we got back in the car I asked
if I could wear 'm now. OKAY.

I feel so great bout havin my very own guitar an I'm still in shock
bout the boots. My stomach's tite with nerves. I'm afraid if I fall asleep

tomorrow when I wake they won't be there. I'm so happy. Kathy's REAL mad. She's jus DISGUSTED with ma for lettin me get 'm. I have conditions where I can ✦ can't wear 'm but ma said she'll probly get used ta 'm ✦ let me wear 'm all around.

You know, I think so much…well, not just lately, but for a great number of months I've been interested in homosexuality. It excites me. I think of all types of stories I make up concernin it.

At work things went so slow I had to masturbate. Yup. Nice goin, hey? While pagin thru a magazine I came to a pix of 3 girls in bikinis. That's what excited me. Homo? Sounds like it.

I had this dream: I was in a Christmas Mass singin with all these other girls when I got up an began singin "Ave Maria" solo. Suddenly I was on the stage singin it with all these people listenin. When it ended I swept back to my place, I had a flowin chiffon dress on. Everyone commented on how beautiful, an then Kath woke me up rite in the middle of it all for school. Layin awake I realize deep down I really wanted to be a flitty feminine girl. I felt sad an told all to Patty, reminded me mental beauty was more important than physical an I came back down to earth.

Kath gave me an article on Dylan from Playboy magazine. On the backside of one page is a big story on masochism an I'm typing out the article so I kin destroy the original cuz I masturbated all over it cuzza the big story.

One of my bad days again. Sex-wise, that is. I masturbated bout 5 times at work, drew dirty pictures, wrote dirty stuff—fer my own release. Patty called me she could sense my tension. I of course told her I was jus tired. Later, downtown with mom and Grandmother, I sneak to the book place + page thru dirty books to find the "good" parts (HA HA).

Now that I write of it, it all makes my stomach sick. I nauseate myself right now.

I find myself daydreamin an awful lot. My hearin goes off, I stare at somethin + I'm in the world of my stories…sometimes watching a young boy being beaten, screamin, bleedin. Sometimes seein a sex-starved, love-starved boy raping a girl, panting, pleading. Today I've been dreamin SO much.

Down to the lake + a guy sits on the wall bout 10 ft away, looks at me, I at him + say hi to him. He comes over + sits down + we talk bout the garbage floatin in the water. He's got brown long hair to the collar in back, a mustache, bushy eyebrows, about 6'2", hazel eyes, thin build.

We went to the snack bar in the Memorial Center + got coffee (both paid for their own, which I like). We read the initials scratched into the table + I whipped out my handy pocket knife + carved "She" into the table. Told him bout the Be-In. Said he intended to go, but didn't. He looked to me bout 20 yrs old. We traipsed around the art stuff, all op-art + we laffed + criticized it.

We walked up Wisc Ave. Singin 'We Shall Overcome.' I had on my cowboy stuff. Walked around a magic shop, the library, in the museum we square danced to music, looked at the mummies. In our fun we held hands sometimes. Told him I hadda be on the bus for work and he rode with me. He showed me his birth certificate: Ralph Henry Kantola, born 1950! He looked older than 17! Told me a lady'd jus stopped him on the street + asked why wasn't he in Vietnam. As he got on the return bus, I gave 'm a quick kiss on the cheek. Bout 6:45 he called and we agreed to meet at the Garde tomorrow nite.

At the Garde, Ralph and I sat in the back. We held each other & he rubbed my neck. He ran his hand over my shoulder under my dress. He leaned back & opened his shirt about half down, took my hand and put it on his naked chest. I was gettin excited so I pinched him by the neck. He got the hint. His hair was messed, he looks so tired, so sad in the dark. He asked if I wanted his bracelet. Said wouldn't refuse if you gave it to me. He took it off & slipped it on my wrist & we kissed.

I'm 16!

John & I went to the drive-in for a coke. He was all worried as usual, as was I. We got out & there was a group of boppers, bout 25 of 'm in a group. They started yellin cuts, "queer" seemed to be the favorite they all began chantin it. "Hey, yer not gonna serve those queers, are ya, Howie?" They all yelled "booo" as the guy gave us our cokes. We walked without a word to them back to John's car & sat & drink our cokes. They kept callin John "hair boy." All the boys, average age 16, bout 15 of 'm, begin walkin to the car. John ordered me to roll up the windows & lock the doors. A few of 'm bash on the side at the car, as some said "Come on out, queer, and let's see how good you are?" "Queer!"

We just sat casually drinkin, not even payin attention to 'm. One big tuffie stood there actin like Joe Coolie 'r sumthin. I remarked to John, "as if they wouldn't do the same thing if their mommies'd let 'm." John said, "No kiddin'." I smile. Joe Coolie saw me smile, he couldn't hear us, an he yelled, "Come on out here an say that?" Oh, lordy!

So John said aw, let's clear out. I agreed. He started up & backed out, much to the hurrays of the boppers. I was so proud, the way John

handled that. He'd've been only showin he's the same as they are if he'd
a quibbled with 'm. I felt 10 ft tall—still do. I sure love & am proud of
my big brother, Johnney.

I knew it all along. Now I know why he looked so helpless, so sad when
I gave him his presents, when I saw him for the last time. His mother
called last nite. Ralph got a job cooking for a family of 10 in Boulder,
Colo. They'd be living in a three-bedroom trailer. She said, "Well, now
you're out an escort," and I was too lost to tell her I'll be out a lot more
than that.

Went downtown shopping and saw a suit at Boston Store that attracted
me, then I realized it did cuz it looks like something Henry from The
Velvet Whip would wear. I got my floor length skirt, put on my big
black earrings and was off with Johnney to the Garde. Bob, who I met
at the Garde, shared the chair with me & put his hand on my shoulder.
We held hands a bit.

I decided this was my last visit to the Garde. The Whip played all
weekend. The place is full of loud mouth babies, even Gordy looked
shot. The place's changed so much, it's jus turned into a teenage
hangout now. And Ogre... Ever since he found I'm against drugs,
he's snubbed me, walks away when I'm talking to him, and I once
caught him talkin behind my back I was skinny and I look bad in my
long skirt. Hypocrite. No one there likes me. I'm jus not like them. I
guess I will always be alone. Am I ugly? Unfriendly? Self centered?
Repulsive? Why don't they like me? Is there something wrong with
me?—No, they must be wrong, there isn't anything terrible about me.
Ralph loves me.

I met a guy at the Garde. He sang some songs on his guitar ᵠ I sang "Suzanne" for him. We skipped down the sidewalk, I warmed his hands. Later, he gave me a feather. On the way home, I threw the feather out the window. Uh-uh… Ralph is more beautiful than truth…

Just as I was going inside the Garde, Gordy stops me and asked if I'm going to school or am I out? I said, "I go to Pius," and "yeah, I'm straight." 'Bout 10 mins. later, Gordy's girl beckons for John to come downstairs and when he came back up, he asked me… "How'd you like to work here?" I almost fainted. That has been one of my long lost wishes—to work at the Garde. Gordy said they'll need someone to wash cups, sweep up, straighten the chairs, etc. So he asked John ᵠ I. Of COURSE we accepted. What an honor!

Tonite I discovered that Richard[5] is everything I ever wanted to be. And I decided not to wear my beads anymore. His wild eyes, his gentle face… I realized he is my heart ᵠ mind in a person. I realized I could never be like him because I'm a girl and cried. What can I do, Richard? I'd do anything. He is the violence and fear of the boy of my stories, yet the gentility and sensitivity of poetry. I began feeling a sense of betrayal to Ralph, yet I know I will have to forget Ralph forever. There is nothing I can do but try to be like him, even tho I know Richard is not sane.

In the back room of the Garde, Barker's wife asked if I'd like to work as a waitress on the weekends when they're real busy. Oh, I can't believe all this is true. "Of course!" I was just flying. I'm hesitantly, almost fearfully, recalling that I held Richard in my arms, I dream I dare not think.

5   Lead singer of the Velvet Whip

Velvet Whip night at the Garde. In between sets, I came from the back room upon hearin a lotta noise ✦ saw Richard, stripped to the waist, leaning over the chair on stage. Tom had the belt they tie the piano with and was whipping his back for fun, but it must have hurt him... that belt is canvas-like. The Whip for me are very much of a sexual outlet, believe it or not. I guess I really am somewhat of a masochist. Even some Whip songs are an outlet for me, mostly "A Little Girl's Dream" which is hard bass music ✦ Richard screams thru the whole thing. It reveals what's constantly sounding inside me. This beating Richard went right over my head when it happened, but now, when I look back, oh, wow. A lot of things Richard does make me feel he is somewhat of a sadist or masochist. Wore my black dress, hair in a bow, black nylons.

Told both ma ✦ dad since ma said she felt I'm old enough to decide my own religion, I won't be going to Mass anymore. Neither of them made too much of it, ma just said she hopes I'll change my mind ✦ go before I die.

Patrick got a "diary" for Christmas (really a diary notebook) and he wrote vigorously in it. He let me read January 1st ✦ that will *really* be a treasure when he gets older if he keeps up in it.

Pat ✦ I wrote in our diaries together.

Talked with a guy who goes to UWM that I know as a casual acquaintance for the 1st time tonite. I think he likes me. He commented on the dress I wore last *Friday*! Name's J.

That J said all he wanted to do in his future was play his harmonica ✦ be with me.

There's a new "performer" out called Tiny Tim. I'd heard quite a few things about him: guy with real long hair, real femmy. But I watched him on TV tonite with Johnney ✝ I think he's beautiful. He's tall and very thin. His face is sunken in, thick dark eyebrows ✝ sparkling eyes, wide mouth ✝ lots of teeth. Black hair that curls down his back, it looks dirty and scraggly. He sings in a very high pitched voice ✝ holds up and moves his long thin hands and bony fingers for expression. Sometimes he plays the ukulele.

When the host introduced him, he said he was a very gentle person. He sat down ✝ crossed his legs. He looked intensely at the host as he talked with him. He talked fast ✝ in a girlish voice. He did act very feminine ✝ I just loved him. He reminded me so much of Richard. I'd love to get to know Tiny Tim better. He told the host people laugh at him but he doesn't care what they think.

He acted just like Richard when he puts on his act. I thought of how once the Whip were in the bandroom, Richard was sitting on Tom's lap, Tom had his hand up Richard's shirt ✝ was scratching his back. Every once in awhile, Richard would wiggle a bit ✝ giggle in a high-pitched girlish voice. And suddenly a member of this CYO band comes in the room. Everyone acted real casual ✝ this kid was so embarrassed but tried to act casual. Then someone said to him "It's not what it looks like, they're really just good friends!" Oh God!!!

But this guy was really "flipped out" as Johnney'd say ✝ we were in stitches laughing. He really was blowing minds ✝ did so beautifully. I'd really like to know him personally. He seems like a real beautiful guy. Now he's another sexual outlet for me—

All day thought of Tiny Tim ✝ I began to think I loved him or something. He was practically the talk of the school ✝ I only talked to <u>one</u> kid who liked him. For the most, everyone found him "revolting" "turned my stomach" "put on." I stuck up for him. His picture was in Monday's newspaper but the garbage man took it. So now I'm trying to get hold of one of those papers! I couldn't stop thinking about him ✝ Richard. I wish I had that picture of him.

I wrote this in school today: For once, you are the person inside me, the person I could never be because I am myself. I love you—because you are me. Because you are everything I would want to be.

He is the wandering lost cowboy inside of me. I really never thought of him that way. And one year ago I sang "Urge For Going" to him.

I'll die if [Ralph] doesn't come back—

Woke bout 10:30 again to breakfast. From there [J & I] took the tandem bike out. He steered & we found a little barricaded path we followed into a little alcove area next to the creek. We walked on the stones in the creek & then followed another path walking up a hill that led to nowhere so went back & sat by the creek. Held each other & kissed. Sat there a long time & then left. Rode all over & came back.

Up in my room. Kissed & did a bit of sexual rubbing. I can't help it. He is so sincere in wanting to make me happy—and I need this so badly. The bodily need is so strong. I feel if we were not meant to touch, why would I need so badly to feel it, so that I almost go crazy? To practice self-control. I find it almost impossible. And he is so good to me. I feel so guilty, yet I just can't help it. We just held each other, hugged & I could feel him. I can't remember much about it. We listened to records.

Rally for the Milw 14. Some people talked. Candles were passed out to us. Saw J. From there we walked silently to the Safety Building Jail Area. Lined up & down along the block, burning our candles & singing.

The cops got all militant & yelled there's no singing past 8 pm, it's a city ordinance. So then someone started it & we recited the Our Father, then we whistled the Nat'l Anthem. Stood there. Some guy yelled, "sing as loud as you can!" When we started singing against the cops, Kath got scared. The cops began coming in front of us with their billy clubs ⚹ we all linked arms. Kath left in a big hurry. I was all for getting arrested. I'm sure they wouldn't do anything to me if I did.

We kept singing ⚹ I guess then the cops realized they couldn't arrest the whole mess of us. Well we couldn't tell which cell the 14 were in ⚹ we held our candles up. Then, from one dark cell, suddenly a light flickered ⚹ a candle was held up. In the window…them. God I almost cried it was so beautiful.

Walked to Kath's wasn't there, ⚹ then to the Garde. Had my short blue paisley dress on.

Gordy was standing outside alone ⚹ about 2 doors away from the Garde he crouched down spread open his arms with a real evil play look on his face. I acted real scared ⚹ started backing up slowly. Then he rushed me ⚹ I ran at him ⚹ he grabbed me around the legs ⚹ I ground my hands on his back ⚹ we started laffing. What a ball!

He followed me as I kept going towards the Garde ⚹ I spun around ⚹ pulled out the stub of a candle I had left from my pocket. We laffed. I pointed it like a gun. Then J came outa the Garde ⚹ Gordy said to him, "Hey, this chick here wants her fire lit." J looked at me curiously ⚹ I pulled the candle on him.

Thinking seriously of taking off Ralph's bracelet—I'm pretty sure I'll have it off by the end of this week.

I was wearing my blue jeans ⚹ he said maybe he shouldn't tell me this but whenever I wore that to the Garde I was always the nicest to him those days. He said he's so glad "everything" turned out all right—I think he was so worried about making me cry last night that he'd blown it or something. We hugged in happiness ⚹ I told him how I really feel we are made for each other—and I really do—how I can just feel it. J said he could feel it, too.

He is so tall ⅋ thin ⅋ graceful. I love to just watch him standing there. I told him how I wished I was him, and he said no one has ever told him that before.

So he got the 2 throw rugs from his floor ⅋ I took the one from the kitchen. Went outside to beat them. I watched him in the dark wildly throwing the rugs against the side of his house ⅋ pounding energetically ⅋ I had to look away because it was really freaking me out…watching his tall, thin body running over ⅋ swinging the rug up against the wall… in the dark. I got all dirty from the rug I did ⅋ he was all sorry but I told him what's the fun if you can't get dirty! I sat on his bed as he got the dust mop ⅋ dusted the floor, got out a jack knife ⅋ scraped glops of wax off the floor, cleared the table ⅋ wiped it with the wash cloth ⅋ carefully replaced every item. I can't describe how I love him as I watched him. He was so engrossed in pushing that dust mop. I moved so he could stoop to reach way under the bed even. I thought of how probably no one stood to appreciate him as I did when he swept in school there. No one watched his shoulders ⅋ back ⅋ hands.

I think maybe for the first time I really realize the Avant Garde is gone.

Ma told me tonite I can't see J tomorrow ⅋ I just don't know what to do. I live for the next moment to see him ⅋ he's the only reason I can take school ⅋ the bullshit ⅋ the idiots ⅋ senselessness there, and home ⅋ all the useless hassle there. When I found out I just laid in my bed ⅋ thought of the waste I'm living now ⅋ of the Garde days…how I loved my Garde ⅋ every weekend I'd run up the steps so glad to be part of it. And the Avant Garde is my whole world…and I cried so hard. It's gone, it's all gone. Dave Kay, Sleepy John Ester, John ⅋ I driving down together ⅋ I was actually asked to be a waitress! Imagine! My wildest dream! The pride of washing the dishes, making the drinks, going for ice ⅋ walking thru the audience with the bag of ice thinking I work here everyone, this is my place!

Vowed we'd never have a fite ✦ if we did we'd probably both bust out laffing rite in the middle of it. Then we made supper of soup ✦ buttered noodles ✦ faked like a typical marriage fite ✦ laffed so hard.

Well, tonite I cleared out a lot of junk in my room. Plus—and this is why it's memorable—I threw out *all* letters, gifts, etc from Lar which I'd kept all this time *and* all letters, cards from Ralph and the gifts he gave me including the once beloved bracelet ✦ aspen leaf necklace. With it I threw out Ralph's picture but retrieved it later to put in my '67 diary since it is the only picture I had of him.

And I don't care...

I don't want all that junk when I move out. I want only me ✦ all my future—

The more I think—I'll need a phone when I move. Necessary evil. But I REFUSE a TV. That I won't need. What a drag. A phone.

An incredible day—my last day of school!

Man, I slopped around there with a give-a-shit attitude I've never had before.

I ran outa there at 2:15 saying out loud as I stepped out "Go fuck yourself Pius High School!" ✦ ran out, my face lifted to the sky. J ! J ! Oh, I'm free *forever*! I threw the uniform in the middle of the living room ✦ told ma to destroy it, so I never see it again ✦ I disposed of all that reminds me of that place.

Oh, it's beginning.

I'm not wearing nylons anymore ⊹ am gradually eliminating my dependency on having a purse. I'm gonna sew nice secure pockets in my coats ⊹ finally rid myself of a purse altogether. I hope.

Not even one apartment on the east side in the paper below $140 rent. Shit. We'll see. Hope I have one lined up before J comes back [from California].

He kept telling me "don't worry" cuz he'll be back soon. His hair was cut short. He just pulled it all back to a little ponytail at the back of his neck ⊹ chopped the ponytail off. He had a bag in the garbage with all his hair in it ⊹ I confiscated it cuz it was really outasite, and I feel close to him when I have it.

I never had a boyfriend during the summer—I began feeling summer once more.

June 1969 – August 1970

"I've got a thing where when I make a change, I can't imagine how it was before I had the change."

East Albion Street and North Franklin Place
Milwaukee, Wisconsin

They've got the urge for going
and they've got the wings so they can go.

Joni Mitchell, "Urge for Going"

—I just can't believe it's all for real. I mean I realize I'm all moved in ✢ all but I can't believe I'm here for good—I live on the East Side, I got my <u>own place.</u>

I just keep looking around ✢ biting my cuticles.

I guess I've got a thing where when I make a change, I can't imagine how it was before I had the change.

J ✢ I have been sleeping together on ✢ off at Albion U. How grand ✢ beautiful it is. And this is even more far out…Last night we had intercourse. I guess there's different stages for boys or something cuz he wasn't full erect ✢ had no ejaculation or anything. Far out! We laid there like that ✢ talked. Too freaky. I can't believe it.

I am overcome with wonder, joy, emotions I do not know.

Two men have landed on the moon today.

I cannot comprehend this all. Two people sitting on the moon… tomorrow they walk upon it…

I got my kittie today. She's 6 weeks old and I will not name her.

—don't let it be on the moon as it is on earth.

She's gray with a few faint brown spots & white legs, feets & tummy. She's a real good one. I'm not going to name her because she's too good for a name—

J & I trekked all over & found the old Shag house & the old For Frails boutique house for rent. He took a room & I took a huge 2 rooms right down the hall. We scrubbed & painted his place immediately & he moved in about 2 weeks ago. He's happy with it & I'm moving in.

So the winter won't be terrible & we're together. My love & I are together. What a peaceful gentle love we have!

J makes pictures but what good are they? It's like he's obsessed insane and making thousands of little pictures for no reasons. What good are thousands of little pictures?

"I'd like to be a kitty. They're so dumb. They have the key to success. Complete oblivion.
No understanding at all.
They just go sleep & lay down."

Some good things happening.

Belinda, the girl who moved into Albion University after J & Bob moved out, is moving out. So out of site—I called the landlord immediately the next day & it's mine. Oh, it'll be just perfect! I always wanted that place. Beautiful huge kitchen with a big cabinet for dishes & pots & food and a big wonderful sink with ample hot & cold water ! ! !

I'm so excited I don't know if I can wait a whole month. Another out-of-site thing is in the 2 yrs I've known that place no-one has ever seen a crawly bug, only flies. Not even a spider. I just hope the carpet beetles here don't hitch a ride over there in a sweater or something. Drag.

And the rent will only be a bit more. For this place I pay $65 a month ↟ for Albion also $65 but I have to pay electricity and heat there. But that won't be too much.

I just can't wait to start moving in. But I'm not sure what J's gonna do. From what I can get from him, he plans to stay here at Franklin Pl at least thru September.

So yesterday night J, Michael Evans (the guy J's moving in with), another girl ↟ I were walking down a busy street here on the East Side to go eat ↟ these greasy-looking kids drive past, yelling at us out the window but so what, that happens every day. But I knew they were coming back—they turned around ↟ pulled the car up ↟ got out of the car, bout 3 guys about 17 yrs old ↟ 4 girls or so.

So the guys come up ↟ the other girl with us ran away. One of the guys said to J "What did you say to me back there?" you know, just to start a fight and J said "I didn't say anything to you" and the guy runs up to J and gives him a shove which almost knocked J over.

I stepped between them and said to the guy "You leave him alone!" And J, Michael ↟ I just kept walking down the sidewalk.

The guys shouted after us "Come on, try and beat my ass, mother fucker" and J said to him "I don't want to" and they yelled after Michael "I'm gonna pull that pony-tail right outa yer head." Michael had his hair back in a rubber band.

Anyway we just kept walking and they got in their car. Which when I think back now was super-strange they'd just back off like that. Really far out.

So all 4 of us kept on to the restaurant, Michael said stay off the street or they'll try ✦ run us over. Such a drag! But we were surprised they'd try something like that, especially on a busy street in the freak district.

September 1970 – January 1975

"He was beautiful but I felt he wasn't sincere."

East Albion Street
Milwaukee, Wisconsin

*I knew that it was in a kind of turbulence
that that self must attempt to find itself.*

John Rechy, *City of Night*

Once we finished moving my things, I closed my door and went to bed and J had left, too. He went to take his mattress over to Michael Evan's. And he didn't come home... didn't come back to Albion for so long. I laid there wanting him so bad in the same place he laid exactly 2 years ago without me.

Now it's "my house," "your place," "your home," "my home," and I have to stop saying "our home," "our mailbox," "our kitchen."

I need something badly but I'll never find out what it is I need. I'm tired of old thoughts, old actions, old thoughts all the time. Rotting in my mind, in my body, rotting poetry, rotting, smelling, and now to the point where it is becoming one with all the other rot in the world. It has no distinctness, no goodness anymore. Rot has taken over every part of me.

... he'd already reproached me for babying him so much, just about "buttering his toast in the morning"...I always wanted to be him ✦ be free of myself

Just all day & all night to smother myself in him.

You know, he never picks up his harmonica anymore.

He has abandoned poetry. And poetry is all I care for.

I just read back & can remember nothing of this fit of depression. They come & go, for no reason it seems. So how can I justify or even explain myself. Today I feel love, gentleness, happiness & none of the feelings of [the previous entry]. Can I blame it on the supposed "two personalities" of the Gemini ? *Ha, ha!*

Bridget's dearest friend, Kathy Steininger, had a baby boy. The day after grandpa died. He's real cute & she's keeping him tho she's only 17 & unmarried. I love the kid! I'm happy!!!

I just finished reading *City of Night* by John Rechy. Excellent book. A long time ago I saw the Gay Liberation Front recommend the reading of several books on homosexuality, which you know I have always been strangely attracted to. One of the recommended books was *The Gay World* by Martin Hoffman. It was real good & it recommended *City of Night*. I got it immediately. Story of a male-hustler, a male prostitute for homosexuals. The whole story was so sad & lonesome… my heart & soul is with the "drag queen."

And how can I help. The last week or so I've wanted to go & leave everything & join that world. But where do I fit in. I felt so deprived & sad & lost. Last Monday I came home on the bus alone (J had a late class) & I was so so close to "cruising" Brady Street & trying to get picked up. So damn close.

I think it was Wednesday nite J & I lay in bed, not able to fall asleep, talking. I cried & told him I was so restless, so unfulfilled & starved for excitement. I tried to make him see what I'd been thinking of, but feeling him out cuz I didn't know how he'd react.

I told him maybe he shouldn't marry me cuz he's taking an awful risk cuz I don't know what I'm thinking, which way I'm going (thinking as I spoke, that what can become of a girl whose real desire + passion is with male homosexuals. That *I want to be one.* That I fancy him to be one + I pretend I'm a man when we make love).

He told me he doesn't want me to feel trapped. That for him ideally he wants our relationship to be a totally free one. To come + go as we please. Not to, say, go somewhere only cuz the other person is going there. He wants a relationship where "everything goes…" I was silent thinking what he would feel if I had got picked up on Brady Street but afraid to ask, but he continued as if reading my mind: "…except probably unfaithfulness." I almost sighed in relief. That is what I had been yearning to hear so long from him. Our love is so real that there is already a sin such as adultery in it.

Oh what can I say? I don't want to marry becuz I'll then forever be deprived of many of those beautiful compliments, I'll never be sought by another. I still yearn for that world—that world I know nothing about—a serious threatening sad ferocious stormy lost world.

The doorbell rings + some girl in a Santa Claus suit pops in. She's no one nobody knows. Gives everyone a wrapped gift with their names typed on 'm, wishes Merry Christmas to everyone, very jolly + ho ho ho + walks out + leaves. Very beautiful gifts—even expensive. We were all in shock. Complete insanity + then Bridget + Kathy Steininger admit they set it all up + Kathy + Bridg got the gifts + got a friend to be Santa. I was so taken.

I think I'm even in love with Kathy in a strange way. I was so taken I cried in her arms. I don't know why. All I could think of was, *And if somehow you could pack up your sorrows and give them all to me, you would lose them, I know how to use them. Give them all to me.*

I said to her so no one else could hear "It's so hard to separate happiness + sorrow—sometimes they're almost the same thing." Cuz I didn't know which I felt.

She's a phantom—she seems to suffer all & always smile, always quiet—she barely speaks. She's radiant & she wears flannel shirts & is beautiful.

And I'm no good. I work 40 hrs a week & spend money like nothing. I can't get out of it & leave it either. I can't be beautiful becuz I don't know how.

For Christmas I got a pair of white Levis haven't had 'm since my cowboy Garde days.

J & I took Baby Tips to the vet for ear mites again. Mama Tips is pregnant again & really *big*.

I told J in the dark while laying in bed, that I wished we could get married. He immediately got angry & turned off & said sternly how stupid & needless it is. I felt so lonesome. I had told Mom that J & I sleep together & I'm getting pills soon. It freaked her out & now I don't have a family. I want to belong somewhere, be part of something. J isn't my *boyfriend*. He said he's my lover & I should tell everyone he's my "lover" if I don't like "boyfriend." I told him how I felt. I want to *belong*. He said I'm just grasping at some false security. Said he just DOESN'T want to get married—he wanted to once but he's changed his mind cuz it's *stupid* & it wouldn't change anything anyhow.

We didn't talk anymore & fell asleep.

I commented to him that he's been acting so weird lately I don't know why. He said he knows he's been feeling strange—he thinks it's the class he's taking on Mysticism. I guess he's really getting into it. I couldn't understand half his rap as he spoke in such ambiguous language.

I hugged him, feeling kinda scared & told him I wish sometimes he worked in a factory 40 hours a week & never thought of this stuff.

That I really try to avoid such subjects cuz you can never really *know* if there's a God or not. So there's no use fucking your mind over trying to find out. He gave some rap that you CAN know it ✝ then began saying how you CAN'T prove 2 + 2 = 4 ✝ that belief ✝ proof were the same thing. He said he thinks I'm just scared of the subject ✝ I agreed with him. Told him I think he's just too idealistic ✝ hasn't been fucked over by enough people yet. He said that could be so.

I took Maryellen to Madison for the day as my birthday present to her. Found she's in a lotta ways like I was at her age. Freaked out ✝ fucked up. I got my boxes of writing the other day from Bluemound Road ✝ all those desperate, lonesome things—really crazy. All those years I was only waiting to bust out at 18 ✝ find total happiness. Here I am almost 20 ✝ I feel like I've come to a dead-end.

Found a lotta lonely writings from the Ralph era ✝ it crossed my mind to collect them ✝ arrange them in book form *To Golden, Because He is There*. Or is he??

When I had that talk with J he said some people are really interested in sex ✝ get books about it ✝ read up, etc, but that he simply is not INTERESTED in the subject, there's better things to spend your time doing. To me, I don't think it's a matter of being interested in SEX but in your fellow human beings. And especially about the goddamn person yer supposed to goddamn LOVE. Also times like these make me sure he's a latent homosexual.

Yesterday he saw this guy he once met at the store ✝ who he thinks is real beautiful. J told me when the guy passed him in the store he felt his heart beating faster. I don't know if he was kidding or merely emphasizing the guy's good looks but seems a funny thing to say to me.

I mean stuff like saying you just don't care about sex is just not normal. It's fucked up. How am I spozed to communicate with someone when I don't even know where he's at? Specially when I don't even know after being with him almost 2½ fucking years! When I asked J who he thought sexiest in the world he said he doesn't know—(he forgot about the guy in the store. I wish he'd admit to me he's gay. It'd really turn me on). He's definitely hiding something man. *NOBODY* can dig fucking books that much.

There's a really weird guy who hangs around the University. He's real tall, has long brown hair ✦ a beautiful face ✦ wears dark black eyeliner ✦ gorgeous clothes.

Some guy offered to give me a ride home from Kathy's Tues nite ✦ then took me out of the way ✦ tried to get me to make love or do something with him. He was a super ugly fucker ✦ I graciously let myself outa the car ✦ walked home. If he'd looked better I mighta gone down on him at least. Shit.

I wish I knew J. He's probably a very interesting person if he'd only be honest with me.

I mean he's the type that if he starts warming up to ✦ getting turned on ✦ I say "no being nice" (what we call making love) he can say ok ✦ go about his business without a second thought—take it or leave it. Far out.

There's a deal where they say some people want a girl with a penis so they get a girlish boy. Maybe J wants a boy with a vagina so he takes me, a boyish girl. I don't know. The whole deal's screwed up.

So these are the kind of things on my mind.

How come I always get the weird-o's.

I was restless ✦ felt so trapped that I told J I needed a vacation from him ✦ I think he should sleep at Michael's a little more ✦ not see me for lunch all the time. He said ok, he does think it'll be best.

Monday I didn't see J all day. Watched for the one guy I'd seen around. He really was strange-looking. Looking like he wore eye make-up ✦ he always wore a long red corduroy coat. Looked really elegant ✦ almost like a male homosexual. Felt real daring all day ✦ finally about 5:30 pm saw him walk by with 2 friends.

Followed them down to the bookstore ✦ when the guy stood alone I reached out ✦ took his hand. He was real shocked ✦ asked what was going on. Told him I liked him. He didn't quite know what to make of it. We stood around ✦ talked bout an hour. Really an interesting person. I had a feeling he was kind of talking down at me like I was a little suburb chick who got a crush on big freaky him. I left myself wide open ✦ hoped either he'd come with me or I could go with him ✦ spend the nite. I really didn't want to be alone.

He said some good stuff to me—like he said if I really dug blues music I should sell my record player ✦ live ✦ *BE* the blues. Well, he took my address ✦ phone ✦ said he'd come over someday with some people I might like to meet. Shit. So went home ✦ downed a glass of really *bad* wine we had laying around ✦ listened to some music, contemplating how I could live ✦ *be* the blues.

Tuesday George's (his name) friend gave me an invitation to a party at their house but I had to turn it down because I'd promised John Connell I'd visit him in Rockford that weekend.

Tues nite I went thru "withdrawal" for not having seen J so long. Cried ✦ kinda freaked out, called J but he wasn't there. Kath called me ✦ cheered me up a bit. Anyway by Thursday afternoon at lunch J ✦ I decided to end our vacation. Was so glad to get back to normal ✦ was surprised to find out the whole idea was mine ✦ I had actually hurt J's feelings.

George walked right passed me—looked RIGHT at me ✦ kept going. Fuck you! The 1st time I ever made a pass at a guy ✦ it all turned out a flop.

I was thinking too that probably the best person to show me how to be a woman would be a queen as they probably got women down more than women do. It's real ART for queens.

Tues morning my piano was delivered. I bought an old Upright piano from Mel Billings for $170. By some miracle they actually got it into the place. I play every night. Haven't played since 1963 so I'm a bit rusty.

Bridget moved into her own place with her best friend Kathy Steininger. Bout 1½ miles from Albion. Really am glad ✦ I visit them every Saturday I can.

Ma came over ✦ offered to drive me home whenever I wanted ✦ even came in to see Mama Tips' new litter (she had 'm July 4, 5 real good ones—all different colors).

Came to the conclusion that I must establish some freedom from J— mental freedom, not physical. (Physical relationships must have a love like ours to be worth anything.) And the only way to establish this freedom is for me to begin acting independently of his consent—by that I mean I have to do things I want to do without worrying or hesitating that he might not approve of it. I'm not real conscious of doing that, but I guess I do it a lot—always cuz I think him to be so superior in style to me that I want to be as much like him as possible. But I gotta quit that ✦ begin forming *ME*. (Whatever the hell that is.)

That decision (maybe it's more of a realization) has made me very happy these last few days.

We went to Randy's garage where we helped him fix up his Fiat car. I waxed the car myself + cleaned it out. Really liked it, working with the guys as a guy.

Got all grungy doing the wax job but did it real good.

So after that went for pizza all dirty as we were. I really like it—I mean, it's like an extension of when I used to play "boys" when I was younger. I like to play "boys" now. I know how to be one of the boys, I never knew how to be a *chick* + I'm *glad*! Yet I think I can still be one of the guys + keep my identity as a girl, I hope, to make a pleasant combination.

We got some Mateus wine (my favorite) on the way. When we got there it looked like it would be a drag—a lotta draggy party-type people there…girls all decked out + guys with he-man cologne on. Then we found out no one had a corkscrew for my wine + when I told J he said oh well, just forget it then. Real cute. "Got any *lemonade*??" Yippeeee. Cuz all they had was beer + Cold Duck which I hate. But Randy, gallant as he is, worked at it for a long time + finally pushed the cork in for me.

So I commenced to drink the whole bottle for the 2nd time in my life + got really really ripped. I only remember bits of the nite. First I got into the music + started dancing around by myself + teasing people like telling Ted what a sexy shirt he had on.

Pretending to flirt with Kathy + Diane + then would point to them, to me + then to the bedroom + nod my head "yes?" They knew I was teasing + would apologetically shake their heads no + I would act real disappointed + shrug my shoulders + walk away. I like to do gross things.

Only saw J a few times all nite + he told me he wanted to talk to other girls + I said I doubt whether anyone even knew we were together. For some reason he + Mike traded shirts + the sleeve got torn off J's.

I got real tired + slumped in a corner to rest + Randy comes + throws some beer on me to "wake me up." Dragged him in the bathroom + poured water on his head. Can't remember why but he took a piss when

I was in there too. We were rassling around ✦ he tore my shirt. I got cigarette butts outa ashtrays ✦ walked around dangling a butt in my mouth. Randy ✦ especially Paul, would say "Sheila, what're you *doing*?" and would grab the butt from my mouth but I just got another.

Then back to Randy's to crash. Fell asleep IMMEDIATELY! Had bad dreams all nite bout big parties ✦ being so drunk, lying in an alley ✦ cats running around with hunks of hair shaved off (one of our cats has a bald spot on his hind ✦ it looks like it was shaved rite off) ✦ someone trying to ether me so he could rape me. A real hassle of a sleep.

J said no one can ever be totally happy, that bad things are still always there. That he'll always have something hanging over his head "...the draft...next year it'll be something else..." That after sex you always return to your troubles, but the trick is to transcend all hassles—to be unaffected if your life is disrupted. He said to me: taking acid is a lot better than "fucking" (he kept referring to it as "fucking"). Man, I coulda shit. *Groovey*!

He says one must let their inner world come out ✦ take over their outer world. I said Christ, if I did that, God...man, they'd have to take me away! I mean I'd just go off the deep end! He seemed surprised ✦ said well, it all depends on what your inner world *is*. (I was gonna tell him that I would have killed him if I let my inner world take over. There were times he slept at Franklin Place that I could hardly stop thinking of pushing a knife into his chest ✦ watching the sheets get red ✦ his gyrations).

There is no happiness
There is no good
There is only tears
       and suffering
       and death

I don't remember how ⚡ what happened but then we made love ⚡ he was so good ⚡ we satisfied each other ⚡ fell asleep with the little red light on.

He slept an hour longer than I did this morn ⚡ I put a note in his books:

> *Dear Tuffy*
> *I love you so much*
> *Snuffy*

J ⚡ I just made love in the back office of my work to which I have the only key. He was frightened like a mischievous little boy, worried we'd be caught. But his eyes sparkled ⚡ he came in my mouth quickly but still kept his hard-on. I love him purely. I would have him wrapped in soft white sheets ⚡ sent to heaven. He ran off right away but with a saint-like smile ⚡ radiant face. If only I could speak to his ghost-like soul.

Took speed last night. Nice high but a bit insecure. J ⚡ I made love for 2 hrs from 3–5 AM this morn. He's really been liking it lately. We've been real free ⚡ imaginative ⚡ it's so outa sight.

While speeding, J, Randy ⚡ I sat talking all night. Randy told me I really freak out all the girls around there when I come into places "all snaked up on Mateus." Randy said they all think oh I could never do that! Which means they can't be themselves, Randy said.

Talking to ma on the phone, she called me at work. I had nothing to say to her. When I hung up I realized that it's cuz everything I do that means anything to me is either immoral or illegal. *HA!*

Randy had a birthday party ✦ we decided it would be "formal attire" only. I have this old black lace dress that's all ripped up ✦ goes down to the floor ✦ looks like a vampire dress ✦ these black lace elbow-length gloves that don't have fingers in them! J got a top hat he borrowed from Metzger.

When we got to Randy's place I really felt glad—they really went all out—had a *PUNCH BOWL* with lemons ✦ limes floating around it, a relish dish with sliced dill pickles—the whole scene. Randy had a suit from about 1920 that fit him just perfect ✦ an old hat that made him look like Mugsy or Big Louie or something. They have a pool table in their dining room so all night they played ✦ we all called it "*billiards*."

Well didn't take me long to get good ✦ fucked up on the punch ✦ really get into it. When my glass ran out I hand it to one of the guys ✦ I'd say "Darling, would you be so kind as to get me another glass of punch?" said in a real stuck-up tone. They always got it too! Or "*DO* get me more punch, *darling*."

It seems I am always reminded how young ✦ inexperienced with thoughts I am. This past Sunday we went to the theatre ✦ saw *Death in Venice* by Visconti. It was absolutely beautiful ✦ I cried practically thru the whole thing. There was so much depth to it—so little action—the whole thing dealt with emotions ✦ thought. And to be able to get this across in film was amazing. Seems that so few people could apply themselves to it tho. All reviews ✦ people who saw it that I came in contact with invariably remarked on the "homosexuality" of the movie, a subject that never even entered into the picture. Sexuality has nothing to do with it! And it irritates me becuz people cannot associate beauty with males unless introducing homosexuality into it.

I've been having lots of feeling that something new will occur this summer. Last week J ✦ I decided once again to see other people of the opposite sex. This time I brought it up. I think more ✦ more how I'm gonna really be sorry I spent my whole youth on one person. And I don't think I'll ever forget that beautiful boy who tried to pick me up at the bus stop last fall, I guess I never wrote about that.

Well, J ✝ I had it worked out that he'd get on a bus to Randy's after work ✝ I'd wait for that same bus at Albion ✝ get on ✝ we'd both go to Randy's. So I was waiting for the bus ✝ it was a block away ✝ all of a sudden "do you always stand around looking in windows?" ✝ I looked up ✝ God, one of the most beautiful, handsome faces I've ever seen??? Nice ✝ tall ✝ thin with marvelous eyes ✝ blonde hair curling around his face. I just stared at him ✝ got real nervous ✝ said *oh no*! see *I'm* just *waiting* for the *bus* ✝ it's *only* a *block away!!!* I felt like an immediate idiot. Christ. He said oh where'ya going? I said something bout going to the South Side to get drunk. The bus was right there ✝ I just wanted to die as he walked away.

All night I realized I'd regret not going with him for the rest of my life.

Such a beauty!! Anyway I've seen him 2 times since, once he was downtown hitchhiking—me shopping with Grandmother—the 1st time *I* ever did in a year. Anyway I stood ✝ just looked at him for a long time. He's got such a fine body ✝ long lithe legs ∻ he wears knee-high black leather boots that make him look like a prince ✝ with his golden thick curls. Saw him the 3rd time when I was walking home with groceries. He was going the opposite direction down the sidewalk ✝ I tried to give him a real nice smile ✝ he looked at me like *who* the *hell* are *you?* Anyway haven't seen him in a few months ✝ I wonder if I ever will again.

Plus J said he ✝ this other girl have had a eye-flirting affair ✝ he'd like to get to know her ✝ I think he should. I do think it will make our relationship better to have open honest affairs instead of being guilty ✝ sleazy about them. I swear if I ever see my blonde beauty again I'll invite him to my place if possible. I've had so many daydreams about making love to him. But I don't know if I'll ever see him again. I really blew it.

Saturday afternoon just for liberation's sake, I cornered Ted's little brother Lorin in the bathroom ✝ kissed him real good.

Saturday I made my second attempt (1st one was last year) to pick up a guy. J, Randy ✝ the guys ✝ me went to Sam's Bar on the South Side to drink. There was this insanely good-looking boy there—probably about 19 or 20, marvelous shiny thick blond hair ✝ dark smiling eyes. I stared at him as much as I could. He was real flirty ✝ bubbly, dancing around talking to his friends ✝ playing pool, etc. I didn't know what to do, I was practically wetting my pants.

So the guys wanted to go eat so I waited til they were all out ✝ said into the guy's ear "I want you to know that you're very good-looking" and left real fast. Everyone wanted to go to Randy's when done eating ✝ I knew J planned on staying there overnite ✝ spending Sunday there so I asked to be taken back to Sam's, saying I just didn't feel like crashing yet. So they dropped me off there alone. He'd left. My heart was pounding like nuts. Figured I'd wait a while maybe he'd come back. He did. I just about died.

Didn't know what to do. So went up to him ✝ said hi. I said "I want to proposition you." He said "what's the word." I said "sex." His mouth fell open ✝ he *looked* at me like *WHAT?* ✝ looked real amused or something. He said we'll have to go somewhere ✝ I said yeah. He was real flustered ✝ said well I have to do something with my friends but I'll be back later. I said I won't. He asked why ✝ I said cuz I don't live around here. He said well just a minute ✝ walked away so I waited.

He was gone real long so I started sauntering around the bar ✝ couldn't find him for about 2 hrs. Finally found him playing foosball. I figured well maybe he wants to hang around a while yet. So I just stood around. When he finished his game I asked him "Yes or no, I'd like to leave." He said after hesitating "Maybe some other time." I nodded ✝ left immediately. Was kinda relieved.

When I told Kathy Steininger ✝ Joyce they just about died. The way I felt about my approach to him—I just wanted to lay it on the line, get an answer ✝ split, I was so nervous. I didn't have any confidence to flirt my way into getting him to my place. Joyce said I just can't take the male role like that. That you have to come on real easy ✝ relaxed ✝ not like a bomb. Like make flirty eyes ✝ strike up a petty conversation ✝ maybe say "I've got some real good weed at my place, wanna come over

+ smoke some?" (Guess I'll have to keep a little weed around). I asked if it was ok to go up to a guy + offer to buy 'm a drink. Nope, that's the male role again, but I can share my drink with them??? It's so hard to play these roles.

Went out drinking with Joyce + to a party. I didn't want to go to the party but decided to try it. Lotta jerks. One good-looking boy. So when he borrowed a cigarette from Joyce, I snatched it outa his mouth, asking what he'd give me if I gave it back. He laid back on the floor supporting himself on one elbow + named all kindsa things, like a world of people without minds (told him we already have that) + everything he offered I said I didn't want. He asked what I did want. I said "you." He said OK, you got me + I thought bargain deal. So gave him the cig + we talked about cats bout 5 mins + he got up + left, talking to some blonde chick. Thought fuck you. He didn't come around the rest of the night (ditched me like the last guy I thought) so I left. Figured that's as cute + flirty as I can get + if that doesn't work, too bad.

Walking to Kathy Steininger's after my piano lesson, someone yells to me from a parked car on the other side of the street "Hey, do you like cats?" I yelled "Yeah, why?" + then recognized the same guy. I just about shit. [Jeffrey] said do you remember me from that party + I said "yeah + you ditched me." He said I did not + I said "BULLSHIT." He said "come here" so I crossed the street + stood by the car. He asked where I was going, told him + he said he *was* gonna go to a meeting but the guy he was going with didn't show up. Asked if he wanted to come to Kathy's for a hamburger + he said that sounds good—then I said "or we could go to my place." He asked who's there + I said no one. He said ok, real eager! So we drove to Albion. Told him bout J + me but that he wouldn't be home tonite. It seemed he was really at ease.

So when we got inside he began plunking on the piano + asked if I'd play something. Told him I didn't want to. He asked what I wanted to do ✦ I said "kiss." He said ok, real eager again. So we stood in the kitchen ✦ began kissing ✦ he began lifting my skirt ✦ blouse. So I pulled his shirt out ✦ in about 2 seconds we were all apart. I said "we're moving" ✦ took him into the bedroom.

He said was I sure my boyfriend wouldn't come in. I said of course, I wouldn't want him to come in either. He laid on top of me ✦ rubbed his dick on my cunt ✦ came on the bed in a few minutes. He asked if I had anything he could wipe it up with ✦ I said "what for?" He seemed amused, relaxed, nervous ✦ everything all at once. Couldn't tell what he was thinking. I couldn't believe how small his dick was, but he was small all over.

I just giggled thru the whole thing I was so glad it was all happening at last!

He just laid there real quiet smiling thru the whole thing (a lovely boy smile) ✦ then he "got alive" again ✦ began rubbing again. I asked if he could come again ✦ he said yeah. I said good. He had strong arms ✦ he thrusted real good—I like that a lot. I laughed ✦ bounced on him ✦ he smiled ✦ I don't know if he came or not but we were done.

So I sat bare drinking the tea ✦ he put on all his clothes ✦ drank a little. I would've like to have sat there a while bare with him (we did sit after fucking a while ✦ I couldn't help touching him) but he seemed to want to go.

I was on Cloud 9, still am. I'm so glad. I feel so *pretty* or something.

I told J all about it ✦ he was SUPER interested ✦ got every detail outa me ✦ wanted to know how he rated. Told him he's definitely a better fuck, Jeffrey didn't do very much on his own. So J talked ✦ talked to me, being almost nicer than usual ✦ when we got to bed he fucked me *real* good ✦ long, asking was he handsome ✦ was he good at making love. He's got a wonderful dick, told him so too! I really feel happy!!!

He said he feels bad cuz he can't stay with me here anymore. I asked why not? Says that if he's gonna at all be able to socialize with people *+* change, he has to get away from me, cuz he comes to me *+* is all secure *+* I protect him *+* he doesn't feel like a "man" with me, but like a "boy." Told him I don't know the difference, that men *+* boys are all the same to me. He said he feels real at ease talking to males *+* females he regards as males, but not when he has to talk to someone "feminine." I told him not to make all these distinctions, that people are people, not girls boys women *+* men. Then he got mad *+* said he's not gonna talk to me if I'm gonna be ludicrous. That pissed me off *+* I let him know—said I'm *not*, I'm perfectly serious. He said he still feels like an adolescent with me *+* he's just beginning to see what it feels like to *"be a man."* (Jesus Christ???) That he feels I'm much older *+* mature than he.

I feel like an old hag when I'm with him.

Wed I took Mama Tips to State St Animal Hosp. cuz her right eye was so swollen, plus I'd run out of medication. So I told the vet I'd like him to try *+* do something bout the one bulgy eye. He said there's nothing he can do anymore for her, she'll be completely blind very soon *+* she's in EXCRUCIATING pain! I told him she certainly was giving me no indication of being in such pain. He said well, there's nothing he can do *+* I know what his advice is *+* it'll have to be my decision.

I almost died rite there—my heart just sank. I told him I'd go in the waiting room *+* think awhile. (I knew she wasn't in pain *+* that she still wanted to live. She eats well, comes to be brushed, the only thing different about her was she moves slower. I felt it'd be murder to put her to sleep.)

I was with Maryellen *+* told her I'd really like to go to this one vet I heard was super-excellent. So we left.

I could hardly hold back tears on the way there. She doesn't want to die yet—she'd let me know when she does, just like the others. Why can't they do something to at least TRY to save her? But I figured if this Lakeside Animal Hosp. gives me the same story as State St, I'd just have to do it. How could I give up Mama Tips, my favorite & best tipsy, when she wasn't ready to die?

When I got to the vet, he immediately began an intensive examination of her. He asked a whole load of questions on her environment, attitude, eating habits, etc, which the other vet never even asked. He looked at her with machines, the other vet never did.

Then he stepped back & said he was gonna give me medication to get some light in her eyes & try & arrest the disease in her left eye. Said the right one pretty much was a lost eye but they'd try & see if we can regain anymore vision, the nerves are so shot in her eyes she feels nothing there. Said he's got a personal interest in this cause cuz he did his residency in feline eye diseases.

I coulda shit I was *so* happy. I had a fighting chance & someone who gave a shit about it.

Today, 3 days later, her fever's gone down & there's a hint of clearing up the cloudiness in her eyes. She's walking around more than usual (otherwise she constantly sleeps) & I think she's getting better.

I'm so fuckin happy I could cry!

Cheyney, Johnney & Kathy Steininger's little boy, I've gotten to love him a lot. Every afternoon after work I go to visit them. Cheyney's gotten to know me well, even cried when I left Friday afternoon. He'll be 2 end of October. He knows & understands SO much, he never ceases to amaze me—no lie. Kathy & I have become best friends too. I admire her inner strength, independence & she's really a *good* person.

J's talking more seriously of grad school[6] ⊕ us moving there.

Mama Tips died Saturday. Took her to the vet, he said she was worse despite all the medication I was giving her. Her fever was 104° compared to 103° last visit. Said he could operate ⊕ close her eyes but she'd still have the infections ⊕ fever. She was hardly eating at all since Wednesday.

He said nothing would make her better if the stuff I gave her didn't. Her "good" eye (the one she could see half way out of) began getting a white clouding in it real bad Thursday ⊕ then the bad eye got it Friday. He said the disease was just lingering on too long to have any hope of the fever going down ⊕ the infection to at least stop spreading any further.

She just laid on the table ⊕ put her paw on my hand ⊕ her head down. I could see it was hopeless. No, she wasn't to the stage where she had to be force-fed ⊕ wouldn't go to the litter box, but I felt she should be able to die with the bit of dignity she still had left.

I was prepared for it. I knew it was coming all along. I wanted to keep her more than anything but it would have only been cruel ⊕ selfish. My favorite sweet Mama Tips—she went through a lot with us. I loved her very much.

And so Dumbo is the only tipsy left. I can't believe I've lost 4 tipsies in less than a year. I almost feel there's a curse on me. All different diseases, all caused by unknown "viruses," all deadly, 2 of the diseases horribly contagious, but no other tipsy got them. What do I do?

We got into this whole big thing. He began accusing me of being a big woweeee with all the guys ⊕ how I *lure* them on ⊕ try to get picked up

6   University of California, Berkeley

by every guy in town cuz I wear short skirts ✦ I never did that before. Told him he's full of crap ✦ no guy has ever tried to pick me up other than horrid gila monsters that I feel like vomiting on.

He said he just gets SO jealous when other guys look at me ✦ if I were doing to him what he's doing to me (with Sara) he wouldn't be able to bear it ✦ so he doesn't even think I'm jealous about her.

Well, the whole conversation got me so pissed, he was trying to make like I'm the big floozy trying ✦ succeeding in getting 1,000,000 guys ✦ he's the innocent little boy who just *never* done <u>nothin</u>. Told him I just couldn't buy that line. The only thing I ever got was a handful of gila monsters goin "hey, cutey, how d'ya like *me*?"

I can't remember in what context, but J said he's harbored a lot of sexual feelings for Paul. That's pretty heavy of him to admit.

He was real cold ✦ matter-of-fact—I felt like shit ✦ tears came. I said I never thought he could be that cold ✦ unemotional. Said he just didn't wanna get carried away ✦ start crying too. That he couldn't help it—he's sorry he's hurting me. Told him I couldn't be friends with my ex-lovers cuz it's too hard—maybe in a year I can be just friends but not until then. That I didn't want to see him at all or talk to him ✦ that it's just unfortunate we have the German class together.

He went ✦ took his bike outside, came back ✦ asked wasn't I gonna come in the kitchen ✦ say good-bye. I was crying hard, he took my arm ✦ I said no, he's making it too hard ✦ so he said OK real sharp ✦ gave me a shove back into the couch. He came back, sat down ✦ took my hand as I was crying ✦ said real gently, "How do you think I feel, huh?…pretty guilty, that's how, pretty guilty." As he left I said "J I love you" ✦ "If you ever wanna come back you know where I am." He said if I wanted to come back I knew where he was too ✦ left. I can't remember if he said he loved me too.

Tues was our midterm German exam. In class we always sat together in the 2nd row on the far left. I got there before him ✦ sat way off on the far right. I didn't look up but saw his feet go over to his regular seat. We did the exam ✦ I saw his feet leave about 5 min before I did.

But I feel good. I feel relieved ✦ more of a person now…like I'm NOT a piece of shit ✦ I do have some pride. I feel I have some say in my destiny. I'd like to gather up his stuff at my place—take it to Michael's when J's not there.

I really hope that by the time he decides he wants me back (I say a couple months…well, Sara's leaving the city in January…we'll see how long it takes him), I just might be fed up with the whole goddam thing ✦ not even want him, or have my defenses up so that I won't be able to trust him not to pull it again.

You know, I really don't think Sara knows a thing about it. I bet she just figures J's a friend of hers ✦ doesn't even realize he's floating on Cloud 9 over her. Bet she doesn't even know she broke us up. Doubt if J'd tell her. I really don't feel any hostility for her…she seems to be an innocent party. He's the asshole.

Last week Monday J wasn't in class ✦ Tues before class the teacher comes up ✦ asks me which section J transferred into. Told her I didn't know he *did* ✦ if he wasn't in class today I was gonna ask *her* if he did. Told her I think he transferred cuzza me ✦ that we've been going together 4 years ✦ had our 1st big fight ✦ I think he transferred to get away from me. So I really felt bad he transferred ✦ pulled out a kleenex ✦ she told me if I wanted I could just leave the class.

So I went home, practically staring at the clock, trying to fall asleep cuz I was so confused ✦ tired. I really felt I lost him ✦ I didn't wanna go on.

I called back at 10:15 ✦ who answers but *J*! I was so shocked ✦ all I could say was "you wanna come over?" He said yeah real much but it's so late ✦ he has no way to get here, excuses, excuses. I kept begging ✦ he said well if it meant that much he'd come.

So bout 11 he came ✦ we couldn't stop hugging ✦ touching ✦ I was the most beautiful person in the world ✦ he could never be away from me that long again ✦ he's so sorry ✦ he loves me so much he could never love anyone as he loves me, etc, etc. So we went to Chico's "to celebrate" he said ✦ he bought me a drink.

We came back to Albion (oh yeah bout the 2nd thing he said was he just doesn't wanna live with me anymore, is that OK? I said yes, yes) ✦ we fucked real good. He said I should come stay at his place sometimes too cuz it's only fair ✦ he wants to move his stuff there. Shit, I'd've agreed to anything—anything was better than never seeing him like that when we both loved so much. I told him that I knew all this time that he loved me, but I didn't think *he* knew it. He said yeah, that was it—he just didn't know how much he loved me.

Sunday was Bridget's baby shower. I felt like a young man in disguise there, sure wasn't into the cute little baby clothes scene like everyone else there. *Bore!*

So today bout 6 pm I'm walking to the store ✦ this really good looking guy comes walking the other way ✦ when we pass each other we both look twice ✦ he asks where ya going?? Said the store ✦ asked where he's going. So we plan to meet outside the store in 15 mins. We go to

Albion, my heart was racing. We ate ½ of a pizza I had ✦ then put a record on ✦ sat on the couch. He really was fine looking, even stood like a beauty. Talked about nothing. His name was Bo.

So I began telling him how good-looking he was ✦ we began kissing ✦ making out ✦ took off our clothes ✦ off to the bedroom. He sure had a small dick. J's is twice the size, no lie. So we fucked. I don't know. I felt kind of funny, cuz he didn't seem to have that much fun. Kathy said guys are freaked out when the girl admires them ✦ touches ✦ tells them how beautiful they are. Guess that must be it.

So when we were thru we laid there awhile ✦ all of a sudden he gets this hard-guy line, "Never turn down a Southern man." (He's from Florida.) I said well I won't if it's you (said that mostly cuz I felt maybe he felt like he was no good cuz he had such a small dick). So he jumps up ✦ has his clothes on in about 5 seconds saying he has stuff he has to do. I said well thanks a lot!

He was a hard guy from the end of the fuck til he left. Asked me for 55¢ for cigarettes ✦ I said brother! ✦ he said I didn't have to give it to him if I didn't wanna. Told him that's OK, I like the criminal type. When he asked what I meant, told him it's my secret. He said next time it might be $20 ✦ I said it'd be worth every penny. Asked if I'd be round tomorrow ✦ I said maybe. Told me he'd put the 55¢ on the door frame if I wasn't. And he left.

Saturday I took myself to the lakefront. Was sure feeling lonesome. A girl came walking by. We said hi ✦ she sat next to me ✦ we talked. Turns out she lives bout 3 houses away from me. It was so easy to talk to her for some reason. We have a lot in common, like feeling more masculine than feminine. She was real at ease ✦ at peace with herself. Didn't seem to have the stormy feeling I've had lately.

We walked on together ✦ went to a bar ✦ she bought me a drink. Name's Dorey. She suggested we buy a quart ✦ spend the evening so we did ✦ went to my place. She's 27 ✦ told me how she'd been married ✦ had a child who died. I really liked her a lot ✦ got a lot of lesbian (yick I hate that word, I'll just say homosexual) feelings from her that I didn't find unpleasant. Kathy phoned ✝ I invited her over ✝ soon she, Cheyney ✝ Joyce came in. Talked ✝ drank ✝ smoked dope ✝ let Cheyney entertain us. I invited Dorey to Chico's but she declined ✝ went home to eat. Told her I'd stop by sometime ✝ she told me I was welcome anytime.

It takes me til today to write about all of the wonderful things that happened to me this weekend. Thurs J came to Albion to stay over ✝ bout 2:30 am I hear a faint knock at the door. Knocks at the door in the middle of the night always scare the hell outa me but I figured if it was someone sleazy J was there to save me. Crept to the door ✝ asked who it was. "Bo." Jesus Christ I almost shit! Threw on a robe ✝ opened the door. There he was with another guy. I said "Oh bad night." He said why is it a bad night? I said oh it's just a real bad night. He got the hint cuz I left him standing in the hall ✝ he said oh, we better leave then. I said how bout tomorrow? Said he'll stop back tomorrow. I just covered my face when they left I was so freaked. Got back into bed…J didn't even wake up to ask what happened. I was so glad he came back!

Bo was at the door. He sat on the couch in the living room ✝ asked me to give him a body rub. We began making out ✝ landed in the bedroom again. Said he had to pick up his laundry (turns out he's got some girl doing his laundry for him ✝ another taking care of his dog) ✝ I should order a pizza ✝ he'd be right back.

So he came back with the friend he was with Thurs. YICK. We ate ✝ drank rum (I love freaking people out by taking shots). He really liked my cowboy boots ✝ said I should wear my hat too. So when the food ✝ liquor was gone they left ✝ he said he'd be back later tonite.

I went to Kathy's for a few hours. At 3:30 am he came back to Albion. His friend crashed out on the couch ✝ Bo ✝ I made love in the bedroom. This time he really got it on ✦ fucked *real* good. He tried to come in my ass ✦ I told him I never did that before ✦ he said OK, we won't do it tonite then. I'd really like to learn to do that (I like to make love like a man…I want to be a beautiful man making love to another beautiful man.) Then we slept.

I woke up mechanically at 7 am. So I laid awake for 2 hrs just looking at Bo sleep. He was so so lovely. He smelled like a bar of soap…his body is so firm ✦ hard ✦ smooth…✦ his golden curls all over the pillow. Ah, he was lovely. I touched his hair ✦ smelled his shoulders ✦ waited for him to turn so I could look at his beautiful face. He was the pure beauty of youth…✦ I was so graced as to have him next to me for a night. I think he could have any man or woman he wanted.

I left the door key ✦ a note telling him to put it under the wastebasket outside when he left ✦ that I hoped to see him again. He wrote on it "Later." Things like that…just his style ✦ manner are so princely ✦ elegant…"Never turn down a Southern man" he once said to me. He likes me to suck him (I wish I could suck him better than anyone ever has). I like him to thrust in me…he has such strong control of his hips. He's such a lovely thing. I think he'll be in Milw all winter…he asked where he could get a job full time for the winter.

I don't feel a betrayal of J either. The entire thing between Bo ✦ I is physical…J knows nothing about him yet.

Beau (I found it's not "Bo," I'm so embarrassed…wrote him a note once addressing it "Bo," that luckily he didn't see!) came over late, bout 3 am. He couldn't get it on again but tried anyway. He's strange…even tho he *can't* he acts like he *is*. So what. Wed morn I wasn't even in the mood to go to work ✦ called in sick.

We got up bout 11:30…his dumb friend Jerry comes over all the time ✦ sleeps on the living room couch. It was really nice…when we woke he called "Hey Jerry!" from the bedroom in a particularly forced low voice. He really wanted to sound like a big MAN. It seems they kinda play serious hard guy games with each other…like once Beau said to

Jerry "Are you *asking* me or *telling* me?" I can't remember what it was about but Jerry said I'm *asking* you. That kinda shit turns me on about him…guess it's my asshole femaleness.

He told me Wed morn he ✦ his friends invented a name for me cuz I didn't look like a Sheila…it's "cowgirl" cuzza my cowboy boots. He's freaked to see a Northern girl wearing 'em.

I really like Beau. He sure enjoys being admired ✦ lusted over. He just lays back like a king ✦ enjoys. What a prissy!

I guess I can consider myself ditched. Creep. I keep thinking maybe he went back to Florida for a while, maybe this, maybe that. Well *maybe* that *did* happen—but shit. So I've pretty well given up thinking he's coming over again. I've hit the bars pretty often lately tho ✦ haven't seen him so it's entirely possible he's not in the city.

J phoned ✦ asked if I wanted to go downtown shopping with him. I did ✦ he bought an $80 white ascot-like scarf ✦ a $40 white sport coat. I never saw him dress up so before. He's getting wonderfully vain I guess.

I really wonder what's gonna happen next year when J wants to move out-of-state to go to graduate school. I don't know if I'd want to do that with him under present conditions. I don't want to be thrown into nowhere with only a boyfriend to date once in awhile who lives a mile away.

Told him I'm not talking bout gory details but I would like him to know…I have been seeing another guy for a couple of weeks…

He got real taken back ✦ said real fast "OK!!!" He started squirming in his seat ✦ I said he didn't have to be freaked out about it ✦ he said real sharp "All right!! You don't have to tell me all about it!!" I thought well good… that'll just put a bee in your ear…smoke on your pipe ✦ put *that* in!

So Fri nite I put a note on my door that I'd be back at 2 am ⚹ went out with Kathy. At 2:15 Beau knocked. He walked in with his Doberman Pinscher dog. I hugged him ⚹ told him I sure thought I saw the last of him! We sat on the couch ⚹ talked…he *had* been in Milw all this time, living on the West Side he said. He got a job on an assembly line.

In a little while we were in the bedroom making love ⚹ after a while he asked if I "came yet." I said yeah (I didn't). He said good cuz he was getting dragged out. I said well you don't have to come here just to fuck me…he said he knew but it made me happy ⚹ he likes to make others happy. I said it didn't make me happy when I know he was bummed out…he said he's not bummed out but it's just that different people get turned on by different stuff ⚹ he didn't think I could get into what turned him on. I said he should try me. Well, I said he sure is strange ⚹ I never heard of anyone making love in a way they didn't like.

So nothing was settled ⚹ he fell asleep. I was really puzzled…how do you handle something like that?? He said when he started making love he wants to but as it goes on he suddenly doesn't want to anymore. I think he was just making excuses cuz he couldn't get a hard-on again.

Well, guess who's *living* with me?

Wed nite made a meatloaf ⚹ once again no one showed up til late. But they came. Thurs I bought some food ⚹ I knew Beau has a key (I left one for him to lock my door cuz he left after me once more) so I left a note that I was staying at J's ⚹ they are more than welcome to stay there (Beau already had his back-pack of clothes in my living room) ⚹ eat anything they wanted.

Thurs at J's house he was so romantic ⚹ loving ⚹ then Michael comes home from work early. What a drag! But we went in the bedroom ⚹ he made love to me like never before ⚹ I love him so damn much. It's so strange. I hope J never finds out the nature of Beau's ⚹ my relationship.

It would really hurt him bad. I love him so fucking much. I understand a lot more now about why J left Albion ✦ still loves me very very much.

Bridget had her baby yesterday. We saw him when he was bout 20 mins old—what a wrinkly purpley blobby guy—big huge eyes *looking*, a little dark bloody hair ✦ a real mean expression like "I'm gonna get you guys fer dis!" Bridg took no drugs or anything ✦ was wide awake thru it all ✦ after the birth ✦ said she was walking around bout 4 hrs later!!

Birth is so incomprehensible. I don't believe all that happened *did*.

Friday Beau got paid ✦ gave me $25. I had borrowed him $18 in $2 here ✦ 50¢ there. He said he, Jerry ✦ I were going out to dinner Sunday nite…but I had to tell him I couldn't cuz J was invited to a party at Dr. Ross's home (his Greek professor) ✦ asked me to come along. So he said we'd make it another time. We fucked Fri nite too.

Sat morn Bridget ✦ Jacob were coming home from the hospital bout 11:30. Kathy ✦ I made a little "brunch" of bakery ✦ coffee. Sat nite Beau *woke me up* to fuck ✦ he really got it on too for a change. He sure is good when he's in the mood!

Sunday J ✦ I went to the party. It was kind of a drag…lotta nowhere people talking bout their scholarly endeavors, etc. Not even any liquor…J was pissed about that. So we went to his place…He loves to undress himself slowly in front of me ✦ pose his lovely body…he knows so many fine things about loving. It's as tho all our time together has made him see that he is as graceful ✦ sexual as anyone can be ✦ he gives me much pleasure. We made love…it's a lot different than fucking. When Beau fucked me Saturday I found myself saying "J" to myself…

Monday when I came home there was $30 worth of food at Albion. I had never had that much food in the house. Beau bought it…a turkey, 4 loaves of bread, soup, milk, eggs, orange juice, hamburger, pancake mix, cereal, lettuce, luncheon meat, cheese…on & on…I couldn't believe it…even toothpaste. That really made me feel good. They aren't living off me!

When he came in I just hugged him! He brought his dog over. I guess he ran outa people who'll take care of it. The little tipsy gets real spitty at the dog but Dumbo just sits & looks at it…then comes over by me real close.

The other day I was in the kitchen & Beau had just woken up. He came wandering into the kitchen with only his pants on, rubbing his eyes & said "Mornin babes." The only thing I could think to say was "You look like shit!" when he was the most beautiful creature in the world right then. His small hard shapely chest…brown from Florida's sun…and his brown curls streaked with golden blond falling around his face… his pants clinging to his small smooth hips…his squared thin boney shoulders…What a beauty he was…I told him he looked like shit while I touched & held him to me. Jerry is always bitching at him in the morning becuz he spends so much time in the bathroom in front of the mirror. I have a brown corduroy waist jacket that he sometimes wears…I pretend I'm wearing it.

Last night I went to Kathy's & J came there bout 8 pm. He'd drunk a *lot* at work & was pretty drunk. He told me about a guy he works with who flaunts his homosexuality & J thinks he's really cool…how he met the guy's "roommate" & he was a blatant homosexual. And J is so "snakey" as Randy calls it when J's drunk. He moves around gracefully & sensuously & smiles invitingly…So Kathy, J & I went to the Saloon to drink & he was beautiful… he gets real feminine when he's drunk & flirts & laughs nervously…

As we left there were 2 guys leaving ahead of us…one a tall very thin guy with shaped black hair around his face…he had tight blue jeans & a black quilted jacket that came to his small waist. He was laughing

⚘ hanging on his friend graceful ⚘ feminine ⚘ swaying his hips as he walked…he called behind to J to have a nice nite or something ⚘ when they saw us hitchhiking offered us a ride. J sat rite behind him…He turned ½ way in his seat so he was ½ facing J, the radio blasted a Rod Stewart song…And J ⚘ this guy sang it to each other.

The guy used his hands to make motions of feigning love to J ⚘ I saw bracelets all on his wrists…J leaned over the seat close to him playing the role of the lover…I realized I'd never be able to participate. No matter how I tried I could never have joined their game. I felt a deep sadness at finally realizing I'll never have my deepest secret dream fulfilled, ever. The guy lowered his eyelids ⚘ took J's hand as we left the car…I had an urge to lean over ⚘ kiss the boy as I left the car… but I knew I could never be part of the life ⚘ I had just admitted it to myself…I left the car hoping he didn't notice I was female…

As I made love to J, I pictured him in bracelets ⚘ necklaces…I told him I wished I had jewelry there to put on him…(I'm thinking of going tomorrow to buy him a bracelet for Christmas…I wonder if he'd wear it).

Sat morn as we recalled the nite before I said I really liked that one guy…he said with the quilted jacket? I said yeah. He agreed he was really cool ⚘ said quietly "he was a little swishy"…I said I know, I like that, I think it's really neat. J said "yeah."

I want to make him the lovely boy I wish I could be. I want me to desire him ⚘ try to kiss him. He told us how he was at this one bar ⚘ there was a blatantly gay guy there ⚘ J overheard 2 guys saying how they were gonna kick that fag's ass when he left the bar. J said so as the guy is leaving the bar, he leans over to the guy checking I.D.'s ⚘ kisses him right on the lips…slowly ⚘ deliberately ⚘ walked outa the bar. No one followed him out. J said he really freaked out…it was so excellent he did that to freak everyone.

When I came back to Albion this afternoon Beau asked me if I'd talked to J yet. I said yes, I was with him last nite. He asked what did he say ⚘

I said "not a thing, we had a good cry together this morn but didn't say a word." Beau asked what J cried about ✦ I said I didn't know. But that I've cried so much over J so now he can cry over me a little. He said, it must be love. I said yeah.

Why is J so insistent on us being apart if it hurts him so when I have another boyfriend? When he knows I'd rather be with him all the time.

Beau asked me if J was "the fighting type." I said no, he's still an altar boy at heart.

I told Beau how J sure was curious about him. He asked "why did he pick me?" I said what d'ya mean? He said why didn't he think you were with Jerry? I smiled ✦ said "He knows my taste."

I was so happy ✦ in such an elated mood when J left. I felt like a weight was lifted off me. It turned me on to think the two beauties in my life held each other's hands ✦ looked into each others' faces. Now I really think things will turn out OK...

When I asked how he could tell I liked it he said when you're with someone for so long you just know. He said we can do such wonderful things together ✦ we'll always be together. "I'll be the woman ✦ you can be the man."—that's what he said. I said, yes, yes.

It was an insane nite. He said he's gonna cut off his facial hair!!

In the morn he laughingly said we could go out whoring together ✦ make some extra cash. Also that he'd seen a very beautiful youngman (I steal "youngman" from John Rechy...it's a good word) in the Union a few days ago (he had blond curls ✦ a shirt opening low on his chest. J said he wasn't sure for a long time if he was male) ✦ did a double take ✦ the youngman noticed J looking at him ✦ looked curious. J said he thought him haughty.

Lately J has told me stories of acquaintances & youngmen he's seen who're gay. At the dishroom where J works is Jerome who is blatantly gay & uses it to freak people out. (Jerome looks like a clown. I wish he were a beauty.) J said he used to dislike him but now likes him a lot. His roommate always waits for him after work, which annoys the bosses. One asked what he was doing & he answered "I'm waiting for my man." J told me the above stories with affection & approval. I listened to them eagerly & greedily hid them in my soul.

Saturday I took my jewelry box & made a bracelet for J from an old broken necklace & the clasp from a junky pink charm bracelet. The beads are a deep green. I haven't seen him to give it to him yet. I hope he likes it.

He told me he tried again & again to get the bracelet I bought him for Christmas on, but can't. I guess I could return it…maybe I'll ask him to go with me & we'll return it for something else.

Sunday at Randy's J shaved his mustache & beard but left the small clusters of soft hairs on his cheeks as I suggested, because they are beautiful. He knew he looked beautiful & I told him how lovely he is, how he's so lucky becuz he has the secret of youth. His face glowed, he said, "really?" a smile lit up his face embarrassingly & he tossed back his long hair. (I think of Kathy in Rechy's *City of Night*, of her ghostlike beauty, of the man who kissed her & reaching under her skirt, realized she was a man).

Beau has left. Saturday nite I slept at Albion & he never came…the first time since he moved in that he's slept elsewhere. Sunday evening bout 5 pm I came to Albion & all his stuff was gone cept 3–4 things. Haven't heard from him at all, he left no note or anything. Bye-bye.

I've been with J every other nite [for eleven days]. He asks for me to.

Monday & Tuesday I was almost completely under the spell of Beau's beauty. Every spare second I recalled to mind his soft golden back, the curves of it…his deep golden curls on his smooth shoulders…the way he arched his back and spread his legs when he wanted me to suck him…and the last time I had him and, in the dark, moving my hands over his cheek, I touched a tiny chain around his neck. Its discovery made me come almost immediately. I ran my fingers between his neck & the chain…I told him I liked him to wear it. And the next morning I only caught a glimpse of the little golden chain. After a few days he was gone.

And I remember how he told Jerry about the girl in the bar who was "crying" just for a reason to get her hands up his shirt.

Still haven't heard a thing from Beau (rotten shithead). He must have come over Thurs nite or Fri afternoon but Fri nite I noticed the rest of his shit (camera, clothes, etc) was gone & I was overnite at J's Thurs. But he left no note or *anything*. Real sleazy.

J went to see Lou Reed, lead singer of the Velvet Underground (an Andy Warhol discovery…Andy Warhol's outasite…his films…his people…they're all fine as hell) Sat nite. He said every queen in town was there & the audience was more interesting to watch than anything. He said he had the best time he's ever had in a long time. He got together with some guy he thought was "AC-DC" (bisexual) and they were buying each other drinks all nite, etc.

I was real drunk myself Sat (went out with Bridg & Kathy) & went to J's place hoping he'd be there…fortunately he came just as I was giving up pounding on the door. We sat up & talked to Michael who came in a few mins later. I told them during our conversation that I wanted to dress up in female drag & be a queen but I couldn't since I AM a female…so I'm frustrated.

I wish I was J—he's such a lovely male. I wish I'd have seen him in that crowd. I want him so passionately.

Well, he finally showed his mug, Beau, that is. Came wandering in yesterday nite. Said he'd stopped by many times before (I doubt that). About the first thing he did was give me back the key to Albion. So he stayed a while, he quit his job & is looking for another & he acknowledged the fact he owes me $60. I felt kind of like I didn't know how to act, but we kissed goodbye. Said he'd stop by again.

A miracle happened last nite too. I had a dream J & Paul Lemmen (his friend, a guy in Randy's crowd) were having a love affair. I was Paul sucking J off in the dream. That's the only real detail about it I remember. But so today I told J I had an "erotic" dream about him & he said he'd had a dream last nite too, a "homosexual dream." I said "really? I had one too!" & told him bout it. He said he dreamt he was making out with some guy (but didn't know who it was supposed to be) & that the dream turned him on & when he woke up he was all turned on & had a hard-on (he usually does when he wakes up tho). We said how strange we both had the *same* dream !!!

He moves so gracefully, his long hair flows, his deep brown eyes flirt but in a sacred way. He is not ordinary and he recognizes he isn't. His grace is pure. He is a saint, a boy saint.

What can I do to encourage him to get a lover? I am beginning to like his all-white get-up he's wearing lately. He wears all white (even shoes) & a black topcoat. Really looks freaky.

In "Toby Dammit," Fellini's short film, a TV interviewer asks Toby, "What do you think is the factor that has kept you and Miss (don't know name…insignificant) together for so long?'

Toby Dammit answers, "Well, I'm feminine enough to please her and she's masculine enough to please me."

So it is with J & I.

He teased me by singing Lou Reed songs… "vicious, oh baby, you're so vicious…." He looked at me thru lowered eyelids and touched his hair, his long bare neck with his jeweled fingers… And then he'd smile. J… J… How can I deserve you? We went to his place & made love crazily, insanely, happily, lovingly… J. He lets me make love my way & he's happy. I put all the jewelry on him… My long long black necklace, over his shoulders, his back, his chest. I came & came & came and he did, too. He slept with the jewelry on. He lets me without any objection. He encourages me.

How do I fit into all this? Even if something did happen…what could *I* do? I could only imagine or wish. Never participate the way I want to.

Yesterday at J's. Told him I knew a certain bar, Fish's Harbor, was a gay bar. Said he knew that for a long time, way before I did & I think he even laughed & said "Do you think I wait for you to find out about that stuff first?"—or something like that. Then he said we should go there to eat sometime & I said OK, that'd be pretty far-out tho. He agreed & after a pause said we shouldn't go there. We shouldn't if we're just gonna go for fun or something. I wanted to say…but I said yeah, I guess yer right.

Why does he torture me like that. He was strangely moody all day Monday. He invited me to go to Randy's pool league game with him yesterday nite. Friday nite Bridget gave me a beautiful old ring of hers I liked…when we got to J's I gave it to him & told him it would look much more beautiful on him than on me. He was real taken back, at first he refused it but later accepted, thanking me so. Monday I commented how nice it looked on him & he looked at it appreciatively & said in a quiet & super sincere voice (I've never heard such sincerity) "That was really nice that you gave me this…it really was…I have to get you something real soon…" J. Imagine how mixed up I am…how I don't even know *what* I want to get, much less *how* to get it. But you have everything open to you.

You could go to the bar any night alone & come back with a beautiful youngman. I wouldn't even be welcome into the bar…and even if I got in, I'd be so ashamed that I was a woman that I'd leave quickly, lost, apologetically ⊕ want to cry in desperation. I don't even know if there was anyone that's ever felt as I do…how they coped, what they did…how do I find out what someone like me does? (I remember writing this same question many diaries back…in probably one of my first ones.)

He teases me ⊕ then looks at me so I don't know if he's angry or indignant or repulsed by me…I want to get away ⊕ come back a youngman ⊕ take him in my arms…

—How's this all gonna work out?

Friday afternoon J ⊕ I made love at his place, like about 3:30 or so. It was superb. I asked him if he really wanted to do all these things or was he just trying to please me. He asked what things? I said like wearing jewelry ⊕ singing Lou Reed songs. He said of course he wanted to do them…did I think he would do all this just to please me?? I said I wasn't sure…that it was all so good.

We were walking to his place ⊕ while crossing a street J ran across while I walked. There were 2 high school age boys next to me ⊕ one of them, seeing J run across the street in all his beauty remarked to the other "Look at that fag." I was instantly turned on, ran after him ⊕ threw my arms around him…he'll never know why.

Today J's sister May phoned ⊕ told me how he'd gone over to his mother's for dinner ⊕ she rebuked him for wearing the tight-fitting black, girls' cardigan sweater. May commented to his ma "Well maybe he's queer" ⊕ J said "I don't know, I haven't decided yet."

I still think of when we were arrested ⊕ J told me the police escorting him to a different room had said to him "Come on, faggot." Lovely fat for my fire.

This past week J slept *at Albion* for the first time in months. It was strange having him there…really good. He's really changing—Shit—a real lot. He found a girls' black cardigan that fits him real tight ⊹ he looks super sexual in it. He said he knows that ⊹ likes it. He always wears one of his bracelets now— has a green ⊹ a black one. We went downtown yesterday morn ⊹ he bought another girls' black cardigan that'll fit him better. We looked at some gaudy rings (he said "how decadent!") ⊹ then he seemed to want to leave real fast (??).

I think a lot about myself lately—my identity as a woman, what's happening ⊹ will happen with my life, how I'll live ⊹ what I'll do. I would like to do something significant in life but can't think what. Nothing holds my interest long enuff to make it a permanent gig. I think how I relate to men ⊹ if my feelings about them are healthy ⊹ good…that is, if I rely on men being around too much, if I could survive alone. Like if J doesn't want me to go with him to grad school. He acts real funny when we talk about should I go or not. Sometimes he says no ⊹ 2 seconds later yes. It's real sleazy.

I don't feel like I'm gonna be 22 in 6 months, I don't feel at all past 18…time stopped for me when I turned 18. But 22…shit, a person should be somewhat down by then—but I kinda feel not all together yet…pretty much together but not all. I guess things'll work out.

It's so strange how things change—yesterday the Vietnam War as good as ended ⊹ in 60 days everyone (POW's–everyone) will be home. It's like I can't picture how to feel after all that's happened—I remember the Wash DC march…all the marches…how emotionally involved I was for so long. Now it's over ⊹ I don't know how it feels to not be at war. So many changes.

Yesterday went to Harley-Davidson Cycles ⊹ tried on their black leather jackets. Excellent! Hope to get mine by this weekend.

I love to blend female & male—I think of myself as 2 people finally coming together in peace with each other. Of my other half I sing "Nobody loves me but me adores you!"

It's funny to look at me now in comparison to bout a year ago. I think if J asked me to marry him I'd definitely say no. In a way I'd like to live with him again, but in another way I like to have these secret adventures (like Beau).

He's so loving lately. We almost had free tickets to the Performing Arts Ctr for a concert of symphony music & I said I would go if we'd go both in "high drag." He laughed & later we talked how excellent it'd be if he went in mink & I in leather. Freak people out!

I went over to Dorey's the other nite to invite her to supper & had in mind asking her to sleep over if I got those vibes from her again like I did before…but she had plans for the nite. Pretty strange, heh?

Since I got my jacket, it's all I wear. Also, I've been wearing black levis everyday cuz color pants don't make it with the jacket.

Guess who just appeared at my door—Prince Charming! (Beau) Showed him all my "drag clothes." Had to explain what "drag" is ("It's when gays wear what they like…"). I'm not sure he got it. But he laid back on the couch, his hands behind his head, stretching his body & looking over himself with admiration and approval. Waiting for me to first show my desire for him—as always was. I submit to his narcissism. I admire & kiss & undress & lick him eagerly—he leans back & smiles, closing his eyes contentedly. And then only after a long while will he lazily begin to undress me.

He lifted me, my legs around his waist, both naked ⚬ walked me in there. We fucked... He came while we were in my favorite position... Me on all fours ⚬ him kneeling behind me... I am the youth making love to this other lovely youth.... Then he had a cigarette. We laid naked ⚬ I showed him all my rings—he said I should give him one. (I would give them all to him if he'd wear them all at the same time.) He said he wasn't a person of big words, just says what he feels. Then, like an angel, he dozed off to sleep, lying there naked.

J ⚬ I went to hear a lecture by Christine Jorgensen, the first guy to have a sex-change to a woman. It was pretty interesting. It took some courage for me to go cuz I guess I'm still a bit hesitant to admit publicly I'm interested in this male/female thing. J didn't let on he was interested til the last minute.

Lou Reed yesterday. Started drinking Saturday noon mainly cuz I was so bored. Started to get sick ⚬ dozed Sunday afternoon but took speed ⚬ came around real fast. Randy, J ⚬ I drove to Chicago for the concert. I couldn't believe how straight the audience was... I was one of the heavies! Small contingent of drag queens, tho.

Lou was beautiful... All in black with silver heels... Once in a while he'd begin to dance slightly or he'd put his left hand on his thigh while moving his hips sensually ⚬ break his right wrist into a limp rose stem ⚬ wave it around... Lovely! The crowd didn't seem all that excited, altho on the ground floor kids were dancing. The drag queens were making out, etc, in the dark.

I was speeding but felt completely straight which was a drag. Began thinking about what I have to do... I have to go to New York. Myself. To find Rechy's FASCINATION lights. It scared me when I realized it, but it had to be by myself cuz anything less would be a cop-out. Began thinking what I had to take with me, which clothes, etc ⚬ where would I start? Which section of town? Which hotel? It would be scary, no doubt. But I have to do it. Maybe this summer.

As we were leaving the concert, there were pretty many heavies...

I'd've liked to hang around but the guys were in a fat hurry. Some pretty little thing was standing around with his shirt all open, blonde shoulder-length hair, smooth white hairless chest. We both stared at each other on by ("I'm heavier than you are" stares) altho of course I'd never compete with a beauty like that. I wanted to reach out & touch his chest but I was scared of course & the guys were way ahead of me & I didn't want to lose them. Yet I think our stares would have softened. They were frightened, defensive stares, but on the same wavelength...

That's why I have to go to NY Alone. I can't have anyone or anything in my way when I find what I'm looking for there. I'm not sure myself exactly what it is...But I'll know. And I really do feel whatever comes, whatever I'd run into in NY, I'd be able to handle. I'm only afraid of being shot down...Being told I wasn't wanted on the scene...It's a pain in the ass being a goddamn girl. Being told, or getting the feeling I wasn't wanted on the scene would destroy me.

But then this afternoon, Liz Marshall[7] comes out of nowhere. She's a guy I went to First Semester Russian with Summer '70 (I think it was) & who came back to visit me in drag months later. Been thinking bout her lately a lot. Told her I was so glad to see her & had such an identity crisis... But the only thing I'm sure of is I like real femmy guys but I don't know if it's a cop-out for my desire for women. We talked an hour. She's trying to get a sex change operation. Told me the gay bars in Milw & that I maybe should go to the Gay Peoples Union meetings. But I was scared. She said she'd go with me this Monday. We made it a date...

My horoscope says I should go ahead with what I'm doing... that I "will be rewarded."

7   Elizabeth Marshall

2 am Beau comes over. Lost no time in getting in bed. He tried butt-fucking me again but I just couldn't... It hurts so. He just jammed in me ＋ I pulled away ＋ I told him I wanted to but couldn't cuz it hurts so. He said just try ＋ relax but I couldn't cuz I knew he wouldn't be gentle but would jam again. So I just said I can't. (Felt bad—I'd like to so I can make love to him like a boy but I couldn't...I'll never be a boy anyhow... It wouldn't be the same, I guess.)

Went to Teddy's, a bar where James Cotton Blues Band was playing. Spotted a cute little thing there, real soft light brown hair and a shag cut, tall ＋ long-legged, blue jean jacket over an undershirt, swaying ＋ enjoying the music. Stared at him about ½ hour but that didn't work so went over ＋ stood RIGHT next to him ＋ stared at him ＋ kept trying to rub against him so he'd notice me but after about 20 mins of that, I wondered if I had to grab his cock to get his attention. Yet he didn't move away when I rubbed against him ＋ I finally figured he knew damn well I was trying to hustle him. FINALLY he looked at me ＋ smiled ＋ I smiled back ＋ he said, "Dynamite band, heh?" I nodded, still smiling ＋ put my arm around his waist ＋ he put his arm around me ＋ we began kissing real juicy ＋ I began feeling him up ＋ the music playing ＋ he was still swaying to it ＋ I rubbed his cock a little.

Finally asked if I wanted to go out in his car ＋ I said well, I only live a block away. He said so did he, I asked where. Turned out to be more like a mile away ＋ I said I live A block away! He said OK ＋ "I don't even know your name." I said you didn't ask. His was Rick. So we split, I told him I'd almost given up on him there, but I've been cruising him the last hour. He smiled he was just digging the music. So my first successful hustle. Felt good. He put on a Howlin' Wolf album ＋ we began kissing on the bed. Had a super tiny cock... J must have colossus for a cock cuz the three others I've seen, his is twice as big. But this guy took the cake, but he was super cuddly ＋ gentle. Was real quiet though ＋ kept his eyes closed the entire time (what a let down!). Seemed he was trying to hold back coming ＋ in fact I don't know if he even did! Pretty cruddy fuck but nice ＋ warm ＋ soft.

Thurs Lou Reed! Started drinking at 3 pm—Patrick, Johnney, Kathy, Bridg ✝ I going. High drag, for sure. Did Alice Cooper eye-makeup trip. Drunk enough to do a shit job ✝ Bridg took over with some liquid stuff. We got there by 6:30 ✝ had to wait in line 2 hrs. During which we continued drinking. Good and fuckin drunk. Then Johnney started getting sick ✝ slouching down on the steps, Patrick holding him ✝ they begin letting people in. We got him to a bathroom. Ah-ha! Liberate the men's can! So the second band played, Johnney lay on the floor, slouched over a toilet, P sat next to him ✝ I stood around. First time I saw a real urinal. Guys'd come in, look at me stand at the urinal, not piss ✝ leave. Pat ✝ I'd laugh!!

I felt fantastic. Hardly watched Lou at all, too into myself.

Then I see a group of pretty guys ✝ *the loveliest...* Long black curly hair with glitter in it, a red velvet jacket all open, his naked chest smooth. Somehow I went up to him ✝ had him! Don't even ask me how—I don't know!

I think we smoked some dope. Then we went to his room, he was just moving in ✝ we had to line up a sofa ✝ chair cushions to form a mattress. We made love good—I don't remember even what we did. He was beautiful ✝ we made love slowly. I remember once I said something on how we were "fucking" ✝ he said no, we're not fucking, we're "making love"... ✝ I started crying. He was a real romantic like that, talked ✝ made nice noises ✝ got water for us. He was real into an inner existence type deal ✝ kept saying "astral" projection ✝ "astral" this ✝ that.

I said once what beautiful eyebrows he had ✝ and he looked away bummed out. Asked why ✝ he said I was only complimenting his body ✝ he didn't want to think like that. That's how he was—real strange. We made love several times. There was still glitter all over him.

As we hugged goodbye, he said, "My Lou Reed" and I really wanted to be.

Have been reading my head off: *Tea and Sympathy, Dancing the Gay Lib Blues, Tearoom Trade, Towards a Recognition of Androgyny, Is Gay Good?, Gay Mystique*, and the latest *The Transsexual Phenomenon*.

Sunday at Mom's she ✦ Maryellen and I read an article on a girl who had a sex-change to a man. Ma said she thinks if they'd've had those in her day, she'd've definitely thought of doing it, cuz she always felt more like a man. The conversation encouraged me and about ½ hours later, I told her about how I felt, etc, ✦ she was very understanding ✦ even said she felt that way, too! It was pretty strange ✦ rather nice... When I left she told me that she only asks I dress up for big family deals ✦ she wants me to be me ✦ be happy ✦ that if I'd even decided to get an operation, she'd be behind me all the way! Told her I don't think I'm to *that* point yet.

So I've just read ✦ read the transsexual book ✦ as I nearly finished it last night, I began crying... Needing J. Thoughts came pouring out: I want to be him, I don't want me if he doesn't, if he doesn't want me I don't want to live but I'm too scared to die so I'll just bury myself. I realize I'd dress up in beautiful female clothes ✦ go to him, but if he'd reject me I'd never be able to wear them again. But if he came back to me I'd be able to easily switch back ✦ forth as I've done before, but I'm escaping into myself, lost, hiding, afraid now. That I need him ✦ if I can't have him, I'll become him so I can always be with him...

Crazy thoughts. Crazy interpretations that made me cry ✦ cry ✦ phone ✦ phone but no answer until I fell asleep. It all happened when I realized that I'd never be able to be a pretty girl again until he came back to me... And if he doesn't I'll always be like I am—a symbol of mangled, violated sex. Destroyed in a strange way...

Friday a woman named Jay propositioned me. Told her I'd never been with a woman, she said she'd make me feel fantastic, but there was only one requirement: that *I* didn't touch *her*. Why? That's just her hang-up... shit. Told her I don't even know if I'd want a lesbian experience... finally told her I consider myself a male homosexual...she was pretty grossed out about that but I've seen her since ✦ we're still friends. She's

32 & super mannish... she insisted on paying for everything (coffee, drinks). That bummed me out, too. She said she knew the first time she saw me I wasn't so butch.

Smoked 2 joints to loosen up.

My high made me lose my inhibitions and I tied my breasts down so they wouldn't jiggle, although it did little to make them appear smaller, plus rolled up a few socks & made myself a penis, pinned it in my underwear.

Eldon[8] calls & asks if I can get hold of Liz, & that he has someone we'd probably both like to meet. He picks us both up and we pick up this 44 year old "woman" who's really a man passing in society as a woman for 23 years without any operation or other medical aid. We four went & ate lunch & then to Eldon's where he taped an interview with Betty. She was about 5'2" & less than 100 lbs so very frail. Said she always liked the femmy stuff & at 16 decided either she had to be a femmy little faggot or switch to a woman. Stayed & nursed her sick parents & when she was 22 they both died & she put on her women's clothes, had her brother drive her to the bus station & went to New York & has lived as a woman since.

Also Eldon told us of a time Winnie was doing strip shows in a straight place where no one knew he was a man at all! Twelve drunk guys from a stag party came in & asked Winnie, who's a *beautiful girl,* if she'll do a private strip show in their apartment for them. He said they were all beautiful athletic bodies & he agreed for $75, knowing a show wasn't all they wanted. After doing a private strip down to the last pieces, he ran coyly to the bedroom. They all crashed in & Winnie puts his hands up & hollers, "Stop right there! *What* do you think I am, a *whore?* ONE AT A TIME!" Gave the excuse she wasn't a whore so

8   Eldon Murray

he wouldn't have to fuck them, so he sucked them all off ✝ they never knew he was really a guy!

I held myself ✝ stroked my skin like I always do ✝ imagining I was a beautiful boy I was sleeping with ✝ then it began to get too real ✝ I felt my mind ✝ my body separating. Got so scared ✝ realized I had to get outside ✝ talk to someone if I wanted to stop. Got dressed ✝ rode my bike by J's tho I knew he probably wasn't there.

Mentioned to J that he won't have snow this winter ✝ he said he'll be back in December.

And so I had to sleep with the boy I am ✝ make love to myself, like I have every nite. I pretend I'm a boy in bed ✝ think how it feels. I've done this for years—as long as I've had sexual feelings. I have to go to bars often if I'm to find myself a boy to sleep with. In times I can't, I can become a boy to sleep with. But it's so much nicer with a real one.

Went to the GPU[9] meeting ✝ about ¼ of the way thru it, a really fine youngman came in I've never seen before ✝ sat in the pew next to me. I immediately thought he was gorgeous ✝ when a guy popped up next to him to welcome him I thought, "Shit, I'll never have a chance next to all these guys...," not that I thought I even *had* a chance. Whenever he wasn't looking I looked at him admiringly.

So when the meeting was over, as usual some stayed around to chat ✝ I did. He told some people he was from New York ✝ came to Milw

9   Gay Peoples Union at University of Wisconsin–Milwaukee

to dance with the Milw Ballet Company. Yes—he looked a *lot* like a dancer, had that classic, statue face + body. He offered to help draw for *GPU News*. As they talked I caught his eye + we stood looking in each other's eyes about 15 seconds + I thought "Hmmm..." Kept a close eye on him. He was staying at the YMCA, he said to someone.

When I saw him leave I "rushed" out after him. He was walking down Ogden Ave toward the lakefront + I rehearsed my speech. I don't know why but he just struck me as not being untouchable like most gay guys, I guess from that stare we had. Suddenly he stopped in the middle of the sidewalk + I walked up to him + he asked if I had change for the bus. Gave it to him and we kept walking together + I said, "You wouldn't happen to be bi, would you?"

He looked at me startled + said *"What?"*

"Bisexual." I didn't look at him at all, so nervous. "Well, I've been known to go out with girls... Why?"

"Cuz I'm interested."

"In me?"

"Yeah."

He was pretty surprised + we just kept walking + he asked me what I was into. Told him my lover, a male transvestite, left last week for Calif + it's pretty hard to replace someone like that. He asked me when did he dress, I said it only when we were together. He kept going, "Oh, this is really strange," etc. He said he hadn't gone to bed with a girl in 5 or 6 years. I felt like saying as far as I'm concerned if he went with me he wouldn't be breaking his record, but didn't. He said, "Well, OK, let's give it a try." Asked if I was getting myself into something cuz he sounded so hesitant + he said no. So we turned + went to Albion. His name was Charles. I was just in a daze.

At Albion he asked if I had beer or something so he could relax, but I only had grapefruit juice. We sat on the couch and drank that. We chit-chatted about shit + he said "I feel like I'm in high school—I don't know what to *do!*" Told him he's making me more nervous than him ✢ we begin kissing ✢ he leaned back ✢ was the first to undo my clothes. Was freaked at my elastic band to flatten my breasts. (I'm surprised I forgot to mention that his skin, back ✢ chest ✢ face is like Johnney's, all fucked up by acne.) So we kissed ✢ petted for about 15 mins ✢ he still wasn't hard, altho he acted like he was enjoying himself. He asked if I wanted to go to the bedroom. I asked if he did, he said yeah, so we did. He opened my pants ✢ was freaked by my jockey shorts. I opened his ✢ he was naked. We got in bed ✢ made out... Still not hard so I went down on him ✢ sucked him. He was hard in no time. He pulled me back up ✢ we fucked superbly.

Anyway he was gorgeous ✢ we slept together like babies. In the morn we ate breakfast ✢ I gave him my phone no. He always whispers "beast" to Little Tipsy lingering on the "sss" —

Tues bout 10 pm he phones.

Went to his new place ✢ he showed me around. The heat wasn't on at his place so we went to Albion. He wore his brown leather jacket!

He rinsed out his tights, etc. I washed my hair.

He laid on the couch naked ✢ I sat at his feet ✢ he wrapped his legs around me ✢ I pet them. He made little "ooohhh" pleasure sighs ✢ I told him how lovely he is. After a long time I bent over ✢ sucked him real good (he'd been hard before I started tho). He stopped me cuz he was gonna come ✢ said he didn't want to yet. In bed we made love ✢ he used his hand to make me come ✢ then fucked me from the rear. I love this: he whimpers ✢ cries out quietly when he comes. I always loved that. We curled up after sex ✢ slept.

I got to look at him while he slept Wed morn...what a beauty. I still can't believe that I could do it—get a gay man ✢ make love to him.

Told him I wasn't into women ✢ I want to go to a gay bar ✢ get men. He said I could. Asked how? They're there to get other guys. He just said I could, without explaining how that could be!

After sex Monday I asked why he came with me. Said he thinks cuzza my leather jacket & my approach. Told him those are the things that usually turn guys off to me cuz they think I'm gonna chop their dicks off or something.

Bout 1:15 pm he had to leave for rehearsal & I went outside with him cuz I have to tighten some screws on my bike out there to go to Bridget's. He asked for a kiss before he left. Said he'll call Saturday & we'll go dancing, OK?

Around midnite J phoned.

He asked me if I could come see him & I said anytime—now or later. Said if things don't work he'll come to Milw the end of the year & forget school & if they do work I should come there. He was very loving & said he couldn't remember how my body looked.

I'm such a gross pig & I have to make boys be heterosexual to have sex with them.

How do I describe that I deceive myself all day & night that I'm a boy & I feel I am—even tho I'm not even passing in society?

I'm so used to talking about everything! All the thoughts & wishes-dreams Charles guesses & accepts & fulfills! That I'm not going to be satisfied anymore with J's half-flirting pretending games. I know I can get exactly what I want now—to fantasize is no longer good enough. Before it was beyond my dream—it was the worst perversion that I wished to have a penis, to fuck a boy, to be on top & inside! But now it's only a matter of time. Because Charles wants it. He wants me. J doesn't even know that I *am* a boy now. That I just don't read about pretty queens anymore. I'm afraid J's in for more shockers than my letter about men's underwear even hinted at. How am I going to all of a sudden be closety again after coming so far out and so successfully.

Here I am in Berkeley. Four hour flight ✟ I saw the Rocky Mountains ✟ all kindsa shit from the plane, the view was so clear.

J comes bee-lining in ✟ we walk out together. He was super speedy ✟ began talking ✟ barely stopped for about ½ hr. Seems he'd had his first homosexual experience last night. He acted like he wasn't really all there ✟ I kissed him ✟ he said he really liked my haircut ✟ I'm so beautiful ✟ he loves me so much, he really does.

He put on his clogs ✟ a pair of silky textured black knee-high stockings (which gave him a hard-on the first time he put them on, he said!). He looked so beautiful as we went out to eat, his long hair flowing ✟ he walks like a girl in heels with his clogs.

I sure feel bum. I'm really lovesick. Left the GPU mtg tonite about ½ way thru. I began feeling persecuted etc. For one I was teasing around with a lesbian who's always super friendly to me ✟ I said I hoped her lover wouldn't get jealous becuz she ✟ I had matching cups for our coffee ✟ she said real sharp something like "No, thanks, I know what YOU'RE into" like I was some gross pig. I felt like saying well fuck you I know what *you're* into too! And No Thanks. Shit. Then last Thurs I gave Eldon my new article I was (*am*) so thrilled with ✟ all he said about it was he liked it but the beginning ✟ ending quotes from Rechy have to go. And that was it. Fuck. Who the hell is he?

I don't know—I think maybe I'm just being touchy. But when I came home I get a phone call from a male TV in Michigan. I guess TV/S[10] gave my name as a correspondent. She was older (admitted to late 30s but gave me some shit how I shouldn't ask a lady her age) ✟ feigned a

10   Transvestite / Transsexual

high voice. She was OK, but I could tell she was from the old school as she was surprised I had no male name, no mustache or beard hair pieces, + I didn't make a man's voice. She spoke of her male side as her "brother" as do older, more conventional TVs. She was pretty interested in me + when I told her a little bout J she thought our relationship was interesting. I really didn't know what to *say* to her but she invited me there this weekend. Told her I'd phone her Thurs. But I don't think I will. For one it's $44 round trip by plane (the boat doesn't cross the lake anymore). Another thing I don't wanna get stuck having sex with a 45 yr old grandma... grandpa? So I think I'll just blame it on the $.

Anyway she got me to thinking + I just can't see splitting myself into my he + my she side, tho I realize male TVs probably have to. But I just can't see having a fake name etc. As for a beard/mustache I don't like them + I'd only look like a 16 yr. old boy with pasted on hair anyway. Ugh.—I'm so damn lovesick.

She said it was nice talking to me, that it was fun to "look in the mirror."

Had supper with Charles + his lover, Jeffrey. Charles looked so goddamn good but I couldn't do anything about it. Had to watch those 2 snootling around + it just made me more horny + alone.

We 3 went out to the bars + and at the RQ[11] a tall queer I see there all the time complimented me saying he *loves* the way I walk + he saw me walking on the street + asked his friends if I was a boy or girl (they told him girl) + he just thinks I'm so cool + he'd love to ride on the back of my motorcycle if I had one. Told him he wasn't too bad himself + if I had a cycle I'd like him on the back too. He said *REALLY??* It was really an ego-booster.

Charles, Jeffrey + I also went to the Wreck Room, the gay leather S+M bar. I've always been scared to go there, being a girl, but once inside wasn't. Mostly older guys in motorcycle + cowboy getup + no one paid much attention to me. And after a while I began seeing how un-hard the whole scene was. Like they had some kind of raffle + all the hard guys were looking at their ticket to see if they won + then

11 River Queen

they announced everyone with a motorcycle cap or a cowboy hat on could get a free drink. How high school! I just leaned up against a wall acting hard & it was fun. We're all girls pretending we're big shot boys! HA HA

That Mich drag Loretta sent me about 10 pictures of her so I wouldn't think her a "decrepit old lady." But too bad—she looked like someone's biddy aunt. Ugh. I phoned her Thurs & told her I couldn't afford to come there. It was really weird. *He* answered the phone, I asked for Loretta & he acted like he was getting a different person & then *she* got on the phone. Gives you the willies. She was disappointed I wasn't coming but said I should send a picture "not of you, of your 'brother.'" When I explained I didn't feel that split in half she was real shocked & said then I wasn't a TV, "not that there's any one way you have to be to be TV," which made no sense to me. She harped on my getting a masculine name for my "brother" like John or Bob ("but not Bobby"). Shit. Told her I was called Lou a while but she felt that just wouldn't do, it's "too ambiguous." Man, what a drag (ha, ha). A drag drag.

Eldon set me up to go to the Ball with this other male TS Eliz used to hang around with but ditched cuz she feels he's just fucked up. But I talked to him over the phone & and he seemed rather embarrassed til I told him I cross-dress too. Name's Greg—female-named Linda.

I had Charles & Jeffrey over for supper & then sat around. The other day I expressed a wish for handcuffs & so Johnney bought me some. We played with those. Then Jeff & I went to the RQ where I'd made a date to meet Linda. He didn't come in drag & turned out to be a real serious, depressed, boring person. Just the while I talked to him he impressed me as just a TV who can't handle it, not a TS. He's hetero too. Wants me to go with him this week to buy women's clothes cuz he's embarrassed to buy them alone.

Jay & Donna (2 older married lesbians) took me to a benefit the gay motorcycle club was holding at Wreck Room. I was hesitant to go, first, cuz I felt women weren't welcomed & I wouldn't know anyone, and, second, cuz I didn't want them to think I'm a lesbian too cuz I was with

Jay & Donna. But it turned out to be a good time & Liz, Alyn[12], Eldon & other friends were there.

Donna also told a story how a nun propositioned her in a lady's room offering money each time Donna comes & she's already made $5,000 off her. The story is human enough to be true. So I'm going to rent a tux to go to the Ball. Over the phone I asked the clerk "Well, should I just come in for a fitting then?" & he said "Yeah, just send the fellow in next week sometime." Even when I *told* him he didn't get it.

Donna said she & Jay are invited to a lotta parties where they're the only women & would I be interested in coming along sometime. Sure! So she was real wonderful to me. Jay was getting drunk & began telling someone how I was her type but she's not mine & I said "yeah, she threatens my masculinity" & Jay said "and I love you for it!" Another queen was there joking around & I got him & Paul Safransky to dance & I watched him (pretty) & Paul says now he gets it: I'm a voyeur!! I told him wait til my lover comes back, that he (Paul) will really like him.

Elizabeth phoned me & we got a ride with all the drag queens to the opening show at the Factory. Good time. Walking home I got stopped by the police for wearing my handcuffs on my belt. One cop yelled out of the paddy wagon to the cop questioning me, "Is it male or female?" They hassled me about 15 mins, calling on a police call box to see if my cuffs were illegal. The redneck cop asked me if they were some kinda fetish or something & I answered yeah. Turned out the cuffs weren't illegal.

So at 4 AM Sat J phoned me. Said he'd wanted to phone before but made a promise to himself he wouldn't call before Feb 1st. I think he'd been drinking a little & kept saying over & over how very much he loves me & he thinks of me all the time & that he doesn't want me to forget him. That he wanted to be with me so much & would be back real soon. That he loves me as much mentally as physically & I'm the best person he knows. Told me how chaste he's been lately & I told him how I've been so good I could join the nunnery.

12   Alyn Hess

Charles is going back to NY on Monday. I haven't had any sex with him since Dec but we go to the bars together ✦ now I'll have to go alone. Also Tues at the bar some kid asked if I was a "communist lesbian" ✦ I said no, I'm a communist transvestite. He was freaked ✦ then asked if I was male or female. He was so drunk he felt my chest (I wore my binder) ✦ he still couldn't tell. He then felt my hips ✦ crotch ✦ I told him I had an operation. He said I'm female, "aren't you?" He asked my name but only to tell him if it was ambiguous so I said some people call me Lou. He approved ✦ said I was the best drag in Milwaukee. Really great!

I had stuffed a sock in my crotch for a cock ✦ one of the drags noticed the bulge. "Hey where'd you get the basket?"

"I figured if the girls can stick out so can the boys."

I also said a few words to a little blond queen who's had a looking relationship with me for a while now.

When I went in to rent a tuxedo the clerk asked "Is anyone helping this fellow?"

Eldon took Michael to the bars ✦ as I walked into the Factory, Eldon pulls me over ✦ introduces me to him ✦ Greer pulls a chair over for me ✦ I spent the rest of the night next to him. He was a super nice guy (later Alyn ✦ I agreed he sure "knows how to butter his bread"). At one point he said I'd look "like a dressed-up hippie" in a tux. I said "Fuck you" ✦ he said "well, if I thought there was a chance…" I said "there is" ✦ he was surprised ✦ said laughingly "oh I was only kidding" ✦ I said "I wasn't." He laughed ✦ laughed, squeezing ✦ hugging me saying "oh that's marvelous!!!" Sure took him by surprise.

I was so excited about my tux ✦ told ma this made up for all those high school proms I could never go to. Soon as we arrived Eldon put me at the table to register those entering the costume contests. Some of the costumes were fantastically gorgeous. I was getting compliments all over how good I looked ✦ several drag queens kissed me including Duchess who *asked* me if I wanted a kiss!

The contests were first ✦ Duchess won the comedy contest ✦ I was so glad. And when Eldon got up to introduce Greer he (Eldon) got a standing ovation ✦ I was so proud of him. Greer's act was great, as funny as he was beautiful ✦ he sang some real serious ✦ touching-to-gays songs like "The Way We Were" (*and if we had the chance to do it all again, tell me, would we? could we?*) and one he ended his show with no one seemed to have ever heard before about gays ✦ being gay with the refrain "*Tell me if you can, what makes a man a man.*"

Sunday went to mom's wearing my tux ✦ she took pictures of me, suggesting all these butch poses, etc ✦ real interested in the Ball ✦ wanting to see my transvestite magazines.

At Monday's meeting a lesbian told me she got a call on GPU's phone from a hetero TV who wanted counseling but there wasn't much she could do ✦ in the end he got scared ✦ hung up ✦ would I be interested in handling these calls. I really felt bad it had happened ✦ told her yes please send them to me! Now I'm thinking of getting something together for counseling them ✦ will tell all phone answerers to send hetero TVs to me.

Charles, Jeffrey ✦ I took a train to Chicago to attend an opening party for a new gay bath. There were tons of people but only about 2 cuties. Charles said he's going to start calling me "he" ✦ "him" ✦ I told him to call me Lou tonite. So he introduced me as Lou ✦ I didn't talk ✦ was really fooling a lot of people into thinking me male. The rooms were like little closets, a bare mattress on the floor ✦ I think a chair. That was it ✦ barely room to move in.

At the end of the evening got heavily heavily cruised by this old guy in leather. I was in my leather too ✦ wearing my cuffs on the left side which in Milw means you're the aggressor ✦ suddenly I realize someone told me that it meant just the opposite some other places ✦ I wasn't sure if they'd said Chicago or not. Shit!

I finally had to flee ✦ break up Jeff ✦ Charles' kissy-kissy to save me from this man. He'd just *stared* at me, standing there looking hard ✦ I tried to look everywhere but where he was but then he stepped in my line of vision. Yuk!

At midnite they began getting ready for business ✦ everyone left but those who were gonna stay. They all went to get undressed ✦ walk around with only a towel wrapped around their waists. Jeff had been cruised by this guy ✦ wanted to stay a while but Charles said he didn't as he was embarrassed cuzza his bad acne. So Charles ✦ I waited in the lobby for Jeff to get screwed by this guy ✦ no one tried to kick me out or was freaked by me there ✦ I was sure they all thought I was a guy.

So I got as far into a gay bath as I possibly could, being what I am. Doubt if many women have.

Found out my first article published in *GPU News* was reprinted in the *Detroit Liberator*. Will get a copy. I submitted my new one to *Ms.*, who sent it back with a form letter saying gee we just can't use it, and *Playgirl*, who sent it back saying they already "assigned a piece on the same subject." Fuckers. I'm trying others tho.

Got a great letter from J last Sat, too. It described all how he ✦ his new boyfriend Alan had an argument. He also said he's beginning to hate women. The letter set me off to crying ✦ feeling so alone ✦ I wrote a freak-out letter, thinking how rejected I felt. (I had complained to Charles how I thought Robert was acting like such a baby by pretending he didn't know me. Charles said "Well, there *ARE* some exclusive homosexuals!")

But Saturday nite went out with Charles ↟ Jeffrey ↟ Robert was at the bar. Another gay I see a lot ↟ is real nice came over to me ↟ said "If I was ever going to… if I ever did… if I ever went straight I'd turn queer for you!" I hugged him ↟ told him "well put." So I snapped out of my depression ↟ wrote J a normal letter too ↟ sent them both.

Linda saw the picture J sent of himself ↟ when I told him it was J he was really surprised—thought it was a girl—he said you really *do* like femmy guys!

Thinking all the time of J lately since Charles left—well really before that. Thought last night how excellent it would be to support him. I don't know why I'd just love buying him all kinds of things, having him at Albion when I get home from work. He'd be all beautiful for me, and we'd go out together. Two and a half more months ↟ he's mine. He said he was going to do all kinds of wonderful things for me. I'll always have plenty of wine around—and a new needle so my stereo'll sound better. I'll bring flowers home to him. I want to court him as a man would a very beautiful virgin. Pay for his dinner, his drinks, and he would have to kiss me. I'd buy him jewelry and flowers and wine, scarves, perfumes, strawberries.

Last night while vacuuming I found one of J's bracelets under my bed. I put it to my lips ↟ cried. Remembering our lovemaking, his beauty—the way we were.

Jeffrey ↟ I got the 6:50 train to Chicago Friday night. We got a private compartment ↟ drank wine ↟ talked as we watched the moon.

Stayed at a friend of Jeffrey's place ↟ we 3 went to the Gold Coast, *the* heavy Chic S ↟ M bar. Bought the belt I'd been dreaming of since the baths. While waiting for it, a 60 yr-oldish man put a note in my hand. I looked at it, then at him ✦ he gasped "Oh, please take it!" When he left I read it: "Master, please, I beg to train as one of your slaves! Master, please, I beg, train me to ream, suck you dry! Your slave, Tom." Too too incredible! He *must* have thought me a boy!

Bought handcuffs for Jeffrey to give Charles as a gift from me (he went to NY to visit him Tues). The clerk said "Can I help you, Sir?... uh, Ma'am?" Jeffrey ✦ I got along famously. Bought him makeup for the evening ✦ he did himself up extravagantly with glitter around his eyes ✦ rouge ✦ wore only a white sequined jacket meant to go over a sleeveless gown. Told him he was my contribution to art.

And then I saw him. Said to Jeffrey "that guy is really strange I don't know what I think of him." He was dancing: thin, my height, very short 1 inch long David Bowie haircut all standing up on top, reddish, a small round face, tiny kissy mouth ✦ large gray transparent eyes... the kind you feel you're looking through. Make up enough but not overdone. Like a girl. A silver ✦ black top, buttons open down his chest ✦ a long lilac-purple chiffon scarf around his neck pinned on the side by a diamond circle pin. Nice, blue jeans. Black platform shoes. He looked like he wasn't real—not of this world. So ethereal I was afraid of him. But the more I watched I couldn't stop.

Jeffrey ✦ I danced ✦ I could see him watching us. I had to talk to him. Stood off worrying what I should do, lost him a while, then saw him standing off—somehow alone—looking out onto the dance floor—the lights assaulting his beauty, his eyes.

Pretending I was walking by him, took his arm, said in his ear "I want to tell you you're beautiful" kissed him quickly on the ear ✦ was going to run off in case he vomited or something but he took my arm ✦ said he'd watched me dance ✦ couldn't believe it. He was smiling, acting so pleased. Asked if I knew Suzi Quatro. Said no ✦ he said I look just like her—she's a British singer ✦ dresses like me. Well we each kept up the conversation, I bought him soda. Told me how he was to meet someone there who didn't show ✦ he had no way to get home. (What a line.)

Lately Duchess has been real nice to me ✦ calls me "Butch" all the time.

Finally someone beautiful ✦ soft came in ✦ out of my life. Saturday there was a party at Jeff's place ✦ they hassled me til I came. Lot of not too bad looking boys there but when M came in I knew right then: *him.* Very thin ✦ feminine, brown hair fluffed around his sharp featured face. So I began cruising him. Seemed he was with no one in particular—finally *he* came up to *me* ✦ asked to see my handcuffs—had them hooked on my belt. Asked my name ✦ introduced himself ✦ I kind of touched his back. From then on it was a kind of flirty-cruisy-what's next deal between us. He'd walk by me, turn to see if I was looking at him (which always I was) ✦ then keep walking.

He came up ✦ asked what I did. Taking it sex-wise I answered "Just about anything." I asked what he liked ✦ he said money. I asked how much ✦ he said $50 grand. Told him he wasn't worth his weight in gold. Later he took the handcuffs ✦ said he'd put them on me—I said no, *I* put them on *him.* He said no.

Curious, I let him put 'm on me ✦ then he asked for money. I told him first he takes the cuffs off ✦ we argued back ✦ forth ✦ finally I got 'm off. Like every 20 mins something'd happen between us. Finally I asked him if he was a lost cause ✦ he asked how I meant. Told him he knew damn well—for *sex.* He said, well, to tell the truth he's kind of asexual ✦ I said well then we'd get along good. He asked was I too? I nodded. From then on he was a lot nicer. He kept kissing this one girl tho. Then he sat alone smoking.

I stared at him ✦ he kept looking over at me ✦ finally I went over ✦ asked if he was so asexual why does he keep teasing everyone ✦ he said he likes kissing ✦ touching. I kissed him ✦ stroked his hair. Later he came up behind me ✦ began kissing me real hard.

Finally about 4 am he came over ✦ shook his hand ✦ said bye. I asked if I could come with him ✦ when he didn't answer I said too bad, I'm coming anyhow. So the one girl he'd been kissing real much, some gila monster guy, him ⊹ I left. Walking alone he was with the other girl ⊹ then a car with a friend of theirs drove up ⊹ we all went to a restaurant. I got to sit next to him ⊹ every few mins he'd ask me a question "Why are you so contrary to your image?"

"So people will leave me alone."

His attentions to me were hesitant, afraid, yet I *knew* he was attracted to me. As they were driving me home I asked him if he'd like to come with me. He asked if I had music ⊹ booze ⊹ when I answered yes, he said OK, for a little while.

We sat on the couch ⊹ drank wine, listened to records. He pulled me over ⊹ we hugged ⊹ kissed. I stroked his hair, touched his face. We laid together in each other's arms, high, drifting but not sleeping.

He asked more questions: my age, if I lived alone, where I worked. Told him I was TVic[13] ⊹ a little about TVs. Told me he was looking for someone to share their money with him. He told me I was beautiful inside ⊹ I told him he was very beautiful, that I wished I was him.

Said he liked my music and the way it touched him. It began getting light out ⊹ he went ⊹ looked out the window awhile. When he came back to the couch I asked if he wanted to go lay down with me ⊹ he said we could for a little while (but we didn't) ⊹ he went and phoned a taxi. (When he said he wanted to share someone's money I said then he could be a "kept boy" ⊹ he said *he'd keep himself*!)

Seemed in seconds the taxi arrived. Leaving, he asked was I sure I didn't have any money. I hit him on the butt ⊹ told him to get out, that all I've got to say is he's lucky he's getting out of here alive. He left.

Somehow I think he'll be back—but then I thought that about Beau too. So I've been toying with the idea of keeping him. Maybe if he comes to see me 1st I'll talk it over with him. But he was absolutely beautiful ⊹ it was like we understood each other in some strange way.

---

13 Transvestic, meaning possessing transvestite-like qualities. Term typically used in a medical
    context.

Who needs a lover on the run all the time.

To the RQ with Jeffrey. Many pretty boys there. But one approached me ✦ asked about J, saying he'd seen us 2 together for years. He was mystified by us both. We danced, were both very drunk ✦ he said I could do anything with him I wanted. He was small, thin, soft brown hair, made up eyes, David.

Took him to Albion. He told me I reminded him of his adolescent jack-off fantasies. I told him that's all I was. He was afraid of me ✦ I played on his fears, which he wanted, the fantasies. He'd ask if I had whips. I'd say you'll see. Undressed him but his necklaces, bracelets left on. I refrained to remove any clothes (didn't all night—fantasies). Told him I was a hermaphrodite. He doubted me so asked didn't he think there were people like me? Did he think we all went to NY?

He told me to fuck him then if I have a dick. So I made him lie on his stomach, he turned to see if I was removing my pants, but I roughly turned him over ✦ violently shoved 2 fingers up him. He cried out, begging me to take them out, asking if he was bleeding. I held them quietly in place (tho I wanted to cruelly pump them in ✦ out, add a 3rd finger) and he got used to them there...Later I put 2 fingers in his mouth, he closed his lips over them. I said in his ear, "Suck." (Genet) His lips, his tongue moved, he lightly sucked. I drew the fingers in ✦ out, fucking him with it. "Suck it." His mouth tightened, he sucked harder. I was immensely turned on by my words, his submissiveness. Genet's words were caught in my throat, never said—"Go on, suck it, you little bitch." (Rechy's "fantasy words" : "Suck me, bitch.")

I need a gun. Instead of my fingers (Genet) I would fuck him with the muzzle—make him suck it—"Suck it til it shoots." Turn him over ✦ force the end of it up between his buttocks, pump him with it, and if he cries out in pain, begs me to stop, only force it further in him, pushing it all the way in, bring it almost all the way out ✦ shove it in again— savoring his cries ✦ pain. If there was blood I'd like to lick him clean after the rape, hoping when I turn him back over to gently kiss him I'll find silent tears.

At one time he was laying on his back ✝ I was kneeling between his legs. Took his foot ✝ licked it, putting my tongue between each of his toes ✝ licking there. Somehow he started telling me he wasn't a "faggot." Doubted him, asking what he was doing at the RQ then.

He said looking for sex—he didn't care if it was from "a girl or a boy or a boy-girl or whatever."

His nakedness while I was clothed bothered him. He argued with me about it a long time. When I sensed his curiosity waning, I opened my pants, revealing my jockey shorts. He was surprised ✝ I kissed him, his kiss now stronger, more persistent. As he got more forward his fingers touched the edge of my binder. "What's this?" I moved his hand away.—I told him he shouldn't get so drugged cuz little girls shouldn't do that. He asked if that's what he was to me, a little girl. "Uh-huh." Then he asked if I had anything I wanted him to put on. "No."—I watched him as he slept.

I slept 2 hrs ✝ went to work, leaving him there. When I got home at 5, of course he was gone, but had left a note that he'd taken a copy of my article, "TV Liberation."

I went right to bed, buried my nose in the pillows—his scent still lingering there.

And so I finally got myself a cock. Charles gave me the catalog some months ago but I didn't order. Some kind of fear prevented me. The only thing I can imagine was I felt it would come to mean too much to me ✝ the whole thing would get outa hand. But lately I've been getting out of hand anyhow. I've begun lush masturbation scenes, performing anal rape on myself, a boy. Needed something to do it with. Finally gave in ✝ sent for one. Got it yesterday ✝ I was even afraid to open the box. But finally harnessed it to myself ✝ it was like it was supposed to be. No big deal. It felt real ✝ I wished it had sensation. Slept with it on all nite.

Have it on under my clothes now, writing this. I fantasize it is erect becuz I am alone with a beautiful boy. I want to wear it to the bar tonite ✦ let some beauty see that he gave me a hard-on. I fantasize being fully clothed but with my cock bulging in my pants as I lay in bed beside a beautiful youth—we are two boys together, tenderness, we kiss, I stroke his hair ✦ he thinks I am really a boy—can't understand why I won't undress for him, desire to make love to a boy with him. I fear it will come to be as important to me as my jockey shorts ✦ I won't be able to be without it. Embarrassed to let J know about it—just as I will want to use it in anal intercourse on a pretty boy. Afraid. Want J to touch it, stroke it while I'm wearing it, as tho it were really me. Afraid. He will be back soon: 4 wks. I want him to love me, accept me—all of me. Let me be his youngman.

Last Saturday Eldon had a private by-invitation-only porno movie showing ✦ I was the only girl there. All male movies. All a turn-on.

Haven't been honest, undressed with anyone since J at Christmas ✦ then we hardly did. I'm so ashamed of my breasts ✦ C, I don't want to make him heterosexual being with me. He couldn't get sick looking at me cuz he does know what he's getting into ✦ he initiated it. I wish at least I had no breasts. What if it was a joke ✦ when I get to the bar he ✦ his friends laugh because I really came. I just have no confidence left. I want it all to turn out so nice. I want to feel loved but I'm afraid of the risk I must take. He was so so lovely ✦ I want him to like me, think I'm attractive, stay a while ⸻

John Tom commenting on how I'm dressed in a gay bar, "Sheila, *nobody* likes a FAGGOT!" My reply "*I* do! What'd'ya think I'm *here* for??" We laugh.

Feeling pretty damn good lately.

[J] is indeed beautiful. His hair he has slightly tinted red with some ancient herb solution. He wears his clogs, his legs long + lithe, graceful. It seems he walks more from his hips, his little ass rounder. He uses his hands gracefully. We visited Eldon. Then, as we walked to a restaurant we got harassed on the street for the way we looked + J has a policy to confront his harasser.

A group of 6-7 hippie guys called us (me) greasers, said we better get to the south side cuz this is the "freak" section of town. I burst out laughing... J in clogs, earring, flowing hair, rings, these "freaks" the reverse of the whole idea that bore them.

Originally the long hairs were the rebels against the macho, the embodiment of freedom and femininity for males. Now—confronted with J, who's several steps further in this quest, they feel their masculinity threatened. They, like the greasers of the 60s, ready to macho the "hair boys" out of existence. One of their girls calling out to J "you're beautiful!" They also thought I was a boy.

J + I had beautiful sex. He stayed last nite + we were all over each other almost the entire time. One of the first times I've really been turned on KISSING. I swear his body's more lovely. He's wearing these wonderful bikini underpants that are so full. He's really gotten to be an anal-erotic too which I just love. He wears an earring all day long! Somehow his back is more muscular, his waist smaller, his ass rounder, his arms more graceful, his neck longer, his lips fuller.

I can hardly believe I have him for more than a few fleeting voyeuristic hours.

He swears I've gotten more beautiful + I can't understand how he thinks. I have no fear or shame of my body when he is around, but I can't feel the same way he does about it. Wish I could see myself as he sees me.

Eldon said I was going to kill him for asking, but what did I wear to work? Freaked when I told him my usual male clothes.

This afternoon we leave for New York. I'm reading thru the NY section of *City of Night* and remembering how, a little over a year ago I was so alone, desperately trying to find where I fit in this gay world—where I knew I belonged somehow. And how, grasping in the dark, I knew I had to go to NY. I just came on this line in *City of Night* that I'd marked then: "*Because even before I got there, New York had become a symbol of my liberated self, and I knew that it was in a kind of turbulence that that self must attempt to find itself.*"

I remember so well my desperation at that moment. How I somehow had to throw myself into that world because I didn't know how else to find it. And, again in Rechy, only a few sentences later:

—suddenly!—*with the excitement of someone exploring a new country I discovered that world. As abruptly as that, it happened; that sudden, that immediate: One day, nothing, and the next it was there...as if a trap door had Opened.*

And now, a little over a year later, I find myself on my way to NY but not in desperation. In a self-assured easiness I know I can go into an insane no-rules fag bar in NY & become part of it like that. Am going to 2 male lovers whom I dearly love, who mean so much to me—and I, somehow, to them. About the 3rd thing Charles ever said to me when we 1st talked was that he thought I was from NY—that I really looked like I was. It happened so different than I felt it would. Me, ready to go crashing in. But the world welcomed me without the fear I had of it.

Saw so much—but on the whole was disillusioned about NY. It wasn't all as exciting or different as it had been cracked up to being. All the tourist sights were just like I'd seen in pictures 1,000 times & I felt I'd seen them before. All the myths (subways sleazy, Central Park

dangerous, "Every night is Saturday night") were proven bullshit. It was
fun + new to be in a place like Times Square where all the lights are,
etc, but not worth moving out there + giving up what I have in Milw.
In fact, by the end of out visit Charles + Jeffrey decided to move back
to Milw in Sept.

I'm still in shock after being there, haven't adjusted back to Milw yet.
But I had a good time. It was a miracle how well Charles, Jeffrey + J got
along. They all fell in love with each other + that's not bull. I had been
worried (so had they)—figured they'd *like* each other but never dreamed
it would be so easy. Fact is Charles + J plan to get an apartment together
when he returns + I'm really glad.

They hesitated at first, Charles said he was reluctant becuz they could
very easily become involved with each other. But I feel Charles will
have a definitely good influence on J on such things as taking care
of his health, getting away from drinking so much, getting a better
outlook on his future, etc.

So good to be with those two again. They love *me* so much too + we all
said over + over we should all move to the same city cuz we're so happy
together. I needed Charles too—he's so good for talking out problems
+ he likes to too. He has a lot of emotions + feelings + isn't ashamed
to express them—that's so important to me.

Jeff cut both J's + my hair beautifully. Sometimes J + Jeff and Charles
+ I would pair off, sometimes vice versa. We all hit it off so well.

So saw gay NY. Went to 12 gay bars including leather + glitter ones,
to a gay movie + to the cruisy gay area of Central Park twice. Saw the
hustlers in Times Square (where *were* they all??), to the gay dance at
the Firehouse Community Ctr, saw the Stonewall Inn. Our attempts
to see a drag show were foiled: the big show bar I knew wasn't there
anymore + when we went to one place where we thought a drag was
doing impersonations of female stars, it turned out to be a real woman.

I even passed a few times: once in the leather bar. A burly leather man
grabs my arm as were are leaving, hostiley, "Are you into the real leather
scene?"

"What'd'ya mean the REAL leather scene?"

"You know what I mean!"

Didn't know what to say so said "Well, I'll tell you one thing—I'm a girl."
His teeth drop, he's shocked. "Now do I have to answer your first question?"

"Oh, that's really wonderful! Do you know Libra & them?"

"I'm not from NY."

"Well come by tomorrow & I'll introduce you to the girls."

"Ok, if I can." But it just didn't work into the schedule.

And another time at an uncrowded gay bar, me wearing my suit. I ordered a drink.

Bartender: "How OLD are you?!!"

Charles: "She's at least 19."

Bart: "That's a girl??!! Oh my goodness, I'm sorry! I thought you were a young boy!"

Other guys at the bar. "A girl?? That's fantastic! Oh wow!!"

Bet I pass more than I realize. J said he really likes me in a suit too & he never says if he likes something I wear or not.

When J came to Albion I was so glad to see him we had beautiful, loving sex for about 1 ½ hrs! He even tried anal intercourse on me for the 1st time. I felt so close to him & loved him so much I never wanted to let go. We went out fancy for supper & actually had a heart-to-heart about our personal feelings.

Told him how I contemplated a sex change & he said "don't do it, Snuffy," but said that if I did get it he'd still come by me as a boy & be my lover. I was so surprised & pleased he said that so seriously & lovingly. Told him I doubted I'd go thru with it, but what's most attractive is the mastectomy so I could have a nice flat chest.

At first he said no, but soon he seemed to realize how sensuous that would be & said I'd be like a boy with a girl's doodie (what we call it) & I said yeah. The image came to him & he smiled & said yeah, that *would* be naughty! He really was attracted to the idea.

(Told him how I felt somehow in puberty I failed to accept the different body girls got then, while boys keep their same childhood body through life.)

(Haven't worn my female clothes since last year, about April. Am making plans to have them cleaned ✦ packed away—maybe at the parents'! It strikes me as a Big Step.)

I just sent off a letter about myself to Elizabeth's psychiatrist Dr. Houghton thru UM's Student Health Ctr. What prompted me was Liz's urging ✦ reassurance that he wouldn't try to take anything away from me or do anything I don't want—such as give me exercises so I'll get to like my breasts better. Yek! She says he'll only ask me what I want ✦ then help me do it. I told her no way am I going to be able to go in there ✦ tell him I want to have my breasts cut off ✦ for him to help me be a femmy homosexual! But she said he will. Anyway I'm still pretty skeptical.

She said it was good I had diaries ✦ also told me in confidence as a friend that I was not masculine ✦ my "masculinity" is as studied as Linda's "femininity" (a statement she later retracted). Both Loren ✦ Liz asked why I buttoned the top button of my shirts all the time ✦ I told them cuz that's how J does it ✦ I like it, it's almost like a fetish to be like him, to be all the beautiful things I love about him. They advised me to leave it unbuttoned as I looked dumb with it buttoned.

Got an answer last week from that letter to Houghton. Said I should probably see someone but his drift of the letter was he'll see me if I pay. Fuck 'm—last nite I felt so damn confused—couldn't keep the tears back. Felt like such a non-person, a nothing, fitting nowhere.

J came ✦ we talked til 1:30. Told him I really felt like I have to see someone about it all ✦ all I really need is someone, anyone, who'll talk ✦ be unbiased—like Liz ✦ Linda just make it worse. Told me I shouldn't seek to fit myself into a definition of "what I am," becuz I don't want to tamper with my body—I'd rather learn to become as detached as I once was: disassociating what I think of myself ɟ what I actually am. I'm now trying to actualize my fantasies of being a guy which I know I never could, even if I did take hormones, etc. I'd still never be the guy I wish I was.

Was upset cuz I didn't know why the gays accept me so readily, like me so much ɟ he said how many people can you really say WHY you like them. You just do. Said the only crowd I feel relaxed in is the gays ɟ I can't be 40 yrs old ɟ still hanging around them ɟ he asked why not? He was so logical, I realized I was building it all up in my mind. Why not indeed!

I said I should maybe stop reading all I do on the gender identity subject ɟ he said no, keep on, he feels I'm doing something really valuable. Told him I like the gays so much that I wish I was more like them—the old problem of wanting *to be* that which you admire. (I do love them so much: the lesbians made me be in a skit they put on at this Monday meeting's "Talent Show" with Alyn in drag. So fun!)

We also talked a little bout going to Calif ɟ he said he's getting excited about going now again. I sure hope we do. Told me a few more of his experiences with people calling him fag—one man next to him in a restaurant bitching at him to move his coat, etc, and "you kind of people don't *have* to advertise!"

He brought up how he enjoyed anal intercourse the first few times but doesn't see how a guy could come without being jacked off at the same time. Said sometimes he gets the urge to go to the RQ ɟ that maybe one of these days he'll put eye makeup on again. The 1st times he did in Berk he got super turned on ɟ got an erection from it.

Loren came up with a term I really like to apply to myself: sissy butch.

Says it's used to describe lesbians that come off with the real butch trappings but actually aren't—like me. J liked it too.

At work, in the hallway, I wore all black but for my silver belt. A black T-shirt over my bound, extremely flat chest, black leather jacket, silver mirrored sunglasses.

Walked past a boy ✦ girl walking together. When I was out of earshot, the boy said, "What's *his* problem?"

This told to me by a gay guy friend Willy who overheard ✦ called out to me "Hey fairy!"

I hope they heard.

Saw Lou Reed last night ✦ he left me so high, almost where I'm not in touch.

Only one thing bothers me: that's boy's gonna die. He looked like a fuckin hype, his nerves all shot. I run into my old prejudice against drugs. I mean—if he'd've been all fuckin' drunk it wouldn't've bothered me at all. But god, that boy was shaking ✦ sweating ✦ the few times he moved his sunglasses his eyes were all sunken, his face haggard—he looked like 40. The last few songs he removed his shirt, his chest was all bumpy ✦ scrawny ✦ his veins all sticking out, his muscles twitching. God, I hated to see him all crazy like that. He didn't stop shaking ✦ twitching ✦ running his hands all over himself. But I try to trust him—I try to believe you can dope ✦ not turn into a fuckin vegetable.

We had fabulous seats (went with Jeffrey) ✦ could see him very clearly. He was forever slam-banging the microphone stand ✦ twisting the cord around himself. A perfect blending of the macho-queen.

I like watching everyone running around on stage taking care of him. He seemed so small ✦ frail ✦ everyone was all over him taking care of him, getting him things, babying him with towels while he stumbled around submitting to all their attentions.

I came outta there wishing I was him, thinking I am, wondering what he is.

Knowing how important he is to me the way I see him. Knowing my fantasy of him probably isn't much like how he really is anyhow—but he's MY fantasy. Maybe that's all idols are.

And it came to me how I've always had a male idol. Since I was 6 yrs old ＋ thought I was Davy Crockett. Memories of others are gone but Cheyenne, another cowboy star I fantasized I was; David Janssen on TV as "The Fugitive;" Paul McCartney (my original boy-queen); Bob Dylan; now Lou.

Lou made me see the beauty of getting old. I don't worry about wrinkles anymore—his had such class.

I wore my black leather ＋ silver. Jeffrey wore all white ＋ sequins. I was James Dean, as usual. During intermission a kid passed by me ＋ said "Hi, Lou. When you going on stage?" I smiled like a greaser—didn't say nothin, I was too heavy. Knowin he thought I was a boy ＋ so did others. Hopin Lou knows what the fuck he's doin.

Afterwards we went to the RQ ＋ it was packed. Saw M there ＋ we talked. That fucker is such a tease—he spent a lotta time complimenting me on how beautiful I am (as a person) etc etc, touched my hair, asked if he could sleep on my couch if he needed to sometime (they moved outta upstairs) talked about how he likes to kiss. I actually had hopes (again) of sleeping with him that night. But suddenly he said he's gonna leave ＋ does. Just like that. Shit.

We talked about how we both liked vain people (told him that's why I like him ＋ I think it's an important step to self-sufficiency). Told him of my fancying male hormones ＋ he said he'd feel uncomfortable about me if I did. Couldn't understand that ＋ he said he must be prejudiced. Turns *me* off to *him*—that my being a boy would turn him off.

But I have begun to think of those damn hormones ＋ have stopped fearing them. The changes would be so erotic to me—to think I'd get a boy's voice! And I read they will decrease breast size slightly if you're in your early 20s (and I only need a little "slightly" before they're gone!) But the changes that make me hesitate: enlarged clitoris (ouch!) ＋ an increased sex drive (god I can't stop masturbating as it is). I've resigned myself pretty much to the fact that I'll never want children—I just doubt I suddenly will, if the hormones would fuck that up (they may). But then the Pill may also. So I'm risking that already. I could really see a redistribution of fat to more male contours (tired of my fat ass) + I've begun to build up my arm muscles—oh those arm muscles ! I only fear exercising will firm up my breast tissue + make them harder to flatten down.

I would be such a pig if I had a mastectomy ! I'd always want to walk around with my shirt all open, or none at all. Be hard to get me to cover up.

But I'm sick of hearing of all these F-M TSs that have the mastectomy + the hormones but still have all their genitals in-tact + still use them—still get off on the sensations, etc.

That's what I want but I get these guilt feelings I can't be half + half like that. Wish there was a fucking gender clinic in this asshole city. ———

Laying around thinking last night: wish I had the mastectomy right now. I know I'll be sorry in 5 yrs for all the time I wasted *thinking* about it + not *doing* it, trying to delude myself into thinking they aren't there, worrying if my binder is making me flat enough, it hurts like hell, it slips down, trying to have an orgasm fantasizing like mad I have a flat chest—I'm a boy kissing J. I want it all so much. And if I ever in 40 yrs regret it, I can get silicone inserts or something.

M from upstairs has been sleeping on my couch. It's pretty easy to have him around—he puts himself out to do things for me like driving me to + from work etc. It's hard for me tho at times to keep my hands off him cuz he's so lovely, but I must.

(Did I write he's on the County Hosp. methadone treatment to kick a heroin addiction?)

J + M hit it off excellently (I found out later both are attracted to the other). I can tell when J is attracted to a guy—he gets very embarrassed

⌁ his voice gets higher ⌁ he smiles with his eyes lowered ⌁ he laughs nervously—very coquettish.

I love him like that.

Last night we had sex when M was sleeping in the next room. I wonder if having an attractive guy close by turns J on—cause we haven't had so much sex since he's been back here.

Jesus would I love to see them in each other's arms.

Don't remember exactly how but earlier M asked if I felt there'd be room in the bed for the 3 of us ⌁ if J'd mind. Said I wasn't sure.

M went to bed ⌁ J ⌁ I sat up ⌁ talked. Told him I myself wouldn't be for 3-way sex.

Out of nowhere he said he wanted to sleep next to M ⌁ I said yes I want him in the middle. The more he thought of it the more he seemed to like the idea. Said it'd be the 1st time he slept with a boy since Berkeley. In bed he laid facing M, wrapped his legs around mine ⌁ put his arm over the sleeping M ⌁ that's how we slept.

I was too tired to fantasize—couldn't even keep my eyes open. Also didn't want to be too obvious I was looking at them sleeping together. I just felt content ⌁ fulfilled *knowing* it was happening.

Just as I thought, it came out he felt like an intruder. He said he just wasn't used to sleeping with people ⌁ maybe he should get used to it, heh? The 3 of us in bed, he smoked in the dark ⌁ said very quietly how it was freaky cuz every time J slept over at Albion when M was there, he had a dream about J. He said this in kind of a pitiful tone ⌁ I flashed on how it was making him face homosexual feelings he has but finds hard to face. I know he likes J a lot. He's talked to me several times how he likes the way J moves his mouth, how gracefully he uses his long legs, how he wraps his arms ✦ holds them up against his chest when he laughs, how he likes the way he dresses, etc. Specific things he admires about J. We leaned over J ✦ kissed each other ✦ slept.

We all went to see Holly Woodlawn, one of Andy Warhol's superstar drag queens, do a nightclub act. On stage, the MC, a real campy queen, spotted J's earring ✦ asked if he always wore them. He said most of the time ✦ the MC made a remark how good J looked ✦ how lovely his skin was, now all he needed were some rollers for his hair (J's hair is always unruly, thus my nickname for him of Tuffy). The MC gave J a pair of dangly rhinestone earrings! Really was good for his ego!

Woodlawn was wonderful.

I was passing left ✦ right with the individuals in the bars—2 times I talked to guys who were passing as girls—they couldn't believe I was a girl. But each time I worried—I wanted to talk to them about passing, etc, but I didn't want to bum J out.

We went to 2 after-hours bars—super illegal places that look like they're closed from the outside but inside serve liquor til 8 am or so. At one, where they have a sex room in back, a doorman was bitching at another that absolutely *no* women were allowed in the place, no exceptions, that's final, etc, etc, while I was walking past them.

At Albion had nice sex ✦ tried anal intercourse but it hurt me so much. We agreed to try it more often so we get used to it.

Monday came the bomb. Letter from my landlord that I'm evicted from Albion at the end of Dec, bye-bye. I was just in total shock, cried. Called ✦ asked why ✦ he said they're "remodeling" the apt ✦

need it vacant. Phoned J immediately ✦ he ✦ M came right over ✦ cheered me up.

The more I thought of it the less awful it sounded. Talked to J bout SF—if we're really going. He says he's 75% positive yes.

By Wednesday I felt much better ✦ actually began to think it's best I move. It'll be a good transition between security at Albion ✦ total insecurity in SF. Decided to sell the piano.

The whole deal of having M at Albion is getting worse ✦ worse. My obsession with his beauty has become almost unbearable—I can't take my eyes away from him. His hair, his mouth, his back, his shoulders, his waist—they all terrorize me.

His innocence and vulnerability overpowers me, defeats me; his childlike naïveté trust ✦ dependence makes me incapable of letting him down in any way.

He came home from work early and found Little Tipsy very ill. He phoned me, I rushed home immediately, but she had died in front of him. When I came in he was bent over her body, crying. I couldn't participate—I was in complete awe of him—and I still can't erase the sight of him before me. His eyes were red ✦ wet ✦ when he looked up at me helplessly, my actions were ridiculously unworthy. I felt like a fool.

I can just feel it: soon I'm going to have to tell him. I'm going to have to say look, I love you, I love you so much I can't bear it ✦ either you have to give yourself to me completely ✦ forever or get out of my sight.

At Albion last night with M ✦ I felt such good close feelings between us. I guess my affection finally was defined to myself ✦ so I could at least relax with him. Anyway maybe he picked up on that cuz at one point as I washed the dishes, he stood very close while I teased him, showing him "the *right* way to wash dishes" and he put his arm around me. I kissed him, he kissed me & I stopped washing, put both my arms around him, kissed again.

I felt so good—free at last. We decided to go out & J was going to meet us at a restaurant. And it seemed so simple: at last I finally realized how I felt for M & unashamed to act my feelings, and he accepted them. But then when J walked in! Oh, he was so lovely. My heart and attentions were his. I knew I could never leave him. I realized then & there I must do what I feel—I can't rationalize this one out, it seems. How could they <u>both</u> spark such deep and intense feelings in me?

We went to a straight bar cuz M's friends were in the band there. We barely got in & it was bad news. Some slob in a leather jacket came up & asked if I was in a motorcycle club. No. Do I have a bike? No. Well, what am I wearing this leather jacket for? Told him it was a fetish. Well, of course, being straight, he never ever *heard* the word before, didn't know what it was. I said you know, as in sexual? Well he wandered off perplexed & then his friend, also in a leather jacket, tells me if I'm not in a cycle club I better not *look* like I am cuz he's gonna kick my head in, etc. Real hostile, threatened, hard-guy trip. I tried to just say "yeah, yeah" but he was more threatened then & saying he better not see me on the street looking like that cuz he'll beat the shit outa me, etc, etc. Really!

So finally I asked him "Look what'd'you want me to do? Kiss your ass??" He looked at me amazed. So I asked if he'd heard of the Silver Star Motorcycle Club & he said no. (If J & M hadn't been there I'd've told him well it's a *fag* motorcycle club ! but I was fearful they'd get on them if they knew we were fags.) But he says have *I* ever heard of the *Outlaws* (*oh come on!*). Finally I just said look, I'm a girl. Well, he blurts the usual come-back to that when he realized he fucked up: "I don't care WHAT you are!" but that got rid of them.

So M went over & explained to him I'm a transvestite (I'm sure he didn't know *that* one either) & I'm not trying to impersonate a cycler, but a boy. M later told me the guy was embarrassed about his little display & sent his apologies to me. What a joke. M tried to tell me I have to show a little more respect when someone hassles me & that'll calm them down. But fuck it, let them go kill themselves!

Told M now he knows why I hate straight bars. I never get hassled by gays. Asshole straights, man, are so untogether *+* fucked up on roles, scenes, etc. They think they really MEAN something!

We stayed a while, bored, *+* left. Passed the jag on the way out *+* I smiled hard-guy style and kissed him. That freaked him. As I walked out he said "take it easy" *+* I answered "you too." I swear—males are so fucking insecure it's just unreal.

Back to Albion *+* M slept on the couch with no protests from J.

M said some girl at the bar asked him why he had his shirt all unbuttoned.
"Because you have a hairy chest?"
"No because it's pretty."

She was real put off by that *+* left. But to *me* that would have been the height of sensuality—that answer. It would've turned me on to no end!

I think J, M *+* I are really performing a service by just being in public —showing them there IS something different as an alternative to themselves.

I was wasted, wanted to sleep, J was determined to regain my love by making himself sexually attractive to me. He put on make-up, nylons, panties, a dress. He was beautiful but I felt he wasn't sincere—he couldn't get hard. Told me he always told people he has a "man," that he can't call me his girlfriend. That he wanted me to be his boyfriend *+* seduce *+* fuck him. I began thinking hormones, hormones, I want them so bad, I could be his man then, it would be true then… He asked me if I liked boys—he's not even sure of that ! Really ! I would be able to get thru these hassles so much easier if I took hormones *+* were a boy.

If I see that Veenhuis doctor I'm going to ask for hormones. I feel they'll help me through this time—that my fears of J leaving because of them are gone. That now is the time to test them—seeing as they're so many other changes also.

Today ✦ last nite I look at M—my fantasy: "faggot junkie," "junkie faggot." I think of him hitting up—his stories of taking too much ✦ lying on the kitchen floor when he lived upstairs. It's so sexual to me, somehow, the fact that he was all hyped up—thinking of him alone sticking the needle into his vein. Lou Reed. "*Cuz it makes me feel like I'm a man, When I stick a spike into my vein….*" I couldn't do it: somehow I feel I'd be a man if I could. A fucked-up insecure junkie hype, afraid but desperate, no attachment to any reality.

Fucked up ✦ afraid—
            like a male.

M, M, M. His back is so small, his hair is so soft.

The guy had a hard-on ✦ was real turned on but M couldn't get into it—he could feel the guy's whiskers when they kissed, etc. Told M he has to get a soft little queen like I like. Esp thought how M said the guy was "breathing real hard." Excites me to think the guy was so excited by M.

—Now when I read back on my fantasies here they sound really dumb, really off. But last night they meant everything to me ✦ I couldn't have done without them. If he only knew how close I get to holding him down ✦ pressing my lips against his hard ✦ long, kissing his eyes ✦ cheeks, burying my nose in his soft, soft hair ✦ drinking his warmth, locking his soft warm fragrant shoulders in my arms ✦ sleeping with him there against me.—I don't understand how he hasn't gotten anything ✦ everything he ever wanted. Beauty is always used to achieve goals. Could that be only for women ? ?

Last night J & I had anal intercourse & I pretended I was M.

I would love more than anything to enter M's small little virgin ass like that.

I won Secretary of Gay Peoples Union for 1975 unanimously. I can't believe *everyone* there likes me. I just can't believe that. Loren drove me, Duchess & Liz home after & M entered into the conversation. Dutchess asked if he was gay, straight ? ? Told him he's super asexual & into narcissism. He said *that's* something different & I said I just really get off on his vanity.

Sensed a change in M's & my relationship. I've tried to cope with it by drawing the analogy that I'm a gay male who's fallen for his het roommate… and there's nothing he can do to express his feelings for him. It's really hard for me to watch him make like he's trying to date all these girls—he even had me "feel out" one girl to see if she'd say yes if he asked her out. All the while my arms ache to press him against me.

The change in the relationship is shown by the fact that he's gone to the couch again when J's not over. Says it's cuz it's too warm in the bedroom & cooler in the living room—but when I slept at J's he stayed in the bedroom. Also it's been a while since we went out to the bars together.

I sense he's been reading my diaries. I've been keeping '74 & '75 at work just cuz I felt maybe he would go thru them.

I'm sure now I was imagining all that bad shit I wrote about yesterday. Last night M slept with me & it seemed like I'd just dozed off when suddenly M moved over & put himself in my arms, laying his head on my chest. I held him close, but gently, my heart began pounding & I began breathing irregularly & felt like I was trembling like an earthquake. Was sure he'd notice but he stayed there a long time & then moved away.—I wish I knew what limits he wants. Only a while before I fell asleep, I'd run my hand down his bare arm & he'd moved away immediately.

I went & waited for J to get off work & his boss, who saw us once together, told J a guy was waiting for him. We had anal sex that nite & it was absolutely fabulous. I got into it SO MUCH. —And I still think about a mastectomy, about male hormones to lower my voice, give me hair on my wrists, sideburns.

February 1975 – July 1975

"Can't believe how sincere
people are in saying goodbye."

North Warren Avenue
Milwaukee, Wisconsin

How do you think it feels
When all you can say is: if only...
How do you think it feels
And when do you think it stops?

Lou Reed, "How Do You Think It Feels"

M called off his date ⊀ we laid around Warren ⊀ watched TV. He was super nice ⊀ congenial. We had a playful wrestling match—the epitome of male affectionate physical contact—Fellini's *Satyricon*, it was hard, when I held him down, not to press my lips against his. He said this was his favorite thing to do on Sat nite—"lay around ⊀ watch the tube with Louie."

Last night he talked on the phone with his girlfriend while I "slept." Then he came to bed ⊀ did something unreal. He was laying on his back, completely nude under his little blanket ⊀ he moved the blanket all down ⊀ brought it up between his legs so the only part of him covered was his immediate cock. I couldn't believe it! I don't know whether he was doing it on purpose or what—the whole side of his hips ⊀ butt were naked ⊀ I was just going nuts. Jesus Christ! All I could think of was how much he called *Charles* a slut—SHIT!

He turned his head toward me a few times under pretenses (to pet the cat, etc) ⊀ I couldn't tell whether he was trying to see if I was looking at him or not. And then one time he lifted the blanket to "adjust" it ⊀ I got a glimpse of his little cock—I was freaked how hairless it was—I'd imagined him to have a literal bush of hair, based on his chest. Anyway the whole display kind of pissed me off cuz I'm sure he knows I desire him.

He was beautiful—his hair has begun to fluff ⊀ curl again, the light from the television shadows his hollow cheeks.

I think so much of what a relief it will be to move to SF & get away from him.

I need a good trick for a night.

Bummed out last nite. Beginning to think I'm going to break down & tell M I can't flush him out of my system. He sat with me as I ate supper, both of us in very pensive moods. And in the middle of our conversation, out of nowhere, he says, "You're really a very heavy lady but you're still fucked-up."

I was really surprised & all I could come back with was "you should talk!"

Without saying anything more, I got ready to go to Eldon's to drop off some typesetting. He asked where I was going & why. I said "whaddaya mean, *why*?" Walking there & back I thought of how he said I'm fucked up & realized that that's a relative observation: what he might view as fucked-up, I might see as an admirable-desirable quality.

I walked into Warren & he was all showered & dressed up & beautiful & and I said "you know I was just thinking—being fucked-up is a relative term…" He stopped me right there in the middle of the room, put his arms around me & kissed me. And finally I could wrap him in my arms & I just held him, grateful, relieved, feeling the all pent-up emotions just draining out of me. Gently I kissed his cheek, his lips, this good, good, beautiful person & I was cleansed, released, purified. It all lasted less than a minute.

He says "You gotta teach Diane how to kiss…" & I said as he smiled back at me, "Shit! Let her get her own!" —Yes, he knows what side of the bread his butter's on.…—Then he went to the bedroom mirror & I came up behind him & threw my arms around him & said, "Hey, I like that!" He was smiling, "What." "Kissing you."

Talked about SF & M said he felt it was too bad J & I are dependent on each other so that I felt I couldn't go out there without him if he decided not to go.

Tonite, Valentine's Day, I'm going to buy roses for my two ladies, J and M—

He decked himself out in jewelry to tease me (in the dream) & then just laid there laughing—laughing as I watched him, knowing I desired him, laughing at my powerlessness to do anything about it.

At the bar Fri nite he was sitting off by himself with his eyes closed & J told me M'd do anything right now for a hit of smack. And I realize now that the desperation, disregard, cold self-centeredness & lack of connection of the junkie is still a large part of M. Told him I'm pissed that he's imposing his REAL self upon my image, illusion, fantasy of him.

Bad dreams Sat & Sun nites: fires, bugs… wandering on the sidewalk with a torn open shirt, people grabbing me, I switching within seconds from boy to girl's chest, then back again & I wouldn't tell them anything… rooms full of people I wasn't allowed into. Just fears & fears & confusion that carry over into my waking hours.

You know it really helps to write all this stuff—I can see & understand it all more clearly & all at once. I can see a pattern or general mood where in just thinking of it, it's all jumbled up.

J told me I should get a dildo cuz he wants to be fucked—told him I already had one & showed him, but expressed my hesitation to use it on him—rather suggested he get a boyfriend. He laughed, "Charles!"—but I'm really ready to go to SF. I'm honestly plain old tired of Milw, my friends here, GPU, my job, everything. I've been making excuses not to get together with friends, been very lazy & irresponsible at work, haven't visited the parents in so long, sick of the bars, GPU people, the streets—buildings & weather in Milw. I need a new atmosphere & I finally am ready.

I throw myself in J's arms. It always comes back to us. His long legs & pretty eyes. Been thinking a lot about his wishing I could fuck him anally. I feel such a lack—I wish it & I'm powerless. I spoze I could try to get a decent dildo & at least attempt using it, but it's so dumb—I want to be real, I don't want to pretend when I make love to him. We will run away—in SF it will be all new.

How did M suddenly become another groovy straight glitter boy doing drugs with his Bette Midler girlfriend— *like everyone else at that party*! I even began to wonder how I could have been so taken with him. He's no longer the detached forever sought-after & never-attainable goddess. He's no longer shrouded in his mysterious "asexuality"—no doubt it was the methadone, he's no longer acting under it now as his dose decreases. Obviously he doesn't even realize how fucked he really is.

I guess I'm carried off only as long as whoever it is feeds the fantasy—if they act blatantly contrary to the image, it's shattered, & so is my passion, infatuation. (Somehow I think of Beau & how he never destroyed the fantasy.) But of course it's best it happened this way. Sigh. How strange now to have this *guy* living at my house. Uncomfortable. I don't *blame* him—but why did he have to turn out to be a real person ?

M comes in the bedroom as I'm dressing & sits on the bed. He's drunk, tells me I have nice legs. He reaches out for me, looks like he's gonna cry, & in a wavering emotional voice says "Do you believe I love you, Louie?" I kissed him & looking into his sad beautiful eyes, said, "No."

We kissed, he whimpered real sadly, "I do." I hugged him, kissed him. And as tho he pulled himself together, he suddenly said flippantly "you're okay for a guy!"

He'd told me yesterday one reason he hangs around with Diane is he knows he could never get serious about her. But "yer more stable for me, heh, Louie?"

"Yeah, but I can't bake bread."

It's a clear, cold, sunny day. I feel like I used to when coming out of confession as a child. This morn told M he has to move "for 2 reasons—J ♦ me."

He'd taken pills to fall asleep ♦ the more drugged-out he got the more he babbled how much he loves me. He asked do I believe him ♦ this time I said yes. Said he was glad. That he's sexually attracted to me but not in a "normal" but a "perverted" way ♦ it's as tho I'm his first homosexual love ? That I water my plants ♦ make sure everything is OK, ♦ tho my life is all upside down, it's so together, ♦ he wants to be infested with these roots.

Auntie Sis, while looking at Christmas photos, asked Dad why I was wearing those clothes (a suit). Dad told her "She doesn't like wearing those girl's clothes, they're too feminine." (!)

So he left without much fanfare Sat afternoon. Liz was over tuning up my bike, so her presence eased it. He initiated some playful pokes ⁊ jabs at me ⁊ a few times put his arm around me affectionately ⁊ I stroked him gently.

I have neither good nor bad feelings about it. Without the constant stimulus of his presence, I'll forget him.

My first night alone at Warren without him. I felt guiltless freedom—vacuumed when he'd usually napped, etc. I felt like spring is here—that's the only way I can describe it. As tho all the cold ⁊ snow has vanished ⁊ I can run outside now without a coat—all of which is not true of course. But I felt as I did as a child ⁊ for some reason remembered the shrine I used to assemble around the statue of Mary on my dresser top each May. I felt like Sheila again. —

In bed alone, finally, no one to catch me, I can hide as before if they came in unexpectedly. I found a shirt M had not taken yet ⁊ wore it to sleep, masturbating, having sex with him with myself all night over ⁊ over. Dreamt about him, don't remember how it went but woke ⁊ masturbated again. I felt like the teenaged me—it was just as it was then. Hope he doesn't take the shirt (maybe I can be liberated ⁊ ask him to leave it for me—but wouldn't tell him the masturbation end of it).

It's been a long time since I've been alone all night, free to make love to myself at will. And so much better thinking about him being there than his actually being there.

I love myself a lot. I love to enjoy the feeling of being alive ⁊ having a body ⁊ secrets. I feel such a better feeling for him too—*my* feelings *my* way. And J in the springtime. He appears with the summer, the spring, just like last year. He brings me outside into the warm ⁊ we walk together.

When I'm with him I just feel like a part of myself is walking around in another body ⁊ we're out together. I'm turning over a new leaf—no more running around, etc. I don't even want to—it's so unsatisfying ✝ I'm only looking for J anyway. While sitting around Warren we were kissing ✝ suddenly it got heavier ✝ we tumbled into bed fully clothed—both in suit coats ✝ we only loosened our clothes leaving them on ✝ had the most intense (for me) gay male love. It took only minutes til we came ✝ laid, two boys together, exhausted.

Sat nite went to a bar with Elizabeth ✝ Linda. There I met a lesbian friend of Liz's, Dawn, who promptly put the make on me ✝ I figured it's about time I tried it. We drove to the RQ ✝ she parked, we kissed, she jerked me off. That's all I can say. It was like masturbating but I wasn't doing it. Put my hand down her pants but didn't *do* anything. And I thought of gay men to have my orgasm. She wants to get some kind of relationship going but I'm going to be real cool about it. Just get together a little for the experience ✝ see what happens. She's pretty ok, but comes on a little strong.

Seems the 1st week in July we leave for SF. I don't know what to do with my apt, job, cat. But can't wait to go.

Reservations for the 12:20 train to SF July 19. J ✝ I beautiful. Seems all I want to do is be with him ✝ everything else bores me to death. To the bars with Linda ✝ Liz ✝ had a perfectly horrible time. Linda such a cunt ✝ Liz so irritating. Swear that's the last time I go out with them.

Ma telling me she wants to get me a going-away present. Told her she could take me to a tailor ✝ get me fitted for a nice gray suit that fits me just so. She said *ok*!

Haven't seen M in weeks. Everytime I want to think or fantasize about him ✝ picture him in my head, all I see are his eyes made up in the smeary way that he wore them, imitating how Diane wore hers. How distant I feel from that scene now!—It's becoming more clear to me that gravity of "moving forever." But I feel so distant now from family, friends.

Ma said she'll get me a nice suit as a going-away gift ✦ we shopped around, realizing we'll have to go to a tailor. She talked to one today about how-to ✦ they questioned her so much *why* her *daughter* wanted a *man's* suit that at the 2nd tailor's she checked she said it was for her son, knowing I'd have to go in to be fitted. I think she gets a kick outa what I'm doing. They'd even made comments what a "little guy" I am size-wise ✦ she went along with the whole thing.

24. It doesn't seem I'm this age, yet it's the age I feel I should be. Only 4 more weeks of work, 5 more in Milw. J ✦ I went out to 2 quiet bars Fri ✦ got along very well.

Sunday 11 am went to the laundromat ✦ 2 boys (bout 11, 12 yrs old) began hassling me "Juneau Park is that way," "queer," "fag" ✦ shooting squirt guns at me. Tried to ignore them sitting inside, but they pounded on the windows trying to intimidate me. Tried to confront them, "Tell me what's wrong with being gay?" But nothing got rid of them.

Suddenly 2 more kids joined them, one saying, "That's a *girl*" but the others assuring him I'm a boy. They got bolder, coming right into the laundromat ✦ squirting me in the face. Spotted them hiding water balloons. There were about 5 other people in the laundromat but no help. I was trembling by now, they'd been after me at least an hour ✦ knew they were waiting for me to come outside.

Decided to bee-line to Eldon's only a block away, but on my way they hit me with 2 water balloons, the back of my head, shirt ✦ laundry sopping wet. Burst out crying as Eldon let me in but only a little. A friend there drove me home after half an hour. The initiating kid has seen ✦ hassled me before—"Look at that fag! Is he a fairy!" shit. Eldon told me there's no "right" way to handle situations such as these. Sure I'm glad I passed ✦ I love to be thought of as a fag, but *really*!

Spent the day at the parents' for my birthday ✦ got several "dear brother" cards. J ✦ I slept together, I babied him cuz he felt sick— loving each other very much.

One minute he's <u>so</u> glad to be with me, kissy-kissy, ⁊ the next minute he tells me right out he doesn't care if he's with me or not. Speaking of "throw-away kisses!"—decided then ⁊ there that if he pulls some funny business how he's changed his mind about SF, I'm going alone. I'll do it. I'm tired of being his lap dog, his puppet.

Waiting for the bus Fri nite in my leather jacket ⁊ tie get-up. An old queen comes up to me thinking I'm hustling or being available, saying with a little effort I could pass as either boy or girl. Finally asks outright which I am ⁊ told him as it was difficult to get rid of him. Then he found it hard to believe I'm female, saying he's still game for sex with me, but I put him off. First time I've ever been so blatantly approached on the street. He said my ID bracelet clued him into my being gay.

Sun to Steininger's ⁊ gave her Jeffy Tipsy.

Last night during sex J became bolder with the isolated slaps on the ass we've been giving each other lately during sex ⁊ really gave me a sharp spanking. Loved it! Sleeping, had a dream that home I folded out my belly-button ⁊ there I had a tied off blob of skin (looked like a testicle tied at its base) ⁊ I wondered in the dream why I hadn't played with it before, cuz I figured it was probably by indirectly rubbing it that I masturbated ⁊ seemed to understand very clearly, then, how I'd been able to get off while masturbating.

Can't believe how sincere people are in saying goodbye.

August 1975 –
June 1976

"Already my eyes are darting about."

―――――――

Leavenworth Street
San Francisco, California

How many questions that passionately interested the world, that seemed, in their time, vital, seem idle to us today, not because they have been solved, but because they have collapsed; yes, collapsed to the point where we can understand but very dimly how such chalk could ever be taken for cheese.

André Gide, *Journals*, 1937

This is really the 1st time I've been alone to write—J just went out to apply for a job. The train left at 12:20 pm July 19—the trip was nice. Glad we had a sleeper car—most of the scenery was barren land. The 20th we just sat in the observation car & drank. Arrived about 5 pm the 21st, and we stayed with an old acquaintance of mine.

The 22nd J & I went looking for apartments thru the newspaper & by walking up & down inquiring after For Rent signs. There were tons of them, unbelievably! After an hour decided to take the first place we looked at. A studio—kitchen, bathroom, living room with couch that opens to a bed. $165 month and about 6 blocks from the main downtown street, 5 from a major gay area. Perfect location & the apartment is clean & in a "ritzy" building.

Since then we've just been bumming around the city, getting acquainted with it & the transportation system. Because J drinks too much we've enforced upon ourselves "dry" & "wet" days every other day & on "wet" days we check out bars, "dry" days no drinking at all!!

Got it into my head that I wanted a *bird*, but settled for getting a bird feeder I just attached to the fire escape out our living room window (on the 4th floor). Within 1½ hrs there were 7 birdies eating out of it at one time!

Neither J nor I have been harassed for being fags, etc, and it really is amazing how many queeny men there are just mingling in the masses *all over*! Even saw an outrageous bull dyke on the bus. It's as tho we just blend in! Each night, especially on our dry days, we go out for a little walk in the night air. Beautiful weather here. The fog can get so thick that it's misting. I'm beginning to feel very much at home here.

J *&* I, as I've said, have been together constantly, doing everything together. Not one bad feeling has passed between us. We split all costs in half, except items especially for one of us alone. Sometimes we eat together—sometimes we each make our own meals.

We're very much like male lovers living together.

Last week both of us half-heartedly went job-hunting.

Exchanged addresses with a woman I met in a bar cuz we had such a good conversation (she's disillusioned by men) *&* J was tee-ed off, but he was so drunk I took his attempt at an argument lightly. We both applied for Calif State ID cards *&* I got a library card—we've both been reading a lot in the evenings. I've been checking out André Gide. A few more when-am-I-moving? have-I-missed-the-date? where-am-I? dreams, but I love it here. Not a regret in my bones!

So here it is a month later. I haven't written mostly because I've been writing letters to nearly everyone in Milwaukee and figure those should suffice—I keep them all, letters received *&* copies of letters I send back. And also because J is constantly at my side *&* today was the first day nearly that we've been apart—he went somewhere with his friend Larry *&* I had things to do, also I felt it's about time we had a day away from each other—too much really *can* be too much.

Neither of us has jobs as yet *&* J felt desperate enough a few days ago to engage an employment agency to help him find something. I'm in no fat hurry. At this point I'm really feeling Leavenworth is home. Like it here in SF tremendously. We've stopped going out drinking except once or twice a week, and have turned to reading in the evenings & I like that *much* better. In a way I very much miss the flirting, running around, being totally unattached feeling I had when J was in Berkeley, but in the long run & considering long-term affections and dissatisfaction that behavior causes me—I have to say this "monogamous" bit is better.

But right now it's time we get jobs or something cuz we are *always* constantly together and I can see it's wearing on both our nerves. And a lot of the time I just don't know WHAT J wants. A few weeks back some old guy flirted heavily in a bar with J & J promised to meet the guy that weekend for a dinner date. I was pissed & forbade him to go & he argued that we can't just set up housekeeping & act like we're married & end living! I agree totally—but he won't allow me that same privilege.

Few days ago, very drunk, in a *straight* bar with a *straight girl*—she & I hugged & kissed & it was all over in minutes & J was pissed as hell. So *I* don't know. I'd really like to work out some individual freedom—but I'm afraid to bring the topic up, afraid it'll blow up in my face. But at the same time I think he wants it, too.

It seems he doesn't trust me. Even today when he left I told him I'd probably go downtown & come right back & he scolded me, worriedly, "And no Snuffy business either!"

Well, that was a short-lived monogamy.

Guess I'll follow the dictates of my stomach—I have diarrhea & flaming asshole this morn. Will avoid J's company as much as possible this weekend until I feel less like vomiting.

J & I went downtown, then to some bars. When I got good & buzzed I asked what he'd think about my seriously pursuing a mastectomy. Said he couldn't understand why I wanted one & I said because they're ugly. He agreed breasts are strange, but said he looks at them as being "kind of funky." I told him I feel if I had one this whole deal would never have happened, & he mumbled it probably would happen much more. Boy, that was an eye-opener. Sure struck a responsive chord with me.

And somehow this new feeling's come over me, I'm suddenly finding it a little easier to be a girl. I almost feel pretty. Something snapped where I realize being a girl isn't so ugly after all. Actually tried to dress less butch & when we went to bed I stripped naked—something I rarely ever do because I think I'm ugly. Altho I don't think I can bring myself to have sex with J for a while—too close to "trading off." And I think he knows that & is waiting for me to make the first move.

J told me a couple of times that I had been "the hit of the party," tho I can't see why as I pretty much stayed away from it. I told him they'd asked me to pose for pictures & I knew he'd be jealous of that. I seriously wonder if they will actually call me.

I realize that people never put any worth on day-to-day activities, no matter how difficult they are. (It's capitalism! I thought. One has to *have* something to prove themselves.) Thought of Elizabeth Farley, that transvestite I met about 3 years ago who'd been living in drag as a woman 22 years & her saying she couldn't imagine why anyone would ever want to interview her—she's never done anything exciting in her life! Incredible! And I decided I'm like her & she, to me, is much more worthwhile than any of those "artists." So since I've thought that I feel much better & think I actually will pose for fun—*if* they *do*. I'm a 24-hour living art form, unique unto myself & that's a damned hard thing to be!

The logical conclusion, I guess. J ⁊ I will be getting separate apartments. Last night he didn't come home until after 10 pm. I sat there like the night before ⁊ cried, I felt so unhappy. When he got home, cheery ⁊ drunk, I told him we had to have a talk. "About what?"

"Getting separate places."
"You want to get separate places?"
"At this point, yes."

He was quiet for a while, then said he thinks it's a good idea, that he's been thinking of it too. Said I just couldn't stand another night of waiting for him to come home ⁊ won't do that in my own place, "You said you're not the type to come home after work to the wife every night, ⁊ I'm certainly not the type to sit home waiting up for hubbie every night."

Wrote to the landlord today giving notice for June 25.

I can already see signs of J rearranging himself, directing himself away from the alchie doldrums he's been in. But I know I will have to make an effort not to fall into my old desperation rut of trying to find someone to enliven the hours I'm alone. Already my eyes are darting about.

July 1976 – January 1977

"I like to call him her because it allows me to identify more easily, to really grasp what he is. I cannot help falling in love with him. I feel he is my soul."

Post Street
San Francisco, California

*Well I'm not a scientist. But I know
all things begin and end in eternity.*

The Man Who Fell To Earth, 1976

Yesterday was the Annual Gay Pride Parade & it was spectacular. The papers estimate 120,000 watching & participating. I didn't march—maybe would have had I felt in a cheerier mood, but it didn't take long for me to get all choked up by it & when the Gay Fathers Group contingent went by & a youngman holding a little kid like Jakey on his shoulders & the kid holding a sign saying "I'm Proud of My Gay Dad" I just couldn't hold back the tears any longer. I felt so deeply that they are my people—tho I know I can never be accepted as one of them.

Sunday nite slept over at J's. Monday had off work but he didn't. I took a nice bath, washed my hair, dressed in all black & wore my binder for the 1st time in a long time—black pants, black T-shirt & black long sleeve cotton shirt, tucked in but open. Silver pens in pocket, silver ID bracelet, silver sunglasses.

Went downtown & some guy comes up to me & says he's a photographer (gives me his card) compiling a book on people in SF & he thinks I'd make an interesting addition to his photos & would I sit for him? & he'd give me copies of the pictures he took. I said ok & we took the bus to his place.

He was close to my age, very clean-cut, looked intellectual. We barely spoke to each other. His place was very close to empty but for his backdrops, camera, some other of his photos tacked on the wall. I hardly even combed my hair. He stood me there, arranged the lighting & took about 36 pictures. I hardly moved, he never told me what to do except "just turn your head slightly this way" stuff. I just shifted, gave my usual dirty looks (remember I used to call them Bobby Dylan looks?) & punk postures.

When he finished I got the distinct impression of those people they say have sex with you & then want you OUT of their sight immediately. He almost rushed me out, I said I'd get in touch with him. Went back downtown feelings 100 feet tall & so punky. Outasite I'd been *discovered*! So much wanted to tell someone. Knew J's reaction would be one of jealousy & why couldn't it have been him, instead of happy for me.

My motto, since I decided we had to get separate places, has been "let go." Not "let go of J," but just "let go."

Sat aft went to see David Bowie's movie. Came outa there envisioning how beautiful he is & how I could look just like him if only I'd…more thought of mastectomy (that word sounds like a species of dinosaur) & sterilization. There's a TV-TS drop-in rap group in Berkeley at a reputed Center[14] every 1st & 3rd Wed of the month. I should go & talk this out, get it settled in my mind once & for all, one way or the other.

Wandered to that certain bar David thought I'd like. It's funny how it happens but I'm standing there, casually surveying the crowd, really not OUT for anything & then my eyes fall on this gorgeous thing & I'm star-struck → "HIM." I sidled up to him, asked if I could buy him a drink. He says "Oh I'd just love a Coca Cola !" Oh my God he's a real live doll. So incredibly thin & graceful & tall & giddy, his face is perfect, Rudolf Nureyev, when he was beautiful.

We danced sexy a little, I got him another soda, I can't believe how slender his hips are ("And oh dear God he has slim hips that could go

14   Pacific Center for Human Growth

into a small bottle"[15]). He is smiling, laughing, gyrating to the music. He kissed me ✦ I proceeded to continue kissing his perfect neck, his bare neck, his bare chest at his partially opened shirt. He was fragrant with perfume ✦ make-up ✦ he was smiling, still ✦ quiet, his eyes closed as I kissed ✦ tasted him. Oh God. Pleasure I hadn't felt since (dare I say) that fart M.

It was near bar closing time ✦ he went off to "make the rounds one more time." I saw him circle past once ✦ wink at me, ✦ then he disappeared. Ah, sweet moments! Another vanishing angel in the night. (Such a sentimental fool! I figure I got my buck's worth of kisses off his neck!)

On the street we ran into some guy who used to work next door to J's work. J introduced me to him as "Lou" we shook hands, ✦ then the guy leans his arm on my shoulder ✦ says "Hey man, no offense or anything, but the first time I saw you come in (to J's work) I thought you were a girl in a tuxedo!" (Tuxedo ? ?) But I said, "oh, *no*," like how could you *possibly* have thought *that* ✦ J just smiled. That does it! I had been going back to introducing myself as Sheila, not using Lou anymore ✦ I'm causing as much controversy trying to be Sheila, as I feel I am trying to be Lou.

Told J I was going to a doctor at this TV/TS group to get this question straight in my mind ✦ he was obviously against it, even said I was wasting my time hanging around "with all those…..", but stopping short of whatever he was going to call us.

Yesterday I phoned the psychologist I'd seen, when going crazy trying to find a job, at the Center for Special Problems. Told her I thought I was ready for their TS group. She asked me to call the group coordinator tomorrow ✦ she'll tell her to expect my call. So I phoned

15   Oswell Blakeston, *The Male Muse: A Gay Anthology* (1973)

her today. She warned me the group was all male-to-female, if that bothered me. Told her they're the only kind I've had contact with so far. We made an appointment to meet *&* talk next Monday.

I really hope it helps to go thru this doctor bit. I'm so weary of considering it. I just want a mastectomy *&* to get sterilized *&* continue living this half *&* half life. I don't feel this surgery would make me a better man or woman, but I know it would make me a better person. I don't believe I can successfully live as a man or as a women.

But I have to do all I can to live comfortably *&* this surgery would do that. I have never felt as sure of that as I do now.

It's really difficult for me to write down what's been going on, my feelings, etc. The 2 weeks between when I first talked to Claire Capor (the counselor for transsexuals) *&* our first session were ridden with hectic downs *&* euphoric ups. My thoughts were so laden with this switching-over idea I could barely function at work. I tried unceasingly to step outside myself, see myself as others would, trying to imagine what I'd be like as a male, how I would pass, how it'd be different, how I'd be different, could I really make it, what about my job, J, etc, etc.

And then, like an angel sent just for me! Saturday morning's paper on the front page, just for me:[16]

I knew immediately that I had to talk with her *&* she could set me on the right path. Just the thought there was *someone else* like me!—I told J I would write her to meet with her *&* we had our first real discussion. The two things he said that stuck in my mind were "What are we going to be afterwards? Friends ? ? I'm basically *straight*, you know!" and "I'm going to use as much of my influence to stop you from doing it as other people are influencing you *to* do it." And that in essence if I do go thru with the change I will have seen the last of him. He said that. I felt pretty bad. Later that night we had a second, similar talk. He said my ambiguity was one of the few things that made me "interesting." Afterwards I

16 "Sex Change Uproar in Emeryville" article about Steve Dain taped in diary

cried while talking with Charles about it, saying I don't want to be interesting, I want to be happy.

He pointed out how J & I go back & forth threatening to leave each other—me because of his alcoholism, he because of my transsexualism. That it seemed absurd to him that I was ready to part with J forever only a few weeks ago & now I'm trembling at the idea of him leaving me. And that he felt I was mostly upset because this is the first rejection I've gotten because of my wish to switch. Good point.

Sunday I penned my letter, Monday I mailed it c/o the high school.

And Wednesday at 6 am my morning paper brought me a picture I'd so wished for & a beautiful beautiful article. I re-read it over & over, stared enchanted at the picture. He was so so beautiful. I felt as tho I were seeing myself.

Took the paper to work, vowed not to discuss it because I was so high on it I couldn't trust myself not to burst. The women at work gathered around one of their desks over the article & I could see them discussing it, laughing, but all I heard was one say it was probably harder to switch to a man than to a woman. No one said a word to me. I was too high to go sit outside & have lunch with the warehouse foreman like I've done for the past few months.

J phoned & asked if I'd seen the article, saying "He really looks good"—me just holding myself back from bursting with emotion. Counting each minute to hear from her, each phone call I got I knew it must be him.

Thurs the foreman asked if I was going to have lunch with him cuz there's something he wants to ask me about. At lunch he says he wanted to ask me about the women who had a sex change, "Can they really do that?" I said "Oh yeah!" & launched into an outline of the procedures, etc, & finally said, "Don't tell anyone this, but I've been thinking of doing that same thing myself." He lent his support, saying when I first came there the women had talked about me, "I wonder which bathroom she's going to use" & he told them I could use the one in the warehouse if I wanted.

He confided "don't tell anyone this but" he has a "homosexual" son. I felt so great after our talk, felt I really had a friend. Since then he's said things like "That-a-girl…er, I guess I should say, that-a-boy," and that I'm his "buddy" and "pretty soon they're not going to let you in there [the women's room] anymore!"

Monday my session with Claire Capor. I felt something like an insect under a microscope ✢ weighed each word I said, knowing what could be read into anything I said. We discussed my background, how I felt about the parents, my first boyfriend, how I found out how men ✢ women have sex. She asked had I ever seen 2 men having sex with each other ✢ I said I don't remember ever having.

Afterwards I asked her what the point in rehashing all this was. She said to try ✢ see why I'm doing what I am ✢ if it's worthwhile for me to continue. That I had to admit it wasn't a "typical reaction." Ok, that sounds harmless enough.

But talked later with Charles, expressing my apprehension at the worth of it ✢ my fear that my defenses ✢ securities will be destroyed. That no matter WHY I'm doing it, I want to continue doing it ✢ that's that. So why find out why? Etc, etc. But I knew that that's only fearing the truth ✢ if rehashing all these things in my past (that *I've* tried to interpret as causes *years* ago) will break me, I better find that out now.

I don't know how often I've re-read it now. And now I realize my biggest hang-up is my lack of self-confidence, lack of respect for my own judgement ✢ my inability to make a decision that will affect my whole life. I am plagued by fear of the unknown future, tho I know in my heart I feel the same way now as I did 10 years ago. With this new awareness I've decided to look into the possibility of getting myself sterilized. Even if I have doubts of my ability to live as a man, I have no doubts of my inability to live as a woman with child. Haven't told J ✢ won't until the day before the operation ✢ am finally resolved to not let his reaction change my mind. Went to Planned Parenthood but they were closed, will call them Monday. It's incredible the feeling of oneness ✢ peace with myself I have once I make a decision like this. You don't have to be a transsexual to get sterilized *&* I want it badly. No more intense fear, horror at the thought of what I'd do if I became pregnant, disgust at the thought of bearing *&* having to center my life around this child, out of guilt *&* the feeling I should be responsible, guilt identifying with how J would feel about the kid. I know he's very against abortion, therefore must want his children. But even though—they'll have to be someone else's. I can't.

J *&* I had our first decent discussion on my problem. He said a lot of stuff that makes sense *&* I really feel good about the whole talk.

He said he didn't feel any operation was the answer for me because he sees my problem as being "mainly one of fashion," i.e., I am tired of the *look* I have now and just can't think what to do next.

He says (and it's true) that if I were to switch over it still wouldn't solve my social identity probably because, like him, I don't know how to be a typical male, that I'll never dress like everyone else or act like everyone else. No matter what, I'll never fit in with either the male or the female scene.

He compared my obsession with surgery with his alcoholism; saying I go toward that direction just because it's so easy for me to give in to my desires, just as it's easy for him to wander into the bar.

He said no matter how many operations I have or bodybuilding courses I take I'll never look how I dream I want to, that I should rather look toward an ideal I can reach, like Romaine Brooks. That maybe I should try wearing some women's suits like I used to.

I must say that since this talk with him, it's the first time in months I've really felt the idea of switching over is not right for me at all—that I should try to look in another direction.

He said he thinks it's a good idea for me to see Steve Dain but that I shouldn't go into it with a hero-worshiping attitude.

Somehow I have to learn to love myself as the weirdo boyish female I am.

It's impossible for me to avoid becoming deeply attached to her (Dain)—I like to call him her because it allows me to identify more easily, to really grasp what he is. I cannot help falling in love with him. I feel he is my soul. Anyway at the rate his hassles are going, I'll never get to meet him. I wish somehow I could be of some help to him.

I had my 1st gay infatuation. It's so fucked up I feel nauseous even thinking about it ✦ it really tears me up inside. He was about 43 yrs old, small, attractive guy. J ✦ I met him in J's favorite straight bar. Name was Cal. I just feel so shitty. He was pretty drunk by the time we got there ✦ began talking to us, saying he's seen us "two guys" ✦ watched us several times—that we reminded him of two hitmen out of Dashiell Hammett (some 1940s detective story writer) and "I really like you 2 guys…you got a certain, ah…class."

Then he began to "read our beads" saying he's observed us often ✦ he sees J as "a villain," not very flexible or open ✦ a cynical person. But he sees me as a man with a sense of humor, much more open to different things, that J can't adjust to change. But that I have a whole realm of possibilities to choose from. That J is basically happy with his job ✦ his life, but that I'm not. Well, of course he knew how to hold our attention, as everyone likes to talk about themselves.

Something very girlish about him. He had lovely expressive eyes ✦ brows and almost involuntarily he'd look in mine. I'd look back and he'd wince, a visible hurt as he studied my eyes, and then he'd look away.

It's as tho my whole inner core of who or what I am is totally stripped away. I wonder how much longer I can continue to function, and that's the truth. I feel more ✦ more alienated from *myself*. How can I gather up the pieces of my mind? I can't think of anything, *anything* but this switch over. It just permeates my entire mind. And I'm so so tired of it.

Ridiculous when my whole crusade was to be a feminine gay male. And also my inability to merge into a male-male relationship with J, even tho I know now it would have been impossible. *I* knew I was acting strangely toward him, that I wasn't relaxed or really *me*...that with the only person I've really felt at ease around. Maybe I *would* have fallen into the Miss Plastic Surgery syndrome—always blaming one thing or another for the fact that I'm not a "real man." I hate to face it, but it's true: I would never be entirely comfortable as a male.

Because in my heart I know I am nothing.

And so the big trip to Milw turned out OK.

Eldon talked to me in length about my identity crises & ended up telling me I am a transvestite & why don't I just relax with that?

Had an in-depth talk with ma about my conflicts & out of nowhere she said she thought sterilization would be right for me, after she'd made such a scene when Johnney wanted a vasectomy.

The only real low of the visit was trying to deal with dad's depression because of the divorce, his business failing, etc, but when I tried to make realistic suggestions he finally said "Sheila, don't try to help me too much." So that ended my sympathy.

I've returned to SF feeling pretty free of my gender conflict & with an acutely raised sexual desire of J. I must pursue my own ideal of the perfect male/female balance & not try to oust one for the other. Somehow my clothes have regained their fetishistic quality & I guess Eldon is right. I am a transvestite.

Eldon had said to me, "What happened to the Sheila who went after Charles after that GPU meeting?"

I laughed, surprised he remembered, but he told me he *& Lowell were in a car *& had offered me a ride *& I'd told them to get lost. Eldon said he knew right then I was after Charles. Eldon asked, what happened to that person?—

After work went to the bar I like best in SF, Sutter's Mill. Haven't been there in a long time. It's in the Financial District *& is where the gay businessmen go after work in their suits *& ties. No one interesting, bore, bore, and *then,* he was about 35, dressed casual, obviously as alone as I. I moved to get a direct view of him leaning on the bar *& I cruised my heart out.

Stared. Wondering what I'd do if it came down to it. And I'm pretty sure he was aware—he kept looking in my direction but not sure if at me. I decided if it did come down to it, I'd make the stipulation that I don't like to be touched *& then I'd just do him, suck him.

The guy was really good looking, rather male model. After a long time of me staring, cruising like mad, he puts on his coat *& I got ready. He had to walk right in front of me *& I grasped his arm, "You leaving?"

"Yes," he smiled. "I have to make a phone call *& then go to a meeting," *& he looked down, "unfortunately." I said "Too bad." He said, "Well have a nice evening" *& left.

I really would've gone through with it.

I honestly think I'm beginning to lose my mind *& something has to give soon. Yesterday *& today wandered around the streets looking for I don't know what—anything to save me from this empty sinking. It's incredible how lonely I am.

The gays—but how are they to accept me? how do I fit in ? The feminists— they always object to my dress, they won't embrace me. The lesbians—but I like men ⚨ don't want to jeopardize J's ⚨ my relationship by getting a female lover. The straights—no way. The transvestites— they're all male → female ⚨ put the make on me, no friendship possible. I can't relate to *anyone*.

I've "broken" the 3-year spell I've had over myself.

I went downtown alone ⚨ went thru the women's depts. My counselor told me if I do go to take my time looking ⚨ trying things on ⚨ not to panic. I kept that in mind. Had no bad experiences with people at all. Tried on 2 dresses at the 1st store—lousy. Nothing at the 2nd one ⚨ at the 3rd one I bought a dress for $25. Very much like the kind of dress I used to wear. Then to the 4th store where I looked more ⚨ bought nylons.

At home I put them on ⚨ I couldn't get over how the whole experience was no big deal. It wasn't strange for me at all. I felt like the person I was 4 years ago—not that long. I parted my hair and smoothed it back instead of pompadouring it. But I had to wear my boy's "ROTC" shoes (as one salesman at Wilson[17] called them).

Phoned J at work ⚨ said "Guess what?" I could hear his reluctance to ask, he must be so tired of my "decisions." "I went ⚨ bought a dress ⚨ I'm wearing it right now." He was thoroughly freaked, "Really? Oh, my God! (Laughed incredulously) Oh, my God! Does it feel weird?"

I was a little offended he was so shocked.

I know I'm really going to have to be strong to juggle my 2 halves, but I can get thru anything after the torments of the past summer.—I

17   Sullivan worked at Wilson Sporting Goods

phone the doc ✸ called off the sterilization ✸ had him prescribe B.C.
pills for me.

Feeling so much better, in general, than I have in months ✸ months.
Have gone to the women's group therapy session twice now plus am
still seeing my counselor on an individual basis on Mondays. Already
I have had an awakening at the group sessions. There are 5 other
women besides me ✸ 2 women therapists. This last session they talked
mostly about feeling you have to *do* something with your life or *make*
something of yourself. I didn't say 2 shits ✸ was getting pretty bored.

Right at the end the leader asked why I had been so quiet ✸ I said I
didn't get what this group therapy was all about, it seemed to me it
was just a bunch of people shooting the bull. The one girl I like best
there asked if the reason I thought they were just shooting the bull was
because they were just women. My first instinct was to immediately
deny that, but I said yes realizing if this had been a bunch of gay men
talking about what they should do with their lives, I'd've thought the
whole thing terribly interesting.

When I told J how I was bored listening to women talk when I wouldn't
had men been saying the exact same things, he agreed with me, saying
he feels the same way. Which really made me feel put down ✸ I wonder
how much of my self-hatred of my female side has been fed by this same
outlook. He said he found it self-indulgent. I began thinking how he ✸
I aren't really getting along all that differently now that I'm being a girl
than from our conflicts when I felt I was a boy. J looks down on women
(and that includes me) just as much as I do. Big help he is.

We had somewhat of an argument on machismo ✸ I realized that
whereas I romanticize it, fantasize it, though never would want it to be
a reality—he would. He believes it all ✸ takes it seriously, where I don't.
Scary. He's worried I'll "turn into a lesbian" if I begin to hang out with
women, yet he isn't making himself too endearing.

Told my shrink how I'd cried Fri nite so unexpectedly. How I really felt I had let myself down by not going thru with my desire to be male. She asked how much of my giving it up had been due to the fact that I would lose J had I continued. How much of it was because of him ✝ how much of it was because I felt it wasn't me. And how much of the feeling that it wasn't me was because I didn't have the support of the physical attributes of a man.

She asked why I abandoned my pursuit of the switch-over ✝ I told her becuz I felt smothered by my own fantasy. That as a man I felt whole inside but uncomfortable on the outside, trying to communicate with others, etc. Now as a female I feel empty inside but feel freer to relate to others. That I always felt had J not been around, if he got killed by a train, I would definitely go towards being male—that I'd even hoped somehow he'd get out of my life so I'd be free to be a man.

February 1977 – June 1981

"Because one is into S + M doesn't mean they have to live the rest of their lives in leather."

Hyde Street
San Francisco, California

*They had identified themselves with their limitations;
they were making a career of them. They had turned
from all other reality, and curled up in them snugly,
as in a womb.*

Mary Renault, *The Charioteer*

Went to see Pam & Julie & had a nice evening with them. They are very interested in me & we ended up spending a lot of time discussing me. They both surprised me a lot by stating that they felt I was one of the strongest people (in character) they knew.

I felt it was important to see my friends while wearing women's clothes & each time I was amazed at what little difference it made to them in the way they responded to me. Like they acknowledged the fact I was wearing a dress & then we proceeded to talk about other things & I felt totally comfortable with them & my self-consciousness left.

Saw Linda & Liz on Saturday & Linda was the only goober to do something to me—she brings out a camera because she "doesn't have a picture of me." I refused to comply but told her I had a nice picture of myself in a man's suit & would send her a copy of that. She said she didn't want that. What a jerk!

Later we 3 went to Eldon's & by then I had no fears of being in a dress, while he was the main one I felt I'd feel self-conscious with. He simply said "Sheila, I never thought I'd see your legs." Told him how I'd feared presenting myself as a female would somehow change our relationship, but he seemed not to quite understand how I meant. He was due to run a showing of gay male porno films to collect money for *GPU News* that evening & I was so happy when he invited me to attend.

Nothing has changed between us! Even with me in a dress he didn't hesitate to accept me for what I am. However I felt really uneasy at the thought of attending in a dress ⊹ of going to the men's bars that evening in a dress. Thought hard what to do—should I confront this fear?—but decided to be easy on myself ⊹ just have a good time so I went ⊹ changed into a suit.

One man I knew from GPU talked with me ⊹ asked if I came to the films for the social angle of it, or did the films turn me on? I readily affirmed they turned me on. (Later told this to Claire Capor ⊹ she asked why did I find it so hard to say that gay male sex turns me on if I'm in a dress, but not if I'm in a suit? Why would it have been so hard for me to go to those films in female clothes? It's a known thing that lesbian sex is a big turn on for straight *men*.)

The bars were rather depressing. Somehow they were 70% straight couples there. Eldon, Liz, Linda ⊹ I went together. The big event was that I saw M. Had been thinking of him the last few days, wishing I could see him again. Well, in the bar saw his girlfriend who told me he was in the men's can. I went in there to see him ⊹ he grasped me from behind in a hug ⊹ I turned ⊹ we kissed real good. I was almost in ecstasy until I opened my eyes ⊹ saw him—the same he was 2 yrs ago. Layered in make-up, the same clothes, ⊹ he immediately begin rapping how he's now a hairdresser at this exclusive shop. My heart sank ⊹ I almost felt ill. We danced one song ⊹ midway I said to him "M, it just ain't the same."

Just read all thru my 1973 ⊹ 1974 diaries. God, what an insane fucked-up scene. And I'm still left over from it.

Claire Capor said it sounds like J holds on to me by putting me down ⊹ that he's afraid I'll leave him if I have any self-confidence.

I got dressed up real sharp female & went to a semi gay-straight bar to write a letter to Charles. When I finished, this man came over & asked if he could sit down. He seemed OK so I said sure. We talked for a long time & he was easy to talk with, had a good sense of humor, was about 40 yrs. old & not bad looking, tho no gem. But he was straight, and I thought I could see having sex with him.

Later, his friend came over & joined us. He was very interested in what my story was & I was very candid with them, told them I was a transvestite, etc. His friend was just as nice, if not nicer than the original guy. I bought them drinks, upsetting their hetero stereotypes a bit. They were surprised I was so "aggressive" (as when I went to summon the waitress). Phil, the friend, was probably in his late 30s.

After about 2 hours Phil asked if I'd be interested in a ménage à trois. I said yeah but that they'd have to do stuff with each other to fulfill my fantasies too. Joe said he could see that, but Phil said no way could he have any contact with Joe. So I said ok, then forget the ménage.

We talked about something else, but then Phil brought it up again & said well maybe we should see what they could do. I said well let's just try it & if it turns out goober, we can all just laugh it off & not be embarrassed or anything. OK.

So I'd spent 3 hrs with them before we went to my place. Put on the TV & Phil goes in the bathroom for a real long time & finally I went & held the door closed & told him if he was going to hide out in the can, he can just stay there & sleep in the tub. Then he went down to his car & got a shaving kit & cut himself shaving. He was real nervous.

But Joe was putting records on & dancing by himself & acting real free. Then we sat & watched TV on the couch (me in the middle) & Phil quickly stripped down. Then Joe stripped. So I did.

We were teasing around & laughing & I felt real unembarrassed. Finally I leaned over & sucked Phil, & we started messing around, but the 2 guys kept away from each other. (J must have the giant dick of the century. They were both so *small*!) Phil knelt to lick me & I guided Joe's hand on top of Phil's hair, but he ruffled Phil's hair real roughly, not at all affectionately or gently. Finally we got in the bed.

They never got too near each other, nor did either of them get a hard-on for more than one second.

I got my handcuffs ❧ my long thick chain. Joe very cooperatively chained his hands behind his back ❧ laid on his stomach. I ran my fingernails up ❧ down his back, and gave him a few sharp smacks on the ass. Told Phil to use his nails on Joe's back—but he had no nails?? Then I got Phil in Joe's place ❧ he reacted with more pain at the scratching ❧ more fear ❧ tried to wrestle out of the chains.

I laid on top of him ❧ held his elbows down ❧ Joe got behind me. This was the most erotic time for me, as I held Phil down as he struggled ❧ Joe began fucking me from behind. Joe's ❧ Phil's arms were rubbing against each other ❧ I pretended Joe was fucking Phil ❧ really started to get off. Finally Phil quit struggling ❧ I kissed ❧ sucked on his neck.

We messed around insignificantly a while longer interrupted with their making coffee or smoking cigarettes. None of us came. At the end I had them both laying side by side on their backs ❧ Joe pulled Phil over playfully. Phil nested his head in the crook of Joe's arm ❧ shoulder. I knelt, facing them, between their legs ❧ stroked them simultaneously ❧ we talked.

So Phil was upset because he thought I'd thrown away his phone number he gave me ❧ I showed him I still had it. Joe was teasing that Phil was in love with me. Phil made coffee ❧ sat on the couch ❧ Joe ❧ I laid apart in the bed. They began talking about poetry (Joe writes) ❧ I brought out my beloved Swinburne ❧ Phil read "Erotion" aloud ❧ I read some of my choice excerpts from "The Triumph of Time" ❧ "Anactoria." About 1:00 am they left.

He cannot be married. No one can have bedroom eyes at 7:30 am on a bus ❧ be married.

Am I over-sexed or something?—Gave Phil a call last nite ⊹ he rushed over from the East Bay to meet me at a bar. Dressed in my best suit ⊹ tie.

I wasn't sure why I'd called him ⊹ I told him right out because I enjoyed his company. He agreed we'd be "buddies" just out on the town tonite. I said great. We drove to Sausalito, hit a few straight bars there ⊹ talked, mostly about sex. He assured me there was no hope in converting him to bisexuality, but said if I really was interested in such a 3-some, he could arrange something that wouldn't include him, with his friend Nick, who is "ready for pretty young boys."

And on into the evening he said there was no way he could think of me as his "buddy" because he was too sexually interested. I was finding it hard to relate to him—he a straight man, me a ? How do gay men relate to straight men? But a straight man trying to make you? I couldn't be on the receiving end of his male attitude ⊹ treatment of females (freaked that I bought drinks, opening doors for me oh so "automatically") ⊹ I told him I felt that was a power game men played with women. At the same time I found his ways charming ⊹ I couldn't help but identify with him in his role. (Mlle. de Maupin—having seen the ways of men could never go back to being a female.)

I vacillated between feeling male-buddy to feeling sought-after youngman to feeling turned-off female. In my sought-after-youngman mood, I leaned over ⊹ kissed him passionately in the bar, aware of his arms encircling my suit, touching my shoulders. And a bit later I invited him to stay over-nite. We went to the men's can together in the bar.

Once again he was a shitty fuck. Said I should call him every other day when I'm not with J. Forget it. Maybe once a week.

Happy birthday, man. I'm 26 and no longer a member of the American youth. Let's hope this year I'll get my brains unscrambled ⊹ be the outasite hot lady I am.

I've discovered what the emptiness I've felt lately re: cross-dressing is all about. I've been feeling so void, like on a long lost road abandoning full-time dressing. I've wondered if I should maybe go back to dressing full-time—what have the past 3 years meant to me, what was it all about, what does it mean to me in relation to my female dressing. What am I doing by presenting myself as a *female* dressed in *men's clothes*, not as a male ? What am I doing to replace whatever purpose cross-dressing served in my life ?

And now I finally see that when I began full-dressing 3 years ago, I did not seriously consider the inevitability of one day having to stop, to go back to women's shit. I had not planned, seen what I was doing in the long run. It was not irreversible, so I never considered the chance of one day having or wanting to reverse it. I did it so easily. I think just now has been the first time I've SAID to myself "Yes, I *used to* dress full-time & did for 3 years."

It's as though I'm a newborn with no before. All new land.

I was wondering "haven't I become accustomed to San Francisco yet? I don't feel really *at home* here." But maybe I've been transferring my alienation to my surroundings rather than to the new fronts I'm now confronting.

Because one is into S & M doesn't mean they have to live the rest of their lives in leather. It is meant for one thing only.

I said to my counselor "Maybe I should be a private cross-dresser only, as it is the public display & confrontation that has made it uncomfortable for me." To save it for special "field trips," occasions when I want to pass. Instead of feeling I must pass.

Just spent the afternoon in a long masturbation session, just like I'd done nearly all last summer. Imagining I'm a boy & masturbating endlessly. Read some from my '74 diary of J, me, M. My passing. This part of me is still very much alive. What can I do with it?

Lots happening. Probably most important is that I received a letter from Elizabeth a few weeks ago saying that she has decided to go back to being a man and has stopped taking hormones and that she has gotten rid of all her female clothes, after 7 years. And that she is moving out here to San Francisco in early January.

I'm so happy for her, so excited, and I immediately wrote back welcoming her ⚭ offering my assistance. But as the time approaches for her arrival, I'm a little worried. I'm afraid I will cause her some conflict while I am trying to adjust to her being a him and getting used to calling him Eliot. I know it's hard enough adjusting to a new identity without having other people reinforce what you are trying to change. But it'll probably work out. J isn't thrilled by the idea—says he's afraid she'll be taking up my time and horning in on our time together.

So much happening I hope I remember it all. Most importantly, the beginning of February I got a letter from *GPU News* saying that they'd give permission to reprint my "Looking Toward Transvestite Liberation" article in a book to be published this fall. And this time it's not a small press publication, but the revised edition of the *The Gay Liberation Book*, edited by Len Richmond and Gary Noguera. My article will be alongside ones by Gore Vidal, Allen Ginsberg, John Lennon, Huey Newton, Alan Watts—unreal!!!

When I read that, my mind soared to the sky—like the first time I was stoned on hashish.

But one bad part—I haven't told J about this (the article being published) and won't until it has been or close to it. He's been waiting for a year now to get some of his short stories published in a small press magazine in San Diego and has been so frustrated. I know that if I told him about mine, he wouldn't be happy for me, only resentful. So it's turned out to be a wonderful secret garden of my mind.

Ma ⚭ Dad finally got the divorce. When I read that it had been finalized in a letter from Bridget, I cried really hard and bitterly for about 5 minutes. I'd always fantasized what a happy childhood I had, but this divorce brings all the terror and unhappiness of those years to light. Suddenly your past is obliterated, Ward and June Cleaver have gotten a divorce. I'm so glad I'm how many 1,000s of miles away from there—I don't think I could bear it.

Gave my 3-week notice that I am quitting the group therapy sessions. I've discovered that one does not have to be a social being to be a healthy being—and I feel I'm at the level of sociability comfortable for me.

We did a tune-up last week in my basic auto mechanics course and I really enjoyed it A LOT. Felt comfortable with the 3 women doing the same car.

I'm really feeling like my apartment is "home" and I'm fixing it up, buying pictures for the wall, cleaning Mr Bird's cage, watering the plants, making my supper instead of eating out, loving J and appreciating him sitting next to me.

I feel really happy with myself and ready to leave the doubts behind.

Well I just can't believe how good I feel lately. It's almost too much. I'm no longer going to the mentie centie and glad. There was about a week after I quit that I felt freaked out and anxious but that's gone now. Upon leaving I told the group how it seemed that everything I did to get better I did intentionally, following a little plan I'd give myself. The therapist told me I should remember that.

So the latest exercise I gave myself was to buy a Playboy magazine to nurture the heterosexuality in me. I look at the bare women ⊄ their bodies are pretty ⊄ sexy ⊄ I look at my body ⊄ it looks just like theirs—pretty ɟ sexy. It makes me feel good about myself. J flipped when he saw the mags, "Why did you buy these? What do you want to look at naked women for??" and when I explained he calmed down. He figured I wanted to look at women because I'm sexually interested in them (God! doesn't he know that's untrue YET).

Doing a lot of different things, mostly in an endeavor to meet new people and thereby form a clearer picture of who I am.

Linda (from Milw) came to San Francisco and stayed at my place [for 5 days]. It's too bad, but, like Elizabeth, I found that I no longer like many of my old friends. I guess I'd felt before that by benefit of their gender dysphoria Elizabeth ɟ Linda were interesting people. But aside from that tiny little part of their personalities, they hold no attraction for me.

Wednesday I went to a meeting advertised as a TV/TS group "for women" in Berkeley. I realized the problem of who's a "woman" here, but half-hoped I'd find females there going to males. No such luck. Turned out to be 5 male middle-aged transvestites, all dressed and talking in their butch voices. I was pretty disappointed but then began talking to the best-looking one. He was very insightful and we talked of the problem of bringing the male side ɟ female side together into one person.

I told him I was more interested in learning how to *separate* the male ɟ female side; that that was my big problem—being able to call upon my female mind when appropriate and set aside the male mind when necessary. That the two sides intermingle to such an extent that I feel I have no control over what's going to happen next.

During the meeting they voted to extend membership to a female-to-male TS (not present) who'd probably be there next meeting (in 2 weeks). This somewhat prompts me to want to go to their next meeting to meet him—but again, it's always a female-to-male *transsexual* and I am, and must remember I am, a transvestite.

I had to reassure J that I was not interested in getting back to that scene, that I'd "learned my lesson," but know I'll always be interested in the topic.

Sitting in my apt crying because I feel so goddamn empty inside. My whole goddamn life is a waste of time—just trying to think up things to do to waste time until I die. Nothing means a goddamn thing.

After I wrote the above I cried bitterly, rested, then went out ✦ washed ✦ waxed the car. Once in a while I get in an awful depression ✦ a good cry usually washes it out of me. A lot of times I feel like living is a real joke. And I think if it weren't for J I'd be absolutely nothing, I wish I had a sense of worthwhileness that so many people have on their own. I seriously think, but cannot imagine any way that I can make life seem more than just waiting to die someday. I lose myself in J's arms and fear the day he dies.

For a fleeting moment I thought maybe this TV group would give me a sense of worth ✦ accomplishment. I told J I was going to the group. He phoned me back ✦ told me he wanted me to be with him ✦ not go to that group because he thinks it's bad for me. I told him he had no right to ask me to choose between him or the group. So I went to the group ✦ my female-to-male friend never showed. I was so disappointed.

Later I talked to the group president ✦ mentioned my wish to possibly introduce some serious group discussions about mutual problems of transvestism, rather than totally allow the group to be a social club.

I continue to feel more like part of the human race, yet less like a person.

Maryellen threw a small party at her apt. I was there about an hour when one of her old boyfriends comes in. He used to play in Cruisin, a 50s band I liked. Well the guy was gorgeous ✦ I proceeded to make conversation. Turns out he's 29 yrs. old ✦ very friendly. I was becoming more drunk with punch ✦ wine and he ✦ I were making eye contact ✦ unnecessary contact. The party was thinning ✦ suddenly it was Maryellen, he ✦ I in the kitchen. And suddenly it was Maryellen, he ✦ I in the bed.

The guy was tall, lean ✦ hard. Absolutely lovely body. For me, it was like my old tricking days—but better because Mary was there to play the female and I was the voyeur, the accomplice, another youngman.

I asked if he'd ever fucked another man ✦ he said no, but he "has been…" most unusual for a hetero first-time to be on the receiving end. I bound him to the bed with belts, and when I only had two, he asked if I couldn't find a third.

With him tied down, I made him suck my fingers, whispering Genet's beautiful fantasy words, "Suck it til it shoots…." His clear soft eyes looking up at me as he obediently sucked and I forced it farther down his throat. Later I took a belt to his butt. He was screwing Mary ✦ I got behind him and fucked him with my finger.

I wouldn't let him enter me, but once he got me ✦ exclaimed, "What muscle control!" or something to that effect. Later he told Mary he thought I was being very loyal to her by not letting him fuck me, because he was supposedly Mary's boyfriend—we laughed at that!

I wanted very much to get him down good, but Mary wasn't very cooperative in tying him down, she later told me she was trying to watch out for him ✦ protect him because she thought maybe the both of us were a bit much for him. I had no such impressions. I could see he would have loved it. I took a scarf and ran it over his soft hard chest. I went nuts! He was incredibly submissive and didn't fight a thing.

Browsing in the SF Public Library yesterday, quite by accident I discovered that I am listed for my "A Transvestite Answers a Feminist" and "Looking Toward Transvestite Liberation" in *An Annotated Bibliography of Homosexuality* in 2 volumes, compiled by Bullough, Legg, Eleano ⊹ Kepner. I couldn't believe it! Listed there right alongside Harry Benjamin ⊹ Virginia Charles Prince. Told J ⊹ *he* even seemed happy for me.

I'm getting the hots to get back into some serious passing. Fantasizing getting together with Emmon, the other F→M TV I met and going to the Castro Street area, as they all know I'm a girl on Polk St. Fantasizing how I *could* pick up a gay guy ⊹ go to bed with him, ⊹ pass, just so I didn't take off my clothes. (But how can I hide an elastic chest and a soft sock cock?)

Just got back from going to a few of my regular gay men's bars with Emmon. He rarely goes out dressed ⊹ is worried about passing, which is ridiculous since he looks ten times better than I do. So I thought I'd take him to some good places. I told him that I've looked so long for other female-to-males, and now I've found her, I don't know what to do about it. Like "now what."

Well, Patrick's dead.

Thursday at 6:30 am Maryellen bangs on my apt door. She got a phone call from Bridget that Pat was in a motorcycle accident Wed nite ⊹ was in critical condition ⊹ the doc said he wouldn't last the night. My first reaction was that this was just another Sullivan freak-out exaggeration. Mary wanted to fly to Milw immediately—I said I didn't. Went to her place, phoned Ma ⊹ Dad ⊹ they were upset. The clincher, tho, was when I talked to Johnney. Bert, his best friend, was driving the cycle ⊹ was already dead. He was crying ⊹ so apart that I realized the seriousness.

Mary was so apart from herself that I made the arrangements ✦ went over to J's. We laid in his bed ✦ I told him I was leaving for Milw that day. We talked about his father's funeral and he was real supportive ✦ loving.

When we arrived in Milw, ma, Grandmother ✦ Kathleen met us crying, saying he'd already died ✦ was hooked up to a respirator ✦ they were just waiting for us to see him that last time before they pulled the plug. So we all drive there. Pat was in intensive care ✦ they said his brain died at 9 am Thurs morn. Bridget was flipped out ✦ said she wanted them to do an EEG on him. The brain surgeon was pissed that she insisted on it because he's done a CAT scan ✦ an electronic brain scan ✦ they both read dead. But he said he'd do the EEG just to please us, but that in any case the EEG "meant nothing."

Went in to see the guy laying in the bed, I got kind of a shock ✦ Bridget's Charlie was there to reassure me. I just wasn't ready for it, it was so horrid to see him laying there—about all I could say was "he looks so tired."

Everyone kept telling me to talk to him—I stroked his hair, plastic tubes down his throat, and could only say "you really blew it this time…." Everyone was upset or crying or in shock.

Apparently, Johnney, Bert ✦ Pat had been out drinking ✦ taking speed. Johnney said while at the bar they all were hugging ✦ crying ✦ saying how much they loved each other. They decided to go to Pat's. They say it was a fluke that Pat got on the back of the bike because Johnney usually rides with Bert, but this one time Pat gave Johnney his car keys ✦ said he was going with Bert. They were going some 60–80 mph down a 30 mph street, hit a car broadside ✦ Pat pushed against Bert, who was crushed into the side of the car. Pat catapulted over the top of the car, flew 100 feet ✦ landed smack clean on his goddamn brain.

The guy didn't have a scratch on his body, but for a few on his left hand.

I went back to the hospital ✦ saw Pat again. This time, instead of looking tired, he looked dead. Maryellen lifted his eyelids ✦ the guy's eyes looked like jello. The whole family was undone. They were to turn off the respirator that morn. Bridget & I went to Pat's flat on the East Side to get his clothes for burial. She'd also suggested that at the wake we have bulletin boards with recent photos of Pat on vacation, with his girlfriend (of 6 yrs.) Jenni, on this cycle, etc. I went to Johnney & Kathy Steininger's & there cried for the first time when I saw Johnney who was really in bad shape. His face was so distorted & red & drawn, his eyes looked so bewildered & sore.

Bridget went to Nanc's & met with the funeral director who told her they'd pulled the plug at 2 pm that afternoon & Pat died 10 minutes later. A lie. Later that afternoon we got a call that Pat still on the respirator & that the doc said that now because the EEG was blipping, they couldn't unhook him from the respirator. And suddenly the EEG (which the doc previously claimed meant nothing) meant everything. That state law requires if you're donating organs you must have a flat EEG reading for 24 hrs. So the guy was still in the hospital.

Friday night babysat for Cheyney, Jake & Brian while Bridget went to Bert's wake. Spent Friday nite at Bridge's & got a halfway-decent sleep. Saturday was torture. He was still blipping. Kathleen & ma got a lawyer who said they could sign a brown paper bag saying they won't sue the hospital for unplugging him & take the kidneys, and it would be legal. So they went to the hospital but were met by big deal lawyers from Madison who said no matter what they signed, they wouldn't unplug him. When we heard this, Maryellen, Bridget & I flipped out & yelled that we weren't going to let our brother wither away into a 12 lb pretzel like Karen Ann Quinlan[18] & that if necessary we'd call the newspapers & TV & get the whole city on our side! Our outbursts won us no favor with Nana.

Later at Steininger's we talked with a doctor friend of hers who assured us that it wasn't "our fault" that we demanded an EEG & now they couldn't unplug him (which is what Pat's doc claimed). That state law requires an EEG on all organ donors. Bridget talked to Jenni's mother (her father is Chief Administrator at St. Joseph's

---

18   The 21-year-old subject of a landmark 1975 court case in which Quinlan's parents fought to
     remove her from artificial respiration after she entered a permanent coma.

Hospital) ⚢ somehow they got it together with the Asst Admin at St. Mary's Hospital (where Pat was) ⚢ the Asst District Attorney. They all talked it out ⚢ agreed to give us a choice: either we forget about donating the kidney ⚢ unplug the guy now, or we wait for however long it takes for the EEG to quit blipping ⚢ donate the kidneys.

Johnney called a "family conference" of me, Bridg, ⚢ Mary. I was the only one who said forget the kidneys, so they decided we'd wait it out, but have the option that if it got real long ⚢ gross we could unplug him ⚢ forget the kidneys. So Johnney went back to them with our decision.

We were doing very little eating ⚢ a lot of drinking. I cried again ⚢ was comforted by Johnney (he turned out to be the fortress of strength after all). I just thought the whole deal of them fooling with Pat's dead body for 3 days was gross ⚢ we should say fuck the kidneys ⚢ unhook him ⚢ let's put him in the ground where he belongs.

The hospital assured us that at the most Pat had 15 brain cells alive (out of the million zillion we have) ⚢ that if he did live he wouldn't be able to see, hear, move, think, talk or anything. Just a living veggie. I also learned we were going to have a "fake wake" at the funeral home Sunday nite even tho the guy was still in the hospital ⚢ I just didn't think I could go thru with it.

Johnney said if it got real bad we could just ditch to the corner bar in our "bereavement." He took me to the basement, we did some cocaine ⚢ had a great talk. I told him I fantasized having sex with him ⚢ we said yeah, someday we'll do it. Saturday morn he had been one of Bert's pallbearers, wearing his black leather jacket ⚢ sunglasses. Spent a sleepless night at Bridg's. We were told no way would those 15 brain cells last the evening.

Sunday morn the family met for breakfast at a restaurant. I felt like shit. My stomach was totally fucked up—I was on the can all Sat nite shitting orange water. Sunday afternoon Bridg ⚢ I put together our bulletin board, heading it "Gem of the Gents" which was what we called Pat to tease him.

From 4–9 pm we had the "fake wake" at the funeral home with a closed empty casket, having to explain the guy was still in the hospital. Pretty gross.

Ma expressed angrily at the Sunday family breakfast that she knew Monday morning suddenly the EEG would stop blipping—she was sure this was all bullshit so the doctors could have their weekend at the golf course.

After the fake wake Bridg had a small party at her place which cheered us up a lot, lots of joking, laughing + drinking. Monday morn what Ma had predicted happened. Suddenly the hospital realized the EEG machine was "broken" + a short in the wire or something was what made it keep blipping all weekend + that he was now in surgery having his kidneys removed. What a relief.

I washed Bridg's kitchen floor to burn off nervous energy.

Tues morn at 8:30 am we had a short wake at the funeral home—this time had Pat's body in the coffin. Johnney + the others put a pack of cigarettes, a pen, a free drink ticket from one of Pat's favorite bars + a joint in Pat's shirt pocket, like he used to always be. Cheyney put a $5 bill ("a fin") there too. Jenni shoved a pair of her sexiest underpants down by Pat's crotch, secretly so only a few of us knew. Pat had always said that if he didn't have a pencil behind his ear, he'd walk with a limp, + I thought we should put one there so he wouldn't walk with a limp to the pearly gates. But ma drew the line.

Patrick was a cabbie + a dispatcher at Yellow Cab + when we got to the church where the services were being held, the cabbies came out in force for Pat + there were at least 30 cabs pulling into the church parking lot. It was a real upper for all of us.

The head dispatcher, a woman, drove Pat's cab first. The cabbies had sent flowers to the funeral home with a card reading "May you ride the freeways forever" becuz when you're a cabbie + you're on the freeway it means you'll be making lots of bucks.

And to our delight, cabbie calls began coming over the PA system in the church. There were just too many cab radios out there! The greatest! Pat would have loved it!

Johnney was smiling radiantly throughout. Mary ✦ I were in the back seat of the limo that took us to the cemetery. Behind us were 3 motorcycles ✦ behind them the pallbearer's car which Johnney drove. The whole way he held his left fist clenched out the car window. Mary ✦ I held ours out the two rear limo windows. A motorcycle cop led the funeral procession ✦ with all the cabs pulling up the rear we were 5–6 blocks long. The cops even blocked off streets for us. The guy went out like a goddamn mayor.

Wednesday Kath picked us up ✦ on our way to her place we passed the cemetery ✦ decided to go in to see where he was buried.

Went to the offices to ask where his plot was ✦ then Mary says, "Well we just brought him in yesterday, so do you think he's already planted?" The lady was so shocked ✦ said oh, yes, of course. That's one real neat thing—the kids took it with a fine sense of humor. (Johnney said they went to a toy store for Cheyney's birthday ✦ there was a game called Brain Wave. He said he wanted to get it to put under the Christmas tree, "To Patrick From Santa.")

Maryellen says she just can't stop crying, but I just find myself preoccupied ✦ staring into space in disbelief. It was all like a bad dream—I can't believe I was really in Milw ✦ this all happened.

Saturday before J came over, I sat ✦ cried, saying to myself "now I'm just supposed to go back to the way it was ✦ pretend nothing happened?"

It'll be a long time before I stop thinking about Pat ✦ about death.

Like Mary said, yeah, I can believe that Patrick is dead now.

But I can't believe that in 5 or 10 years he'll still be dead.

I was in the middle of shampooing the rug ✦ J rang the doorbell. I buzzed him in, he knocked at the door ✦ came in. We said hi ✦ I said I thought he had that luncheon today (with his Japanese class). He said he didn't feel like going. I sat very quiet, not touching each other ✦ said "I don't know what to say."

There were long silences in between each of our statements. I said "well, I don't think we should see each other anymore... You're right, time doesn't mean anything." Tears started down his cheeks, but I just sat there ✦ didn't cry. I've heard this all before, we've been here before.

Well I spent New Years Eve rinsing out sweaters and sewing on buttons and writing letters. Went to bed at 11:00.

I've been going out a lot on my own lately and have already struck up a few acquaintances in the local gay disco. I run into that kid who reminded me of Patrick pretty much and he sure likes me. Put a henna pack on my hair last Thursday night and it turned out *really* red, almost too too, but I love it. I feel like a pretty gay boy with it. It looks great with a white shirt and black suit ✦ tie. To survive this fool J shit, I have to begin planning and thinking "Sheila" instead of always "J and Sheila."

(I made myself a good strap-on cock out of socks ✦ wore it to sleep. Good masturbation.)

I'm finally getting a phone (which I've never had in SF) and Maryellen says she'll be glad to give Ray my number.

I've finally washed that man right outa my hair...

Maryellen & I went out. She went with me to a dirty bookstore and I bought a dildo (finally! was getting tired of those desperate nights searching for something in the kitchen!) We also found the bargain bin & bought some paperbacks.

Later we went to the bar where Ray's band was playing. We saw him there immediately. He talked to Maryellen but hardly looked at me. Maryellen said she thought he was embarrassed. He was a very reserved type. When he played on stage, Maryellen & I moved up front and watched him. He smiled down at us and at one moment I thought he winked at me, but then found he was just winking back at Maryellen. Got frustrated. But when they were done playing, he just about RAN up to us. The bar emptied out and Mary & I stood talking to him for a long time. Finally I asked if he had plans for the evening. He said no. So I said "well, you're invited over to my place for a little Blue Nun—if you like blue nuns." (That's a wine.) He accepted.

We waited for him to get his equipment off stage. Maryellen was a little nervous about the whole set-up but I knew it'd be okay. We 3 went to my place, sat around, smoked dope & drank the Blue Nun. (Before we'd gone out I'd changed the bedsheets & turned down the bed in hopes...now he was there, just as I'd hoped all week.)

Anyway once Mary went to the bathroom & he & I started kissing passionately. Well, I was beginning to think Maryellen decided to stay for another threesome because the wine was gone and it was about 4:30 am and she wasn't leaving. I threw a few unkind hints, which now I'm sorry for, and she left.

Well, I handcuffed him and he was totally passive & smiling. Even though the cuffs weren't connected to the bed, he held his wrists up like they were. I had my clothes off & didn't feel funny. The guy was so electrified—everything I did to him he almost hit the ceiling. I could hardly stop looking into his clear blue eyes, they made me crazy. What a smooth hard body.

I wrapped my chain around his beautiful chest and kissed him all over. He asked for water + then I got the idea and ran an ice cube over him. He trembled and gasped, and when I put it between the cheeks of his pretty butt, his whole body just awoke with excitement. I left it there + kissed and bit him tenderly.

Checked to see if it had all melted and when I found the little piece of it, I ran it up + down the insides of his thighs and then stuck it back up his ass. He just went crazy! He was so incredibly responsive! I fucked him with my finger and he gasped and when I went to find some K-Y he said yeah he was going to ask for some. Almost emptied the tube between his ass cheeks and he loved it.

He asked if I had anything to wear + I said "female stuff or male stuff" + he said female. Brought out my Frenchie bra + little pink slip but I didn't know if he wanted them on him or on me + I put the bra on but the slip just laid there + he wouldn't give me any indication what he wanted, so that fell through.

At one point I took one cuff off him + he got up and I turned over. He knelt behind me + we screwed a little, but he started to act like he was coming, so I pulled out. He was really disappointed, but tough. I kissed him all over again + when I kissed his cock he almost hit the ceiling again! So I took his cock in my mouth and gave him a good sucking, with my finger up his ass, and he smelled so good and his cum even tasted so good. (Oh, I'd brought out my metal eagle belt, too).

Well, it was great to lay there next to him. I turned out the light and after a few minutes I beat off, coming twice. (Oh yeah, I made him play with himself too and when he'd take his hand away, I'd take his hand + put it back on his cock. He was so pretty.) We cuddled together in sleep real good, almost as good as J + I do. In the morning I was interested in a little more action, but he didn't seem to be.

He got dressed + I made coffee. We sat around, drinking the coffee. He asked "How gay are you?" after leafing through my *Advocate* + *GPU News*. I said well I envision myself as a gay man, that the first time I'd been with a girl was when he + Mary + I were together. Again he told me he'd been fucked in the ass by a friend of his and liked it, but another time he was too tight and he didn't like the scratchy whiskers.

He asked me "who do you like to make out with?" and I said "gay guys." He said "you've really set up a challenge for yourself." I said yeah, but when it happens it's so nice! Told him I was into guy's clothes and my big fantasy was to go to a gay bar & get a guy who thought I was a guy to take me home.

I asked who *he* liked to make out with and he said "girls" and told me how he dug wearing garter belts & nylons but never had any around, so I said "well I'll have to get some then" but he didn't acknowledge that. I wish I'd've known that before! That's probably what he wanted when he asked for female clothes??

Maryellen came over in about 45 mins. Her Mr. Right & her are going to move in together. She mentioned that I sounded a little disappointed with Ray & I said yeah, he didn't get my phone number & he could have been a little more initiating and well, he wasn't J. I really felt that. It was fun for the moment, but once again I'm alone.

Saturday and Sunday nights I believe if he'd have walked into my place I'd have brought him to my bed. Monday night I think I'd have turned him out in anger.

No Valentine this year, sucker.

Friday afternoon J gave me a small white box with a pink ribbon around it. It was a 14-kt gold necklace—very dainty ＋ feminine design. He asked "Did you think I forgot?" I answered, "I didn't think you wanted me to be your Valentine."

Yesterday I was cleaning Mr Bird's cage and he was flying around and I was vacuuming and it was stuffy so I opened a window. When I was through vacuuming and turned off the vacuum, the silence was deafening. I realized Mr Bird was gone. I hadn't even been thinking, and he must have flown out the window. It was all too symbolic and I cried because Mr Bird was gone.

Maryellen said, it was like Patrick getting killed and a few weeks later Jeffy Tipsy died.

Last week Ray phoned Maryellen's place twice ＋ asked for my phone number. What an ego booster! But I haven't heard from him yet.

Saturday I bought 2 zebra finches and Sunday the female laid a little bird egg. They weren't sitting on it, tho, and the bird shop told me it probably wasn't fertile, but that I should get them some nesting materials and they'll build a nest and have birdies. Sounds fun—think I will.

I look at other men and try to picture spending years with them, but I can't imagine it.

Bridget and her 2 boys came here to visit Maryellen ＋ I. I had a fantastic time—her kids are so incredibly warm and loving. So for 9 days I didn't have to feel alone.

She and I went to hear Ray's band last Friday night. I even wore a skirt there. Ray was walking around and when he saw me he sat next to me very friendly and after a pause in the conversation he abruptly asked "Could we have another date sometime?" I looked him smack in the eye and said *"Any time.* I'm game."

He said "Sometimes I get this urge to dress up in women's clothes." I said "well you'll never find anyone who will understand that more than I do." And I said, "In fact, I'll stock my place with whatever you want and be sure to have it there for you. What do you like?" He got a little shy, but said, "Oh, garter belts and nylons." I said I'd be sure to have some then.

When his band played, he wore his leather jacket over his bare chest and a diamond-ish necklace and leather pants and he was so sexy and beautiful. This week I spent $9 on a sexy black lace garter belt and seamed nylons and I've masturbated picturing them on him. It's very rare that I get off sexually on men in women's clothes, but somehow I imagine him in that garter belt and nylons and my pink slip and a necklace, and putting eye make-up on him and kissing his lips while reaching under the slip and stroking his penis. It makes me crazy! Sure hope he calls *real* soon.

I've been extremely good to myself, spending a lot of money, buying a 3-foot bamboo birdcage that Bridget & I put together, getting tickets to see Roxy Music in April and Lou Reed in May, and like that.

When I have looked back over the mean things people have done to me in my life, none of them approach the incredibly deep hurt J has imposed on me.

So not much has changed. Last Saturday I got all fem and sat around a rather nice straight bar here, and ended up leaving with a cute-enough young guy. We came to my place but I'm afraid I was too pushy and aggressive and tried to do a Ray thing with him when it just wasn't appropriate. I just can't relax and let the guy be the big make-out artist. I'm afraid if I don't do something, nothing'll ever happen.

Anyway the guy never got a hard-on once, but he was warm and cuddly and affectionate. We laid in bed until 2:30 Sunday afternoon. One thing he did real nice was continually stroke my arm, back, leg, etc. Just nice to have someone laying there. He seemed like a real straight-o guy and I wasn't even thinking of him when I practically attacked him.

We went out for breakfast and I gave him my phone number, but I don't know if he'll call. He was probably pretty embarrassed about not being able to get it up.

Monday evening Ray calls me finally. But his first words are: "Are you a lesbian?" I mean, really.

He tells me he knows some girl who wants to get it on with another girl and he thought of introducing us. I told him in a nice way that I wasn't very interested. We chatted about music, etc. I told him I'd seen him at The Pit and he must not have recognized me, cuz I was in drag. So he starts saying goodbye, and I said well I just want to let you know I've invested in some paraphernalia and he's welcome to come try it out. (Meaning the garter belt, etc). He was very interested, but we couldn't get our schedules together this week. Maybe next. Why do I always *end up* the aggressor?

Last Monday went to a super-straight bar that was having Cheap Drink night. Who walks in but Joe—Mr. No Hard-on of my last entry. We ended up going to his place. I was very passive this time + suffered through his long hard kisses that never ended + you don't breathe for 10 minutes.

Finally got in bed + I was pretty excited + he had ½ hard-on + I sucked him damn good + he stuck his fingers up me + I was going NUTS and finally whispered "Fuck me!" Well, too bad because he just laid on his stomach. I asked him "What's the matter? Don't you want to?" He said he didn't know.

I asked "Don't you like me?" He said "What kinda thing is that to say?"

I got a call from Ray. Can he come over? SURE! I ran around getting ready ✤ trying to think of a way to smoothly do this. He came ✤ we drank wine ✤ chatted, and then I asked if he'd ever put on eye makeup. He said a few times, but someone else had always put it on him ✤ he'd been thinking of wearing some when they play (his band). I said well he'd have to put it on himself ✤ let's do it.

He didn't have to be asked twice. I was getting so hot watching him put on eyeliner, blue eyeshadow ✤ mascara on those incredible eyes of his. He did a damn good job ✤ even got creative, ✤ I just watched him ✤ suggested ways to make it easier. When he was done I kissed him madly.

God he was so beautiful.

Opened his shirt and stroked his beautiful chest. Put the necklace I was wearing on him ✤ kissed his neck where it laid. He asked "Where's that garter belt?" ✤ I said "Just be patient. One thing at a time or it'll be over too soon." Stripped off all his clothes ✤ gave him my red lace underpants to put on ✤ his beautiful hard cock just filled them up. Then gave him the garter belt ✤ seamed black nylons. He put them on, asking where I got them, saying they're "just like mommy's."

What a gorgeous thing!

We stood in front of the full-length mirror ✤ kissed ✤ I told him what a beautiful rear end he has ✤ I got down ✤ sucked him good. He was electrified—like last time—he gets so turned on ✤ his breathing becomes little gasps ✤ he shudders like a child. I could hardly look at him he was so lovely, I said "You make me crazy!"

He took my clothes off ✤ was delighted that I wore lacy black underpants. We laid in bed ✤ he sucked my tit ✤ expertly used his finger to make me cum. And then, oh God, after 6 ½ weeks! he put his cock in me ✤ I just died. We fucked good—I should say *he* fucked *me* good! He took the active role ✤ I watched the muscles in his chest ✤ stomach ✤ arms and it felt so good ✤ when he came he whispered "Oh! Sheila!" which I liked very much.

Ah, it was so good. Afterwards, he took off the nylons + had runned one. He said "now I *really* look like a street whore!"

He slept overnite + I woke every ½ hour it seemed + just looked at him or stroked or kissed him. How lovely to have him there! In the morning he drove me to work + spoke knowledgeably of solar energy + I kissed him + said the evening was my pleasure + see you again.

Went to The Palms Sat afternoon to have a few drinks + began watching this youngman sitting alone not far from me. He was small, delicate features, pretty eyes, *white dress shirt* with *French cuffs* + *cufflinks* (which makes me crazy!), and I watched him hold his cigarette prettily + thought him beautiful, except for his tightly curled blond hair which looked like it needed a combing. (He had a tie stuck in his pocket, too, like he just got out of work.)

He saw me watching him + looked around + we smiled at each other. He went to the bathroom + passing my table said "It's like a maze in here!" + I smiled + said "I'm tellin ya, it's bad!"

When he came back he asked if I'd like some conversation cuz it's no fun sitting alone + you can only look out the window so long. He talked away. He was intelligent, educated, ambitious, motivated, diversified, aggressive but not butch, and interesting! The more he talked, the more I thought "wow!"

We hadn't talked long + he asked the bartender for a pen so we could exchange phone numbers. His name is Tim.

Well the guy was absolutely the greatest. Heaven-sent. A pretty youngman into both men + women, but not in their traditional roles! A guy who digs women in men's clothes! A guy who digs being oral with a woman! Who said "God *knows*" he's been fucked by other men! I mean, this guy was too perfect.

Tim just phoned me tonight to confirm our lunch date. He said he thought of me all day (he had to work) and all night last night which, he said, was the best and very exciting. I felt he was implying he had masturbated thinking of me, & I told him I think we shared the same experience. He said he needed to go clothes shopping & I said to take me along! He asked if I'd tell him what looked good, etc & I told him I was a pro at that & that I never had anyone to dress up before. He said oh, I could dress him up all night!

He's a cute flirt. He's very talkative.

I hope he's as pretty tomorrow as he was yesterday.

I'm going through so many changes! All day today I felt a little down, not at all what one should feel. And I've finally realized that I feel sad over this big change in my life—leaving the era of J. Somehow I feel like I'm falling really hard for this Tim & I know now what they mean about being on the rebound. Yet he's been more wonderful to me in 5 hours than J has in 6 ½ months.

Tim told me on Saturday that he was looking for someone solid, someone to live with, and God I want that too so much. I want to rush into his arms but I'm so afraid—

I just don't think I can ever trust anyone like I trusted J because I can't stand to be stabbed in the back again.

This guy is making it so much harder by being so right, so eager to be with me, so goodlooking, so considerate of me, so cautious and hopeful. I can't picture myself with another lover—but I also can't picture myself with J anymore.

I put a nest in my zebra finches' cage and [the following day] there was an egg in it already. This morning there's a second egg!

John, K. Steininger + Cheyney, and Bridget, Jake, Brian + Charlie are all planning on moving out here to SF this summer. Bridget's house is already up for sale + Kathy's goes on the market next week.

Thurs nite I went to see Lou Reed—my namesake, as Maryellen said—and Lou, oh God, he completely had me. I was lost at the foot of a god. How such a very unattractive man could hold me so really amazed me. At first I felt as tho I had to get to know him all over again from scratch, but as the evening wore on, I knew him, his every gesture, his vocal intonations.

He is the perfect aging greaser, still a smart-ass street punk, at his age. He's getting a little paunch, his butt sticks out, he was healthy as a rat. What a fairy, too! I was close enough to watch him prancing, being quite the queen—quite the *fag*—he's too old to be a queen.

Like Bryan Ferry last month, these two guys just slay me. They are such perfect MEN! Yet they aren't REAL MEN at all.

I never realized how very political Lou's songs are.

There was a militant uprising at the last transvestite group meeting + I missed it. But the 2 originators of the group phoned me at 11:30 pm to appeal to me to be on their side + so as of Fri I am now the "Treasurer" of the Golden Gate Girls/Guys, in name only.

I wrote the above in a bar.

A youngman began talking to me. He was a hippie-type, good conversationalist, thin and strong as hell. We ended up back at my place, smoked his hash + had sex. I told him I could put on a sexy garter belt + nylons. He asked what for? and I said I just wanted to let him know the possibilities involved. A while later he said he thought he would like me to put them on after all. This guy was Mr. Hard On!

So then I asked him to put on this white shirt and tie, and he refused to! I teased him that he was no fun. He said, well I was wearing the garter belt, isn't that enough? I said "oh, big fun for me! There ARE other people in the room, you know!" But I dropped the subject ✦ he was a good fuck.

This guy was Mr. Straight-o. Said no one had ever asked him to do anything like that ✦ I told him he had to expand his horizons. He took my phone no. ✦ left.

I phoned Tim and oh, he'd been out of town ✦ just got back ✦ meant to phone me, blah, blah, blah. Asked if he wanted to go to a punk rock concert Saturday ✦ he had another engagement but he would buck it because it sure sounded much more fun going with me.

So we met Saturday night for a few drinks ✦ out to dinner. I wore my black suit ✦ tie. He looked like a slob, plus buzzed his hair, but for the 1st time I saw what gorgeous muscled arms he has ✦ he probably has a beautiful bod.

Saw Ray at the concert—his band was playing—and he was all alone ✦ I began wishing I'd gone alone so I could've hung out with him. I just was feeling detached and uncomfortable. Realized it was cuz I didn't feel at ease with Tim ✦ decided to "let my hair down" ✦ if he didn't like it, he could fuck off. So I slung my arm around him ✦ began enjoying the music ✦ rubbing his neck ✦ in between bands we ended up on a bench really necking ✦ hugging ✦ God is he a GOOD KISSER. I was getting all hot ✦ horny.

So when we left ✦ walked to my place I asked if he was coming upstairs ✦ he said he was "thinking about it" ✦ I said well you better think fast cuz we're only ½ block away. He said "no, I don't think so." But oh we should go to a movie this week ✦ he'll call me.

So the hell with him. I'm not phoning him anymore ✦ if he likes me so much, let him come to me.

During those first few weeks that J ✦ I were together in 1968, we were in his room at Albion, sitting on his bed. I told him to lay down and I'd rub his back. He did, very hesitantly, and then suddenly he sat up and took hold of me and said "Sheila, don't tell me to lie down and then stab me in the back!"

I'll never forget his fear, and how I understood the importance of what we were getting into.

Tonight it's 3 months since we've seen each other.

Got a postcard from Ray—his band is playing in New York. I wish he wasn't married—the guy is such a perfect sexual companion for me. He is the one truly honest shining star in my life right now—with his intermittent comings ✦ goings.

> And he sent me a postcard
> > He sends me a postcard

I'm crying now. My god, this good good person. Not in ✦ out of your life like a thief, but a good fine youngman who cares.

J phoned me ✦ asked if I wanted to get together ✦ talk. I said well, I don't know, does he have anything new to say other than what we've been saying for the last 10 years? He said "not really."

One of my baby birds had a birth defect & couldn't use his legs & the vet put it to sleep. But the other 4 are big and healthy.

Later I went to Polk Street. A very very drunk 45-ish man began talking to me & ended up asking me to his place. I told him that first I had to warn him I'm a female. He was genuinely shocked but not upset & said, "I don't know, you just caught my eye… you still do…" That was a very big compliment to me. However he didn't want to go home with me then, all the while telling me it wasn't because of what I told him (as if) but I assured him I wouldn't have gone with him anyway because he wasn't fem enough for me.

I've said it before & it's becoming true again this time. Whenever I'm alone (i.e., without a boyfriend) my crossdressing becomes more serious & constant. In my search for the perfect male companion, I find myself. In my need for a man in my bed, I detach myself from my body and my body becomes his; I stroke his hair, I see his wrist. I feel the warm winds blowing my open shirt from my smooth, hard, flat chest. I catch the hungry eyes of another beautiful youngman. I reconsider male hormones—trying to remember why I decided against them before.

I could shave… I could take them! I wonder if I could live as a male without taking hormones, or if I should take hormones but stop at surgery, or if I should just get sterilized and have them remove my ovaries.

And when I think of my future, and what I really want for myself in the years ahead, the only real thing that matters to me is that I be able to dress and pass as a male. When people ask me at work "What do you want for yourself in the future?", how can I tell them that I just want to be a man?

I finally broke down & sent away for those beautiful men's shoes in my size—$70. I have the urge to buy new, better-fitting men's underwear, and slacks. Went to a new haircutters, told him I wanted a DA[19] and sideburns, and that "your ultimate goal is to make me look like a boy."

Bridget said that, what I met her after the haircut, when I was approaching her, it took her a long time before she could figure out who this guy was coming up to her—I was wearing sunglasses, too. Tom Rupenthal from the old Velvet Whip met us too ✻ said, upon seeing me, that I hadn't changed a bit. I try to find a common thread from my past to my present, and he reaffirmed my belief that I have always been like me.

Thinking hard ✻ close about who I am. Just who *I* am and what I am, alone, and what I want for myself. So long I gauged my future next to J's. Now I see what a mistake that was, and that's what makes me doubt that we can ever be what we were before. I can see myself following my own dreams, regardless of ANYONE else's opinions.

At first I wore boy's clothes cautiously. Then I went full-force without any women's clothes, in fear someone would know I was female. Then back again to women's things, and I even felt sad about my wish to abandon men's clothes. Now I find myself yearning for the total male look again, even though I have no fears of being female.

Thinking very seriously of sterilization, admitting that motherhood just is not for me. And that too ties in with my commitment to being a man. To decide between those two—and in looking hard, reading books on deciding to have children, I even wonder why I'm reading such a thing—it seems totally absurd because I KNOW myself ✻ who I am.

I wonder how I could do all this. My brothers ✻ sisters would readily accept me, my parents would learn to relax with it as well as they can relax about anything else. (Johnney once said to me that I am the closest thing to a brother he has left...) I am ready to leave my job anyway ✻ could take another clerical job as a youngman. I could leave my apartment without any problems ✻ rent as a man. It would all be worth the trouble. And as a man I could maybe even learn to be J's

19   Hairstyle called a Duck's Ass

friend, without the torment of needing to be his lover. If I am ever going to do anything with my life that I can be proud of, it must be my success at living full-time as a youngman.

Sometimes I feel as though I am turning inward so much that I am going to turn inside out. And become totally submerged in my own delusions.

Had a GGG/G meeting last night ⁊ I wore my binder ⁊ a T-shirt. With my hair just cut, I looked pretty damn good. Talked to Lin Fraser, who is a psychologist in gender identity, ⁊ she said several times how I looked like a boy, asked how old I am, where I work, if I had any breasts or was that a binder, how I look like a boy from the back ⁊ how I don't "wiggle" my hips when I walk.

I talked to Georgia ⁊ Karrie (who'd just had M→F surgery) ⁊ I told them I'm wanting hormones again. Georgia told me a doctor ⁊ said every effect from male hormones is reversible except the voice—and who cares if you're a women with a low voice? Told her I didn't really want to go to a hack, but to a reputable clinic, ⁊ Georgia said "forget it, they wouldn't touch you with a 10-foot pole." Why? Because I don't have the typical transsexual story they want to hear.

—The reasons I decided in 1976 not to pursue transsexualism were 1. because I was too unsure of myself to take on that major change, 2. I hadn't reconciled my female-male conflict, ⁊ 3., because J said he would leave me ⁊ I didn't believe I could go on in life without him. All three of those reasons no longer hold true. I think I'm finally seeing myself in perspective.

Maybe the stigma comes from being *either* a TV *or* a TS—but there is a middle ground that I've never considered…what Georgia calls a "cross-liver." Someone who takes hormones ⁊ lives in their desired gender role, but who has not necessarily made a decision on having surgery. I truly believe I could be a "cross-liver." If I had hormones to lower my voice ⁊ butch up my face with a few whiskers, I don't believe I would suffer the anxiety of passing.

Another concern I had when previously considering TSism was that I felt I couldn't "live a lie," i.e., trying to hide my past as a female. But many people *don't* hide the fact they are TSs—Jo Dillon even kept his old job, returning as a male—and I could live with telling people when it's necessary ⸹ lying when it doesn't really matter.—While laying awake last nite trying to fall asleep, I seriously thought this all out.

I believe that, if I *am* going to live my life alone, and if it is true that you *are* the only one you can rely on to always be there, I had better make peace with myself. If I am the only one I have, I have a right to make myself happy. And I've been struggling with where I am now for 6 years—and it's time to stop sweeping the issue under the carpet.

I phoned Center for Special Problems this morn ⸹ found that Claire Capor (my old counselor) is on leave til February. In the meantime, a Dr. Leibman is running the TS group there, ⸹ he's the doc Georgia said would give me hormones without much hassle.

I walked back into Center for Special Problems, the 3rd time I've registered there over my crossdressing in 4 years. Began dressing full-time again on this date also.

Talked to this Leibman character about my desire for hormones ⸹ to live full-time. He seemed very suspicious of me ⸹ somehow irritated. He had my old file ⸹ read aloud the last entry—how I had come in as an "attractive female" ⸹ that I'd thought I could live with both sides of me ⸹ had given up my desire to be a man ⸹ he said, "It seems you've had a change of heart." I explained why, that I was no longer afraid of my female half but felt I could incorporate those feelings into my male feelings.

He asked how it would change my life ⸹ I said "not a whole lot, that's another reason I want to do it." He asked me to describe myself as I see myself as a man. I said I was small, had a determined face, was a careful dresser ⸹ basically was a "fruity little faggot." He asked if I had any sexual feelings for women, said no, but mentioned my 3-ways with Mary ⸹ Bridg. He asked how my family would react ⸹ I told him how

I had all "yea" votes—he said real doubtfully "isn't that rather unusual?" I said no, they've all seen me doing this for 6 yrs now ✦ are wondering *what* I'm doing ✦ my one sister said it was this dress-one-day, suit-the-next that made her wonder what it is.

Asked how I felt wearing women's clothes ✦ I told him it was like hiding because then no one would look at me funny ✦ it was like I was getting away with something, that's why I decided to go back to women's clothes. Told him I wore my men's clothes to work, he looked suspicious saying "You go to work like *that*?" referring to what I was wearing, a suit jacket ✦ tie. I said yeah! He kept flipping thru the file, looking irritated, said he thought we should talk some more about this, so I have an appt [in two weeks].

Walked out of there really down, a line from a song going thru my head: *I'm always crashing in the same car.* I just don't want to go thru all this again. What do they want me to say? I felt so sad.

Told Bridg it was like Jack's argument against her moving to SF→ gee, you got a good job, friends who like you, you're an "attractive female," why do you wanna mess that all up by doing this?

I laid in bed ✦ tears welled up. The phone rang—I was in no mood to talk ✦ almost didn't answer it, but turned out to be Lin Fraser. Said she's just talked to Steve Dain about me (I'd just drafted a letter to him moments before!) ✦ he said he'd very much like to talk with me. My spirits soared! Gave me his home phone ✦ I thanked her all over. Said he charges $20-50/hour depending on income. Steep but probably worth it. Told her about my bummer session with Leibman.

Friday left a message on Dain's answering machine. Monday he phoned back. So incredible to hear his voice—like a youngman's, not an older man. Think he's 36 or so. Asked for Lou Sullivan ✦ said "you want to get some counseling?" I said "yeah." Thanked him for returning my call. It was a very male business-like conversation. He thought out loud of his schedule, asked where I live? Made an appointment for Thurs nite. TODAY.

I felt very masculine talking with him, and very relaxed, like for the 1st time I was talking with someone who understood what I meant. I've never met a F→M TS! For all my wanting to do it! I have real high hopes that I'll learn a lot about myself & about what my dreams consist of from him. If I really *am* crazy, I think he'll be the only one who could tell me that. I am nervous, but feel I can be honest with him—no reason to put on a cool front. In fact, I'm afraid that meeting him will be like looking in a mirror & just thinking this makes me want to cry.

I'll go to Leibman [in 2 weeks] but if he leaves me with the same feeling as last time I'll tell him I'm not coming back & why. I need to take an aggressive attitude. Hope this Dain meeting will increase my self-confidence so I CAN more aggressively pursue my dream. I bought 2 pairs of slacks & some new men's socks & underwear. My men's wardrobe is old & unflattering—some I'm still wearing since Bluemound Rd !

—I keep thinking what a relief it will be to be in the gay men's world, finally, as a man. But I realize I'd have to stop short of a physical affair with another man becuz I'll still have a woman's body—but at least my outward appearance & my mind will be together—for the first time!

This is so hard to write because I'm so excited my thoughts are running wild. I didn't eat or sleep much at all last night & am not even hungry or tired this morning. Last night I met with Steve Dain. I was uneasy for only the first minute & he was so relaxed & friendly I was at ease from then on. He is very short (5' or so), very muscular & masculine, grey hair, a thick beard. Sorta built like Jack, if Jack wasn't so chubby. He gave me gum, and we talked for 1 ½ hrs. He asked all sorts of questions. He was super liberal & warm & open. Said being a TS does not dictate anything other that your feelings about yourself & it pisses him off that these docs think you've got to fit a prescribed mold.

Told him about Leibman & Dain said he disliked the guy too & was surprised Leibman even *listened* to me cuz he's such an ass! He couldn't believe he'd told me to come back in a month! He asked about my sexual feelings, my family, my adolescence, my crossdressing life. Told him what I use for a binder & he thought it was a great idea, so I got to help him out, too.

Asked me if I had any questions for him & I asked how much hassle is it to go from F→M. Told me about hormones & that the Institute where he's studying can do the whole stick[20] of getting me a new driver's license, etc. Said hormones will make me a little taller & bigger so I'll go up about ½ clothing size. Great! Then I can wear *men's* sizes instead of boy's. That it usually takes about 8 mos for the effects to really show, so I should stay at my job & save, because there'll be about 3 mos where I'll be too butch for my female job but too fem for my male job.

He said he was behind me all the way in this hormone thing, and that I should call Lin Fraser & ask her to refer me to an endocrinologist who can give me hormones. (He said they have to be injected & they'd show me how to do it myself. Told him Maryellen, Bridget & Kathy Steininger all know how to give injections, so they could help & he said great!)

And he said—which really summed it up for me—that it was incredible how much I've been thru & how well I've gotten along all this time. I really needed for someone who knows to acknowledge the importance of all I've gone through. He said it was obvious to him that I know what I'm doing & have thought all this thru very well. And because all the effects are reversible, I definitely should do it.

He said when he was going thru it, he asked people if he'd be in demand in the lesbian world. I even laughed at that one. But he was told by some gay men that he'd for sure be in demand in the gay men's world, even tho he had no cock. He said it wasn't the vagina or lack of cock that turned gay men off about women, but their soft skin & extra fatty body they didn't like & that would go away with male hormones. That as far as they're concerned, my having a vagina would just be one extra hole for them, which is what Dain said he has—it's not a vagina, it's "a hole." I like that idea.

I explained why I left J & Dain said he admired me for my self-respect in getting out of that demoralizing situation (where J would say he

---

20 Gentile use of schtick

didn't know who he loved better bullshit). Dain recommended The Bisexual Center as a good place to meet bi men open to different scenes.

He also asked about my nephews ✦ said his 3 ✦ 7 year old nephews watched him change ✦ it was very good for them to see. (When I talked to Bridg later she expressed concern for the effect on the kids.) Asked if I had pets ✦ told him about my bird family ✦ he said it's good I have an outlet for my "nurturing" feelings.

He said he was counseling an 18-yr-old female who says she feels like a gay man ✦ who hits Castro St.—so we *do* exist! He said after the hormones I would look "LIKE A MAN," not like an effeminate man. That if I wanted to be effeminate I could incorporate those gestures ✦ looks, but that right now I do *not* have effeminate gestures ✦ I only look very young. That made me feel super good ✦ confident too cuz, I told him, I was worried I come off like a "fruity faggot."

He told me of one incredibly limp-wristed person that was really laying it on thick at Stanford ✦ he thought the person must be a male-to-female but it turned out to be a female-to-male! Dain said I should re-apply to the Stanford program. He told me to come see him regularly (at whatever intervals I wanted) while taking the hormones ✦ that I needn't pay him, just put him on GGG/G's mailing list. FAMOUS. It was obvious he really liked ✦ understood ✦ respected me. It was just all too good to be true.

Just talked to Lin Fraser who gave me 3 numbers of endocrinologists ✦ I have an appointment for next Thursday with one of them. She said she trusts Dain's judgement on my situation (F→M) better than her own judgement.

It's all systems go, man!

Told him I don't feel like "a man trapped in a woman's body." ✦ he laughed ✦ said nobody does, that's just a catchy phrase coined by the medical profession ✦ that being a transsexual does not dictate anything other than your feelings about yourself, and I have a perfect right to be a gay man if that's what I want.

Went to see Dr. George Fulmer, an endocrinologist. He asked me all the same questions about my life & feeling. He was an old guy, but had a sense of humor & seemed sympathetic & understanding. At the end of the whole spiel, he said everything seemed fine to him, except he hesitates because I'm not interested in women. Said he didn't deny there are people like me & I said I know several M→F's who're now lesbians. He said he wanted me to do 3 things—go get a lab test, come back to him for a pap smear, & go see Dr. Wardell Pomeroy, Director of the National Sex Forum. I got the impression that if Pomeroy OK's me, Fulmer will give me the testosterone.

He did ask some pretty dumb questions, like "What typically 'masculine' things do you like to do and what typically 'feminine' things?" I DON'T KNOW! How the hell am I supposed to answer that?? Oh, I put cream & sugar in my coffee, that's feminine; I like to watch boxing matches on TV, that's masculine; I put bath oil in the tub, that's feminine; and I use Brut deodorant, that's masculine. GOD. I just told him I pretty much stick to middle-of-the-road things anyone can do, and that if I weren't a secretary, I'd like to get into printing & publishing & I told him how I enjoy doing the newsletter.

I left there rather discouraged. I first went to a bar (masculine!) and then home to cry (feminine!), but when I reflect I think he'll cooperate with me. Dain said Pomeroy was great & if he gives me ¼ of the encouragement Dain did, I'll be in like Flint.

My one boss asked "How did it go at the doctor's?" just to check up. Told him I had some "female trouble" (yeah, my *body*) & that it would all turn out in the end.

Received Stanford's application & it's the same 15-page extravaganza I filled out 3 years ago. HELP!

So I'm making an addition to my story: instead of saying I'm not interested in girls, I'm gonna say that, since I've really decided to do this change, girls are looking a lot better to me—which is true! Suddenly it's no longer a rejection of women, but an acceptance & almost an interest, because I no longer have to be one of them!

Sudden thought: If that psychiatric profession has decided that being homosexual is no longer a sign of mental disorder, then how come *wanting* to be homosexual is so mental??

Went to see Ray's band. He greeted me with open arms, obviously glad to see me & excited that our leather jackets looked the same. Told him about my plans & he was real excited, saying "Gee, can we be buddies afterwards?" I said "Sure! I think it'll be much more fun that way!"

Well, he lost no time. Monday he phones & comes over about 10 pm with a brown paper bag containing his "new toy" he wrote about in his postcard to me

—an old-fashioned white satiny long-line bra/corset that fit him perfectly, lovely. We drank wine & had a lively conversation—we think so much alike. It was as exciting (if not more because I'm unguarded) than the talks J & I would have.

Something he said initiated my hassling/teasing him that he is no better than me cuz he crossdresses too, except I just have more fun doing it. He looked very surprised & denied it all. I asked accusingly "You think I'm a pervert, don't you?"

I was holding him down on the couch. He said nervously, "Yeah, that's why I come over here!" and then he sat up and acted kind of disgusted with me. He shook his head sadly & said that was really tacky for me to say. I felt sorry & he said that I had better get over that if I'm going to be a boy. Then I *really* felt bad. I said yeah, I know. And he added "because boys have no morals…."

These are the kinds of things you don't read about in a "book about men." (That's maybe what J meant when he said in 1976 that I don't "think like a man.") Can it really be that men in general are that aloof, that matter-of-fact about sex?

Ray says that's the attractive thing about the gay world—the easy availability of sex. He also said one problem with having sex with women is you've got to talk to them beforehand (at the time, I didn't think it, but was that an indirect cut?) Apparently, I got the message, you don't do that if you're two guys who want to get it on. Maybe that's what keeps that distance between gay men—while stable relationships are so scattered. How do you know if the guy's an ass if you don't talk to him? But I guess when you just wanna fuck, you just wanna fuck.

The difference between having sex & wanting a relationship with someone. I gotta learn all this shit all over again. I started with J too young. Never had the chance to be a free & easy guy.

This guy goes for the total role reversal. No holds barred. He isn't the least self conscious about just laying there & letting me do anything I want with him. I rough him up & pet & kiss his stuffed bosom & he moans & writhes, totally succumbing. He said "I bet you could get into girls." I said yeah, I think I could. He said "Girls are fun, sometimes."

I sucked his cock real good (and I've had a sore throat!) & when I stopped, he sighed & said I'd go far in the gay world. Told him that's a really good compliment. I would lay on top of him with him on his back & pretend I'm fucking him, using a lot of strength & muscle to keep thrusting & he LOVES it even when I'm not *even* fucking him! I love that masculine superior position. I had my fake cock (stuffed sock) in my jockey shorts & rubbed it against his cock & ass and he really liked it. I wished I had a better one so he could've played with it & it wouldn't've been so stupid.

He questioned me on how hot my binder must be, especially in summer. It ended up where he turned me on my stomach & slowly gently put his cock in my ass. I was *so* happy! But I was having a hard time completely relaxing & so he withdrew & went in my C. I said we couldn't cuz I'm "unprotected" ✦ was he giving up on me so soon? He asked for some lubrication ✦ that sure was the answer cuz he ass-fucked me REAL good ✦ I'm not even tender today! Ray cums so good, he just stiffens up ✦ trembles ✦ totally loses himself.

So, hey, I can take it in the ass—NO COMPO (think that's short for "no complications"). Was a little concerned about that, cuz it's been so long since I have. I remember that one real hot time with Charles. That was THEN and it was 1973 too. J ✦ I probably did a few times in '76 too.

God, and just laying there while he was sleeping, I wished he was mine. I knew it was out of line ✦ "feminine" to feel that way, but this guy is such a goddamn perfect sex partner—he never destroys my fantasies ✦ it makes me really get into his fantasies. That's why he can put on nylons ✦ a corset ✦ he's sexier than hell, when I'm always afraid it might turn me off.

He is such a SEXUAL person, in total. And despite what he says, I believe he *likes* to talk with me. And he's right—talking like that is a feminine thing because he has to relate to me on the same level, which may make him feel feminine, which is why straight men don't like to do that. Suddenly we're like 2 human beings going to have sex instead of a man ✦ a woman going through a dating ritual. But it's true I shouldn't stay fixated on this one good scene we have, but should have different sexual experiences with different people to enjoy a wide range.

I said to him "You are a *quality* fuck!"

In to see Dr. Wardell Pomeroy at the National Sex Forum. Steve Dain greeted me ✦ I told him how I saw Fulmer ✦ how he'd asked me all this stuff ✦ said it was all fine, but he figures I should like women. Dain gets more perturbed with this stuff than *I* do ✦ he said, "that's why I want to get my PhD—so people don't have to go through this *bullshit*!"

He sat in on our session, as did a female student. Pomeroy asked me a raft of factual-type questions (how old were you when you began menstruating? did you ever see your parents having intercourse? did you have many friends in high school? how was your relationship with your father?). It seemed he had a written questionnaire & checked off answers as I have them. It was very painless, took about ½ hour.

Then he said he had only one question in all this: why am I trying to force myself to be a heterosexual man & like women? what's wrong with being a gay man? ? ? ? I set him straight fast—said I'm NOT AT ALL trying to be a hetero man, I WANT to be a gay man! That all I said was that, as I get closer to being a man, women don't look that bad to me anymore. That when I am doing this, I can see where women might not be so bad once in a while. He said, oh, ok then, cuz it's fine to be a gay man???

I waited in the lobby about 5 minutes so the 3 of them could confer & then they told me they all agreed I should try hormones. But I should go at it gradually and I should put any surgery "on the back burner." Told him I intend to. Said he'd phone or write Fulmer that he supports me for hormone therapy & that I should continue to see Dain regularly while on hormones, say once a week. I said I'd like to. So I got 'm! This Pomeroy was no bullshitter. Fulmer, who wasn't even qualified, put me thru three times the questioning!

I'm actually going to live as a man. I can't believe it. Something I've wanted to do since I can remember—be a boy! God, it's too good to be true. There's no going back now, I just know it. It just seemed everything fell into place—when it's right, it just happens.

Ma said that if this is what I want & it's what will make me happy, that's all she cares & that who is she to say if the doctors & I agree it's right for me? But, she said, the *only* thing that worried her was—how was I going to go into the men's bathroom? I said, ma, I've been going into men's rooms for 6 years—there's no problem. You just go into a stall & close the door, and if there's no door you just have to be quick at pulling the pants down & up. She said oh, of course she hasn't been in a men's room, but, yes, she supposes that's true! (If that's her main concern, it can't be *that* bad.)

When I told dad, he was very receptive + said he hoped I'd be happy + he's glad I'm doing something that will make me feel better + that if I need anything, money or anything, I should just let him know. Dear Jack. When he offers you money, you know it's from his heart! Of course I would never take him up on that offer, he knows that, and that's why we get along so well. I don't test his love... He said that somehow he felt very close to me.

Bridget, Kathy Steininger + I snorted cocaine and stayed up all night Saturday having deep conversations. We talked in depth about my change, about their fears, etc.

Bridget said she remembers when I was about 14 I came to the dinner table with something obviously stuffed in my pants for a penis. When she confronted me about it, she said I pulled a sock out in which I'd put a hair roller + said something like—this is what it is, so what?—or something defensive like that. God! I don't remember....

We talked about my relating to their kids + they acknowledged that I related to them like, say, Patrick did + that I am surely more an "uncle" than an "aunt" and Kathy said she hoped I'd be the one Cheyney comes to to ask questions about sex, etc.

I've been feeling a little apprehensive about taking these hormones + living as a man. Worried me but I tried not to think too hard about it.

Today, I've tried to identify this feeling. And I remember having felt this way once before. It was when I worked at Trade Press, just out of high school, + I'd only been living in my own apt. for a few months. One lunch hour I was walking along the street + I suddenly had this strong urge to get on the bus + go back to Bluemound Rd. + become a little girl again + have mommy take care of me. I just wanted to escape the responsibility + insecurity of adulthood. I wanted to be taken care of + not have a care in the world.

And these last few days, as the appointment with Fulmer gets closer, I have those same feelings. It's so hard to be mature sometimes. Yet I'm still not getting my hopes up. I still can't believe that I'll be leaving Fulmer's office tomorrow with a prescription in my hand.

Took Cheyney to a basketball game last night ✝ it turned out really well. He was full of energy ✝ curiosity ✝ no trouble at all. We were talking about faces ✝ I said I was going to be an ugly grandpa. He corrected me, "grandma," but I told him by then I'll be a grandpa. He asked when I was going to "do that" ✝ I told him I had to take all these tests, but it should begin in a few weeks. Told him my name'd be Lou ✝ he said he didn't like that name ✝ I should pick "Ned." I said thanks a lot!

Told him his great-grandpa's name was Louie. He didn't know that. Asked what he thought of my being a guy ✝ he said he liked it cuz then he would have someone to play ball with instead of waiting around for his dad or Rusty to be there. (I'm always perplexed by people's reasons!)

Later he said he liked me best of all the Sullivans cuz I never told him what to, or not to, do. In other words, I'm the only one not playing mother or father—tomorrow I call Fulmer to see if he got all my test results ✝ then make THE appointment!—Looks like my job is safe, too, til at least the end of the year.

So went for my 1st shot—50 mg of Depo-Testosterone. Was so relieved ✝ happy I could have burst. God, finally. Finally. Got it in the ass, "going right to the root of the problem—right where it's needed most" I laughed to Maryellen.

Fulmer told me he got the sex chromatin test ✝ I came up a "weak positive" which may not mean anything, but ma latched onto it right away, consoled to think I have some genetic reason for feeling ✝ doing what I am ✝ it wasn't cuz she was a failure as a mother.

Steve Dain returned my call ⚢ he said when they heard I still hadn't received my hormones, Pomeroy called Fulmer to ask what the hold-up was! No wonder Fulmer was so cooperative! Dain said I should get the expensive chromosome test done, that maybe I actually DO have XY chromosomes!

When I told him I got 50 mg ⚢ would get 100 in another 10 days, he flipped. Said that was bullshit, that Stanford recommends *200 mg per week* until your menses stops! I was instantly depressed. Felt like crying. Dain said I should demand 200 ⚢ if there's a problem with that, Fulmer should call Pomeroy. I felt so bad—why is Fulmer hacking me around? But I hate to go to a doctor ⚢ tell him his business. Dain said they give frigid WOMEN 200 mg of testosterone! Anyway, told Dain how my boss was there for me ⚢ my parents, siblings ⚢ friends, ⚢ he said there seemed to be no reason for me to meet with him for counseling until I have some problems.

So of course felt ⚢ saw no effects from the 50 mg. On Nov 27th went back in for my 2nd shot. My face was zitsville ⚢ Fulmer zeroed in on that immediately, but I told him it was not unusual for me, especially because I had my period. Told him my counselor said I should ask for 200 mg/week. He very firmly stuck up for himself, that *he's* the doctor ⚢ has many patients who have full beards; this is the way he does it; the medical profession always tries to give the lowest drug dosage to achieve the desired effects; I've waited 28 years already, what's an extra couple weeks, blah, blah, blah. So what can I say? He gave me 100 mg.

Took Kathleen to Polk Street ⚢ her 1st time in a gay bar. Some man began talking to her ⚢ she introduced me as her brother. She made a concerted effort all week to call me Lou.

Saturday I was to meet her in front of the punk club. Wore my black leather jacket, white T-shirt, black pants. Four big hippie bikers were out there drinking ⚢ eyeing up the punkers. They began saying "Hey, is that a chick or a guy?? Tell'm to whip it out, then we'll know. Yeah, let's see'm whip it out... Hey, are you a chick or a guy?" I just looked at them like "oh cut it out!" One of them positioned himself about 10

ft from me ₊ stared at me about 10 full minutes. I looked over at him,
let him know I knew he was staring at me, but didn't stare back or
challenge him.

Then he came over, put his hand up on the wall ₊ leaned over me.
Asked why I was standing there. In my lowest, most male voice, I said
"Waitin' for someone." He said, "Long time to wait." I said yeah. He
commented on how expensive it was to get in the club ₊ I agreed. Said
a few more sentences ₊ he walked away. I had tried to be congenial, but
not passive or cowering.

When he returned to his friends, they asked "What's the verdict?" I
heard him mumble ₊ I heard the word "guy" but I don't think he really
decided what I was. In a while they all began leaving ₊ had to walk by
me. One said, "Hey, Frank, did you figure out what it was?" ₊ cocked
his head toward me. The guy who'd talked to me looked at me ₊ said to
his friend, "It's cool."

They got on their motorcycles, were revving them up ₊ acting real
hard-guy ₊ Frank raised his hand goodbye to me ₊ I raised mine real
butch-like. The guy showed a lot of class.

Instead of going in, Kath ₊ I went to the hot tub ₊ sauna place. We
got bare together ₊ it was real nice. Our roots... We laughed about
how funny we must've looked going in there together: Pacific Heights
matron picks up 17-year-old runaway boy. He asks for $10 and a hot
meal...

Part way through the film, youngman sat next to me, his leg "incon-
spicuously" touching mine. I didn't react or move. He began pressing
his leg against mine ₊ I still didn't move, so he was encouraged. Then
I pressed mine against his. My right arm was on the arm rest between
us and I slowly lowered my hand onto his left, squeezed ₊ stroked it.
Made my way up to his crotch, both of us still intently watching the
film. He put his left arm on the arm rest between us, kind of pinning
my arm there. I tried to open his pants, but couldn't, so he did. Had no
underwear on ₊ I played with his penis ₊ testicles. He was little, but

hard. I wanted to lean over and suck him, but saw no other heads disappearing in the audience ✦ didn't have the guts.

He dropped his left hand and took hold of my bulge—I was a little (but not too) worried my sock-penis and balls might not pass. He went for my zipper ✦ I took his hand ✦ moved it away, while continuing to play with him. Moments later he again reached over ✦ stroked my crotch. I let him rub me outside my pants but after a while, took his hand away again. But a minute later he was at my zipper. I let him open it ✦ reach in, but he began trying too hard to find me under the layers of undershirt, shorts, jockstrap—so I took his hand away again. He fought me, but I was insistent, finally taking my hand off him ✦ crossing my legs ✦ arms so we couldn't touch. I figured he should have gotten that "I would do him but he couldn't do me." Well, he sat ✦ smoked a cigarette, probably trying to figure out what the hell my problem was! Then he left. My zipper was still open, so I quietly masturbated. Another man sat a few seats away ✦ watched me.

Later went to the drag bars. My attitude really changed. Instead of just watching the show ✦ feeling self-conscious ✦ worried I'd be read, I was aware of who I liked ✦ who was liking me. Now when someone's looking, I think they're cruising me instead of reading me.

Caught a not-too-bad queen staring, so I smiled ✦ watched. She showed me some leg ✦ I smiled ✦ admired. She came up to the bar ✦ ordered a drink ✦ I paid for it. She sat down ✦ I was the man, she was a loose woman. She wasn't bad at all, tho a little chubby. Ended up at my place. On the way she said she didn't want to offend me, but I was a little too feminine. Told her I'm taking male hormones, thinking she figured me out then. (But later on she said she thought I was a hermaphrodite!) I said I wouldn't take my clothes off, but she was really free ✦ open ✦ told me not to be that way, that we are all okay no matter what we are. She made me feel relaxed ✦ good about myself ✦ we ended up having pretty good sex. She had a small cock, I got it hard and she ass-fucked me. It was the first uncircumcised cock I've seen. I did keep my undershirt on, tho. She told me I'm going to make a really great gay boy! (She should know).

Next morning bought her breakfast & she asked for a couple dollars to get a drink. Gave her $3, walked her to a bar. She was honest & open & intelligent. (Some teenage boys watched us walking & began shouting. When I left her at the bar door & kissed her goodbye, they began shouting "Ugh! You kissed it!!" I just laughed—if only they knew!)

So finally I've succeeded in getting a drag queen!

Saturday hung out with Maryellen. Feeling extremely sexual & male—wore a shirt with the sleeves rolled way up tight to show off my already-hardening muscley arms. My energy level is incredible—I feel like I'm speeding a lot of the time. Coffee! Coffee!

At the GGG/G meeting I was pretty popular—compliments on my newsletter & attention because the hormone effects are becoming apparent. Told Emmon about my theater exploits & he said it sure sounds like I know my way around the gay scene & should have no trouble. Talked about the self-confidence & ego men have that women don't, that women spend so much energy "giving" to others & nurturing others, that when you're a man you have this looking-out-for-#1 attitude that's the greatest. Told him how, since I'm doing this, I'm feeling very few "shoulds."

Well, I'm doing pretty damn good. It truly is wonderful how good I feel, waking up in the morning, facing weekends, or evenings alone. I feel so so relaxed & self-satisfied. I never knew how fine it felt to feel attractive & worthy, to feel sexual & self-aware. My body tingles all day long. I feel electrified. When before I felt like my body wasn't even there, that I was living in a dream, watching myself as though I were on TV, now I feel so sensual & strong & vibrant.

To the bars. Danced very well with one young beauty but afterwards he split. I was drunk & so damn starved for physical contact. After the bars closed, I took my position leaning against a building on Polk Street, like all the other young hustlers. Watch 2 older men talking to a boy. One of the men rubbed his own crotch & saw me watching. Came over to me, talked a few minutes about the hustlers & soon were touching each other. He was a very "screaming" faggot type, about 45 years old, but with a lean enough body. Told him I live close by.

He drove us there and we sat in his parked car and he took his cock out. I sucked it. He said "let's just do it in here..." I think he was scared I might rob him or something (I had on my black leather jacket policeman-look). But I said no, let's go upstairs, but my conditions are that I don't take off my clothes, that I have a birth defect I don't want him to see, but that I'll do him.

Once inside I sucked him more. I poured drinks, he spent a long time telling me how to cut my hair. And always suddenly he'd push my head down to his cock. I sucked like mad & got so turned on. He kept saying he wish he could fuck my "sweet boy's ass." I decided to risk it...I was so turned on & drunk. Told him I wanted him to fuck me; I planned to lay flat on my stomach and hope he didn't see, cuz he was pretty drunk too.

But he told me to get on my knees & get my ass up & he stood next to the bed while I knelt on the edge & he was fucking my ass, then my cunt. I figured he HAD to know what he was doing, where he was & when I cringed & got worried he said, "Get your ass up and keep it up! It's all okay. Everything is all right. Okay?" And I figured he was telling me he knew, but didn't care. (Of course I kept all my clothes on above my waist.)

But then later it seems he didn't know! It was like he still figured I was a boy, but that my "birth defect" was I had no cock. And he couldn't really tell the difference when his cock was in my ass or my cunt! Too much! When I told him what my scene was, he was truly surprised. He whimpered a few times how this must mean he's really not a queer after all, etc, but I told him to "cut it out, I'm a boy." But it didn't stop him cuz he fucked me like I couldn't believe. Told him I wanted it in the ass, which really amazed him, & he'd always ask if he was in "the right place." I mean, this guy's stamina was incredible.

A few times he got me on my back with my ankles on his shoulders ✦ fucked my ass. I was so hot! Sucked him more. He said I was such a good cocksucker ✦ fuck that I'd put a lot of boys to shame. What a fine compliment! Brought out my dildo ✦ set it down without a word, ✦ he used it on whichever hole he wasn't fucking. He said I had a good waist! Twice he said he's glad I didn't try to 69 with him ✦ I told him I would never have done that. He kept calling me a sweet boy and the whole thing turned out so fine. He actually wore me out and I fell asleep and he snuck out. When I awoke Saturday morn, he was gone.

This anticipation it's just too much. My adrenaline is rushing so much I'm not going to have my usual 3rd cup of coffee this morn... I'm jazzed up enough. Falces this afternoon. I'm not banking on a yes-or-no answer today, but it'd be nice. Figure he'll jack me around a while before deciding whether to do me or not. I'm so looking forward to my flat chest. Dillon sent me a picture of his ✦ it's so beautiful, even with the scars. Karl had his done a few weeks ago. I deserve to have it done! Mary said I could stay with her for a few weeks after the operation ✦ she'll nurse me.

This torture has gone on long enough. I deserve to press a man against my solid hard chest, feel his against mine, and have him feel mine against his. That's what my heart feels, that's what I want to express to him. I have learned to love my body—to finally be able to touch my nipples while masturbating ✦ feel sexual about it—and I think I deserve to have my body relax with me. It will be like a miracle to look at myself, to run my hand over my chest, and to feel me.

I wish I could cry my happiness all out. It's overflowing, swelling inside me. July 15th. I'm not crazy, I'm not living in a dream world. I'm not pretending anymore. I will have a man's chest. I will be a man. Oh, God, I don't know how to believe it's true. It's too good. It's too good. I know now: I can do anything. I can be anything I want. I can challenge the wind...

I love dealing with these professionals. Like Pomeroy, this guy (Dr. Edward Falces) just buzzed into the room, said he'd read my files (Fulmer's records, Pomeroy's letter) and it looks like I'm a very good candidate and under the care of very competent people. He told me the different surgical methods he can use ✦ that I was borderline on breast size where he may be able to do the "key hole" method of just cutting around ✦ working through the nipple; but if that didn't work he'd have to cut across the breast ✦ reposition the nipple.

Asked if there was any history of cysts or tumors in breasts in my family ✦ I told him yes, my youngest sister. So he said he'd remove all the breast tissue so I'd never get breast cancer. Told me to concentrate on skin care—discontinue washing with Phisohex ✦ use Betadine to clear up my acne. Told me to build up my pectoral muscles as much as possible—put my hands on my hips ✦ press in as an isometric exercise. Said I'll be in the hospital 1-2 days after surgery, should take off work 2 weeks, tho I may feel like going back earlier than that.

It's incredible the wave of relaxation that has swept over me in the past few hours. Walking down the street, I didn't even have to concentrate on untensing in my facial muscles (which I realize are so often twisted up). I can look passerby right in the eye ✦ openly smile ✦ face attractive people, instead of hoping they don't see me or feeling totally inferior to them.

July 15th!

July 15th!

How to express how very good I feel. Despite the real traumatic changes my body is undergoing, I've never felt healthier, stronger, more energetic or in higher spirits. I can almost FEEL that female layer of fat dissolving under my skin. My arms are becoming solid ✦ rippling, the veins protruding there and on the backs of my hands. My chest, my hips, my thighs becoming hard. Dark hairs on my feet ✦ toes, wrists, backs of hands, on my stomach, all over my legs, on my ASS!

I lay in the sun on the weekend, my skin becoming rich ✦ golden. My body is vibrant with sexuality ✦ tingling with sensation, electrified by every touch. (A new woman at work—she always calls me "he"—often puts her hands on my arms or shoulders, the feeling lingering long after she's left.) I see a small woman I find pretty, fantasize her arms around my neck, my mouth on her throat, and then a tall lean youngman boldly swaggers into view and warm passion fills my body.

A firm middle-aged man approaches ✦ I imagine my hands on his body, his eyes closed in pleasure. This new interest in mature male bodies has really pleased me. I want to know men's bodies, all of them. I want to examine their shapes, their tastes, their smells, their textures.

I'm experimenting mentally with my sexuality as a man. How does it feel to be a passive receiving man? To have my nipples stimulated? To have my ass used? To have my legs spread? Or to be an active aggressive man? To take a man in my arms? To use my tongue on his body? To put my cock, my fingers in his openings?

Such a new exciting world—the first time in my life I've felt relaxed about being sexual. I masturbate in different ways to experience these feelings about 3 times a day, waking up during the night to jerk off again. And it feels SO GOOD. No more guilt or self-hate. Only total pleasure. Yet my awareness ✦ enjoyment of other people has increased. I love the sound of my voice, I laugh a lot, join in a lot, feel intelligent, worthy of attention, open to new ideas, new experiences. I can be silly, or wrong, or stupid, ✦ not feel ashamed.

Last Saturday night Bridget ✦ Charlie were waiting for a bus to North Beach. J, who was on the bus, saw Bridget recognizing him ✦ when he finally realized who she was, became quite surprised. On the bus she walked past him saying "You know who I am, don't you?" He said yes. She said "How are you?" He said "OK," and she kept walking. Said he was carrying an orange backpack ✦ I laughed until I looked down at the tube socks ✦ athletic shoes on my feet. Yes, we've changed.

Some funny occurrences: Yesterday a male friend (about 60) of my next door neighbor called, bringing roses. She wasn't home so, apparently instead of tossing them, he rang my doorbell. When I answered, he asked where the young lady was who used to live in my apt. I said I'm her. He said no, it was a young LADY. I said well, I'm doing some changes. He said (not getting it at all) "oh, so she's not here anymore?" Giving up, I said no. He said oh, he just wanted to give her these flowers ＋ he's sorry for bothering me. (Am I THAT unrecognizable?)

Just got a call from Falces office firming up my hospital date. He wants to see me for a pre-op appointment. God, I can't wait. What a feeling! My body will finally be mine! I'm to bring his fee of $1,500 then, ＋ the hospital requires prepayment of $2,000 which should cover the whole cost.

This past Friday went to the gay porn theatre again. A 35–40 year old man sat next to me, glancing over at me. I put my leg against his ＋ pressed. His hand went right to my thigh ＋ I went for his cock. Both of us still watching the movie. I played with him ＋ he rubbed me thru my clothes. When he tried to unzip me, I gently moved his hand back down onto my crotch. Again he tried, I let him get just so far ＋ pulled his hand out. He resisted but I was insistent. He looked at me puzzled, but I kept watching the movie. I guess he decided I was real young ＋ this was my first time, because he patted my thigh with a very warm understanding, taking my hand off his cock, tucking himself back in. Then he patted my thigh again, as if to say "it's okay" ＋ he left. God, I would if I could!!! If only I could!!

He went in the backroom ＋ I finally got the nerve to go back ＋ check it out. You had to go thru the bathroom to a very short narrow hallway, off of which were about 8 tiny cubicles, large enough for maybe 2 people to stand inside. I went into one ＋ there's a glory hole! So I took my position, sucked a cock that appeared. When one guy was sucking another in the adjoining cubicle, I reached thru ＋ played with his balls, stroked the neck of the man sucking. It was nice.

After they left, I wandered around & found a big man just standing in one of the cubicles, so I went down on him. Really sucked him good & proper, he reached down once to rub me but I acted like I was so eager to suck that I didn't want him to feel me up. So he gently caressed my hair & neck. It seemed he came a little, then he lifted me to my feet & very lovingly hugged & kissed me. When I turned to leave, I found about 4 other men were behind me, watching. I bee-lined out of there because I was so delirious I'd been sick with my sinuses clogged & had snorted some meth before going to the theatre & now had a bad headache.

Sat in the theatre to recover. Now I wish I'd've felt better & sucked the other 4 while I was there! When I felt better I went back again. I was pretty disappointed at the lack of action & people. Hoped to be a voyeur but there was nothing to see! Found the one larger room which was pitch black, but I could hear noises so knew there was someone inside. My hands found a naked body doing something to someone & I found his ass & fingered his hole. Boring.

In the hall saw a youngish blond back into a cubicle & began following him in, but he gave such a violent shove, I was really surprised! What a goober! I mean, there were some horrid guys grabbing me too & all you have to do is gently move away so you don't hurt them. This guy was really nasty. I hid in the cubicle to regain my self-pride.

Later went down on another short man in a business suit. He caressed my hair, reached down the back of my shirt & stroked my back & shoulders. Felt so good. None of these guys ever really came in my mouth & I was surprised at how small their cocks were. If I get what Dain has, even if it doesn't get hard, it'll still pass off as good as these guys did!

I was surprised & truly delighted to find the display of affections & feelings going on in these reputed dens of anonymous sex. I didn't know that—the understanding pat from the man in the theatre, the gentle caresses and blatantly affectionate kiss & hug I received while sucking these men. Somehow those brief displays of tenderness between two men mean more to me than I can say…more than so many of the undying devotions & commitments spewed out by those who know no better.

Went to a salon to get my mustache dyed black. They'd said on the phone they could do it, though I warned it was sparse & fine. (I darken it every day with mascara & have to keep an eye on it & touch it up throughout the day.) But when the guy saw me he exclaimed, "Oh, what are we going to *DO* with you!" & told me to come back in 1-2 months after it grows in (didn't want to have to tell him it's been this way 5 months!). I still have no whiskers. It seems this past week the hair on the backs of my hands is growing again, after a long lull. Most of this hair is blondish & unnoticeable.

In August when I want to begin looking for a new job, will I be able to present myself as a 29-year-old man? Not at this rate. Went to change my checking account. The guy asked NO questions. I didn't even tell him shit—just that I had a name change. I was out of there in 10 minutes. No lie! So now I have all my IDs changed. Don't have anything left under Sheila, except a life insurance policy.

Maryellen is pregnant & getting married. I'm glad…something other than myself to think about for a while.

I feel so distant from all the people who mean so much to me. Spent the afternoon with Bridget, Kathy, Maryellen…yet there seemed no way to express the reality, the importance of the changes in my heart, in my eyes. To wash my body with surgical soap, according to instructions, washing, washing, and watching my body that is there, that isn't there, that won't be there in 3 days. How can I share this emotion; how can I find an outlet for these incredibly strong feelings?

I went shopping this morning for another new shirt—an expensive white dress shirt—waiting, planning, only wanting it because it would be on my chest…my man's chest. I haven't worn any of my new shirts, not wanting to "soil" them, "jinx" them by putting them on over my breasts. I want them to be pure, to be male, to be me. I want to start new, to be part of the total magic that will be me, that is Louis.

Sometimes I worry (and I know I worry too much, too seriously) that I will have the same self-doubts & uneasiness as a man as I have as a woman. I worry that I will fail to find the happiness I think I will. But as I wash myself & prepare for this surgery, when I buy my new shirts & look at my breasts & think they are sexy (!), I know I'll come out of this a better person.

I've never felt I could love a female's body. Or want to put my mouth on a woman's breast. Now I know I can, I want to. I know I can make it as a man.

I need to resolve the dichotomy of my genitals. To convince myself that it doesn't matter. I read an article by John Money who tells of a kid who'd been considered a boy all his life, but at age 11 began to menstruate through his penis! I need to remember that I have made the choice of being a defective male instead of trying to continue as a defective female. That's when I know I can make it as a man... when I remember how useless it was to struggle on as a woman.

Everyone went through the day as if nothing was out of the ordinary. Couldn't they see it in my eyes? Can't they tell that I'm *not* the way they see me?

It's so nice to allow myself to say I am a man, to know I am a man. It's all real now. I don't have to pretend anymore. I look back on how I was before & all the wasted time that had to be. J was my refuge where I hid for so long. I had him and never had to face my exclusion from the rest of the world.

J, J, J. I pray I'll find someone who will mean as much to me as you did. I miss that closeness so much, though I have no capacity to open my heart unconditionally at this time. This time is so valuable to my heart, in building this solid good person who deserves someone's love and who has something to offer to someone who deserves my love.

My hands, my wrists, my arms.
My body unveils itself
and is simply, quietly beautiful.
Suddenly, magically we found each other

There we were…here we are
I plan to let you happy me
Summer me
Winter me.

So here I am in the hospital. Woke up feeling alive, alert and with a very clear head. I am amazed at how easily my mind has adjusted to this change in my status. I am incredibly self-confident ✝ sure of this decision. As I've said before re: this change, I feel like I'm finally coming out of a fog. A preoccupation is fading from my thoughts. I thought I'd be nervous ✝ have diarrhea, etc, but I'm totally relaxed, am breathing deeply ✝ slowly ✝ clearly ✝ have to suppress the urge to have a silly smile on my face.

All kinds of nurses ✝ others traipsing in ✝ out of my room for this ✝ that. Two asked what I'm here for ✝ were visibly taken aback when I answered "I'm having a mastectomy." HA HA! I tried to dye my mustache last night so it'll be more visible ✝ I'd feel more male. Worked a little—guess that fine growth doesn't take dye very well.

Anyway, I'm Mr. Louis G. Sullivan here ✝ everyone is treating me as such. Though I requested a semi-private room, they said they always give a private room to people with my "diagnosis!" HA HA

Falces came in with a marking pen ✝ tape measure ✝ drew on me where my nipples are in relation to my collarbone, etc ✝ said he wanted to replace the nipple at those specifications as "nature knows where to place nipples." I asked how long before I can begin lifting my weights after the surgery. He said 2 weeks!!! Great! Told him I had fantasies of getting some sun after surgery, okay? But he said he'd kill me if I did, but I should get sun on my back. Said sun would make the scars worse. And I did mention the TS he did who Dain was so freaked about who had a scar from underarm to underarm. Falces looked embarrassed ✝ stammered that I shouldn't have that problem becuz I'm not that big.

Well, you know, I'd written J ✝ told him July 15 ✝ secretly hoped that he'd somehow acknowledge the day. Today I got a long letter from him, saying what I expected him to say. He begged me to "reconsider" (I'm reading the letter on the bus to the hospital, not much time to reconsider!), that he felt I am really "going off the deep end," that he "thirsts for those kinds of discussions we used to have" ＋ that if I go through with this he doesn't think he could have any personal face-to-face contact with me. Yet, he says "I don't doubt you're happier as a man—but I think this boils down to merely 'feeling better' about yourself." MERELY? Poor J. He finishes up by saying "Whatever you decide to do, at least we can carry on a relationship of some sort by mail, I hope. And if you do decide to go on, please accept these words as a get-well bouquet, since I could never be there in person."

Dear, sweet J. He knows I will go ahead as planned. I know, I knew it would be hard for him—but I also know, and so does he, that we will never totally lose each other. The bum is again addressing the envelope ＋ letter to Sheila, tho, all spelled out S-H-E-I-L-A. He's gotta at least cut that out. He also apologized for "the horrible way I treated you in the past, not only actively, but by stifling you, neglecting you, blah, blah, blah." I'm glad he realizes that now—sorry he doesn't realize that he's still trying to "stifle" me. (Bridget says it sounds like his ego's getting in the way.)

I have a beautiful view of San Francisco from my window.

So I can't even believe how goddamn good I feel. Yesterday morn at 6:30 they rousted me up ＋ gave me 2 shots in the behind. I started getting woozy ＋ a very entertaining orderly came to wheel me down to the operating room. They stuck an IV in my left wrist, the anesthesiologist said he was giving me something that would make my eyes droopy ＋ hard to focus. Falces was about 15 mins late ＋ came in saying he was at a great hockey game. That's all I remember.

Next I'm in the recovery room, the nurses telling me to wake up, lay still, wake up, lay still. I was very groggy. Don't remember them wheeling me back to my room, but there were 2 women ＋ a man rushing around saying my blood pressure was 80/40 ＋ it must be lousy stethoscope! I was freezing! She says she can't find my pulse ＋

maybe one of the others should try! Then they're saying, "Lou, take a deep breath! Lou, take a deep breath!" but God, it hurt! Then it was 90/40. Something like that. My pulse was very weak too. I started getting scared!

Then the nurse says "A very good friend of yours just called to see how you were ✝ his name was J." Of course my first thought was—J! Told her it was amazing he called, that I haven't seen him in 2 years ✝ we had gone together for 10 years. She was impressed. (But later I realized it was J, my co-worker at Wilson.)

Next I know I hear Bridget come in to visit. She started marching around, so they consented to disconnect the IV (which hurt more than anything) ✝ finally let me drink water—before they'd only give me a damn cloth to suck on, ✝ my throat was so raw. My blood pressure rose to 104/70 ✝ I began feeling very good. Falces came ✝ said he only had to cut a small incision on the side from the nipple to the underarm, so shit! That's excellent! I have drainage tubes coming from my underarms going to little plastic bottles at my side, containing thick dark red liquid draining out. The right side hurts much more than the left. So hungry! They brought me a liquid lunch ✝ Bridget fed me ✝ got me some candy bars. Funny Hershey bar saying "It's a He!" She stayed several hours while I dozed off ✝ came to. Phoned Nanc, Jack ✝ Kathleen but no one was home. Later Nanc phoned me ✝ I talked to her ✝ Kath. Very supportive.

After Bridget left they brought supper—steak ✝ a butter knife. Fine! I almost wanted to cry cuz I was so hungry. I called the nurse, asking them to cut my meat, but they started bitching how I need to exercise ✝ they just propped me up higher ✝ lowered the table, so I could slowly feed myself. God! Had to piss, so called the nurse to unhook my tubes, but I guess she didn't know how, so she brings me a water-pitcher-shaped urinal. Told her I couldn't use that, you see, I don't have a penis. She was surprised, saying oh well, how about a bedpan? Jesus, you'd think they'd <u>tell</u> them who their patients are, or that the nurses would all be snickering about me. God! Then she yanks the pan out from under me ✝ spills it all over the bed. Then she's got to change the sheets! Unreal.

Then Maryellen came with a thermos of tea ♣ some "smut" magazines for me. She stayed a long time, way past visiting hours, busying around smoothing the sheets, etc. I had to piss ♣ shit ♣ this time they ordered a porta-potty for my bedside which never came. Mary finally helped me with the bedpan.

She left about 10 pm ♣ I turned in for the night, tho had to call the nurse 3 times after that—once my tubes came apart ♣ twice they left the doors open ♣ lights on when I was trying to sleep. Woke up at 2 am, my back sore from the same position. Sat up awhile, the nurse brought me some juice. Slept through til 6 am. So I got out of bed, washed my hair by myself (!)…I can't believe how good I feel ♣ I still haven't had one pain killer since the surgery!

Falces came ♣ took off my bandages. I looked caved in here, puffy there, and very very flat! The nipples looked like chewed-up pink meat full of stitches. He wrapped me up in 2 large pads and an Ace bandage ♣ said when the draining stops I can go home, probably tomorrow or Friday, but let's shoot for tomorrow, he said. Phoned Wilson ♣ Jack. Can't wait to heal up. I look so good, I'm still in a dream.

Spent Wednesday in bed, mostly being reflective. Wrote in you. Rested. Stared out the window. Bridget ♣ Kathy visited and I talked to Maryellen on the phone for over an hour. Had a hard time falling asleep cuz I had to lie flat on my back when I'm used to lying on my side. So Thursday I stretched the drainage tubes across the bed ♣ sat in the chair, reading Rechy's *Rushes*.

Falces' partner, Dr. Kauth, came to see me, said I'm looking fantastic ♣ can go home Friday. The hospital chaplain came in (I guess making his daily rounds) ♣ asked how I was doing. Told him real good, blah, blah, blah. He looked very caringly ♣ gently into my eyes ♣ I returned the sentiment, which I think encouraged him to be bolder. He asked how I'm doing financially, that he saw I had to finance this myself. So I knew he knew what I was doing. I explained that my father was paying for it, that I've had total support from family, friends ♣ my place of employment. He asked my plans for the future, told him I'd need to get a new job & eventually a new apartment. All the while he looked at me lovingly & I felt my whole body flushing & a cold sweat over my shoulders & back. Then he said his ministry was very supportive of this kind of thing & if I ever felt I needed to talk with someone, they were there. Then he left. Incredible.

Emmon & Dianna (who gives beauty talks at GGG/G) visited & we had a lively talk on women/men. After they left, Mary & Rusty came by—Rusty & I downed some of the cognac J from Wilson brought me. Watched TV til 10 pm with them. Woke at 2 am very uncomfortable again.

So this morning this Dr. Kauth comes in to send me home. Unwraps me, lays me down, and I mean I thought I would hit the ceiling. These tubes are about ¼" diameter going into me under each arm. He takes hold of the right one & gives it 2 good hard yanks before it comes out and I was totally freaked. He goes for the left one & I asked him to wait until I regained my composure. Then he yanked that one, rewrapped me & said I could go home. Don't raise my arms above my head, leave the bandages on, see Falces in his office Monday. I was in the most pain I'd been in the whole time, just laid in the bed about 45 min trying to relax & breathe & let my body collect itself. The only time I felt I may have to break my record & take a pain pill. But I didn't.

So I feel fantastic now, though my underarms are sore with those holes in them. Don't understand why they are bleeding profusely—how those tubes were inserted. There seems to be large staples holding the incisions together. Don't really need Mary's nursing, but will stay here through the weekend.

So I don't really believe I have an okay flat chest. Sitting here with this ace bandage wrapped around me, it just feels like a binder. I peek underneath and see no breasts! I'm clean! I'm back in one piece!

Well, well, well. Just got a phone call from J. It seems "that goddamn bitch really fucked him over" and boy is he pissed and did I "really go through with it?" I said yup! He said "you don't have tits anymore?" "Nope, they're all gone!" "Shit! Fuck! Shit!" I just laughed.

He said I sounded different & I just said "of course, that's not all!" There's a lot of changes. Well, so since he just moved in with her, now he's got to find a new place & he's staying at this resident hotel. He said someone he knows is a ticket taker at the straight porno theatre & recognized me when I went in & told J I have a mustache. HA HA HA I'm getting a real charge out of the whole thing. What perfect timing! Now it's on *MY* terms!

Steve Dain was supposed to speak at a sex seminar at Pomeroy's Institute Saturday but couldn't, so I was asked to go. Little scared, but wanted to. Bridget accompanied me & it went well. Said they shouldn't rely too much on textbooks, because according to books, I don't exist (a gay male F→M). Was a small very informal group. They said Dain always bares his chest at these talks, so I peeled off my gauze pad for them. I got a lot of positive feedback on how excellent I pass & even the men with gray hair commented how, even though they knew some TVs and TSs would be speaking, they never dreamed I was one.

Saw Falces Monday & he removed the final stitches. Said I'm healing excellently, put Vitamin E oil on scars, move wounded skin from side to side one minute per day to loosen scar tissue from muscle. Begin exercises to build pectorals again. See him in 2 weeks.

Phoned Dain to tell him how satisfied I am with Falces. Also discussed how I'm wanting to "disappear" now from the transgender community, though I enjoy doing *The Gateway*.

I'm relating to my new body much better. Walk around my apartment with no shirt on and the shades all open—the freedom! Or in the streets with just a thin, almost transparent T-shirt on and I look so good. The lines and bumps of the material over my chest look so attractive.

The very area of the wounds is still very numb and sore, so there's very little erotic sensation there right now. Can't wait til the feeling is back ✦ someone's lips are on my nipples, a man's hands on my chest. God, it will be so satisfying! Have been concentrating in my masturbating fantasies of thinking of myself and another man together, instead of (as before) "those two men over there together." Must incorporate myself into these sexual "scenes" to get myself used to the side of being a functional gay man. My asshole is so full of erotic sensation, it's not even funny! I want a man's cock in my ass, his mouth on the back of my neck, his hands moving over my chest, pressing my back against his chest. GOD!

So this is my 4th day on the new job. Everything has fallen into place beautifully. They don't require a physical exam! Can you believe it?!! I really lucked out. There are in excess of 25 people in our department, which is in a major office building downtown. Tons of people all over ✦ incredibly I am just another youngman working there. There is no doubt. There is no question of my status. God, I am so happy I hesitate to even think about it.

And ah, the men's room! The men's room! I feel so good walking in with a man standing at the urinal in his suit. I'm working on not feeling self-conscious about going into a stall to sit ✦ pee…I try to remember that many men have a physical problem ✦ must sit to pee, and that when a guy has to shit he sits ✦ may pee also. Another reason I feel self-conscious in the men's room is because I feel so very attractive and am afraid if I look at a guy he might think I'm eyeing him up ✦ I can't risk that reputation at my place of employment. I don't want to be known as a flaming faggot. It's probably my second phase of my adaptation in life: I'm adapting fine as a man. Now I need to adapt as a gay man.

Monday evening the old gay man from the seminar called. I knew he intended to bed me. Wasn't attracted to him, tho he had a nice trim body. We drank in the bar a while *r* I finally asked him over *r* I'm telling you I don't understand WHY he came on to me. Once we started having sex it seemed he wasn't much interested. He just laid there smiling while I licked *r* sucked him *r* when I laid back passively he never reached out to please me at all. I was pretty pissed. He never once got hard either. Jerk. But it was the first time I had sex with my new chest *r* that felt super good.

Walking home the sidewalk was deserted but for me *r* a tall pretty boy. He began talking to me *r* it's obvious we're both gay. He apparently was going to hustle Polk St *r* he got me in the mood so I decided to head up to Buzzby's to see if that M→F was there.

I brought out a joint for us to share. But some street jerk butts in to share it too *r* then takes the joint, says thanks *r* starts walking away with it. I got really pissed *r* went after him, saying "Hey, what do you think you're doing? You just don't rip off people like that!" He tried to get away from me but I pursued him until we were standing in the middle of the street, still arguing. I momentarily thought I may get into a physical fight with this guy *r* will my pretty friend help? Suddenly pretty friend is at my side also trying to reason with this guy *r* we get him back off the street, telling him to be cool *r* smoke the joint with us. I was really relieved when he did. Then after that shit he starts telling pretty friend how he's never been in a fight or ever hit a man.

Well I was very proud of myself for going after the guy *r* not fearing or running away from a possible punch-out. God, my self-confidence is fierce? So jerk leaves apologizing *r* pretty friend is underage *r* can't go to Buzzby's *r* by now I'm enjoying him a lot *r* it's obvious he likes me. So I take him to a gay underage disco *r* he was amazed when I paid his way. He was very well-mannered *r* we got along very well. (Name was J—why is everyone named J?) We shared a lot of common tastes in men. So he came over to my place to smoke another joint *r* then wanted to go back to the disco. I couldn't, work the next morn, so he gave me some speed he had *r* took my address *r* phone # *r* I'd really be glad to hear from him again. When showing him to the door, I opened it slightly ⚡ while it was ajar I took hold of him ⚡ kissed him fervently. He returned the affection, but said, "Why are you doing this with the *door* opened??" Ah, sweet beautiful stolen moments! The naughtiness of it all!

I'm loving walking around downtown where I work now. Amazingly beautiful men all over ⚡ not too infrequently one will look at me as intently as I at him ⚡ then I want to melt with passion.

I met a goddamn angel last night ⚡ once again broke new sexual boundaries. Out with Maryellen ⚡ Charlie to the gay disco on Polk. I was feeling hot ⚡ beautiful ⚡ reefed ⚡ speedy. A guy next to me ⚡ I started talking ⚡ soon we were dancing in each other's arms. He resembled Randy in Milwaukee very much, except that he was very unapologetically gay.

In the corner we kissed ⚡ hugged ⚡ felt each other up passionately ⚡ whenever he tried to rub my cock, I turned around ⚡ put my ass against his—hint, hint. Finally he said, "You wanna get fucked, right?" Believe it or not, he's from Houston ⚡ is a 23-year-old sailor docked in SF for the weekend. It was no story either. He was for real. Well, the more I look at him the prettier he gets. His hands on my chest! and he pulls aside the armhole of my sleeveless T-shirt and kisses my nipple. God, the lust in this guy...he appears very straight (is in the goddamn Navy!) ⚡ yet he is completely uninhibited in his sexual desire for a man.

He says he wants to fuck me ⚡ he likes his cock sucked. I said I think I could manage both. He kisses my neck and sucks me until I have hickeys...like a high school boy in the back of a car. He says tough shit, he's gay—"or homosexual if you prefer." His hair is beautiful, thick, black, short in back, a waterfall down his forehead. We go to my place.

In the light I see his laughing blue blue eyes and soft soft little black hairs on his cheeks ⚡ chin ⚡ neck. He is absolutely beautiful. He sits on the couch, his legs opened, completely offering himself, ⚡ I kneel

before him and suck his penis. He is moaning with pleasure ⅋ I suck
his nipples ⅋ his underarms. He responds without reservations, yet
moves at a pace with me, slowly undressing upon my instruction. I lead
him to the bed...I am still fully clothed ⅋ he is naked. I lick ⅋ suck
him all over. Finally he says take off all those clothes! I remove my
pants ⅋ with my back to him, quickly sit on his hard cock as he lay flat.
I still kept my T-shirt on (my scars!) I try to maneuver with my back to
him all the while, yet I know he's aware of my "shortcoming."

He asks if I want him to fuck me ⅋ I said yeah ⅋ laid on my stomach.
He spread my legs ⅋ began fucking my ass royally. Unfortunately I am
literally full of shit ⅋ in no time everything else is, too. He turns me
on my back, my ankles on his shoulders ⅋ he says gently, yet slightly
menacingly, "Stick it in your pussy." So I guided his cock into me. He
asks, "Is it in your pussy now?" I smiled ⅋ said, "What? You can't tell
the difference?" He said yes, my "pussy" is tighter. I laughed that that
was pretty embarrassing (that my ass is looser than my cunt). He asked
which I like better ⅋ I smiled ⅋ said "Well, they're both pretty nice..."
Then he asked if I wanted to fuck him, so he laid on his back ⅋ I stuck
his cock in my cunt ⅋ fucked him good until he came. He said "Let's
go to sleep now."

After the lights were out I removed my T-shirt, we cuddled ⅋ slept.
Or should say, he slept. I was still speeding ⅋ too aware of this sexual
being laying next to me. I touched him all night ⅋ as morning came,
he pressed my hand onto his cock. I scooted down ⅋ sucked ⅋ licked
him for a long long lazy gentle sleepy time. He had never once all night
become soft! I was so happy I enjoyed cleaning his "soiled" penis.

As it lightened out, he got up, sat on the couch a long while it seemed
⅋ smoked a cigarette, still naked. I pretended to be SO TIRED, but
watched him secretly. Waiting for the questions. My scarred chest now
visible to him. Wondering what he's thinking of me. I offer to make
coffee ⅋ gathering up all my self-confidence, got out from under the
blankets ⅋ walked by him naked, my lack of genitals very plain. But he
never said a word to me about it.

When I returned from the kitchen, I slowly slipped my jockey shorts
on without guilt. He came back in bed ⅋ we drank coffee ⅋ for several

hours I sat in stunned admiration as he told stories about his fun drunks ✦ shenanigans ✦ bitch fights on ship. About his best friend Paul ✦ how he knows once they get out of the Navy they'll never see each other again. About his ex-wife, and his ex-lover ("he"). He does not treat me as anything other than a gay man he has spent the night with. His extremely beautiful black hair is streaked with gray hairs and tumbles into his clean sparkling eyes.

He asks me to make more coffee. When I glance in the mirror I am dirty ✦ smelly ✦ my hair is standing on end ✦ I'm zitty but lean ✦ muscular ✦ masculine. I marvel that he'd sit there looking at me. He asks about the Club Baths ✦ looks for his membership card in his wallet…this guy is a real life homosexual. No weekender. I keep watching him closely, trying to learn from him. How does he live 24 hours with these straight macho men, arguing with them, obeying them, sleeping near them, showering with them, and when I complained about my hickeys, saying "I have to go to work, you know," he said, "Just tell them your girlfriend did it. That's what I do."

I want to ask if his friend Paul knows he's gay, yet I want to show him the same respect for privacy as he has shown me. I am so glad not to explain what's the matter with me. I still wonder at this kiss, wonder what he thought I was, and why he didn't care about it. I guess he would have been more physical in the morning had I been an intact male, yet can't know that for sure. Maybe he was just getting back into his "navy" head, though he rambled on ✦ on, his southern accent ✦ intonations making him sound like a Black queen. I give him my address ✦ phone when he leaves. I spend the day feeling his caresses, glad to be what I am.

Had another date with an angel. (Just remembered Rechy used that word…one of his characters "collected angels.") Saturday worked for Paul Walker again ✦ drank champagne there. He finally referred to his being gay, which I had only suspected before. As we both began feeling the champagne, we spoke more openly. Told him I'd had a fun time with a sailor ✦ he said, "Oh no! Are you corrupting our country's finest?"

Leaving there, I was rarin to go, so hit the Giraffe ⚭ began playing pinball. The guy at the next machine started talking ⚭ soon we were playing a game together, buying each other drinks. I had to go home to see the TV show on TSs (that I was asked to be on) so told him I'd be back in ½ hour. The show turned out to be an hour long.

So went back to the bar ⚭ he was still there! A very plain-looking guy, kind of big, 25, very college. But we got along well ⚭ he was very affectionate...patting my arm, etc. He said he was hungry so we got a pizza ⚭ took it to my place.

He is a Calif Highway Patrolman!!! Just like my sailor, I was all over him ⚭ he apparently loved to lay back ⚭ be "serviced." I was more worried about the goddamned mascara on my mustache rubbing off than anything else! He was very cuddly ⚭ not very cock-oriented. Whenever he'd get near mine, I'd just turn away ⚭ do something else ⚭ he never pursued it. He did try to fuck my ass but we were both very drunk ⚭ out of it ⚭ eventually just fell asleep. He never asked about my chest scars, nor seemed to be aware of my lack of a cock.

As usual I didn't sleep all night ⚭ while he snored away I played with his body. (Greased his ass ⚭ easily inserted the smaller butt plug. Then sucked his penis, but he mumbled "no" ⚭ removed the plug.) I spent the night with his penis in my mouth. In the morning we awoke cuddling ⚭ I lowered my shorts in back ⚭ he fucked my ass ⚭ came in me. I thought I was rather skillful all night at manipulating my shorts or being naked on my stomach, etc.

Later we drank coffee ⚭ cuddled more. He then said, "You know, this is kind of a milestone for me, if I can bring it up without any embarrassment." And I thought well, here it comes—this is my first time having sex with a girl. But instead he says, "This is the first time I've ever come inside someone." I said, "Oh yeah? That's really nice!" He said he just never could before, but I had such a "hot ass." That was it.

I sat next to him in just my shorts as we talked ⚭ he stroked my thigh, saying I had "such smooth sweet skin." He was very romantic, loving, warm. He threw some very strong hints about where he would be that evening ⚭ asked when I'd be back home that night. Told me about a band playing in a bar ✦ knew he hoped I'd be there. He said, "If I give you my phone number, will you give me yours?" Told me of his roommate, also a CHP. The roommate seemingly doesn't know he's gay, but Bill has been falling for him ✦ the evening before left a note telling him how he felt about him. So Bill says he's not too eager to to go home ✦ find out his reaction.

I picnicked in the park with the family ✦ later showered ✦ got all sweet ✦ clean ✦ went to hear that band. He was there. We hung out ✦ stood with our arms around each other's waists. He said his roommate had reacted favorably ✦ said he "wanted to share the bed" with him! So I figured that nixed me out of the picture at least for now. He said he'd call me next weekend. A goddamn Highway Patrolman!

Monday night went to see that fantastic fuck film with Charlie (titled *Raw Country*). God I've never seen such an erotic passionate and incredibly tender loving film. These guys were all totally gorgeous ✦ the sex (of course it was an all-male film) just made you hold your breath. I WANT. That's all I could think. I WANT.

Afterwards we closed my favorite bar. Really enjoy his company. He's staying at my place because he ✦ Bridg are on the outs ✦ I'm very complimented he would share my bed with me, be nude in front of me, and treat me exactly as he would a male buddy.

So 6 pm arrives. I try to wear something very masculine, but not revealing. I haven't been putting mascara on my mustache for a week now—I put black dye on it ✦ it looked pretty good this time so I'm satisfied it at least shows. Stopped into a bar ✦ tossed 2 quick ones down, because my heart was pounding so hard. But when J answered the door it stopped, and my first reaction was to reach up and kiss him. Of course I didn't.

He looks exactly the same. (I wish he'd get a decent haircut.) He asked where my mustache was. I said, "It's there!" ✦ he asked "where?" ✦ that "everyone" told him I had a mustache. Then he said I don't look different ✦ I said "I told you!" I could see he was a bit uncomfortable but I was in good spirits ✦ he soon relaxed. We talked easily about music, Al, our jobs, etc.

He asked how my operation was, how they did it, how it looked…so I asked if he wanted to see it. He said yeah. I opened my shirt ✦ showed him one side. He asked, "Did they only do one?" I laughed ✦ so opened my shirt fully. I don't remember that he made any comment. He then asked if they "did anything underneath?" What's the matter with this guy—hasn't he been listening? I told him I've been doing pretty damn good in bars ✦ about my two angels.

He had tickets to the Peking Opera, so we were only in his apt about 45 mins. He asked if I wanted to walk to the subway with him. On the way, I headed for the nearest station, but he kept saying "Let's walk down further" ✦ we ended up going to the furthest one. I mentioned I usually go to music happenings alone ✦ he suggested we go to some together, but, he said, not too often because he has to "put his energy in other directions." I told him that was fine with me, that I'm doing real good ✦ am "not looking for anything from him," that it's just good to see him. He said good, cuz he has "nothing to offer." So, fine with me. I don't think the guy could handle me! HA HA.

So he works nights, so I don't expect we'll be getting together a lot, but it's funny with us. It's been well over a year since we have even seen each other or had a conversation, but once we get going, it's like we've always been together.

I've been in such a weird fuckin mood. Like spaced out. Last week I had dreams of having to go back to being a girl ✦ having to wear a dress, etc ✦ how disoriented I was. I felt uncomfortable all week. I think a lot of things contributed to the mood: my beginning to see J again (the major influence), my taking on this new job at ARCO ✦ its resulting career crisis, the rejection from that lust fuck I brought home, my goddamn hassle having to wear my glasses for a straight 2 weeks (the longest I've ever been off my contact lenses) IDENTITY CRISIS!

When I went to work for Paul Walker last Saturday I told him about the dreams, etc + that I needed some words of professional reassurance from him. He said he'd seen a movie in which the philosophy of the star was, "Fuck'm if they can't take a joke!" That was his advice. I laughed + said hey, thanks a lot, that's all I really needed…some professional words of wisdom.

Jesus! In a lot of ways I think the problem is I spend too much time seeing myself through other people's eyes, + not really being in my body + enjoying myself + relaxing in my image. I guess after so many years off shittin' about how I was coming off, it's hard to suddenly act like there's no compo.[21] I know I'm lonely too. I sure wish I had someone to stroke my chest + suck my little cock. That would really be so fine—to wrap someone in my arms for the night.

I masturbate so so much. My ass is really stretched—I put this big rubber "butt plug" up me + it feels so good. My ass is looking so firm + cute lately—what a switch!

I think I just need the Big One. I wish I didn't have a female crotch. How much easier it'd be to find someone to touch me. I've really got to go out this weekend to the dirty movies and to the bars. Damn.

My chin hairs cut off 1/4/81

Went to the GGG/G meeting because heard other F→Ms would be there. Met Mark from San Jose (finally) + he brought a Steve. Liked them both a lot. Had hoped Mark would offer to show me his phalloplasty but he didn't + I thought it rude to ask. They both complimented me. Steve's been on hormones about 9 mos + had much more hair on his arms than me…I guess I really am not going to be hairy.

21 No complications

Going home, as usual I cruised men walking past ✦ suddenly recognized Paul Walker. We talked a while. Saturday when I went in to work for him, he asked if I was cruising him that nite. I said, "Of course, and you were cruising me too. Except you're worse than me—at least I recognized you!" A while later he asked me to "come play footsies" with him, but he just wanted me to sit in a chair so he could move the furniture a comfortable distance. Then he sat to see if the chairs were too close ✦ he grabbed my foot with his. I immediately grabbed his more firmly, but he quickly pulled away—all teasingly. Hey, I wouldn't mind getting it on with him at all!

Later told him if his secretary ever left, I'd work for him "because I think this is FUN." Am getting LOTS of positive feedback on the F→M pamphlet I wrote.[22] Am still struggling with the idea of joining a men's gym ✦ now one close to me is having a membership sale—so now I MUST do it. God, I'm scared.

Heard a gay therapist on a talk show, explaining how gay men are "searchers" who search all the time, all their lives. That even with a monogamous relationship they search for new ways of defining relationship because there are no role models, as in the het scene. I like the idea of being a "searcher." We are always searching—we see many things and absorb much and look for more.

Read 2 books by that therapist I saw on TV (I think Paul Walker knows him, too). More good theories—one where he said gays spend so much time pretending not to notice…pretending not to notice other men's bodies, or close feelings for male friends, or themselves for that matter. We've spent our youths trying to ignore those things, precisely because they were such strong feelings that they could (*we* could!) not let show. I say "they"—but it's really "we." I must learn to allow myself the pleasure of finally joining the class of gay men, letting myself fit in the way I feel I do. I've spent so much time *wishing* I could join them, *trying* to join, that it's so hard to relax and let it be so easy. Funny, isn't it?

22   *Information for the Female-to-Male Crossdresser and Transsexual* (1980)

Another section where he says gays must learn to enjoy their bodies, because they've spent their youths trying to *control* their bodies, suppress the surges of pleasure and natural reactions to stimulus, while all the hets were out experimenting with their bodies. It seems in so many ways I've gone through very much the same stages as all gay men have, only for different reasons, though not all THAT different. I go through periods of "vegging out," as I've said before, "trying not to think, blanking out all thoughts" and I always wondered why that happened to me. Now I believe it's because I've trained myself not to think of all the things I wanted to be, wanted to do, "knowing" I could never realize those dreams.

Now I know I MUST carry through with all my desires in order to stay alive, aware and HUMAN. *Let* myself "notice." And it's been happening more & more after that I am walking along the street & am looking appreciatively at a man, I see a sparkle in his eyes, and we smile and nod, acknowledging each other's appreciation. And when he's gone, I soar, I feel totally worthwhile, so satisfied with my life, so filled with loving feelings, that the isolation caused by my incomplete body is not all that important. I have more true love in my life now than I ever did—isn't that hard to understand? I can barely understand it myself. But it makes me know that what I've done, what I'm doing, is right, and that everything will turn out well.

Watching TV with Brian & Jake in which a character was named Beau. I said, "I once had a boyfriend named Beau." Brian: "YOU had a BOYFRIEND?!!! Oh yeah. You used to be a girl." Me: "Well Bri, you don't have to be a girl to have a boyfriend. Haven't you ever seen two boys holding hands or kissing? That's what 'gay' means." But he just looked puzzled.

So apparently for real this time, Johnney has left Kathy & gone back to Milwaukee to live with Diane for a few months & then they plan to move here & we 3 will find an apartment together. I'm really looking forward to it. After being with Diane that 2 weeks, I realize how tired I am of living alone ⊹ I think I'd enjoy both of 'm.

In a way I'll be sad to leave my neighborhood, as I am known there ⊹ people are so nice to me, but in another way, I'm tired of the area. Want some different scenery.

Bumped into J on the sidewalk. He's chopped his hair off very short (finally). He was on his way to eat so I invited myself along. What a dud he is. He's back in school. Told him I'd played basketball the day before with Charlie ⊹ his friend Big Jake ⊹ how much I enjoyed that male camaraderie again. He said he really missed that too ⊹ I invited him to join us if he wished (knowing he never would), but he excused himself by saying he was so busy.

So go to hell, who needs him? All he does is manage to make everyone else uncomfortable. My fantasies of getting back together with him are completely gone, and I'm beginning to see how ⊹ why my past relationship with him really stifled and confused me.

"Dear Abby" ran Paul Walker ⊹ Janus' address in her column ⊹ we received about 500 letters in 2 days. I've been answering them all, almost jealously, not wanting to let anyone else do them. Somehow I feel an acceptance or security in reading other TS's traumas especially when they're from tiny rural Southern towns. When I think I have problems!

Last Friday went to some gay fuck films, pretty good ones again. Later that night I found an out-of-the-way parking lot and, at 2 am, stood against a wall, hidden, the warm wind on my electrified skin, and I jerked off. Suddenly I noticed one of the parked cars bouncing wildly ⊹ saw the dark outline of a man humping someone else. After they sat back up, they must have seen me, because they sat a long time in the car. I couldn't really see if they were watching me, but I was sure they were. I unashamedly played with myself, even baring my stomach ⊹

chest a little, until I came. Then I rearranged my clothes & left. I don't
know if they were 2 men or a hetero couple. I felt so very sexual…

My masturbation fantasies have changed considerably, and interestingly.

My male-male fantasies have become more loving and tender acts,
myself in those scenes, e.g., me kissing another man, our mustaches
brushing together (*WHAT* mustache!) or our chests pressed against
each others'.

I don't want to analyze why the change, but it does seem like it means
something. Actually I can see a healthy progression & hopefully my
fantasies towards women will take the same course, i.e., become more
loving as my body enters the scene.

What a fine 3-day weekend. Friday night went to the gay porn theatre,
hoping to suck some cock. Tall, slender man stalking the back area,
circling the back of the theatre, sitting down, getting up, noticing &
returning my stares. I talked myself into the courage to pursue him &
he finally went into the dark backroom, knowing I was following him,
& I immediately went down on him. Sucked him a long time while he
stroked my hair, my shoulders, my arms (God, I love that). I noticed 2
other men standing next to him, watching us. He was very lean & hard.
Finally he whispered, "I have to rest. Let's go sit down."

So we went to the lounge, snuggled in a couch. He reached for my cock,
began opening my pants, but I gently moved his hand away, "Not ready
yet, heh?" he asked, & then asked if I got off in the other room. I said yes.
We sat a long time, kissing, touching, He asked if I'd do a three-way—he
saw another man there who might, but when he went looking for him
after I said sure, he'd gone. I was totally unprepared (my "padding," my
apartment) for an overnighter, but I invited him.

Whenever he'd go for my crotch, I'd just twist around & bend over
to suck him, or some other way to make myself inaccessible. In the

bed he stripped, I stripped down to my shorts ✦ took the aggressive position, licking ✦ sucking all of him. He was obviously enjoying it, yet somewhat troubled (I could sense) by my hesitation to be naked or touched, ✦ then after seeing my chest scars, too. But he told me I was "really good" ✦ he'd bet I would be great at massaging. So I gave him a dynamite back rub, culminating in my giving his asshole a long work-out with my tongue ✦ fingers. He smelled so goddamned good.

Such a drag to have to be on the defensive ✦ not be able to relax ✦ enjoy him. He asked if I'd like to get fucked ✦ I said yes enthusiastically, laying on my stomach ✦ slipping my shorts down just so far. I'm not sure if he saw then, while he was aiming, that I had a woman's genitals, but he did fuck me good ✦ I reached down in front ✦ jerked myself off. I came, too. But I don't think he did. We laid together quietly, snuggling. He left after a while (not having questioned me at all) ✦ I felt satisfied, but sad. I desperately need surgery. This won't do.

Saturday a female-to-male, 48 years old, who just last November met Paul Walker ✦ realized she's a transsexual, came all the way up from Denver just to meet me for a few hours. We talked, went to dinner. She was as thrilled about meeting me (possibly more) than I was when I met Dain. She was obviously impressed.

When I went in to Walker's office last Thursday nite, a youngman walked in ✦ introduced himself as Walker's assistant. He asked why I worked on Janus ✦ I ended up telling him I'm a F-M. He was really shocked. Saturday Walker told me the guy said just those few minutes of talking with me was infinitely more educational for him than all the books on transsexualism he could have read. (My apparent totally unequivocal success at being a man just shocks me—I don't FEEL much different at all.) Sunday ✦ Monday in the parks with Bridget et al, Mary et al, Kathy et al.

My stomach muscles have finally firmed up ✦ I'm so proud of my taut lean torso. I feel so very HARD, my body is so SOLID. Cheyney especially tries to test my strength, my ability to withstand his blows, ✦ I *do*! He ✦ I played ping-pong ✦ he commented I played like his dad.

I phoned Johnney ✝ Diane (who I've decided to call Flame ✝ Therese respectively as these are their chosen names) to shoot the breeze ✝ keep in touch ✝ let them know I really do want to do this moving in together thing.

I think I should mention what an effect world affairs are having on me. I was so wrapped up in the 52 American hostages being released from Iran the day Reagan was inaugurated. I haven't felt this one with the climate of the nation since Vietnam, or so moved by the historical moment since the day the troops pulled out of Vietnam. All around me I see a swing back to the middle class way: family, home, security, life decisions. Flame ✝ Therese, Bridget ✝ Charlie, Mary Rusty ✝ Buddy— it's all over!

And me, I want a "family" surrounding too. All the hippies are 30 years old ✝ realizing they can't be outside society forever.

The press is publicizing the Moral Majority group which plans a big anti-gay campaign here in San Francisco ✝ I'm ready to fight as a gay man. Americans need to calm down in our radicalism but there's no possibility of swinging THAT far back into conservatism. This Reagan era is definitely a New Age, but one that must be watched carefully.

God, I can finally do this! I'm packing up my house to move. I'm finally getting the hell into the world. The place is beautiful. I went there tonight, carrying $65 worth of three Tiffany lamps I just bought for the place. I stood there and tears welled up in my eyes—I'm so happy. As I tried the key to get in, a youngman in a business suit with his expensive car double-parked, was sweeping the sidewalk and said "Oh, hi, Louis!" He lives 2 doors next to mine. He was super friendly ✝ I told him how glad I was I got the place. I'm finally getting out there and being the gay man I've always wanted to be. I can feel myself just floating away into it.

June 1981 – January 1982

"Surely his face is God's."

17th Street
San Francisco, California

How should he greet thee? what new name,
Fit to move all men's hearts, could move
Thee,

Algernon Charles Swinburne, "Fragoletta"

Well, so many good things have been happening for me, and I've just been such a happy man. I've wanted to write earlier but couldn't come down to earth long enough. So I moved into this fine apartment and have really been applying myself to fixing it up nice.

I bought an easy chair for $30, a side table for $15 (another story here), and a nice dresser for $110. Got a really nice couch for free from a friend of Maryellen's. I've really had a lot of fun arranging it all. It makes me ill to think of all the beautiful furniture I left in Milwaukee (that bed! that dresser! that dining room set!) that costs me 6 times now what I got it for then.

All I really need now is a bed (I'm sleeping on a piece of foam on the floor) and a few tables. I lay there in the dark, the street lights reflect in the window and make beautiful patterns on the ceiling. It feels so good to spread myself and my belongings out and see how comfortable everything is.

On the weekends I buy a newspaper, make some coffee and go up on the roof and lay on a blanket with only my undershorts on, sunning myself—all alone, no one can see me, I feel so free. I can sleep with the curtains open—no one can see me, I feel so free. With a place like this, I think it's worthwhile to stay home and clean house!

For the first time I gave myself my testosterone shot. Kathy Steininger coached me and I did it in my thigh. I couldn't believe I was actually sticking this needle into my body like that. I felt faint through it all, but accomplished the task. It hurts like hell today—not at the actual shot site, but that whole muscle is very tender ✢ it hurts to walk. But I'm going to keep giving them to myself. It makes me feel strong and self-reliant and pretty cool. But it sure is freaky to force a piece of metal through your body like that.

Well I guess I knew sooner or later it would creep up on me but this last week or so I've really come to the end of my rope trying to deal with being a twin in my body. I am so tired of trying NOT to be sexual. I look in the mirror ✢ see this fucking beautiful guy looking back at me ✢ I see other men smiling at me ✢ almost reaching out. But I have to keep it on such a platonic superficial level.

I've tried to learn to live without affection, but I can feel it eating me from inside. It seems so foreign to me when I see how free ✢ open everyone around me is with their bodies. I realize that I don't even give potential lovers a second glance, or encourage even the slightest any men who are attracted to me. And I know they are. I am beautiful! It hurts me too much to encourage them, or to even notice their attentions to me. I can't stand to see someone offering themselves, and my having to deal with this fucking body. It's just not fair. I have to start now to pursue the rest of me.

I can feel it's time to see Dain again. All the goddamn questions ✢ decisions ✢ concessions I'll have to wrestle with—AGAIN. Do I want a cosmetic cock like Dain's? Although it has no hole in it and is very tiny…Or do I want to be able to use a urinal like every other guy? Or have an erect cock? Is it smart at all to allow them to start snipping ✢ nipping around down there ✢ possibly lose the sensation I have, possibly jeopardize orgasm—Falces said he was going to leave part of my nipple tips intact but he didn't ✢ the sensations just aren't there that used to be. Do I want to entrust my clitoris to him? Shit. Do I have to resign myself to the fact that I may possibly lose the feeling I have there in order to have halfway passable male organs?

Meanwhile how the shit am I going to pay for whatever I settle for? I can fight ARCO's insurance. I can try to hit up Jack again…but I really don't want to do that ✦ he wouldn't have the amount I need. I just want to LUNGE at someone to hold me. I just get crazy imagining kissing a man. I am a good good person ✦ deserve something better than this. My fucking clit looks like it's stopped growing or something. I've gotten NO more hair on my body than 8 months ago. What the fuck is going on?? I want to sleep with a man. I want to wrap myself around him. I want to offer myself unconditionally ✦ unapologetically. I should be free to feel all the warmth ✦ love I do.

I have gone as far as I can go the way I am. I've very successfully adjusted to being a man. Now I want to BE A MAN.

I think I'm in love ✦ I can't believe it. I mean, this gorgeous boy just told me to go out ✦ find someone who'd be my perfect lover, while he smiled ✦ teased me. He knew it, too. God, is he fine. He's small ✦ hard ✦ eager ✦ logical ✦ quiet. What more can you ask? He ✦ I ✦ Dan ✦ Kooka (my neighbors down the hall) were on the roof of the building til it got so cold Dan ✦ Kooka went home.

On a chance I invited T to my place ✦ he came! He's 20 years old ✦ looking for LOVE. He as much as told me he would get involved in a gay relationship just for the experience. And I had to ignore that—(see what I mean, I'm tired of running, I'm tired of pretending I didn't hear that). I told Dan when we were alone that I was falling in love with T. He said forget it, T's 100% straight. But hear it from T, that fucker's a romantic.

So what do I do now? Try to kiss him? Invite him over for dinner? Ask him to smoke another joint?

It's supposed to work. One day I'll find someone who likes me so much it won't matter. He is almost frightened, but his eyes are so steady. He is so small, so pretty. I wanted to touch his hair. He almost laughed at me. He knew. He said, "Do you think I come on sexually?" I said, "Yes, to me you do." He just laughed ✦ said he knew it.

And so what was I going to say?
"Oh, you little tart...(kiss kiss kiss)"

All I could say was "Do you want more coffee?"

He asked me to go jogging with him tomorrow morning. I said I couldn't. I feel sorry for myself when I have to run for the bus. I can't believe I did that. I said no because I knew he could run farther than me.

You mean, I can really do this? I can really just fall in love all over again? When was the last time I wrote poetry?

I'm afraid to fall in love. I'm afraid to shame myself. To reveal to this guy my secret. And have my world fall down around me.

So the first thing he says when he finally comes over to the party is "You look real nice tonight." What kind of thing is that to say? All night Kooka's hugging him, touching his face, sitting on his lap & he's in heaven. Dan says "Kooka, he's a *youngman*?" I told Kooka I was in love with T, that I haven't felt this way in a long time. She was kinda surprised. She said he really liked me too. I said, "Kooka, give him to me..."

So he & Kooka & Dan are on the roof. I went up there & Dan & Kooka were coming down.

T lingered behind with me. I asked what was going on. T smiled at me, looked down coyly, moved close to me & said, "How did you get involved in this?" I said, "Oh, what do you mean. You've been flirting with me from the beginning—" I caught him around the waist & moved closer to kiss him.

He slipped away, "Lou, what are you DOING?!" He said for where he is right now he loves her (Kooka). We talked about her. He thinks she's beautiful. I said she was a charming lady & had a good bod but (and I shouldn't have said this) "She's got a face like a dog."

Well, he left right after that. That was uncalled for. I should have recognized his love.

So I'm preparing for this party, the door's open, I have reggae on the radio ♣ suddenly I think I hear him singing. But I'm not sure. I hear him again ♣ I think I'm hallucinating. Because I didn't hear him come in. And then suddenly he turns around from my living room into the kitchen in front of me.

And fuckin J didn't show up. I said to Maryellen, "I hate him…I really do…that really sucks that he didn't come."

He sends me a belated birthday card like my mother did.

God, I want to sleep with T. How pure to kiss him. How pure to hold him naked.

And Oh God he has such slim hips
they could slip into a small bottle

I gotta hang in there. I have to bare my soul to him. He said "You should say what you feel. You can't pretend—that's wrong." I wanted to say well then I better say that I think I'm falling for you.

I want to give him a poem Swinburne's "Fragoletta." He says you're supposed to come right out with it. How am I going to give it to him? Deliver it via Kooka? She'd probably give it to him.

This morning I opened my door, had gospel radio music on, was dressing & I hear his golden voice, "Where's the birthday boy?" I said what do you mean, birthday—whose birthday is it? He laughed & stood in the bedroom doorway & said "I want to apologize for being an asshole last night." !! !! !!

I said what do you mean? Who said you were an asshole? He said "You did, three times!"

Oh God his beautiful blue-grey eyes. They are so clear so steady so alive. We finished the pineapple he had cut up for the party, & he said he was going next door to get some breakfast & see ya later.

I got ready to leave the apt for the Gay Pride Parade, and Kooka & Dan's door was open so I wandered in. Dan greeted me & as I entered the room where T was, T shouted out, "Get away from me, Lou! Don't touch me!" I jokingly stepped back & flattened myself against the wall as though his words pushed me back. He snickered, got up from behind the table. I looked at him probably with a questioning look & he laughed. I shook my head & said, "Sometimes I just can't stand the pressure."

This was the best Gay Pride Parade ever—not counting of course the first one. Didn't see much of it but it looked like all highlights. God God God

The beautiful lusty men in this city

At the Civic Center after the parade I finally sat on a ledge. A well-muscled but small man lay in the grass at my feet. Soon he knew I was watching him. He scooted over closer—He said hi first. I offered him a joint & he was soon moving closer & closer. I said "Your body is so beautiful." He said, "*OUR BODIES.*" He began snoogling & kissing & it felt so so fucking good. He said "Feels so good…" I said, "It's been a long time since I've necked in the park." I thought, I've never necked in the park before in my life.

This morning, rushed up onto the roof ＋ laid in the sun, rolling down my jockey shorts so that only a thin strip covered my pubic area. I'd remembered to stuff my basket a little so I was prepared when some doll of a guy comes up ＋ we began discussing the fire in the building yesterday. He stood, looking down on me as I laid there, looking up at him. I felt so desirable. We talked a long time. Then he introduced himself ＋ we shook hands. He was obviously gay ＋ I was obvious to him, too. God, it feels so good.

I walked down the middle of Market Street. The first time I can say I actually felt I "marched in the parade." My opened shirt blew in the wind—The sun tanning my stomach—Feeling lean and alive and beautiful—Saying I am a man—Saying I love men.

T's facial hair is just like mine, except it's black. Just a thin mustache ＋ chin whiskers. Nothing on his pure smooth cheeks. God, what a beautiful boy he is.

This evening I even closed my door, but he rang the bell. I opened it ＋ there he was. We drank tea, he told me about some old girlfriend he phoned, but she's going out with all kinds of guys ＋ doesn't want to get serious with him. Except, he said, "she let me fuck her." Just the thought of this beautiful boy, I was shocked, "LET YOU??" He didn't even get it. He said, "Yeah, she was touching my body ＋ everything."

I had been attempting to start lifting my weights when he came by ＋ he picked up my barbell ＋ dumbbells ＋ said I needed to put more weight on them. Shit, I'd just removed some of the weight because they were too heavy for me!

Again we talked about Kooka ＋ he says he thinks he's getting over it already, and he thinks he should place a classified ad for an older woman.

Friday, July 18, 1980

July 1980
S M T W T F S
1 2 3 4 5
6 7 8 9 10 11 12
13 14 15 16 17 18 19
20 21 22 23 24 25 26
27 28 29 30 31

200th Day — 166 days to follow

CLEAR
CLOUDY
RAIN
SNOW

At the Civic Center after the parade
I finally sat on a ledge. A well-
muscled but small man lay in the
grass at my feet. Soon he knew I
was watching him. He scooted over
closer — He said hi first. I offered
him a joint & he was soon moving
closer & closer. I said "Your body
is so beautiful." He said,
"OUR BODIES." We began snuggling
+ kissing & it felt so so fucking
good. He said "feels so good..."
I said, "It's been a long time since
I've necked in the park." I thought,
I've never necked in the park before
in my life.

　　　　　This morning rushed up
onto the roof & laid in the sun,
rolling down my jockey shorts so
that only a thin strip covered my
pubic area. I'd remembered to
stuff my basket a little so I was
prepared when some doll of a guy

Saturday, July 19, 1980

CLEAR
CLOUDY
RAIN
SNOW

August 1980
S M T W T F S
1 2
3 4 5 6 7 8 9
10 11 12 13 14 15 16
17 18 19 20 21 22 23
24 25 26 27 28 29 30
31

comes up + we began discussing the
fire in the building yesterday. He
stood, looking down on me as I laid
there, looking up at him. I felt so
desirable. We talked a long time.
Then he introduced himself + we
shook hands. He was obviously gay
+ I was obvious to him, too. God,
it feels so good.

I asked my angel in the park
if he worked out + he was very pleased,
saying "Oh, I didn't know if it
showed or not." I said "Hell, yeah."
He said "well, you don't look so
bad yourself."

He who can't even get
my ass in gear to lift
the goddamn weights
I have

My feet hurt
I need to do the laundry
I need to do the ironing
I should write letters

My God, when he stands so near to me I feel like I'm going to be burned if he brushes against me. I can hardly hold myself back from taking hold of him. He looks like he tastes good. He smells good.

I said I was very complimented he came over. He said he's real lonely lately. I debated with myself whether to give him "Fragoletta," but decided against it at this time—no need to rush anything—we're having a 4th of July cook-out on the roof. I just told him I got into a real poetry-reading mood after everyone left from the party.

We drank tea ✦ talked. He sees me watching him ✦ pretends he doesn't ✦ then he decides to give in ✦ looks me right in the eye ✦ laughs.

Why is he always teasing me?

Will I ever be able to kiss him. I wonder if this is all fantasy-land, or after some point he'll actually let me give him some of these physical pleasures he's craving so bad but wants from a true blue female. Ah, those 20-year-old hormones!

"Fragoletta," too gushing, too physical. I found instead "A Leave-Taking" by Swinburne.

So I did it. I gave him the poem. He immediately opened it in front of everyone ✦ asked me, "What does this mean for you?" I answered, "It's a love poem." He began reading it ✦ asked what it meant. I said "It says it all there, better than I could say it." He said, "Then you're putting yourself down." I said don't read it here! He said, "I want to talk with you about this at your place." I was so shocked and nervous, I said, "What?" He repeated it.

COME HENCE
LET BE
LIE STILL; IT IS ENOUGH.

He asked who wrote it, I said a turn-of-the-century English poet.
Suddenly we were alone in the room *&* I said what did you want to
talk about? He's sitting in an easy chair. I'm standing. He says, "What
do you feel—inside—for me?" I answered, "I think I love you." He
asked "Why?" I thought a second, recovering from his question—so
blatant, so cutting, so disbelieving: I said, "Because I think about you a
lot during the day." A smile came over his lips, he smiled at me *&* said
"That's nice. Thank you."

I suggested we all go to a movie *&* he wanted to go get a sweater, I
guess, so was going to meet us at the theatre. I asked, "Can I come with
you, T?" He called back, "Sure Lou. If you want to." We went to his
beautiful beautiful place. It was like Albion, but more beautiful. He said
he built all the wood himself—a loft where he slept. I was enthralled.
Mystified. He lived there 3 years with a 30-year-old roommate.

Suddenly we were sitting on the floor talking about some shit *&* we
lost track of the conversation *&* I was gazing into his face *&* he asked,
"What are you thinking about—RIGHT NOW." I started laughing,
fell back on my elbows *&* answered, "I was thinking how beautiful you
are." He told me that from the start he felt something special between
us, too, and that he liked me a lot and thought we really had something
good between us. That he really felt good that I told him how I felt. He
said he didn't want to get into anything sexual with me, though, and I
said, "Neither do I. That's what that poem says."

We ran together to the movie. I didn't arrange to sit next to him, but
there he sat, next to me.

IF I FOLLOW MY HEART
I'M GONNA LOVE YOU

He fuckin let me kiss him in front of a big group of people, including Kooka. I said, "Look at this guy—he's an insatiable flirt. Have you no shame?—He has no shame, and I have no scruples."

He told me he was complimented by my attentions. I said, "You should be. Because you really did turn my head."

Oh sweet brat boy
Bellyward on my bed
And when the evening was ending, he said Kooka was jealous of me. I asked if she had said anything. He said no, but he can just tell. I asked what she was jealous about ✝ he said, "She's afraid you're trying to turn me gay or something."

He keeps wearing the same shirt, but it always looks fresh on him. Somehow. In certain moments his hair looks like it could use a shampooing.

THOU HAST A SERPENT IN THINE HAIR

I asked if he read the poem ✝ liked it. He hedged around, wouldn't be direct. I asked, "Did you *read* it?" He blurted out, "Yes, three times!" "And did you like it?" "Yes," he shouted, his eyes flashing proudly.

It seemed like every time he was on his way out, I was on my way in, and we'd bump into each other in the corridor.

In the beginning of the evening, I offered him a joint and he says, "Are you trying to get me stoned, Lou?" I laughed, "I'll try *anything*!"

In the morning, I'm walking around bare in my apt, after a shower ✝ having just given myself a shot, ✝ he rings the doorbell ✝ just fuckin walks right in. I scooted to the bedroom ✝ threw a robe on.

Fabulous weekend. Saturday eve J came over ✝ we played records, talked. Wandered over to introduce him to Dan ✝ Kooka. There's T, Kooka ✝ 2 other girls playing records ✝ dancing. T dances so sweetly, a little bit of clumsy with a whole lot of grace. About 5 minutes after we got there, T said he had to go, Kooka "walked him to the door" and they disappeared from the building. So J ↗ I split. I had told J the whole story beforehand ↗ was super glad he got to meet T. J ↗ I went to the I-Beam, a big gay disco.

The majority of time we talked about "us" ↗ I talked a lot about T ↗ he gave advice, saying he could see why I liked T, that I made a good choice to fall for him. J was most complimenting of me ↗ it's obvious this change was best for me ↗ that I'm extremely well-adjusted. He encouraged me to pursue T, saying he regretted he'd split up with me ↗ would have done it differently if he had it to do over again.

We were *very* candid. He saw me shirtless ↗ said I looked real good "without tits!"

This morn I got very dressed up for work ↗ looking great. I hoped I'd see him on the street on his way to work. And there he was, on his bike across the street. I called out ↗ waved. He waved, looking me over good, said something I didn't hear. I kept walking, he crossed to exchange pleasantries with me, but I had kept walking. Dumb shit, I'm so glad I looked so good—first time he's seen me in suit ↗ tie, I think.

Had a dream a few nights ago that Dan, Kooka, T ↗ I were in a room talking ↗ Dan called me "Sheila," ↗ they all sat looking at me, knowingly, ↗ I covered up my face ↗ cried, "Oh no! no!" feeling I had lost my friends.

I can't even present myself as an interesting person. All the interesting things I've done ↗ am doing are TS-related ↗ I can't mention.

For some reason, T said I am a snob. I denied it ɟ asked why he said that. He said "Because you are." I said I didn't think I was better than anyone else. He agreed that I didn't. Then I wasn't a snob, I said. He said I was, too.

Oh, oh and the beat goes on.
          QUOTABLE QUOTE:
                "The girls dress up for each other, and the boys just want to stand on the corner and boogy" -Kim

So Friday night we all go to the bar where Bridget works to wish her a happy birthday. The sweet doll of a man I wrote about last month was there, and it turns out Mary knows him from when she first moved out here ɟ was picking up men in the gay bars! She's had sex with him on several occasions, and I remember her telling me about him! HA HA So he joins our table and remembers me, too. He flirts outrageously with *everyone*.

Mary ɟ I go with him to his car where we smoke his marijuana ɟ snort his cocaine. Back at the bar, I go to the jukebox and he follows me. I say I dislike the bar, so straight ɟ boring. He agrees with me, asks where I hang out. Told him Polk ɟ Castro. He told me he preferred there, too, but guesses he's not all the way out of the closet yet. I told him I was, that everyone at my work knew, too, ɟ once you do come out, it's not as big of a deal as you thought it'd be.

Well, we all retired to Mary ɟ Rusty's to party. Just had a super fun time. He continued to discreetly brush up against me; smile ɟ nod at me invitingly, etc etc etc. Once I was going into the bathroom ɟ he followed me. I caught him around the waist ɟ kissed him ɟ tried to pull him into the bathroom with me. He said, "Not yet! Not here!" and explained that he was trying to get Steininger. I laughed ɟ said forget it! He said no, no, he wanted to see if he could, but that I shouldn't go away because he'll be back for me later! That's all he needed to say!

So as the night wore on, people trickled home and then Kathy was saying goodbye and going home. Kim ɟ I are suddenly the only ones there. I told him I was just going to stay there ✦ he could, too, if he wanted. I turned out the light, laid on the couch and moved over. He crawled in beside me ✦ we cuddled up. He laid perfectly still as I opened his shirt. He rested his arms above his head as I ran my fingers over his smooth, hard chest, kissing ✦ licking his chest, his nipples, and he moaned and his breathing quickened.

Slowly I loosened his blue jeans and reached inside. He was hard. I took my time feeling inside his pants ✦ licking his chest. He wiggled only slightly and helped me lower his blue jeans. I licked and kissed and sucked his testicles, his penis. He put his hand on my hair, or on my shoulder.

Rusty suddenly comes from the back to go to the bathroom, putting us directly in his sight range. Kim tensed up, but seeing I continued on without flinching, he relaxed again. (Rusty later tells the story that he went to the bathroom and "it looked like someone was saying their prayers"... that he couldn't tell which one of us it was. I said "I was kneeling and giving thanks.") Well, he was plenty hard and aroused but wouldn't do a goddamn thing himself, so I didn't sweat trying to make him come, but just took as much pleasure as I could.

When he got up to go to the bathroom, I opened up the sofa bed. We slept a little, but I woke often, stroking him, kissing him. Soon it was light out, I lifted his quilt and rubbed ✦ kissed his ass, still covered by his blue jeans. He moaned in pleasure, encouraging me. I shoved my hand inside, feeling his ass, trying to find the opening there. He moved to let me open his pants ✦ yank them down. I stroked ✦ kissed his ass and licked between the cheeks. When I got the hole good ✦ wet, I fingered it and slowly inserted my finger. He didn't flinch. I finger-fucked him, but soon I got so turned on I had to stop. (I think now... I could easily have fucked him, had I been able. He would have let me put my cock in him, I know it!)

I laid down with my mouth at his hip, and he turned to give me his hard cock, and again I took my pleasure; he moved slightly a few times to put his penis further into my mouth, but again I felt he wasn't working hard enough to deserve coming. So when I got too turned on, or too tired, I stopped. Later I laid beside him and put my hand into my pants and jerked off. He turned his face toward me, and I know he knew I was masturbating.

I came. After I caught my breath, I reached over (with the same hand I had used to jerk myself off) and stroked his tousled blond curls. What a beautiful man! He turned his face the other way. I continued petting his hair. We fell back to sleep.

He had told me during the evening that he had to work at 9 am. At 8:45 he suddenly awoke ✦ when I told him the time, he sprang out of bed and buttoned his shirt, zipped up his pants, grabbed his jacket. He came back over to the bed and held out his hand and said goodbye, hurriedly. I grasped his hand and squeezed it and said "Goodnight." He dashed out the door, and I turned over ✦ fell asleep.

Oh, God. I am so happy. My life as a gay man has been so fulfilling, so perfect, everything I could have hoped for. The beauty of a man loving a man just takes away my breath.

So Cuca (*THAT'S* HOW IT'S SPELLED!) ✦ Dan are in Mexicali this week. I saw T in passing twice, no, three times this weekend and each time he couldn't muster up enough friendliness to say a few lousy nothings to me. What a crybaby. I consoled myself by imagining that he tried to fuck his little girlfriend and he couldn't get a hard-on, and so now he's all freaked out. HA HA This last time I saw him ✦ he walked away real abruptly, I wanted to say, "Well, poo on you! Give me back my vacuum cleaner!"

Later Friday night I go over to T's. A light is on in his room. I knock, but his roommate tells through the door that T's not there. I was going to write a note to leave for him, but his roommate asked who should he say stopped by. I answered, "Lou" and left it at that. I figured T was out with his girlfriend.

Early Saturday morning, we take off north of the city: Bridget, Charlie, Jake, Brian, Kathy and Cheyney, Mary, Rusty, Buddy ⁊ I. I had gone after work Friday to a swank gay men's clothing store on Castro ⁊ finally bought myself a new pair of swim trunks. And I looked beautiful... I look beautiful in it. We got a place about 60 miles north, called Sugarloaf State Park or something, and set up camp. I complained there was no swimming and found out about a swimming area nearby. I was the fun Uncle Lou and watched Buddy, playing frisbee with Jake, Bri ⁊ Cheyney while the rest of them put the campsite together.

I felt very independent, traveling light, only having to worry about my own care... not a family's. We all laid in the sun and, when we got bored, piled in the car ⁊ went to the swimming hole. Spring Lake—do you believe it? It was perfectly beautiful—roped off shallow area for the kids, rent inner tubes, paddle boats, no problem with drinking, smoking, or playing music. It was perfect.

I watched the young men and I felt so attractive, even though I still have to put tape over my scars to keep the sun off them. Who cares anyway. I was still one of the best looking guys around. Maryellen and Kathy both sincerely told me how cute I was, and Kathy said if she were a girl (!) (we laughed), she'd be eyeing me up. Then Rusty pointed out to me the 4 gay men just behind us on the beach. They were older guys, not being blatant, but definitely two pairs of lovers. Thereafter I put on a little show for them and they watched as I pranced around, sunning myself, oiling myself, combing my hair, toweling dry.

So we started cooking up the food and doing quiet things alone. I sat under a nearby tree and read Mary Renault's *Charioteer* (so far a little disappointing in its lack of physical affection/contact). It was about that time that Rusty started calling me "My man, my Main Man," as he fired up a joint for us... a term he seems to use only for his very close buddies. Well, we were all a-smokin and a-drinkin and we all ate and started playing tapes on my recorder. Dancin and a-singin. Even little Buddy was out there!

In the morning I wake up to birds chirping above my head. It was dewy out, but already warming. (This was an open-bed truck.) And next campsite to ours is a very beautiful nearly naked male torso sunning himself in the morning light. I played along, stripping down to my swim trunks and laying on the side of the truck on my back. They were 4 I believe obviously gay guys, all primping and stretching and sunning. I thought—we have always been here. I always wondered where we were.

I was so obviously beautiful, laying there in these tight little bun-hugging swim trunks. I took a special pleasure in being alone, obviously not with any of the women—and seemingly more friendly with the men. One time Charlie laid on my blanket and I teased him loudly. I was beautiful and alone and sexy and happy.

I was home not half an hour when my doorbell rings and I figure it's Cuca or Dan, but my face very obviously lit up when I am gazing at T. He smiles, embarrassed at my obvious pleasure, and says in a staccato tone: "Lou! I'm Very Sorry I Haven't Returned Your Vacuum Cleaner Yet !" I said quietly, nodding and looking down, "Well, yes, you are delinquent in the return of the vacuum." He said "Well are you going to be here a while—I'll bring it right now." I said sure.

I ate bacon and eggs before he returned, the whole while I wondered how I would keep him there talking to me for a while and not just leave. Well, he did not act like he was staying, and then I asked about his car. He asked if I wanted to drive it. I said sure. He almost flew out of the apartment since he has no license and can't drive it. But, I couldn't drive a stick shift, so he drove after all. I found out later it was only the second time he'd driven. We had a great time going all around—he was so serious and such a careful, slow, unsure driver. Asking can he turn right on a red, shit like that. I went on about what a great car it is ✛ all he needs is a tune-up.

He smashed into the side of the garage as he backed into it and I made no notice, telling him how many rear view mirrors I smashed off my Toyota going in ✛ out of the garage. He asked if I had any marijuana and he came up to smoke a joint. Oh, T, T. It was like old times. I'd all of a sudden feast my eyes on you and you'll look right back at me and smile embarrassed but confident in my love, of my appreciation for him.

I asked if T'd ever had sex with a man ✦ he said yes! But that he (T) couldn't get a hard-on, or something. I said that's how I am with women. He asked if I was into S✦M and I said yeah, a little, it's kind of fun to play and have someone who likes to play the same way you do. He asked what magazines I had ✦ I hauled out my small stash (he said "ALL OF THEM!") of Playboys, Playgirls, some beaver mags Mary gave me, some *Drummers*, *GPU News*. He asked if I had any TRANSVESTITE MAGAZINES and I said yeah, but none with pictures.

"Why, you like those?"

He said "yeah, when they look like this" and held up one of the beaver girls. I said, oh but with a dick, huh? He said yeah, they turned him on. I said I had sex with a guy who had a sex change but couldn't fuck her because her hole wasn't big enough. HA HA (It was true, tho.) I held up a picture of a very well-muscled man's torso ✦ I said this is what *I* like!

Oh T. When he finally left, I laid in bed ✦ tears came.
Should I tell him? If he is sincere about liking TV's, maybe he wouldn't so object to me. I wanted him in my arms so bad. Phoned Maryellen at 11:45 and she talked me down, saying I'm nuts if I tell him now, before I even KNOW him, just on some comment he made while paging thru dirty magazines. That I should go camping with him and, she said, she'd be very surprised if he soon didn't put the move on me, and I'll know when it's right. She's right too, I knew she'd know the right thing to say.

This afternoon I went to the roof to bug-spray a table I found ✦ there he is in swim trunks, sitting on a towel on OUR roof, reading ✦ eating a sandwich. He asks if I have a joint to share, says he'd like to go hear a band with me tonight, invites me over for melon.

I love him at his apartment. The feelings I have are so intense. We go over to Lawrence's but he's not home. T says he's going for something to eat, I say I have to do my laundry. I watch as he leaves me, walking down the sidewalk. I go to dress, to go to get some dinner.

I find out he's a Virgo. Exactly like J. My God is he ever like J.

When I sleep I pretend T is lying next to me, and I can touch his hair, stroke his chest and press him up against my body.

Sunday morning I look like shit and don't care. I get a newspaper, make some coffee and he comes to my door. He asks if I just got up (I looked like shit) and tells me he's already had a *bath*. I fantasize how clean and sweet his body is. He shares Mexican cakes with me, saying his landlady gave them to him for helping with the groceries. He says my coffee's good for being instant and I beg his pardon, explaining that it was expensive French Roast coffee. I said "You have a lot lower opinion of me than I thought you did!"

I play Lou Reed, good music, he hangs around in my living room, shadow boxing with himself, leaning out the window, I go into the next room and fold my laundry and I am so aware of him, I love him so much. I try so hard not to panic, but he simply looks at me and smiles coquettishly.

I love it when he gets real serious with me, he knits his pretty eyebrows
✦ crooks his arm ✦ strokes his chin hair—the few he has (like mine!)—

and his eyes sparkle, and he says, "They said they were giving me… no, they were adjusting the valves…" Then he looks at me searchingly, I say, "Well, then they're not giving you new valves." He says, "No." I say, "Well, then you're not getting a valve job." He says he's afraid they're going to charge him for something they didn't do, so he's reading up like mad so he knows about cars when he picks it up from the shop. He asks me what I'm doing Saturday morning. I say what time? Eleven o'clock. I say fine. He asks when I get up. I say ten. He says cuz he needs to get tires & drive the car, but he only has a permit so needs someone to go along. I said, "Oh, you want me to be your dummy, huh? 'Just sit in the seat & shut up!'"

He genuinely laughed & looked at me appreciatively and his beautiful teeth sparkled (actually, they're pretty bad). J phones me! I talk a long time while T somehow takes off his shirt, and with only a sleeveless A-shirt, lifts my weights. I tell J about the great concert last weekend & how I tried to call him to go but he wasn't home. I look at T & he nods in agreement as I described how good the band was. Then J tells me he got a job in an office. Little by little, I begin saying a few things here & there to T, letting J know someone was there. (He never asked who it was….)

We talk so easily when I relax, especially when we smoke dope together. We have a great time. But even when we don't. I didn't smoke any the night I ironed my shirts, tho he did smoke a joint. But, Christ, sometimes I just can't even look at him. I am really unsure of my control of my desire to touch him. When he smacked my arm affectionately, I wanted to take hold of him & press his chest against mine & press my lips & mouth on his smooth boy's cheeks, push my hips against his and rub against him. Oh, T, I'm saving my money to have them make me a cock.

And then I'm going to take your advice. I'm just going to take off my clothes. I want you so badly. I want to bury my nose in your hair when I sleep. I want to lick the too-pink, too-soft nipples on your chest. I told him I was checking the hot spots at the Russian River for our trip. He said, we're not going to the Russian River! I said I thought you *wanted* to go there, you suggested it. (And he did at first, before I told him it's gay city up there). He laughed shyly. I said no, I'm just kidding. We'll have to wait til he's 21. He said, yeah, in September. I said yeah, we gotta go out drinking that day ✦ get you all drunk. He laughed, and I believe he just might go. (Where the fuck would I *take* him ??)

Paul Walker actually went to see *Death in Venice* with me ✦ I don't think he really appreciated it, as he gave me a big lib rap after it, how it was anti-gay because it says youth ✦ beauty are everything. He missed the whole point. (T was listening in as I told this to J, so now T knows I do have other friends.) I still go into Walker's office every 2 weeks for a few hours to answer the Janus Information Facility. He mentioned he'd like to form a female-to-male therapy group, and I could co-lead it with him ✦ he'd pay me. I said, sure, let's do it—but know he'll never get it off the ground.

So I've told T. It was just time. He was figuring out something was wrong with me, and I wasn't going to lie if he outright asked me… and I decided I'd rather have him know the truth than believe the things he was imagining.

It all started coming out like I was a guy who had changed to a girl, and now was going back to being a guy. "Now you're trying to be a guy again?" He asked. "Why?"

I looked at him, sitting there beside me, and it just seemed okay.

I said, "Well, T, that's not really the whole story." I decided I'd rather have him know the truth, than think I had made a decision ✦ then changed my mind. That was too weird. I said, "The truth is, I am a sex change from a female to a male." He asked, "You mean you never were a male?" I answered, "Not until now." He said, "I would never have guessed you were once a female." I said "Thank you…I hope not!" He asked, "So you don't have a cock?"

I told him I was always wondering how I would tell him, but that it was very important to me that people don't know, because they act differently toward me. I asked him not to tell Cuca or Dan.

I tried to act as normal & un-freaked-out as I could. I want to tell him what he means to me, instead I tell him who I am & what I am all about. I hope it will make my feelings toward him clearer and more true. I thought about it and was glad I told him. I asked him if knowing this changed the way he felt about me. He answered, "Not yet" and I pondered on the many ways he could have meant that.

Later Dan & Cuca joined us for a cookout on the roof. T disappeared for a while, later saying he'd gone to see Lawrence. I figured he told Lawrence just because (as his telling me about he & Cuca) he had to tell someone. I really don't care. Dan & Cuca are moving into a house about a mile away in 2 wks. Suddenly it's not so big of a deal if they knew—like Peter & Joyce, who later came over. They both know & I have a great relationship with them.

During the cookout, T & I started flipping pebbles at each other. T said, "Come on, Lou, and fight like a man!" We "boxed" again, but he really didn't put his all into it. I taunted him, "Oh, now all of a sudden you don't want to, huh? It's all different now, huh?" I got a little more aggressive & began looking him in the eye & egging him on & smacking him a few good ones. He finally fought me. When we got tired, he commented, "You're getting better, Lou."

A little later we started up again. This time I really was the aggressor. I even saw him flinch from me a couple times. He knew what I was saying to him: don't you dare treat me any differently now! We even shook hands when we stopped & he said I was getting even better than the last time, & that we should go somewhere & box together for exercise. I said yeah, it might be fun.

I saw him smile a few times at the little double-meaning things I said that applied to my situation. I wanted to relax in the knowledge of his new outlook of me, and I laid back to let him look at me & see me as he always has. I even looked back at him. He was just fine until he left the party abruptly when we came into the building. In fact, as soon as he saw Peter & Joyce, he split. (I can't remember exactly the conversation but we were all talking about how gays make this city & without the homosexuals it'd be a hell-hole, when Cuca turns to T, smiles cruelly and says, "T, you're a homosexual, aren't you?" He looked at her & just turned away from them… She really gave him a dirty jab.)

I think the main things now is for me not to act any differently than I always have. Not feel uncomfortable or touchy knowing he knows. Just think: shit, man. I'm a nice guy & there's no reason to treat me any other way than you have.

Early today he rings my doorbell. When I ask on the intercom, "Who's there?" he yells, "Open up!" He comes in with dirt & blood all over his hand & completely beside himself. Somehow, while pushing his car window closed, he pushed his hand right through the glass. He asked for something to clean it up. I was on my way to the Castro St Fair, meeting Bridget & Charlie, & he offered me a ride.

It didn't take much to persuade him to join us (he pretended it was because Bridget would be there). The 4 of us had a fine time, tho he was still agitated about the window & kept complaining of a headache. He, Charlie & I played pinball in a bar. The whole time I was in heaven, he at my side, having a good time, smiling, joking around with me, flashing his beautiful smile, his beautiful eyes. We made several light-handed or joking references to my change. (I tell him I think women are more hassle than they're worth. He says, "You should know.") He tells me Joyce freaks him out so bad (and I think, "That's why he ran off the night before"). He asks if they know about me.

Somehow we all got separated from each other & my heart sank, thinking I'd lost him. Ran into Peter & Joyce who had seen him going ahead, so I rushed all the way to the end of the street & waited, watching, upset, I couldn't believe I'd lost him, he must be here somewhere, he'd have to come this way… and then I spot him. I rushed up behind him as he was turning to leave & acted like I'd been behind him a long time. He was obviously glad to see me ("Lou! Where WERE you!??"). Turned out when I ran off for beer, he had *followed* me & I moved so fast he lost me.

We drove to a carwash to vacuum the glass out of his car.

We sat in the car a long time, mostly being quiet ✝ laying back in the seats, sometimes talking, laughing. He says women are so weird, and he likes the older ones because the younger ones won't suck your cock. He tells me Cuca was such a great fuck that he ALMOST CAME. "Almost." Said he'd just finished jacking off before she came over ✝ that they fucked for 2 hours. He says all he wants to know is: do women really like to fuck as much as men do...do they want to get fucked or not ??

I tell him they do, but sex is such a power struggle ✝ they don't want to feel they're just being fucked. He tells me he only goes out with Elena because he wants to fuck her. I say, "No wonder she's not calling you." He laughs.—

He sees me looking at him ✝ I know he sees me out of the corner of his eyes. He lifts up his chin ✝ lowers his eyelids. He has a bad hook nose that's somehow pushed in right at the end. I drink in his relaxed body. I love him so much.

I say, "Sometimes you're scary to look at...it's hard for me to look at you."

He says, "Yeah."

He told me yesterday I should shave my facial hair ✝ it'll grow in darker. So I did this morn, even my mustache, which I've never shaved before. I want to reach out ✝ touch him, but I dare not, telling myself it's too early. We drive more, all around the Park. Then driving home, he asks if I'd like to come over to his place. There we lay on the floor in his room ✝ listen to music, pet the cats. He tells me he still has the headache. He was also still fretting about the car.

His fucking roommate interrupts us several times. We eat watermelon.

Finally the roommate leaves ✝ T climbs up into his loft. I can't believe it, and I think, *What should I do* ? God. I resolve that, if he invites me up, he <u>wants</u> it. I ask if he has a light up there, he says, "Come on up, if you want to." I try not to fall over myself, scrambling up there, trying to go up nonchalantly. It is so high to the ceiling you can't really sit on the bed, but are almost obliged to lay down.

He pulls out a girly magazine, explaining that it didn't really turn him on, that it was his roommate's & he was throwing it out, so T just took it to look at. We lay side by side in the bed & my heart is pounding so loud. He had his arms folded under his head, his sweater pulled up slightly, baring his lean stomach. My eyes burn him, I fight with my hands to lie still, he sees me, but closes his eyes & sighs, stretching. I am nuts. My body wanting to touch his so badly—a distinct bulge in his pants. I try not to pounce on him. I try to tell myself it's too early to act. He sees me look away & he closes his eyes.

I say, "Sometimes it's so hard not to touch you." He is silent. He does not move. His eyes are closed. I raise up to kiss him, but he blocks me with his arm, "Don't kiss me," gently, yieldingly. My hand moves across his bare stomach & down his pant leg. Over his penis. I kiss the cloth covering his penis.

I run my hand up under his sweater, over his smooth firm chest, his too-pink soft nipples. He lays unmoving & says, "Don't tickle me to death."

I said, "Oh, I'll try not to." I try to open his pants, but he reaches down, takes my hand away—AND THEN HE QUICKLY OPENS HIS PANTS AND PULLS THEM DOWN TO HIS KNEES, TAKING HIS PENIS IN HIS HANDS AND RUBBING IT. I go for it.

My God, Dan was wrong. He has a beautiful cock! He said, "Oh, it's probably down & it's dirty, too" and I said, "Well, we'll just have to clean it off then" and I take his hands off his penis and suck it into my mouth. I sucked him nicely & felt him harden a little. Again, he reached down & took his cock in his hand, so I licked down to his testicles, but he had them in his other hand. He told me he didn't like the sloppy stuff, that he just wanted to play with himself a little because he's so horny. I stopped myself from asking, "Can I just watch then?"

He handled himself a while saying, "Now, Lou, don't start getting sexually involved with me." I said, "Well, then don't start taking your pants off in front of me!" We laughed.

He said he can't help it, he doesn't want to get involved but sometimes he just wants to have sex. I said, "Yeah, so do it." I continued stroking his body. He sits up and strips off his shirt.

I stroke his chest as he lays back down. I tell him his nipples are so pink. He says, "I don't have much body hair, do I?" I can see he loves to be touched but it was hard to allow himself the pleasures. He asked me to give him a backrub (his famous line) ✝ he said he could feel the tension leaving him, as I straddled him, actually cracking his spine a few times. I rub his neck, he gets up, moving me gently off him. We lay side by side again, ✝ I think, "I'll be damned if I'm going to be the first one out of his bed—he's going to have to <u>tell</u> me to leave!" Then we hear his fucking roommate return ✝ the guy actually positions himself in the adjoining room (the kitchen), puttering around, emptying the garbage—Oh bullshit—with T's room completely visible ✝ audible from where he was, what a rude bastard.

T sits up ✝ pulls a sleeveless A-shirt on—one of the sexiest garments I know. I can smell his body—the taste of his penis still on my lips. I touch his arms, his back. He lays back down. I think again that I'll just lay there until I *have* to go—I'd love to just sleep there silently near him all night. His roommate clatters the dishes.

T says, "Excuse me, Lou" ✝ goes down the ladder. I descend slowly a few minutes later, paying lots of attention to the cat up there. He is nervously washing the dishes while his roommate wipes the counter. What a bunch of shit. I don't want to leave hurriedly. I saunter about the rooms. After a while I say, "Well I guess I better be shoving off." He says, "I'd like to come over to have some tea, if you don't mind making some." I say "No, of course not." I am thoroughly amazed at this incredible youngman, this jewel I have found. T loosens up, laughs, tells him about the car window. He tells me he still has his headache.

We come over to my place. I play Mahler ✝ make hot tea, giving him one of my Tylenol with codeine. He stays 2 album sides worth.

My God! He said he loved me, too. He said it quickly, without emotion, but he said it. And he is not one to say something with that gravity for no reason—I'm thinking of him sitting on the roof, leaning back in the warm sun, his sheer pinkish shirt fluttering in the breeze against his bare chest. I can hardly look at him because I didn't trust myself to control my urge to reach out, to try to capture this apparition, how to control my breathing.

Not only does the thought of him arouse sexual feelings in me, but a deep admiration + a sense of reality, a sense of being part of the world, that I've never experienced before. He makes me feel strong + good + as though I am important.—He says he doesn't think he'll take his brother camping with us. I was disappointed + accused him of changing his treatment of me now that he knows. He denied it, saying with our relationship as it is now, he would feel he was just bringing his brother along, instead of spending quality time with him as he would like to. Fair enough.

We were walking down Broadway. I saw him + couldn't resist taking hold of him from behind, tickling him, as I had done before. But this time there happened to be some broad there from one of the strip joints + he got pissed she saw it. He shoved me off + warned, "Leave me alone, Lou. I'm really a macho guy, Lou!" I looked at him incredulously, (I seem to do that a lot, hey?) + said, "You're really a 'Macho Guy'?" I just shook my head. Later he says to me, "Lou, I like you. I just *like* you, I don't LOVE you or anything." I said back to him, "You told me you loved me!" After being initially startled, he got that intellectual look + said, "sometimes I just say things because they seem right at that moment."

I talked to Dan a little, trying to cool down. Then I turned to T + said, "Man, don't talk SHIT to me! Don't tell me SHIT!" he knew what I meant, too. He put his head on my face, he laid the palm of his hand on my cheek, and said, "Lou! Don't start freaking out!" And the warmth of his touch quieted me.

Earlier in the evening I had jostled him around affectionately + he responded, saying "be rough with me, Lou. I like that." I said, "Yeah I do, too."

He's wearing a St. Christopher's medal. I tried to take it out of his shirt twice, but he kept stuffing it in. I remember Beau. I remember his gold chain.

I watch my beautiful young boy blossoming into a beautiful youngman. I want to write about how my change has opened up a new world of love ✦ happiness for me. We can watch the hang gliders over the ocean ✦ I think I have never felt stronger about anyone... Even J. I feel safe ✦ sure with T. I feel strong ✦ steady. I feel only good things can happen.

We discussed the economies of this magazine we're going to put out.—I said I saw no problem on my end moving in with him ✦ that he should see if there was any on his end and, if there was, then (and we said this simultaneously)

Me: Then we'll move out
He: Then we'll fight it out

I wanted to touch his soft protruding nipple, but people kept coming over disturbing us whenever we had a quiet moment.

He does not become as uneasy as before, and now will meet my eyes and smile at me. He asked if I'd give him a body rub, "all over my body." I said I'd be delighted to. He went to the bathroom (no doubt to wash his cock) ✦ I went boldly to the bedroom, closed the curtains ✦ turned on a dim light. But he turned out the light ✦ opened the curtains, letting the street lights soften the room. He stripped to his jockey shorts. I open my shirt, remove my shoes.

I massaged him all over, even his feet. I cracked the bones in his back. He lay [there], completely offering his body, ✦ I stroked his chest ✦ could feel him flexing his muscles under my touch. I removed my shirt. After a long while, I stroked the cotton shorts covering his cock. Soon he was hard. I took my time playing with it, ✦ then lower the shorts ✦ took him in my mouth. I'm amazed at how long & thick his cock is when he is so small. I could taste the pre-seminal discharge. I sucked as he masturbated & realized he was holding back, not wanting to come in my mouth.

I petted him as he masturbated & played with his nipples until the little tip hardened & I played with it. I lay back, stuck my hand down my pants & beat off next to him, coming twice. I knew he was amazed watching me work out like that—I really do work up a sweat & have violent trembling throughout my sessions. I touched him a few times as I masturbated, and I ran my hand over his, I felt his finger stroke my palm—his first reaching out to me that night, his first return of my affection. I want him to desire me, too. I noticed he had also cum.

We went to the gym tonight. I joined. He was pretty considerate about being with me. Actually I was trying to avoid him so I wouldn't embarrass myself in front of him, huffing & puffing with 15 lb dumbbells. God. Afterwards he told me my shorts were too effeminate. I was embarrassed. Back to my place, where I put a nest in the birds' cage & we watched Mr. Bird fill it. Pretty.

T is like a child. I am, we are speaking more freely & comfortably with each other. I felt I've caught myself feeling too female-like with him lately. It's something that bothers me, but I'm not sure exactly what it is. I should maybe ask T if he feels I'm acting more effeminate toward him since I told him about myself. Anyway we then went to get a pizza & ate it in Dolores Park, overlooking the city, where he says he often goes. He tells me a man at work keeps calling him a "fag." I asked him what he was in therapy for & he says because he was more intelligent than most kids his age. We talk about moving in together—he says he's not bringing the cat. We sit in the car & smoke a joint.

When I finally got into bed I felt like I was floating on a cloud in heaven—I couldn't believe my fortune. My eyes sneakily devour this beautiful youth, huddled in blankets, wearing sleeveless A-shirt, his black curls in disarray on the pillow. I dare not touch him & wanted to show him we could lay together as brothers. My heart pounded loudly as he turned or changed positions, not sleeping.

He asked me to turn on the heater, and I gave him another blanket (I wanted instead to wrap him in my arms and warm him with my love). He slept like a vision, a tender young boy, and I fantasized he was there for my pleasure ⊹ had to submit to whatever I forced upon him. I slept a little. Each time he moved, I had to see him. And then he reached out his arm, laying it across the bed, his hand against my right nipple. I laid my arm over his, we both feigned sleep, and I felt his fingers stroking me once or twice. I needed nothing more from him. We lay that way a long time.

When the sun came in the window, I felt him masturbating under the blankets. Slowly at first. I reached over ⊹ ran my hand over his chest and down his side, discovering then that he wore nothing but the undershirt. He muttered, "Leave me alone." I grunted "Uh-uh," but I took my hand away. He continued pumping himself, I laid still, my face away from him, pretending I dozed off. After he came, he stripped off his shirt ⊹ cleaned himself, then went off to shower. I buried my nose in the fragrant shirt ⊹ pumped my penis ⊹ came. He dressed for work ⊹ left without a word.

Fri nite we lay in my bed (he naked, me with my shorts on) ⊹ watched TV. He lay on his stomach with a small well-shaped butt in the air. We slept with his feet and my head at one end, my feet and his head at the other, and sometimes cuddled up in that position.

Saturday at his suggestion we drove up the coast to the Russian River, gay mecca, arriving so late in the afternoon, we decided to sleep in the car ⊹ stay the next day. We had a beautiful time. Lay in the sun, (he popped a blackhead near my right nipple), went to hear a lousy band, walked around Guerneville, slept in the car. Sunday we found a secluded spot ⊹ did some nude sunbathing—I was not self-conscious around him. And he tried to jerk off at one point but was too nervous about canoers on the river. I laughed.

T told me that being with me has triggered him to constantly have confusing dreams, which linger with him all day, having a negative impact on him; that his thoughts are as constant + muddled as music; and that his feelings for me are mixed: he said he WANTS to have sex with me, but it's hard to reconcile if I'm a man or a woman; that he feels living with me would be too much of a strain on his energy; that he feels speedy + unsure of what our relationship means. It was the first time he outright expressed desire + affection for me. I told him I understood—that I was also going through lots of thought and changes from being with him; that I have dealt with my ambiguity; that I thought this whole experience of my change and relating to people now was a super exciting thing + I loved being involved with it, that it kept my mind from being bored + stagnant, I love the adrenaline pumping through me. Any problems he has with it, I said, are his alone to reconcile.

I said I wanted to continue our friendship (quoting the gay book by that title). I said, " I never should have told you." He was surprised. He asked why did I tell him? I answered, "Because I wanted to have sex with you + felt it better to tell you first, rather than have you find out that way," and also, I said, because I wanted him to know I wasn't a goof-off.

He said he did not want to live with me and, while he wished to maintain our friendship, he felt he has to remove this disturbance from his life. I told him I was somewhat relieved because I didn't especially want to move from my new place. He said he wanted to live alone, + asked why I had agreed then to move in with him. I said for a change I wanted to do something crazy, follow my heart instead of my logic. He asked, "You mean you've never fucked up before?" I said nope, I never have. The room was silent. After a while, thinking of what he had told me, he said, "This was hard for me to say." I wanted to cry, "Don't leave me, T! Don't go." Instead I nodded + tried to be accepting.

He asked me to read the segments from my earlier diaries I had gleaned into a book. I read a few + he asked to hear some I'd written about him. I told him I was tired of exposing my inner feelings in order to feed his ego, when all he does is tell me I'm weird. That I keep baring my soul, when in return he is so cold. He admitted he was, "sometimes."

I said something about his being a lousy lover. He countered that he wasn't trying to be my lover, but I reminded him he admitted he *did* want to have sex with me. I did read some to him as he lay across my bed: the entries of my party, end of the day I told him about me. He smiled, commented, ✦ was obviously ego-fed. He laid there so lovely, as a lump of emotion caught in my throat as I read words of love. I reached over ✦ stroked his chest, his hair. He turned away ✦ I began wrestling with him, trying to pin him down on the bed ✦ accept my attentions. We struggled, laughing, and the mattress slipped off the bed frame. We still struggled— he won—but then he sat on the edge of the bed ✦ said he'd like to stay over, if I didn't mind. My heart soared.

For the first time, we had uninhibited beautiful sex. For the first time, he reached out to me with desire, touching, stroking me. I sucked him ✦ he instructed me how to do it better, how to masturbate him better.

He positioned his cock between my legs so it looked like mine, he told me how to stimulate it, and he said, "There, now it's yours." I looked down ✦ felt whole, like a man, I looked over my muscular arms, my flat chest as I imagine his cock mine and masturbated it. I was raised to incredible sexual highs.

He asked if I wanted to be fucked. I turned on my stomach ✦ he entered my cunt ✦ fucked like mad. It felt so damn good. He marveled on ✦ on what a beautiful perfect ass I have. He asked if I liked it better in the cunt or ass. I hesitated, said in the ass, and he said he figured, "because you're such a fag, Lou." (He wouldn't fuck me in the ass, tho, saying it would be too tight, ignoring my denials it would—he should know what I've had up there!) He rambled on with "dirty talk" which I guess turned him on, about cocks and "pussy." He asked if I liked the taste of his cock ✦ asked what it tasted like. I told him "like going to sleep," and "warm."

He reaches out for me now, but I still must express my desire for him first.

Surely his face is God's. I look into his eyes ✦ I feel that I have seen God. And then he'll meet my eyes ✦ smile, taking me even higher.

We walked around the Tenderloin, into several dirty bookstores. He says it's a funny thing, but in those stores he doesn't get turned on by pictures of cunts, "just the opposite," he said. I asked, "You like the cocks?" He nodded, with resignation. I felt strong & proud in my old neighborhood, showing him the hot spots.

T came home late, stripped & flopped onto the bed beside me. He said he'll begin paying ½ the rent & I gave him a set of keys. We chatted about our day; he jerked off to his TS magazine, commenting on the "gorgeous dicks" on some of them. He said when he makes enough money he's going to borrow it to me for my operation. I am becoming less obsessed with his presence & am finding easy peace. I hope this whole thing doesn't fall through…

One very important difference in loving a man versus a woman: We are not totally free to express our affection. How I yearn to touch him—just put my hand on the top of his head & ruffle his hair affectionately. We look at each other & smile (as we lay on the beach in the sun) and he takes a boxing punch at me, smiling with true affection, and I feel my arms go limp, for loss of what to do. My arms don't say knock him one too. My arms ache to wrap around his shoulders, my hands ache to flatten against his back.

Now I *know* the guy loves me! He spent a long time last night squeezing pimples on my back, chest, neck, face. Then he put vitamin E on my face. Then he took a scissors to my hair, affectionately tousling my hair, rubbing my shoulders. He asked me to punch him in the arm as hard as I could. We boxed & punched him in the jaw a good one. He kept trying to sock me, until I said, "Oh, sure. You'd rather hit me instead of kiss me."

My upper arms are bruised from his punching me all the time. He said he didn't understand why he wants to hit me so much. I said I felt he couldn't handle his affectionate feelings for me ＋ that he shows his affection by punching me or popping my zits (which he does daily). Little by little he has been standing behind me ＋ putting his arms around me, or stroking my back. It's like he can't FACE me ＋ hug me.

But little by little he becomes more traditionally affectionate while having sex, etc. He explained his hesitation was because he said he has these feelings of closeness ＋ affection for me now, but he's afraid I'll be hurt when he moves on to other things. I told him I was in control of my feelings ＋ I know better than to be hurt, that we should enjoy our relationship while we have it ＋ when one or the other of us moves on, that's how life is.

I appeared with Paul Walker on a San Jose TV talk show on transsexualism. I understood San Francisco could not get the station, but they do. Yet I figured it a long shot anyone would see it here.

Yesterday, a woman at Bechtel[23] I've had lunch with ＋ been friendly with approached me, saying someone had seen a Lou Sullivan on TV ＋ was it me. I denied the whole thing. She was very freaked out by it ＋ said she knew it couldn't *possibly* have been me, because she knows I'm not that weird, etc. I assured her it wasn't, but could feel sweat forming on my forehead. She left, but I called her back, asking the name of the person who had seen the show. She wouldn't tell me, saying she'd talk to the person ＋ tell them to quit spreading lies about me.

23 Sullivan worked at Bechtel, an engineering, procurement, construction, and project management company.

(That night I had a dream that he was holding a knife to my neck *
cut me slightly * it bled. I told him he had to move out because I didn't
want to live with someone who'd act that way, and he was regretful,
begging me to let him stay because he had cucumber seeds and this was
the first chance he's had to plant them in the backyard. But I wouldn't
give in.) Today I told him about my dream. He was quiet for a while,
then he said he promises me he'll never hit me again. I said no, I *liked*
him to hit me, just so it wasn't *hard*.

My last day of vacation—I sit on the roof of 17th Street, the sun
glowing over the city, the cool air calm. Sometimes I dream of quitting
my job * making a living off my writing, but it has been only since I've
been with T that I've been hit with the reality that I'm not really a very
good writer. There is so much I cannot express, or find impossible to
allow the reality into my life. Such as T. Our lives together. Once when
I read excerpts from my diary to him, he commented that I "left out a
lot of the humor in our relationship." He's right, but I find it so hard
to take us lightly when I reflect how important he is to me. I've had a
whole week to myself * haven't written shit.

And so my life has turned another chapter. I think we've found an
excellent place to move into. Very large, more rooms than we need. I
think we'll live there very comfortably. We've been very close lately.
Cuddling. Kissing in a way I've never kissed before: gazing at each other,
he looks at me with such feeling sometimes. He says he hopes it's not
just that he only comes to my room * I close myself off to him if he has
someone else there. I said I didn't want it that way either. The other night
he came inside me for the 2nd time. He's really turned on by me!

I get scared sometimes that I'll fuck up this relationship by being jealous,
or by falling mindlessly into old female reactions/feelings/habits. I must
keep remembering there are no rules for the kind of relationship we
have * want to have. I must keep remembering he * I are not like J * I.
That T *wants* me a lot, not like J who kept me at a safe distance. I must

remember that T & I are equals in this relationship, and *both* of us have something to lose, or something to gain.

He's talking about buying nice rugs & good furniture & getting renters insurance together, etc. I'm amazed at the commitment he wants to make, while I see him making decisions against commitments in other areas of his life.

I look forward to moving into this larger place to regain some of the anonymity I've lost while he's been here with me. I'm so infrequently left to my own thought, at this time when I especially need to reflect & digest all these feelings & experiences that I've craved my whole life and am now realizing—my head spinning, my mind working overtime so that I often lay awake at night too preoccupied to sleep, as he lies warm & loving, pressed against me.

Last night T said the reason he liked me is because I "could be a real macho guy," but I was "still sexy in bed." What a fine compliment! I told him I liked him for that same reason.

We discussed how the rooms would be used. The bedrooms are connected by a narrow sink area, and T drew up a floor plan and, via his pencil, indicated that he saw that sink area as open to traffic between our rooms "as long as we like each other and love each other sexually."

He said I am petite!

I said I wish I had a cock so I could stick it up his ass. He said even if I did he wouldn't let me. I called him stingy, but he said someone already had done that to him and he didn't like it. Ah, what fantasies I have! What fun it must have been for whoever had him!

Now is the time for me to begin to say goodbye to this apartment— this place where I learned so many things…where I learned to laugh and to be witty, to relax and breathe easily, be caring and sharing and loving and giving…and receiving. I've grown so much in only this short time. The fears I had when I left Hyde Street! The adventure I feel now, leaving 17th Street. Yes, we got the place I wrote about.

I remember seeing him in those early days, appearing…sometimes like a spirit…every place I'd be. When I'd hear him, or think I heard him, and then he'd be there. Now I hold this fresh spirit who teaches me so much. The adventures we will have!

Last summer, laying on the roof early in the morning sun, coffee at my side, reggae music on the radio, my body browning beautifully—I thought I could never be happier. Can I be? Somehow it all came so easily to me…it just seemed right.

I need to associate with people who don't know! I learn the most and am the most relaxed with them.

Tonight in bed I lifted my little cock out and T opened his legs as I rubbed my cock against his ass crack, trying to titillate his opening. I was masturbating at the same time.

Wondering what it'd be like to be inside, opening him up, using his fresh young body any way it pleased me, getting off and he pushes me off him, complaining, "I don't feel <u>anything</u>!" in an almost disgusted tone.

I said, "Well, *do* something then! *I feel something*!"

So I moved off him, but continued to finger myself as I got off, thinking "Yes! I *do* feel something! And I'm gonna enjoy the feeling!" I am strong.

He said he could really see being a girl because they enjoy sex more than boys, he thinks, because they are more pampered and get into being beautiful & he could really see doing that. I told him he was more beautiful than any girl!

He wanted to know what I was thinking while we had sex ϟ I said none of his business.

He thought it was funny when I tried to get him to describe to me how it feels to have a penis (..."does it feel like a finger?") ϟ he replied that he felt the physical feelings were probably pretty much the same for men as for women during sex. He said I shouldn't get the cock operation because I *am* enjoying my pussy. I agreed and told him what a special person he is.

February 1982 – November 1986

"I gather each tidbit, each lead I pursue as though I am finding someone with whom I am in love."

Page Street
San Francisco, California

I'm flesh and blood, if you'll condescend to such low things.

E.M. Forster, *Maurice*

This fragrant youth in my arms.

I find myself being afraid to love T totally. Already I find myself feeling "too feminine" around him, sinking into his arms too happily, too over-indulgently. This week we've been throwing a log on the fire, and as the evening grows late, we've had sex on the floor in front of the fire. He came up to me and hugged me yesterday! He calls me "Babe." And when I look at him I sink into his beauty and I am consumed and he notices and his eyes flash at me.

This is what I've wanted all my life. I have never felt so relaxed in a stormy kind of way. Is what I am experiencing that which everyone else in the whole world—or even the majority of people—feel? As a daily experiencing? My head is reeling with excitement, yet I look at everything with boredom ⚹ fear. Mostly fear. As he sits near me, my heart beats and I try to see him out of the corner of my eye, and when I do, he looks back at me.

I never felt I was <u>there</u>. I never felt I was beautiful.
He makes me feel perfect. He doesn't want me to change.
Yet he never treats me like a "girl"—(what do I mean by that?)

He <u>never</u> looks down at me
He <u>never</u> looks down at me
And God I laid him down and
the fire shown on his skin
My warm perfect boy
My lost lover
Myself—who I missed!
The curious gentle boy
My lost youth
My loving youth
He was sent to bring it to me
I move the white cotton away
from his golden glowing body
His warm golden breast
The beauty of it
And I am afraid to look
at myself

Going famously. Saturday he bought a bed but never even made it up, and slept again with me.

Life was worth living just to have experienced him—He is a blessed joy.

Last night he told me I'd have to wait til Sunday for my valentine. I was pleased / surprised he was so outward with his affection. And then, as though he couldn't wait, he said he'd give it to me now. He'd made it up himself and printed them in his shop at work. In a homemade envelope (on which he had written '*Louis G. Sullivan*') was the card.

A small cupid shooting an arrow into a larger cupid's butt, little red hearts all over, and inside it said *"You stuck me from behind—Happy Valentine."*

He had made up the saying. Underneath it wrote "*Love, T.*" He sat there as I read it, as tears welled up in my eyes + I tried not to really cry or go overboard, but I told him it was the nicest valentine I'd ever received.

What has it been about male / male love that has made me desire it so?

The fact that it didn't *happen*—that the two people involved really *wanted* to be with each other, and that the other person chose to love him. And in all my apprehensions about who or what I am, and my unhappiness in my incompleteness as a man, I know that T + I have that quality—the most important quality…the one quality that I've always looked up to.

Not so much that it was two male bodies (not to minimize that aspect, though), but that despite all forces against them, they clung to each other with desire. T clings to me with desire—I cling to him with desire.

We had a talk the other day + he said he thought I needed to be with other men, someone who would have sex with me as a man.

I agreed and marvel at his perception. I want to have sex with a man as a man, and fantasizing at the possibility during my upcoming trip to NY, yet even my best fantasy doesn't fill me with desire as he does. And I believe when the day comes when my body can be complete, T will be there.

I've been making a real conscious attempt to take control during our lovemaking.

To be fully aware of his body there, and my body touching his, and everything he does to my body. I've realize that even if I *had* a penis today, I wouldn't even know how to behave with one, and that the first step to *having* one is learning how to behave with one, whether you can use it or not.

I have a feeling I've expressed this complaint once before, but T's beginning to get on my nerves on one subject: he is *constantly* talking about my cunt. I mean constantly. It's always in a teasing light vein, but it's really aggravating me. Either it's he has to take a shower because he's smelling like my pussy, to how's my pussy hole these days, or it's something about how he's gonna "fry my flounder," blah blah.

I'm really getting tired of it. I've told him to stop it, ♂ he just asks why real innocently. Why, indeed. I know even women don't like that shit, but my reasons aren't the same as theirs. It just really turns me off. Sunday ♂ Tuesday nights I've slept in my bed when he's been in his, just to demonstrate my independence ♂ strength. Why, indeed.

I finally defined why: I see that part of me as a defect, an incompleteness of my body.

I also think this constant reference to my female parts is his way of denying he's involved with another man, emphasizing his male role with me, and reminding me of that—and that *really* pisses me off.

$$\rtimes\hspace{-0.5em}\ltimes$$

Saw Fulmer again. My lab tests checked out 100% normal ♂ he mentioned my cholesterol was 198, below the normal 200, ♂ he said that meant a long life.

T urged me to begin writing my book. I told him I AM—I could publish my diaries word-for-word. But I'm not ready.

A woman secretary came up & told me I'd never have gotten the promotion if I were a female. I was taken aback & didn't know HOW to react (I *felt* like saying, "Hey, I KNOW that!")

In bed T opens my legs, opens my lips and uncovers my little penis. He takes it firmly in his mouth and sucks it hard, and it hardens and stands up. He pulls it & sucks it, bites it, until it grows to over an inch. He tells me where to hold the skin so it stands up highest and he lowers his round boy's ass onto it, trying to put it into his hole. I press it against him, but it's too soft, but I moved around so that it wiggles between his cheeks & against his opening.

When he enters me, I reach around & grasp his firm smooth cheeks & spread them apart. He asks me to use my finger (when sometimes he won't let me!) and I insert it and my orgasm is deep & strong.

He calls me a beautiful sexy youngman and he says "I love you very much."—

My facial hair is sprouting little by little. T keeps a close eye on it & tells me constantly to shave off the sparse whiskers because they "rub" him and it's "too weird." I used to shave in order not to offend him, but I'm deciding to [leave] them on more & more.

He hangs out with me all day, all weekend, with or without my family around. We work on the backyard together, make meals, clean the house, go to movies, babysit for Buddy, go to a free concert on our bikes, go shopping, smoke a joint, go for a drink.

He finally took me to the greasy spoon restaurant in the old neighborhood where he wouldn't take me before because it was "too rough." Once there, I laughed & said, "As if…this place is like the breakfast place at The Russian River!"

We had a long talk earlier in the week—my complaint: that I was tired of always playing the girl + wanted to play the aggressive one once in a while. He told me I could do whatever I wanted, that's how much he loves me…that's what he said—

So last night it was assumed we'd sleep apart, but in the middle of the night he comes snuggling under my covers, whimpering that he was so cold + bugs were crawling all over him in his bed (!). In seconds my pretty little angel was sound asleep in my arms.

Yesterday T + I rode our bikes through GG Park, he was leading me through hidden path + trails. Found a secluded spot + laid in the grass. Told me he wished he could introduce me to his family + be open with them about us, but he knew he never could, that he has always strived to be what they expected him to be, especially his ma. He said he felt that way even if I were a normal man + we were together, so I don't feel too bad.

Then he asks me if I have any problems with our relationship + I said yes: I wish he'd turn off the iron by the switch instead of just pulling out the cord (telling him in that way how content I am). He pressed me further + then said I never tell him how I feel about him! I couldn't believe it, and so tried my best to express to him how much he means to me.

He said he wanted to read my diary because it will tell him how I feel about him.

We ended up having loving sex there in the grass, each masturbating the other to orgasm.

He says he can see I'm holding back sometimes + I admitted it— of course I am, when he continues to tell me he wants a different relationship, one with a woman (because he feels he SHOULD, not that he wants it).

He gave me a transistor radio for my birthday so I could listen to it at night like I used to on Bluemound Rd. He also took a self-portrait for me ♂ developed one of the photos he took of me on the roof of 17th Street when we first knew each other.

J phoned me for my birthday, telling me he finally got a job in Japan, something he's dreamed of for several years. He's leaving the end of the month to teach English to Japanese businessmen ♂ housewives. I am happy for him, but feel a little melancholic.

This gay woman at work told me this "terrible" thing some man said to her in a store: he mumbled that she "must be a boy." She was shocked! (I mentioned that someone had called me "her" the other day in a store ♂ this gay woman just dismissed it, "Oh, YOU don't look like a GIRL.")

She continued, "Well, *this* is going in my book! All of these things!"

It amazes me how people think they have such unusual experiences, such exciting lives, when I can't feel that same way about my life. And I remember Elizabeth Farley, who had lived as a women for 33 years without ever seeking medical help, and I thought "What an exciting life!" Yet she couldn't understand why anyone would want to interview her because she hadn't done anything special in her life.

He went to have a drink with the gay Black man who lives upstairs, who said he'd sell his motorcycle for super cheap to T. T showers and puts on his thin cotton trousers—shirtless, a towel over his shoulder, his hand absently stroking his chest, he steps outside into the sunny backyard ♂ beacons to him through the window, asking to see the motorcycle—

> smiling beautifully
> his chest and arms
> smooth as marble
> and as well shaped

He was complaining as we were having sex that my whiskers were "rubbing" him and he *hates* that. I asked, "What's the big deal? Yours rub me, too." He said "I don't like having sex with men."

I answered, "You're not have sex with 'MEN,' you're having sex with *me*."

He sank back into my arms with kisses.

I'm so angry at J because he forced me to so distort my image of love—

We all went to the Gay Pride Parade. T's first time, because he'd always heard there was so much violence at them, so he stayed away (obviously getting the macho Mission District viewpoint before). This was my 7th parade, and I watched it thinking of all the others I'd been to, and how this was the first one I attended with my lover. T stood close to me and I stroked his fragrant hair. Remembering how I'd watched all the other parades alone, wondering where amongst them all I'd ever find someone to love me, feeling so alone and sorry for myself. And here he is, smiling at me, loving me.

J told me it had really pissed him off that I had such a great story (about myself) that would sell even if it weren't well-written, but that he believes now, if I wait a while longer, I WILL have a worthwhile story to tell.

Monday we worked in the yard ＋ got T's graphic arts camera into the garage. Slept by the fireplace so we could watch the total eclipse of the moon out the window. (T said, "Dress me up in drag." So I did as good as I could—his idea of sexy drag isn't the same as mine, so we did it his way—and he wasn't even getting hard, but I was getting excited to be able to be the aggressive one ✦ I worked my cock against his hole ✦ did what I was able to, as a man.)

I'm beginning to think my scars aren't going to fade. They're still pretty wide ✦ red. Two years later. Shit.

We laid on the couch kissing ✦ he asked if I were being male or female at that moment. I thought a second ✦ said, "Neither—I'm just being me," but thinking "mostly female" because I was melting in his arms.

He answered, "Because if you think you're being female right now, then you have something to work out with yourself."

He challenged me to an arm wrestling match ✦ I took him on. Our arms weren't balanced squarely on the table and the table tipped and stuff slid off as I allowed him to bring my arms down to stop the sliding. I protested angrily that he was using the table ✦ rearranged it so we were balanced, and while I couldn't down him, he couldn't down me either. I said, "I know I can't beat you, but I'll give you one helluva struggle."

Just told this gossipy old woman, a secretary at ARCO (with whom I go to lunch sometimes) that I'm gay. She asked me (because she'd read somewhere) if gay men wanted to be sex changes, and if I wished I were a woman!!! I laughed ✦ said, "Not at all!" and told her that sexual preferences ✦ gender identity were 2 different phenomena, ✦ that if a man was attracted to other men ✦ wanted a sex change to be a woman, he would be defined as a heterosexual person (someone who wants a body of the opposite sex from their lover's), not as a gay person.

I also told her if she ever had questions about gays, I wasn't shy to discuss anything. She asked me very seriously, "How is everything going for you?" I answered, "At this point in my life, I'm happier than I've ever been."

She said it really brought tears to her eyes when she read about these people who are men but have the feelings inside of a woman, and "Don't you think that must be a horrible thing?" I said "Yes!" I told her how I'd met Elizabeth Farley & her story as a man living as a woman & how that really opened my eyes to that sort of thing. I tried to educate as much as possible without identifying too strongly with the sentiments. What a predicament! How well I handled it!!!

T took a spectacular picture of me. My face has gone through such a change. When I first started the hormones, my face looked like it got squarer, my cheeks puffed out some. Now my face is more angular—so much more handsome. I'm an incredibly good looking guy, I think, sometimes (but not always). Mostly I need to lift weights & muscularize my chest—it's still so sunken in.

Late last night I got a call from a F→M in So Calif & we talked a while. T overheard the conversation while in my bed & when I returned, suddenly out of nowhere he started this crap again about it's too weird for him to be with me & he thinks he should see a psychiatrist because he's having dreams of being naked & freaking out. I don't know where this all came from! I said I thought that was an insult to me, and if he thinks he needs to see a psychiatrist, then maybe he should, because there's no shame in that.

Just pissed me off. He hasn't come up with *that* rap in a long time. So this morn I resolved not to let it bother me all day like before. I know he's probably already forgotten about it—it's not ruining HIS day. I resolved to change my thinking: every time I thought of what he said, I'd change my thoughts to contemplating how much better *I* feel in comparison to before—with my job, my co-workers, my neighbors, my friends, my family. THAT was why I changed…not to please a lover. I must remember that he'd be giving me this same rap were I a normal gay man, because even THAT is "too weird" for him.

I said I'm tired of being different than anyone else in the world, of knowing that no one is like me, and I'm going to relish these moments of living easy, of responding to everyday occurrences in a correct manner, without thought, without reflection (as simple as not knowing what to do with my hands when I stood there, as complicated as not feeling I was inside my body when having sex with someone) and the constant realization that my thoughts are of my responses as a youngman.

I said I was thinking all day how my relationships with all these people in my life would be so different were I still female, of my boss, of the people I work with everyday, of Dan & Cuca…I would never have made friends with them ("Why?" T asks, "Because I'd have to be 'girlfriends' with Cuca & Dan wouldn't talk to me the same way he does. I wouldn't value their friendship under those conditions; I wouldn't be comfortable"), and that for the first time in my life I feel a part of the brotherhood of man.

"Why," he asks me (I couldn't understand why) "do you want to continue giving yourself those SHOTS?" "Because they are what brought me into humankind."

He told me he loves me just the way I am, that he wouldn't want me to change. I said, "Think of us going into a bar with all men in it, and how that would feel. Then think of us going down the street into a bar with all women in it. How would that be different in there? That's how *I* feel different." I wished I could have put on a tape recorder. Our conversation was so beautiful. I tried so hard to remember each important word.

He finally mentioned the strap-on dildo I purchased that has been in the drawer with our other sex toys. He said he thinks I bought it "to embarrass him." When I asked if he really thought that, he admitted he wasn't expressing himself well. Said he wanted to see how it looked on me, which embarrassed ME (which he was trying to do, I'm sure), so I wouldn't put it on. I said angrily, "It looks STUPID, VERY STUPID."

He said I just was trying to put him down, so I asked if that is what HE does when he fucks me. Of course he said no. The conversation was not heated or argumentative, but I felt irritated and, once again, very impotent. He said he was satisfied with our sex life & I said, of course, he can do whatever he wants, but I'm not because I can't. The way I feel seems so obvious to me.

He says, "but you're NOT a man."

No one wants to admit it's there, but there's no escaping it: to be "fucked" is to be "put down" and "embarrassed." But I don't believe I'd feel that way towards him if I had a cock to put in his ass.—So I don't know....

Stopped into a big hard-guy gay leather bar, the SF Eagle, this afternoon for a few quick ones while in the neighborhood alone. Had 2 drinks & in the middle of my 2nd, I heard 2 drag queens (one a TS, I guess) arguing about how it is to be a TS with some guys, so I moved closer, thinking of adding my 2¢ worth if I had anything to say.

Suddenly I felt some guy moving up close & says "Your place or mine?" I looked up at him, kind of laughing, & he walked away, winking, "Think about it." I looked over at him & called over, "Thanks, but I don't think I can deliver." Realizing he could have taken that in the wrong way, I tried to smile at him more. Obviously I was very flattered—he was a Black guy, probably my age, though built quite chunky (but then I'm used to T's slender torso).

He strutted over and planted a big juicy kiss on my mouth, which I participated in. He asked, "You think you can deliver now?" I said

"I'm afraid not... you see I don't have a cock." We kissed more ✝ then he asks, "Now *explain* that. What do you mean?" I shook my head, "I don't." He asked why ✝ I debated whether I felt like dealing with telling him the truth, but I was even less creative in coming up with a different line, so I simply said, well, I was a female-to-male transsexual ✝ haven't had all the surgery yet.

He said, "Now wait a minute. You were a male-to-female..." But I slowly shook my head, and he corrected himself, "a female-to-male..." and I slowly nodded. He drew me back ✝ said "I don't believe it." I said well thanks for the compliment, but it's true. We kissed again, long ✝ sloppy, ✝ I said while we were kissing, "I'm encouraged. I'm encouraged." When we stopped, he said, "You used to be a female ✝ you still have the..." and I nodded. He said, "Oh, but you don't like getting screwed?" I looked at him ✝ nodded eagerly. He asked "Well, then, what's the problem?" meaning it was OK with him.

I was really surprised ✝ thought how we could get together, because in 20 min I had to be babysitting for Buddy. I wondered if I'd've gone with him had I not had to leave, thinking of T. I told the guy, "Well, now all I can do is come up with excuses" ✝ told him I had to babysit. He frumped like, "Oh, shame!" and asked if I'd be there later. No. He'd told me he was from LA ✝ did I want him to go back without having any fun. He said he was leaving the next day. I shook my head like "too bad."

He said well, maybe we'll run into each other the next time he's here. Well, I really did feel like he didn't believe it as I rushed out of the place. I had to go! He went back over to his pals ✝ one asked, "Well, how'd it go?" He answered, "He says he has to babysit for his sister." That's all I heard. Interesting he told them that before telling them I didn't have a cock!

Boy, I sure needed that compliment. He was a very affectionate kisser, too! Could have been fun. I wonder just how much I want to have female sex with people, tho. Thinking about doing with this guy what I do with T really grossed me out. I could have played boy with him, I guess. I wish T would let me do that more. But it seems he's relaxing a *little little* more each time. Sure takes him long, though.

Went to lunch with Cheryl (my lesbian secretary). She said she didn't care what her 4-yr-old boy turned out to be, just so he wasn't transsexual! Asked why & she said something about fooling with nature. I said I liked the TS's I knew & always thought they KNEW something. She said she's known a M→F in Florida who was the object of ridicule as she couldn't pass well. How often I think, "If they only knew!"

Attended a co-worker's wedding Saturday. Cheryl drove me. Late in the evening, while full of liquor, she told someone if she ever had a guy again, she'd like it to be me! I said I wouldn't mind sleeping with her, either. When she drove me home, she asked if I wanted to "party" but I said I had a "previous engagement" with T.

Had a dream last night. I was at some political gathering with the family & T. Approached a table of lawyers carrying some marijuana. They wanted to arrest me but I walked away with it. One came up to me saying they had my police record file & I've been in trouble before and how come, when they offered me a job in Washington several years ago, I turned it down?

The whole convention was waiting for my answer. I told them because it was hard enough for them to accept my homosexuality (one lady gasped and stood up), but there was also the issue of my transsexuality, and that when they offered me the job before, I was female—but now I'm a man & that's how I'm now living my life. I walked out proudly, looking each of the 3-pc. suited men in the eye. One in the aisle shook my hands. I went looking for T so we could leave, gathering up my reggae albums. Strange.—

I'm beginning to stuff my crotch again in order to feel more masculine. I don't like feeling "vulnerable" when T keeps grabbing me there all the time. Last night he grabbed me ♦ got a handful. He quickly recoiled ♦ was about to bitch at me for having it there, but wisely remained silent. I felt strong and self-assured.

Came alone to a party of some girl I met once through Maryellen—I knew no one here. I'm having a good time being a guy here. Women are so friendly (so self-conscious and aware of me) and they have much better manners than men!—I am methodically rushing home after being at the party. It's 2:30 am and I can hear the foghorns but water is too far to reach. I had many people to talk to, and some I really liked, men and women. How easy it is to be a "man."

Women have so many rules. Men are raised with none. If they grow up weird, they learn, easier than women, to accept it.

T is in bed only yards away from me, as I sit on our front porch. How I love/desire/yearn/LOVE him!

Just got back from talking at the Sex Institute again during their sex course on transvestites/transsexuals. Am now watching a television show on the subject. I think (as the people in the audience look at sex changes in utter awe, wondering how they made this incredibly big *switch* from being one sex to being the other) that I never *was* any other way than the way I am now. It just doesn't *look* funny to other people *and* to me anymore. It's not that *I've* changed, but that everyone else has changed toward me, just because they think I'm a male now. And I feel less self-conscious because of that.

I haven't changed inside at all.

Last night I did my bi weekly testosterone shot and T walked in my room. Later when I joined him he was asking why I keep "poking" myself when I know he doesn't like it. I answered, "Don't even tease me about it," letting him know we've gone through this already. He said he wasn't teasing, that it made him mad.

I finally said, "Let's put it this way: I'd rather lose you than stop my shots." "You mean that chemical is more important to you than I am?" "No, *I* am more important to me than you are."

It pisses me off that we keep having to have these conversations. It's just that he <u>doesn't</u> <u>know</u> what it's done for me…he just thinks if I'd "cut back" on the shots I could be his girlfriend and we could get married and it'd all be great. He just doesn't <u>know</u>.

I'd like to get in touch with Lou alone for a while. Instead of always "Lou relating to T." I guess he's reading that as I don't love him anymore. But suddenly he's been working hard on his projects—in the backyard, on his graphic arts camera, he's making a monster movie with Brian & Jake (what a little boy he is; how I melt into his being and romp in his beauty). His silliness often makes me uncomfortable, like I don't know how to "answer" him when he wants to be silly with me. But see? Again we're back to Lou relating to T.

Again had a female-to-male who is interested in breaking into the gay men's world come talk to me last night (a few weeks ago had one from Ohio came by, too). I don't know if T was listening or not, but later while having sex he really encouraged me to act as a gay man. He really worked at my clit until it was hard, calling it a "hard little dick" and he tried to get it into his ass. We rubbed & pushed & he kept rubbing it with his fingers to harden it.

I tried to keep it hard, get it in, but it wouldn't stay hard or in for very long—just not big enough to get the needed friction to stay hard. He sat on my crotch to get it in, we laid with our legs open sideways. But I could get it pretty hard and it kind of worked. It felt so good—I was ecstatic. He said he could feel it in him. I told him I like it also because it let me look at him more and that really turns me on.

My resolutions for 1983: To take typesetting and word processing classes in preparation for '84 when my ARCO job is over; to eat more fresh fruit (no pun intended)—T sets such a good example that way I realize how lacking my diet is; again, to do more chest exercising...a resolution I didn't keep in '82.

New Year's Eve we lit the fireplace and slept there on the floor. At first I thought, gee, here it's New Year's and here we are at home AGAIN, but then I thought, if I were out in the bars, I'd be sitting there wishing I were in front of a fireplace with someone I loved—and with that realization, I had a perfect evening. Soon we'll have been at Page Street one year! It's all been so fast—like one single magic moment.

Went to Buddy's birthday and partied until late; pretty drunken sleep. Dreamt I was in bed with an older man who didn't have a cock either. He said he had an operation and lost it. He asked me if I did too, but I showed him my enlarged clit and said no, I just have a small one.

Friday night took T to see my all-time favorite gay male porn film, J. Brian's *Raw Country*. He acted bored and irritated throughout it and we left even before it was over. He had a nasty reaction, "Don't EVER take me to a movie like that EVER AGAIN!" I said, "Hey, you knew what it was before we went, what's your problem?" I guess it was his first gay male porn movie, but Jesus! (I was kind of prepared for that reaction, but I wanted to expose him to it anyway.) He was pissed because all it was was fucking, sucking and sex. I said well that's what porn movies ARE.

Finally I told him he was no fun to go out with—all he does is bitch and moan, which is pretty true pretty often. Later, after we both calmed down, I said, "You didn't even like the swing scene??" (Two guys outside on a swing having sex...just great to watch) I figured I really blew it for him, encouraging using my dick on his ass, but 2 seconds later he was trying to shove it in! You figure it out! I like to imagine that he was so mad because he built up so much tension trying NOT to be turned on by the film.

Seems like I've become a sounding board for all the unhappy people lately. Last weekend Bridget, who had been drinking, comes out of nowhere telling me T *&* I ought to go to a counselor! I was stunned! Asked why? She answered that she just doesn't want to see me hurt. I said I knew one day we'd part, but so far there's been no indication and all's fine. She remarked that all the people in the ward where she works think T *&* I are gay lovers. (So?) And then she says, "You know T thinks of you as a girl!" I felt kind of amused and answered, "Well, in a way I sort of am one." Well, she couldn't deal with that one, and I just considered the source—talking to her is like relying on Nancy for marriage advice!

T is forever about. Were I to go off into another room to concentrate on better writing or diary updates, he'd be sniffing around in no time, reading over my shoulder or distracting me, trying to talk. I hope to slip off to the library this weekend to have some peace.

Sometimes I think my life has changed so much I no longer know what is/isn't good/bad or important/unimportant.

I just got high *&* went in front of the mirror, to really LOOK at myself *&* really try to see myself as others do. I immediately see the worry lines carved into my face, now aging *&* showing all the fighting. In my eyes I see a deep sadness—a deep down panicking of always striving toward something you'll never have. I think—I better start slackening up on myself and STOP RUNNING STOP BEING AFRAID OF EVERY SITUATION.

I want so much to relax into being a man, but I just spent so much time running from being a woman that now I've got that hopelessness, that despair and almost horror etched into my face. How will I look in 10 years? Like a frightened man? I need to relax all my muscles.

Maybe I need to perfect some comfortable stuffing for my crotch, because I haven't been stuffing because it's so irritating (plus few of my pants fit correctly then) and then the thought goes through my mind as I'm talking to someone too long, or else I'm afraid the longer I speak, the more time I have to fuck up & reveal myself or worse, have them not like me. So many of the men genuinely do like me, though.

I can never be a man until my body is whole and I can use it freely and without shame. I may appear in all outward ways to be a man and I may feel in my heart all that a man feels, yet my spirit is hampered and my dreams of being a whole man will always be just dreams… I will always have to back down…my shortcomings will always be a factor. I do not mean that I am not a man, that my living as a man is a lie. I mean that I cannot even fool myself when I stand face-to-face with another man and he is full of pride & privilege & confidence that has been his birthright.

Or is it all a lie? Is male pride & confidence only a front to protect them, and inside they envy my passivity? Or should I (once again!) defy all "fate" & go to school to "become someone" & build my confidence & pride? I've lost so much TIME! I am approaching life as a 32-year-old man and am GLAD I can TYPE well in order to earn a living. I see many men (even older than me) in the same position, but it doesn't make me feel any better about it.

I do feel resentful for having had to waste a good 10 years fucking with my head!

Just told T I need my space. Told him I was going thru a macho head trip and need some time to myself to figure it out. I said sometimes I wish I hadn't told him about myself. He said maybe he should just move out. I poo-pooed that off, and said it's not that I don't love him or anything—I just don't like him treating me like a girl & grabbing my crotch every second and calling me "Fifi." *Come on!* He says he treats me like a guy. I said, well, I want him to *more*. He said that's the only way he knew how to treat me. He said he guesses he just shouldn't hang out with me then, because he's bothering me. I laughed and said well if that's how you want to put it. He huffed away to his room & the TV.

I'm missing the pleasure of living alone. Haven't I already written, "Must I be alone to be happy?" Well, this is one reason I was so happy with the layout of this flat. We can each have our own rooms and I even have a living room off my bedroom. Like my own place where no one is watching me or grabbing me or demanding my attention. He pissed me off by not having something around here for dinner when I got back from class. Same thing Tuesday. I would've had something here for him. He wanted to go on his motorcycle out to eat and I said fuck that, I've only got 2 hours left for myself today.

Johnney and Kay[24] call me on the extension phones, trying not to scare me but acting pretty scary, to say Jack's in the hospital since last night with a broken blood vessel in his brain. I tried to find out all the facts. Is he conscious? They said yes, but he can't remember who the president was before Reagan (I stopped to think, "Who *was*?"). I asked if he was going to the bathroom by himself or was using a bedpan (I figure if he's shitting in a bedpan, that's pretty bad…if he can still make it to the bathroom, he's OK). They said he was using a bedpan.

They truly alarmed me and I started to cry, saying "I know he's going to die sometime. I just love him so much! I think about him almost every day!" Well, then Kay says he hasn't "moved his bowels" yet. So maybe if he's just peeing in a bottle, he's just taking it easy. Johnney said he was still cracking jokes; Kay said he was pissed at her for not staying overnight in the hospital with him.

I asked them to call me before he dies because I'll be flying back there to talk to him. Johnney said snottily that he's not going to die!

---

24   Married Jack Sullivan after divorce from Nancy Sullivan

The experience of Patrick has prepared me, because I know this isn't as horrifying, but I am now at SF Airport awaiting a flight to Milwaukee. All I could think of was "Dad! My dad!" He's only 63. He's had such a shitty life, living with ma & us kids through it all. He would STILL be there if ma hadn't moved to end an obviously bad relationship. He spent years mourning and now he's finally found solitude / peace—had his hip operation only a few years ago, and now this.

Bridget called his doc who said 15% chance of his dying during the operation, another 15% he'll live with a serious side effect (blind, can't speak, maybe even no mind). I couldn't stand it and called Kathleen. But no one else can go to Milw except me, so I'm going. Kathleen made sense when she said, "First go for yourself, to ease your mind; then next go for John, who needs support; then if dad happens to recognize you, go for him."

Why is it always something with the BRAIN —like with Patrick?

I remember standing at grandpa's bedside and knowing he was dying.
I remember Patrick there.
My dad...my dad.

I'm sitting here alone in the hospital with dad while he sleeps. He moans and winces in pain even as he sleeps. I am much encouraged, though, considering what I expected to find left of him—still visions of Patrick when it really <u>was</u> too late. He looked so fallen there, lying in that bed, just flattened. But he's not connected to any tubes, other than a catheter, or any machines; he is strong (he held my hand with his left and squeezed mine tightly a long time).

All I saw of my dad was a brightly shining spirit stricken with a fallen body. He talked to me a lot, silly things, kidding around—he is so glad I came; that alone was worth the $400 airfare. He didn't say one lefty thing to me the whole time I was here yesterday, but he is disoriented, as is expected with any intense head pain.

He said, "Lou," there's only one thing he wants to say and that's, "Do what *you* want to do and don't give a fuck! What anyone else says, just *do what you want to do!*" (And I just wanted to say, yeah, dad, you should know—you waited too long to do what you wanted.)

Kay asked me about myself and, in front of John, I recounted to Kay my usual rap, like I give at the Institute sometimes, about how I got to where I am. She thanked me for telling her.

How we are encumbered by our bodies! How burdensome our bodies are! I said to dad, "Too bad we got to lug these bodies around with us, isn't it?" He mumbled, and John chided me for saying that. It's true!

I am amazed at all the truly beautiful old brick buildings and cement buildings in this city. Kay and John and I left the hospital and a huge storm was moving in—it really thundered and lightning and I took some photos of incredibly beautiful Milwaukee. Dad's Milwaukee. I got a shot of the after-storm rainbow over the city from dad's balcony.

The operation is tomorrow morning and I told dad tonight when I fed him his dinner that it'll all be better after tomorrow.

Today dad is slipping further + further away. He's not moaning or wincing, or playful as before.

When the doctor left, Bridget + I went out to eat dinner and do some heavy drinking. It was a good time to reach Kathleen at home and I dialed, but was delighted to turn the task over to Bridget. I spoke a few words, but she was near hysteria. She knew he was dying and it was going to be like the Patrick scene all over. We told her that we only felt it our duty to let her know.

Bridget laughed, "Boy, Maryellen just banished me from dad's room and said 'I want to be alone with my father!'" as soon as she arrived in his room.

At 10 pm tonight John & I got a call at the bar below John's apartment—it was Kay saying it's almost over and he won't last the night. We raced to the hospital (me urging John to be careful driving) where we met Kathleen, Maryellen & Kay.

I kissed him goodbye and told him I'll keep playing his records. His chart said he had some sensation in his feet (I don't know how they could tell), so I massaged his feet as we all gathered around his bed waiting, I guess for us all to be convinced by the monitors for them to remove the air pump. He's not even in his body anymore. Maryellen sobbed desperately over his body.

Aunt Sis said she couldn't watch Maryellen do it and I said neither could I, so she & I went on the other side of his curtain—surrounded the bed and put our arms around each other. His body seemed to quickly grow cold and pale. Everyone wants to sit with his body, but I feel him inside and in the air all around us. I just want them to take out that air pump. If he can't even breathe on his own, what are we doing to his body? It's gross.

I sat outside the curtain, only a few feet from his bed and wrote feverishly all my thoughts, which I am copying here.

I went to the pay phone and called T to tell him dad was really dead. It was hard to believe there was a loving place waiting there for me. T said he went to the ocean today and I love him so much and it made me happy and peaceful to envision him there by the water.

I said to the other kids, "So far we've all been 'despondent,' but I think tonight we've entered official 'bereavement.'"

I need to go forward with T and make things right. Jack says, "You just gotta stay cool," (one time when I expressed doubt at being able to keep a drum beat).

Jack was a religious experience.
Jack is a religious experience.

For many years us kids had private jokes/lines between us. One is a take-off on how children speak in front of their elderly parents as though they weren't there—now we say it to each other with a new meaning:

> Q: What are we gonna do with dad?
> A: He can't stay here.

I was blown away at just having read, only a few weeks before leaving for Milw, William Wharton's *Dad*, about a middle-aged man watching his father deteriorate and die. But my dad was snatched away from me when he was only 63, and I am only a youngman of 32.

On the plane returning to San Francisco. I know once I get home I'll have to begin to grieve all over again, once I realize that dad is dead. This has all been like a bad dream. T & I had put up a bird feeder in the backyard shortly before I left—no birds had come. But as I've phoned T these past 2 weeks he's told me about the many birds there now, & I crave to be back there with him in my arms.

Sitting in the sun in our backyard yesterday after work, T & I talked about the meaning of life. I am not so much sad about dad as I am reflective on the question he asked me so often, "What is it (life) all about?" T says he believes dying is just like being born—we don't remember how it was to be alive. T says we are all like all the other living creatures and our lives mean no more than theirs; that all we can do is what makes us happy while we're here. I said it all sounds so senseless—what's the point of going through life then? He said, "Aren't you happy to be here in the sun of our backyard with me? Isn't this worthwhile?" Yes. Yes, it is.

That Sunday night when we all stayed in the Intensive Care ward, the evening I believe he died, at 6 am. Monday, left the hospital to go to breakfast together. We stepped outside and were bathed in the new dawning sun. Somehow that sun just keeps coming up...somehow it just keeps coming up.

What a riot! Went to lunch with the bitchy old ARCO secretary and we talked a lot about dad, etc. I told her I had to face his relatives for the first time since they knew I was gay (it's so easy for me to substitute "gay" for "transsexual" and still have the story come out the same).

She said with a shy, knowing look, "And you're not even sure about that!" I was so surprised, I asked, "What?" She clarified her statement, "You're not even sure you're gay, are you?"

It's amazing how people zero in on my ambiguity and misinterpret it.

My thoughts are dominated by what happened with dad, with Kay, with John, with Kathleen. I've been dreaming every night of dad. I remember leaning over him in the hospital and kissing him, and saying a line from a song (a song that echoed in my mind all through Pat's death), "I want to kiss you all over." Dad's weak sleepy face immediately became playfully "shocked." I tried to feebly explain, "No! That's a line from a song!" but I'm still glad I said it to him. John was there and laughed. I guess I said that line to him because I knew in my heart he was dying, like Pat.

I just can't stop thinking about him. Lying there, probably knowing he was dying. "It's not in the cards," he said, and we all hoped we'd heard him wrong.

John & I emptied the trunk of his '73 Buick convertible and I found a beautiful black cashmere coat that *almost* fit me. I've brought it back to

San Francisco & had it cleaned. I also have the bottle of vitamins that I'd purchased & taken to the hospital for him. The nurses agreed to give them to him, but he only lived to take one.

I've just finished reading a book that has changed my life, entitled *Life After Life* by Dr. Raymond A. Moody, Jr. It's by a doctor who interviewed 150 people who had "near death" experiences or who were clinically "dead" but were resuscitated, and they tell what it felt like when they died. It is so incredible that it was hard for me to read, but what it was telling me! I saw dad going through so many things they described— they all described the same kind of experience—and I wonder how much he was really floating above us watching us care for his body in the bed. Like dreaming (and dad told me he was dreaming so much).

As I look in the mirror, I realize, I'm already having an out-of-body experience! I cannot believe that that is who I am…it may be *what* I am, but it certainly isn't *who* I am. If I were to look at myself and have to form an opinion of where that person was at, it certainly wouldn't be where I believe *I'm* at. That's why I love to look at T. Because that's where I'm at inside. He's the kind of person I would judge myself to be. I guess I've spent my whole life dreaming I was someone else, but no one else would believe me. So I have an operation & now they all believe me, but they can only give me part of my body.

I think of Genet, who wondered what two beautiful men thought when they faced each other.

Last night Erik Clark from Cleveland & Sean from the East Bay, both female-to-males who feel they are gay men, came over to talk. Both are in early stages of the change, i.e., are passing as men only sometimes. I see so much of myself in Erik physically.

Unfortunately a new book has come out *Female-to-Male Transsexualism* by a psychoanalyst Erik knows, which seems to be very derogatory & misleading. Of course I need to have / read it, but I hate to buy it & support this jerk's work. Just the few sentences Erik read made me so mad (e.g. he wrote that testosterone doesn't change one's musculature & that the only treatment for the acne side effect is discontinuing the hormone).

It's the ONLY thing published on the F→M and will be used as an authoritative text all over. Just meeting with Erik & Sean makes me feel like our situation *is* improving (at least we have each other to talk to, not like when I was first coming out), but then this book! One step forward and two steps backward.

We received the inventory of dad's worth & my calculations show I should get about $18,000—after taxes, lawyers, etc, it'll probably be closer to $10,000. I'll have enough to give T $2,000 toward his print shop & the $5,000 needed for genital surgery. I saw a F→M who had Laub's "wrap"[25] in which the labia minora is wrapped around the clit, silicone balls put in the labia majora, which is sewed together leaving the vagina a bit open. I've been pulling & stretching & rearranging, trying to conceive of an acceptable method for my own body. It truly shouldn't be so hard. (The F→M I saw was still very swollen from the operation—looked like he had 3 big blobs at his crotch, all looking alike). If I get the $$ in a timely manner, I may have it so that I'll be available for the operation after I leave ARCO & before I get another job as I'll probably be laid up about a month.

Well, as 1984 begins, I can't complain. T and I spent a quiet New Year's weekend…planted flower seeds in the backyard, shopped for a TV stand, went into some 25¢ peep shows, had fun sex—in fact, at

25   Procedure developed by Donald Laub (Stanford University Gender Dysphoria Program) similar to contemporary metoidioplasty.

midnight New Years Eve, T was shaving my pubic hair. We made a wish on a wishbone. I wished I'd have my surgery this year ✦ T would accept it ✦ it'd all work out. I won. Would be nice. I sent flowers to Kay, writing on the card that "Jack made me do it."

For our whole lives, our bodies are the only things we have here on earth. Life here is the body. Death is leaving the body behind.

I remember Beau: he had never seen snow ✦ he got up early to go to work, like T. His body was always warm ✦ sweet. T is Rich reincarnated. Trying to be real macho and cold, but really being soft and warm inside.

I think about myself ✦ cock surgery. The money will come from dad's estate. Now what am I waiting for? I no longer can dismiss the question with, "I don't have the money for it." Why do I hesitate to go for it now?

Once T asked me, "Haven't you ever felt like you wanted to stick something in somebody?" (or did he say "stick yourself inside something?") Anyway, I was really perplexed at the question. I would have to answer "no." When I see someone pretty, I just want to touch ✦ stroke them and tie them down so they can't even move an inch and run my hands all over them and use my finger to reach in his hole as I grasp his hard shapely cheek.

I guess that means I'd like to stick something inside somebody, but it doesn't mean I want to "stick myself inside somebody." It would be interesting ✦ fun to get my hips involved in that searching and reaching in him, and I'm sure if I had a cock, it would be a lot of fun to do that. But at the same time it's not a natural urge.

I just finished a marvelous masturbation session with my newfound jock stuffer. It's a cylindrical water balloon the very size of a cock that slips inside itself in a continuous motion, feeling much like the skin over a limp cock. I think a limp cock is so much more erotic than a hard one.

I put one in the jock cup-supporter pouch and I let another hang halfway out over the top of the pouch and hang it into a cup (fantasizing the cum will squirt into the cup to be eaten later) and then I reach underneath ✦ rub my clit like it were a little cock ✦ the limp cock hangs into a cup where it will soon pump out a white thick cum.

I remember when Kathleen's best friend Linda told me how women get pregnant. I was so relieved because I had imagined that a man urinated into a cup ✦ the woman drank it ✦ that's how she got the man's contribution into her "stomach." Maybe the eroticism of those childhood fantasies still rings my old bell.

Realizing I'm more turned on by a limp cock has opened a new reason why I should get cock surgery. One gripe is that the new "cock" doesn't get hard, but who cares? Just so when I touch it it's as good as an orgasm as I get now and, I tell you, I get WET when I cum. More now than before testosterone. If they could only reroute that fluid out my cock! If I could only be SURE I'd retain my ability to orgasm as deeply as I do now.

Sometimes I feel that I'll have to lose T in order to have cock surgery, like I felt I had to lose J to take hormones. Maybe yes, maybe no. I must think of *me*, tho.

I just don't think I write enough on how much I enjoy life lately. This change, this SEX CHANGE that is supposed to be so *weird*, has in reality made me feel LESS weird. I can relax ✦ laugh ✦ not THINK before I say or do something ✦ it all comes out right ✦ I'm relaxed ✦

I think, "My God, if they only knew..." I feel I should write about it (but who could relate to it? who is my audience? can they really accept anything I would say? Obviously they would think them the words of a mad person). It saddens me so much to think I am such a "freak" deep down, when I know I'm just like all these other guys.

Later for the first time I can remember, T let me "have" him. I was feeling him up ✦ he asked what I was doing. Told him I was feeling him up and asked, "Don't you like it?" He said yes, but he gets so tired. I told him he didn't have to do anything, just lay there. I got bolder in my kisses ✦ caresses ✦ concentrated on pleasuring myself.

Rubbed my little hard cock on his asscheek ✦ he obligingly laid his arms above his head submissively. I laid him back ✦ got on top of him like a man does ✦ rubbed my crotch against the bulge in his little underpants. Anyway I felt I was "using" him as he was limp in my arms ✦ it turned me on immensely until I, in fact, came. "Now was that so bad?" He said no. What a turn-on he is. How can I deny him anything?

The more I sit around thinking of what I want to do, I realize how important it is for me to seriously begin pursuing the penis surgery. I will begin by masturbating more ✦ looking at what's there now ✦ which parts are involved in sexual arousal. Not only does a man have a penis, but he's got his piss hole right on the end of it and, since reading *The G-Spot*, I've really noticed how touching or pressing my piss hole increases arousal. Can they close up the underside of my clitoris, inserting a semi-hard extension from my pisshole to its tip? I could stand to urinate then ✦ use my clit for sexual stimulation—wouldn't have to be big.

I made an appointment with Dr. Michael Brownstein, who does chest surgery on female-to-males and has a great reputation concerning scar revision techniques and he may be able to put something under my areolas to point them out and I'll just talk ✦ see what he can offer ✦ $ involved.

It's not how others perceive me that matters to me; it's how I perceive myself.

Can any remaining family sue me for telling [Garland's] story. How to find them...

Am making fabulous strides in my book about Jack Garland. Saw Allan Bérubé again at his new lecture ✦ he came to talk with me afterwards ✦ I showed him my research. I said I felt guilty like I'm moving in on "his" story, but he said emphatically, "Oh, no! No!"

Told him I'd phone him next wk ✦ we could get together. He was pleased. Said I was the best person to do a book on him. I'm considering the possible consequences of doing my book under my real name. So what? Just because it's a story about him, doesn't mean I'm one too. (Sorry, Jack. Survival. You know it well.) I'd like to have some accomplishment to show for myself. I feel if I really do get this book out ✦ selling, I will have made my life a success. And my diary could easily be edited ✦ published from beginning to 1980 under L.G.S Reed.

Entitled:
Jack Garland: The Daughter of SF's First Mexican Consul

He came in my bed last night ✦ this morn we had sex HIS way again, except he just lays there while I "fuck" him now until he comes in me. Then he asks me if I "like that," as tho he had done something for me. Ok, T have it your way. Judy Van Maasdam told the other F→M gay man I know that they don't think a F→M can make it as a gay man cuz they showed slides of the cock surg to a bunch of gay men ✦ they all said they weren't attracted to the cocks. Can you believe it? My answer to that is, if they'd showed the gay men slides of pussies, they'd've liked those EVEN LESS!

Despite what T says, I AM lonely. I feel like I'm the only one with this problem—a gay man in a woman's body—and so alone, so left out. I gather Jack Garland's remnants with delight ＋ think of his life compared to mine ＋ it does make me feel better. But not much.

T spent Sun nite ＋ Monday w/ his girlfriend. Mon nite I "waited up" for him, but truthfully I just couldn't sleep ＋ when he still wasn't home by 6:30 on Tues morn I broke down ＋ sobbed really hard, anticipating losing him. I know I will. I feel so helpless ＋ sorry for myself. So alone. So lonely.

All I can do is get more butch. Reapplied to Laub for the cock surgery ＋ my letter came back undeliverable as addressed. Guess they've moved.

T says he has no intentions of moving out of Page St. Neither do I. How'd he react if I suddenly found a side partner. I don't even want to face the issue of explaining my GROIN again ＋ having to deal with it.

Going back to Brownstein for surgery again. He'll put a silicone gel filled implant under my right nipple too it's not so caved in. $450.

T ＋ I had a very good talk this afternoon. He's laying on the couch watching TV ＋ SHE calls. I can tell immediately because his voice gets all giggly and soft. While he's talking to her, he beckons me to lay beside him on the couch. I do, after my first reaction of not wanting to.

After he hangs up he asks if I'm mad ＋ I ask him how'd he feel if I were saying, "Okay, baby, I love you, too" to someone else on the phone in front of him. Seriously, the expression on his face changed. I told him I felt sorry for myself because I have a fucked-up body ＋ anyone is always going to look better than me.

I told him if I'd've had a regular guy's body, I wouldn't even be having to think of these things. That I just want to get this weiner operation.

He said I should do what I have to do, but that after I did he would no longer be attracted to me sexually. I said I didn't think he only liked me for my pussy. He stumbled around his words, but finally ended up saying he didn't know how it would affect his feelings for me sexually. I felt a glimmer of hope that he just might not find it so awful.

I said I was tired of always pretending I'm a guy when I have sex and he said, "That's OK! I don't always think of myself as a guy when I'm having sex." I asked, "then why won't you be my girlfriend?"

T says I've got my priorities mixed up: I should buy a typesetter before I get this weiner operation. What a riot!

Am working hard on Garland's story ✦ almost come to tears going thru her parents' personal letters now at the Bancroft Library in Berkeley. Have discovered more about her family. Piece by piece.

Went to see Brownstein yesterday ✦ the implants do have to come out—he's going to special order one with half the fill of silicone, as now I have too much "projection". I'm pissed, but it's feeling less sore and this morn I notice my nipple is real sensitive and I definitely feel that sensual bee-line to my crotch when I stroke it. So glad the feeling is there—in fact has intensified. Gives me good vibes ✦ hopes for good feelings after the cock op.

How about this ad?

Sensual 35-year-old with child-sized pee pee seeks fun guys.

Write J re: lipo ✦ gays.

I gather each tidbit, each lead I pursue as tho I am finding someone with whom I am in love. Jack Garland is my dad. The coroner's report said he had cancer of the liver ✦ spleen. When I first read it, I thought it said she had iron-gray eyes, but today I looked closer and it said brown eyes ✦ iron gray hair. She had hair like an old man… and I think of dad's beautiful white locks.

Wasn't even going to go to the Calif Historical Society a second time, because I found out the first visit they didn't have anything. But wanted to see if they had any of the newspapers missing from the libraries. They didn't. So I am aimlessly wandering through the newspaper file and saw there was an index to a SF newspaper from 1896–1903! So far there's been no indices to the newspapers… I've had to just view the microfilm aimlessly to happen on an article by or about her.

(I like to call him "her" because it reminds me where I came from and how lucky I am… how Jack Garland wanted to be Jack Garland! I wonder if I'd've had the strength to live full-time as a man before the luxury of hormones/surgery. I feel I want to have all the surgery—to go all the way, in memory of Jack Garland.)

The index had one article on her I didn't, described as story on Babe Bean with portrait. Of course when I looked up the newspaper reference the article wasn't there. So now I'm following another lead. I know there's another article with more more precious info—and a PORTRAIT. Not just a "cut," as they described the line drawings.

Tomorrow I go to an all-day (T asks "all-GAY?") workshop on how to get your book published, conducted by a literary agent here in San Francisco—they've been recommended to me twice. Called Chris, who's another F→M gay man moved here recently from Cleveland ✦ is my age, and who's trying to get his stuff published, ✦ he wants to go, too. I'm gonna get this book on Jack published.

Tomorrow I see Paul Walker to try to enlist him in my quest for Laub's surgery. I'm very nervous about how to state my case and know I must try very hard to keep my personal feelings about Judy Van Maasdam's unprofessional conduct out of it. I've gone thru my copies of my correspondence with Laub's office, and the whole thing is even more absurd when I see in 1981 they did agree to "evaluate" me with Fisk and now, after 4 ½ years living as a man, they won't even do that. I've never been very good at manipulating or politicking, but that's the phase of transition I'm in now.

In one hour I must leave to go meet one of the respondents to my Personals ad. He sounds FANTASTIC and even had experience previously dating a F→M gay man in NY!! This is too good to be true. He's a singer in SF cabarets ✝ sent a photo ✝ is very cute!

We have 2 choices in finding a mate: someone who is just your type, or someone whose type *you* are; that is, someone *you* choose, or someone who chooses you. Impossible to find that special person who meets all those requirements.

You can't always get what you what, but if you try sometimes you find you get what you need: Thursday had good sex and orgasms with Joseph, the cabaret singer, and last night with Monica, the male-to-female transvestite. They both think I'm sexier THAN!

Finally got my computer ✝ am inputting Jack Garland's story. How easy it's going! The typesetter is finally working ✝ T ✝ I are going to get this business going. He still spends weekends with his girlfriend ✝ I go on ✝ off being jealous. I haven't put any time/effort into getting together with my other sex partners—just lack of interest. T says he "likes having a girlfriend" which I think says it well…it's not so much that SHE'S so great, but he likes being the male ✝ probably likes having access to female finery.

Cuca *&* I went out last night *&* T gave us a ride to the Mission District with his girlfriend in the car—most unfriendly *&* cold *&* I even felt better about his "having a girlfriend" now that I've spent a few minutes with her. As Cuca put it, it didn't look like they were going to have a very good time and "T deserves better." I feel so very unsexual lately.

So much going on I can't believe life moves as quickly as it does. Kathleen does have multiple sclerosis *&* I've been haunted by the thought of her. She's still in the hospital, but now in physical therapy where they're showing her how to dress herself *&* how to walk. She still isn't making it to the bathroom…I guess she can't feel it coming.

I made reservations to go to Milwaukee, then cancelled them—I can't face going back there again for another bum trip à la Jack *&* Patrick, but I can't think of it that way—she's not dead. But she is there in Milw all alone with mom. Anyway I've made another reservation *&* will be going to Milw [for two weeks]. She's sounding better on the phone—her voice isn't so slurred and monotone.

Meanwhile I landed a fuckin GREAT job. The ACLU never even called me for an interview, but the guy I worked with at ARCO for whom I've done some freelance typing referred me to his neighbor. His neighbor, John Woolsey, has a 2-floor flat…the upper floor of his offices for his sales promotion/premium/sweepstakes business he's moving out here to SF from NJ.

He *&* his rich wife live on the bottom floor. He's got an IBM computer just like mine (but a better printer) and needs someone to input his data *&* "grow with the company" and he hopes to have a location *&* 7 employees in a year. I'm working 2 days a week for him for $12 an hour! So I've worked 4 days so far *&* got paid $309…OFF THE BOOKS…CASH IN HAND. Am still collecting unemployment *&* looks like my cash flow problems are over.

I've completely typeset my 1985 edition of *Information for the Female-to-Male* and need to paste it up *&* get it to T to print *&* place ads in gay/women's papers, etc.

Meanwhile I'm on the Newsletter Committee of the newly-formed San Francisco Bay Area Gay and Lesbian Historical Society, but haven't really had to put out yet. I will, though, in the beginning of June. Will typeset ✦ paste up what others have written ✦ T will print so it'll be ready for this year's Gay Parade.

Meanwhile T's alternately telling me 1. he doesn't want to have sex with me anymore, and then 2. having sex with me. I feel really awful that he doesn't desire me anymore, but try to remember that I didn't change my sex in order to have a great sex life, rather in order to live comfortably from day to day.

I talked with Steve Dain on the phone during one of my "down" days and he always makes me feel better. Seems the topic of rejecting me (because I'm gay) for the surgery is becoming something people are discussing ✦ are also angry about. I feel too wasted to pursue surgery right now—will save my $$ and wait until after September as Paul Walker recommends.

Meanwhile my sex partner Joseph phoned ✦ is "so busy" being a successful cabaret singer in SF that we haven't gotten together, but we will in the future I'm sure.

I am ashamed to admit that I shaved off the whiskers Grandmother stroked ✦ encouraged me to grow out ✦ shape, just for T, because he promised that, if I did, after we had sex he would sleep with me.

Just saw Paul Walker. Went to see his secretary (I was in the neighborhood) for some addresses ✦ Paul was right there alone, xeroxing transsexual pamphlets. He invited me in to "chat," told me he hadn't forgotten me, but said he hasn't been able to get into a long discussion with Judy Van Maasdam about it yet, but "it's not only Fisk, it's Laub, too. They said they want to free the world of homosexuality by offering sex change surgery."

Told him Dain suggested I not be so honest with future doctors about my perception of myself as a gay man, but that I couldn't do that. Walker said I shouldn't lie.

I didn't tell him this but I've been having some very educational masturbatory sessions to see what is doing what, and think I'd like my future surgeon to watch me masturbate to see what is doing what, and to make it all where it should be.

I just realized that I use my hands a lot as a sensory extension (typing, writing, I just bought an old upright *piano* for $375!) to compensate for the lack of a penis as a sensory extension…

Reaching out to stimulate my body as a way of feeling alive.

Everything is going my way. Got my piano. Practicing Mahler. T finally finished printing my F→M booklet. And today I bought a 1985 Honda Rebel motorcycle for $1,350.

Well, I just feel so goddamn cool on my new motorcycle. It is a "dream machine." So easy to handle and just *glides* me from here to there. I'm plenty happy with myself. After all this time, I finally got a cool motorcycle. I've wanted one since 1973. No lie. And after I get my permanent cycle rider's license and get more comfortable on it, I'm a'ginna join a gay men's motorcycle club and see iffin I kin find myself a motorcycle daddy! YEE HA

Sunday morn I awoke feeling very down.

Took my coffee into the back room where my finches were, fed
them and sat watching them chirping around. Sunday eve I covered
their cages because it's been especially cold lately, and more so in
that backroom where we put them because Kath's in the front room.
Monday I ran off to work hassled and had to stay overnight house &
dog sitting for Woolsey's.

Tuesday T said he glanced into the room & thought to feed the birds,
but was in a hurry & decided to do it later. Wednesday, this morning, I
uncovered their cages to feed them and all four finches were dead. I am
so full of grief.

T was the only one home with me at the time & I'm so glad. We sat &
cried, knowing they'd died from our neglect and they probably starved
to death in those few days. T told me to put them in a box "and put a
paper with a prayer in it and tell them that we're sorry."

We've been so busy taking care of everybody and everything else that
our sweet Little Guys were the ones to suffer. Only a few weeks ago the
clerk at the pet shop marvelled that my guys were nearly 7 years old
when they usually only live 2 or 3.

We put our faces together and cried.

T & I drove to the Cliff House & buried them in the forest of trees nearby.

2 days T tried his damndest to have pussy sex with me... just constantly
tried to stick it in, but I just kept moving away. Guess I can't blame him
for trying since every other time I've made that rule I've allowed it to
be broken.

Last night T had me take some photos of him in his print shop to take
to Puerto Rico. When I offered to have the film developed, he said
there were some pictures of his girlfriend on the rolls & she wanted to
take them for developing. I felt hurt & I cried for a long time alone.

Told him I felt I didn't belong with him—that he's ashamed of me ✦ after all these years together I don't deserve that. He got upset ✦ denied being ashamed ✦ asked for evidence. I said "No one's taking pictures of ME to take to Puerto Rico." He got mad ✦ stormed down to his shop.

Set up the camera to take automatic photos of me ✦ us together (his arm around my shoulders) in the shop. In bed I masturbated while playing with him ✦ he didn't try anything funny. He really wants to keep me.

It's 5 am and I'm wide awake fuming about something Paul Walker said yesterday during my appointment. He acknowledged that Laub's refusal to operate on me smacked of homophobia ✦ that someone needed to challenge that for the sake of gay rights. But in order to challenge him they needed a "squeaky clean" case like Matlovich in fighting gay discrimination in the Army. But that I've been "doing everything with everybody" ✦ so they can't challenge him.

What in the hell does he mean?

I've hardly been doing everything with everybody. I've still never had sex with a female as a female. I've had 2 long-term relationships with men who consider themselves bisexual ✦ with whom I felt as a gay man, and all my other flings on the side have been with gay men. I've felt ✦ acted consistently as a gay man since I "came out" in 1973! I'm going to phone him ✦ demand further clarification on that one. Is it because some of these guys stuck it in the wrong hole??

Walker said he only recommended I should get a girlfriend cuz he was worried I have "fem-a-phobia" or an intense fear of females ✦ I'm wanting a sex change to run away from women.

When I got up to leave he said he wanted to give me a hug, and did.

His fees are $85 per hour.

This whole week it's been pouring rain—I've been caught in it while on my motorcycle more than once.

Bought some piano music books—old Beatles and old Bob Dylan. Am really looking for Joni Mitchell songs.

Finally bought an 8 mm movie projector tonight to view the old porn movies Howard Beck sent me. They sure turn me on (gay and straight films) and I can see this film collection will be a valuable outlet for me for the rest of my life.

Thursday evening I bumped into Leon + Russell, the 2 gay roommates upstairs (not lovers) in the gay bar on Haight. They know nothing of my past identity. I spilled my guts to Leon about T, etc, even got super drunk (coming on quickly) + puked in Leon's toilet. T came upstairs to see what I was doing but left quickly when we began watching a movie. Sure gives me insight to talk to Leon as a gay man-to-man about life + relationships.

Yesterday afternoon took my motorcycle to The Eagle, the gay bar that's the headquarters for the motorcycle clubs. Lots of really nice-looking men and I felt really cool to be able to park my bike out there with the rest of them. I felt like I was among friends though I knew no one, and I know I'll be able to be among them and things will be OK after I get the rest of my body done. I'm so goddamned tired of being a freak. Life is passing me by and everyone else finds their slot, but I'm always on the outside looking in.

I was so tempted to approach one of the guys in the motorcycle club to ask about joining up, but at that time I still didn't have my permanent driver's license + besides, maybe I'll try to find out about the requirements for joining before I humiliate myself face-to-face with one of the guys. Maybe they don't accept wimps. But I think I'll hang out there more often. My kinda place.

Another good thing is it's sunny ✦ warm ✦ today's the second day in a row I've been able to strip off my shirt ✦ sit in the park ✦ get some sun on my chest ✦ back. Almost better than sex.

On a 24-hour notice I flew with Kathleen's Jim to Milwaukee to get some of their belongings ✦ drive back to San Francisco.

Because we're towing something, Jim has to drive slow. Cross-country truck drivers in their rigs come up behind him and pass us. After they pass us on the left Jim gives them a signal that they are clear of him ✦ it's OK for them to change into the lane ahead of us by flashing the van lights off ✦ on. Then the trucker puts on his right turn signal and pulls in front of us. Most of the time they will flash their truck light back at us to thank Jim for signaling. It's such a warm sign of camaraderie—

Plus it's exciting because each truck has a different configuration of lights on them—some along the top, or along the sides and bottom— some trucks look like Christmas trees, they're so lit up! And when the truckers flash back their thanks—their flashing shows something of their personalities.

Yesterday T appeared at our door with an actual armful of carnations, pink, red, lavender. He teased me saying a secret lover of mine asked him to give them to me, but later admitted he'd found them in a garbage can!

Saw Brownstein yesterday ✦ I may be able to get this cock operation by him here in SF *soon*.

WOW it's like before it would never happen, and now suddenly it's happening NOW.

I'll be in the hospital only one night. He said $5000. Great. So his secretary phoned in the order for the implants ＋ made sure they could get 'em soon; then phoned ＋ scheduled me into the hospital for surgery Tuesday morn 4/22.

I look between my legs to say goodbye, like I said to my breasts, but I don't see anything to say goodbye to.

The tight pants I have that I may not be able to wear anymore.

T had a terrible reaction when I said next Tuesday. He said it was too soon and he needed more notice than that! I asked what the hell HE need more notice for!

Know I cannot rely on him to do anything for me while recovering from my surgery. But Bridget ＋ Maryellen are very willing to be on-call for me and even Jim/Kathleen are offering their place for me to come over + Jim will nurse me, too.

I AM READY

T asks how do I know I'm ready. I can just tell. I am finally finishing what I began 6 years ago.

I feel like there's so much to do to prepare, but can't think of what. Pack my pajamas, have food in the house, get some reading material. I may have to lay in bed a week ＋ TV is too much to bear that long.

So I'm finally a <u>MAN</u> ! Went to the hospital yesterday morning. Brownstein came in dressed in 1930s-style gangster clothes (he's really handsome) carrying a box. He asked if it was OK if he took photos of the surgical process because it really is innovative. I eagerly consented, hoping it will benefit others. I don't remember anything after being wheeled into the operating room.

I couldn't see of course, but Maryellen said it looked really good (she could have just been saying that, though—she sure couldn't tell me it looked lousy!).

So with catheter bag in hand, I came home Wednesday afternoon.

Waddled into my place; T gave me no special notice or attention. Bridget dashed in about 7 pm to give me dinner. Maryellen came later & I got up & washed my hair.

In the middle of the night I took my first painkiller. My crotch was burning! I had a bad dream that the catheter came out & I was peeing all over everything. This morning Bridget popped in with coffee, donuts, & a newspaper. Steve Dain called back & we talked a long time. He takes care of people who have no one else after Laub operates on then, so he knows post-surgery well. Said I could probably take a shower.

T said he didn't want to see it until I was all healed & the hair grown back. I don't blame him, cuz it ain't a pretty sight right now, and I sure don't need him to get that first impression of it.

OOCH - OUCH

I keep trying to think all this discomfort will pass, won't this summer be great, etc etc but right now I'm too worried about being able to piss.

Got 3 blissful hours of rest. Awoke feeling like going to a restaurant for breakfast, but after washing my hair in preparation, I realized I was acting a little too hasty & spry, and had better take it slow. So I cooked my own breakfast, then went outside & laid on the deck in our backyard, with my robe discreetly open in order to get some sun and air on my wounds, to dry up the sore tissues.

Maryellen came by and took some photos of my crotch, so I'll have some "one week after surgery" views.

This is all going to be

PERFECT!

I just want to make those muscles contract until I'm exhausted in dizzy sensuality.

Testicles! Balls ! ! Balls !!

Well, ball now.

Appointment to see Brownstein cuz I wanted him to take out a few stitches and take a look at the deal.

I laid back on the table. I had only had 2 sugar donuts ＊ 2 cups of coffee all day ＊ I was feeling the vapors! The fucking guy tells me he's going to remove the implant on the spot and then I really *had* the vapors.

He said he'd replace it with the next size smaller ＊ I just felt like I'll just lay right there until he gets it by 24-hour express delivery.

So the whole aftermath of this is that I have to go through probably the next month with only one ball.

Oh, I just felt awful. I FEEL awful.

I was ready to ride that big wave of loving my body and wanting others to love it, and to loving and wanting *theirs*. But the humiliation of my incomplete body continues to plague me.

I can't tell you how sorry I felt for myself, I dragged home like I'd been butchered ＊ went right to bed, I was shivering cold. So glad T wasn't home cuz I didn't want to talk to anyone.

I felt closer to crying real tears than I can remember. Since dad or Kathleen or whatever latest tragedy—I guess the finches dying when T & I cried so hard together.

I'm glad I beat off as much as I did when I could these past few days, cuz right now it's hard to feel real gorgeous.

I'm healing up, but somehow I think, slowly.

He said he'd put a smaller size testicle in my left ball and I'm glad. It's sexy to have a bigger & a smaller ball.

Kathleen went to the hospital about a mile from my place for 2 weeks of chemotherapy.

What in the hell can be done ?

What I see when sitting back and looking down at myself.

Terry phoned last night. He asked what was happening with Paul Walker...that he's "shutting down his business" and rumor is he has AIDS! I was really shocked but not surprised. Of course, now I have to think of a tactful way of finding out if this is true or not. If so, I will really be able to say this AIDS epidemic among gay men has really touched my life. Over 1,000 gay men in San Francisco have died so far of this..."venereal disease," as I see it. I'm going to really feel bad, too, if it is true, because usually a man dies within 2 years of discovering he has the disease.

I'm so glad to be 35.

Ma phones today, says I'm "getting to be an old broad" and that she remembered two things about me—my pink tutu and purple leotards, and when I was in the pool alone because I disliked being splashed. Not hard to understand, as she made a videotape of us as children and those were the 2 scenes I was in—with the tutu, and in the pool.

I remember my 4th birthday party, when I was Davy Crockett.

Saw a 1919 German gay silent film this last weekend. What a treasure to be in San Francisco and have such an opportunity to see such a gem. The film speaker said that, in those days, being gay meant being "in the Life." I like to think of myself that way—of being in the life.

This afternoon had my surgery—it's 9 pm now. It hurts as much as it did the first time, except this time I don't have the catheter. I've smoked 2 joints, taken a Vicodin ＆ I think that reefer took the pain away.

I feel like I've been cut up, which I have.

YOUCH!

I'm still nursing my precarious left ball.

I lay in bed hardly moving all day ＆ even T finally took pity on me ＆ boiled some eggs for me, made me some cereal ＆ tea, brought me a banana.

Thought about a lot of things yesterday... Jack; Kathleen; Bridget ＆

her kids are moving to Pennsylvania next week; J; T; I'm really feeling I need to fall in love with myself before involving myself in another intimate relationship. That's why I wanted to change my sex in the first place...so that I could love myself, sleep with myself, know myself and enjoy everyday living. It's as though I'm playing my favorite game all day, and now it's just become so easy ✦ natural ✦ fun that I don't want anything else. I want to learn to love my body ✦ feel all its sensations, to be with other guys who look at my body and they want to "dick off" too. It sure is hard when my body won't cooperate with my quickly changing psyche.

I'll tell you one thing—
I'll be plenty pissed if I'm not plenty healed by the time I finish you, diary, and begin another book...and I'd say that's giving me PLENTY time.

Yesterday, upon first glance and without any question, Brownstein removed my left ball again. It wasn't as painful as I'd expected and almost immediately I felt a whole lot better physically. Maryellen has been very supportive, driving me back, having me over for supper.

He says I must wait for 6 months before he'll try to put in another testicle. I feel the year is shot...that I better re-prioritize all those things I've been putting off "until I'm all healed up." Doesn't seem that that will be til 1987. Of course I feel sorry for myself. But I am happy I have *something*.

Yesterday 1,000 gay men marched through the streets of San Francisco chanting:

"WHAT DO WE WANT ?"
" SODOMY."
"WHEN DO WE WANT IT ?"
" NOW!"

I met with a 22-year-old female who feels she is a gay man. How wonderful it was for me to be there for her—telling her she's NOT the only one and she HASN'T invented a brand new perversion that's never been heard of before.

She's been prowling the libraries as I had, trying to find a single mention of such feelings. She's seeing a psychologist in Berkeley & finally told him about 2 months ago how she felt. Her shrink phoned Paul Walker to see if he ever heard of this, and Paul referred him to me.

We talked for several hours and she said I don't know how great it was to meet me, but then quickly added, "well, maybe you do."

This evening met with 2 FTMs: John Leiken (who I met maybe 5 years ago at Christopher's apartment here in the City) and Brice Roycell, 39 yrs old, who started hormones 12 yrs ago (an old-timer). We spent several hours talking, of course. They wanted to see my genitoplasty. It was fantastic talking to these "more experienced" guys instead of me being the one further along the way. I know they both really liked me & somehow treated me with more respect & acceptance as a gay man than I sometimes feel from my hetero peers. I gave them both a copy of my book & John expressed an interest in doing some publishing.

Last Friday Jim Burrell & I were coming out of a movie theater after seeing *The Mystery of Alexina*, based on the book *Herculine Barbin:*

Being the Recently Discovered Memoirs of a 19th Century French Hermaphrodite. A Black FTM gay man, Chad (who I met last year at the FTM picnic) was with his white FTM lover (who says he likes girls better) and recognized me. We all went out to a gay men's bar on Polk St. + talked a long time. Chad will see me Monday about typesetting for some things he wants to publish.

All of a sudden I have a million FTM contacts.

I feel like I'm choking back the tears, I am so proud and happy to be in San Francisco.

I've gotta find somebody to play with and am very acutely aware that, once I find someone, I'll beat myself over the head for the months (nay, years!) I've mourned over T.

I think the open wound in my left sac has finally healed closed. Poor Lou.

I've been putting in some volunteer time working at the "No On Proposition 64" campaign headquarters. It's a California state proposition to put victims of the AIDS virus into quarantine—a super vicious and anti-gay measure perpetrated by right-winger Holy Rollers.

Went to sign up today for a therapy group forming for "gay men with hidden disabilities" and sounds like I certainly qualify. I told the coordinator nothing of my female past but was totally honest in all other respects.

SOME OF MY CHIN HAIRS
CUT 9/24/86

John,[26] a "well-known" F→M phoned me to say he'd like to get a
female-to-male group going ϕ someone suggested he call me because I
might want to, too. I was so flattered he'd call ME.

I'm very excited by the idea of calling a gathering of F→M's just to talk
to each other, exchange information, ϕ just "be there" for new F→M's
coming out.

I'm very excited...oh, I already said that...but I *am*, about maybe even
getting a small newsletter going ϕ I'm sure it's possible if we can get
other F→M's to "sign up." And you know how I LOVE to put little
newsletters together! I've been xeroxing old 1980 issues of *The Gateway*
I did for Golden Gate Girls/Guys and I must pin roses on myself ϕ say
they were great little publications!

26   John Armstrong

I laughed to Terry, "Gee I never really thought of myself as one of the old timers!" I feel really proud of that status.

Have put in quite a few hours cataloging periodicals at the SF Bay Area Gay ☽ Lesbian Historical Society and will meet tomorrow morn with a lesbian who will show me how to use a database program on the computer so we can log this info.

Jan Morris, a renowned travel writer from Britain, was signing her travel memoirs downtown. She had changed sex male-to-female many years ago and wrote a short autobiography, *CONUNDRUM*, published 1974! I took my old beat-up paperback copy and apologized to her for its condition, but that it had come a long way with me. Told her I'd changed female-to-male 7 years ago. She seemed pleased and asked "have you lived happily ever after?"

Can't wait to get my other ball!

I wish I could stop loving T, but he came into my bed yesterday morn ☽ initiated sex. As usual the main activity was try to put your dick in Lou's cunt. I said no ☽ he said "everyone gets to have fun but him." I asked who he was talking about.

In the *5 years* we've been having sex we've ALWAYS done it his way ☽ NEVER what I want. God, what a selfish lover.

I know it's just that I'm so starved for a gentle touch that I'll put up with his selfishness.

So Jim Burrell & I just rented an apartment at 124 ALBION ST. If you can believe that ! ! ! It's perfect & I feel excellent & with no hesitation about leaving Page Street. Decided yesterday for sure that it's time for me to move, and this was only the 4th place we looked at.

I talked seriously to T yesterday about moving & he was very amiable & took my hand & hoped we can remain friends & I can keep my office room on Page Street at no rent & I can take the television, etc, etc and I didn't have to be out right away but could move stuff at my leisure, etc.

I thought it would take us at least a month to find a nice place, but there it was & the landlord/lady didn't even check our references, but took Jim's check & gave us both a set of keys! Jim and I just clasped each other & jumped for joy in the kitchen!

I look around the place on Page Street & see very little I intend to take with me, as far as furniture, etc. We should have no problem dividing our possessions—it's fairly clear who owns what.

                                        1987 has GOT to be a good year...

T actually was getting choked up that I'm leaving and said he doesn't think I'm ugly & disgusting & should have TALKED with him about moving out. I told him we've had this same talk for a year & a half now and I DON'T WANNA TALK.

He never really thought I would go...

I can't believe I've lived with this guy 5 years and the last two have been so sad...

T says there's two kinds of sadness: 1. the kind where somebody dies in your family and 2. when you see something sad on TV. That almost made me laugh.

He came over and hugged me & I hugged him back.

December 1986 – March 1991

"I still would like to believe that a few simple carnal pleasures can still be mine."

Albion Street
San Francisco, California

Goodbye is too good a word, babe
So I just say fare thee well.

Bob Dylan, "Don't Think Twice, It's Alright"

I'LL BE ON
ALBION
AND TURN THE PAGE
ON PAGE

Somehow I feel so light and free, sitting in my bed in our new apartment. Stayed overnight here for the first time last night and no way could I fall asleep.

I was helping T in the print shop and the perfect song came on the radio. I sang along aloud to him.

Oh, this freedom is going to nurture me.

Amazing how relaxed ✦ at home I feel on Albion St.

Jim ✦ I are getting along famously. He can be a rather "excitable" person but I just ignore that. Am still sorting ✦ arranging ✦ organizing the apartment…it is a bit smaller than Page ✦ I think I better start getting rid of some of the stuff (especially clothes) that I've had for 10+ years.

I have noticed several times a day I have a shortness of breath, as though I cannot take a deep breath…Maryellen says it's because I don't breath properly ＋ I should take some *yoga* breathing classes. I guess I'm "excitable" in other ways.

I don't think even I realize what a stressful thing I did by busting outa Page St. Five years living with T…I almost feel ashamed at having stayed there that long.

He was a sweet boy, but became the kind of man I can do nicely without—

Well, diary, I didn't think I'd be writing the Last Chapter so soon. My penmanship is pretty bad because I have an intravenous needle in my right wrist ＋ I'm in the hospital.

I have AIDS.

How in the hell could this have happened? I, who have been a sexual recluse for so long, contracted a disease associated with promiscuity…a fatal disease.

I guess I first noticed my weakness ＋ shortness of breath when I was moving. I explained it away as a chest cold, as a lack of proper diet, as being "out of shape." Sometimes I'd be walking ＋ have to stop ＋ wait until I caught my breath. I was taking decongestants ＋ figured my sinuses, which were clear, were draining into my chest.

I went to the Gay Historical Society meetings ＋ a friend said it sounded like I had "walking pneumonia" ＋ should see a doctor pronto. I made an appointment to see Fulmer, my endocrinologist, on Dec 31. But by noon of the 30th, while working on a temporary job downtown, I felt like I just couldn't take one more step, my heart was beating so fast, I was panting for air.

Rode my motorcycle to the Haight Ashbury Free Clinic, but they had no doctor there ＋ referred me to another walk-in clinic. With great effort I rode there ✝ found a "we have closed this location go to another location" sign. Rode my cycle there ✝ they immediately took chest X-rays ✝ said get to the hospital <u>now</u>. The doc didn't want me to ride my cycle to the hospital so called Maryellen ✝ she came to get me. But didn't want to leave the cycle on the street, so I rode it to Mary's while she drove behind me. Went to UC Medical Center Emergency ✝ [they] almost immediately assumed it was AIDS…pneumocystis carinii pneumonia.

I was put on oxygen ✝ the AIDS antibiotic right away ✝ it looked bad. They said my case was well advanced. I don't remember much of the first few days in the hospital but had fitful sleep where I dreamt that a Boogie Man was after me. Maryellen slept on the extra bed in my hosp. room.

Was it Wednesday or Thursday morn? they took a bronchio-scope. Shot me up with morphine ✝ deadened my throat ✝ stuck a camera down my mouth into my lungs. They shot some fluid into the lungs ✝ scraped some tissue out for analysis. The doc even let me look at the pictures they were seeing inside me. Maryellen was falling apart ✝ I urged her to call Bridget ✝ I'd pay her airfare from Penn. so Mary didn't have to face this alone. Ma said she would come, too.

Friday T was visiting me, brought me a holly plant, when the docs came in and told me the test results were positive that I have AIDS— Acquired Immune Deficiency Syndrome. They explained every case is different, but prior patients have lasted from a few months to a few years. That I would surely be in ✝ out of the hospital often before I die.

I guess it was Saturday that ma ✝ Bridget flew in.

I'm sure I've been in just a state of shock ✝ disbelief. How in the hell did I get this when I haven't even been having sex with anyone. I can count on one hand the number of sex partners I've had since I moved in with T. My main thoughts were completing my Jack Garland story ✝ publishing you, diary. But it appeared even that wouldn't happen. And I guessed that this would definitely prevent me from ever completing my surgery. What a rip-off.

Of course the whole family is stricken with grief. The misfortune in the Sullivan family has just been too much.

The last time T visited I could see the terrible sadness lined into his face. He said he lit a candle for me & that the flame burned high & strong for a long time so he was sure it was a good sign. Kathy Steininger's boyfriend came in to visit & T kissed me goodbye on the forehead right in front of him. He tries to project optimism but I know he's hurting inside.

Each day I'm feeling stronger. I get intravenous antibiotics every 6 hrs called Septra. I had a fungus growth on my tongue & mouth but it went away with a few tablets. It was pretty gross, though.

Jim & Joe came to visit & Jim's eager for me to come home & still wants me as a roommate.

I phoned Brownstein on Monday & told him. He was very upset & said he felt awful. I asked if this definitely nixes giving me my left ball & he said he wouldn't completely rule it out, but that he has to talk to a lot of people & find out a lot more before he could make a decision about what this means.

The docs say I could be out of the hospital maybe even next week, but that I almost certainly will return with Pneumocystis again. They gave me permission to bring my computer to the hospital so I can work on the Garland book. I will be put on disability and state medical aid & guess I never have to work again.

It really hasn't hit me that I am about to die. I see the grief around me, but inside I feel serene & a certain kind of peace. My whole life I've wanted to be a gay man & it's kind of an honor to die from the gay men's disease.

I'm recovering & feeling so well that I'm beginning to think this is all a big joke! Wednesday & Thursday I threw up once each day, but yesterday kept my food down without any anti-nausea medicine. I've been taking showers by myself without getting winded ＋ venturing out into the hallway, altho I wear a surgical mask to protect myself from other people's germs.

T comes to visit every 2–3 days. I urged him to wear a rubber when he has sex to be safe. He said it's too late for the relationships he's in… they've been exchanging bodily fluids for 2 years…but he will wear a condom if he has sex with anyone else. I'm sure he's not telling Paprika anything about my condition or his possible exposure to the virus.

The thing that hurts me most is to think that I will never know a man's loving touch on my whole completed body. That even though I may still be able to undergo the surgery to get my left testicle, that because of my disease I will never find a lover who will suck me, lick me, kiss me there.

How close I was ! How good it feels to have even one ball! a miniscule cock!

And now I feel like a leper, something diseased ＋ fearsome ＋ unlovable.

Monday afternoon they discharged me from the hospital. I was so excited to go home, I was completely exhausted once I got there. Maryellen has been by my side on a minute's notice ＋ really an invaluable assistance at all times. I can't imagine how I'd get through all this without her.

So good to be home, but rather frightening. I feel like, hey, I got this deadly disease ＋ no one can give me any guidance as to how to manage it or what I should do differently—other than eat well, get lots of rest, wear gloves when I change the newspaper in the bottom of the birdcage.

It's impossible to watch TV or read the paper without hearing something about AIDS ✦ how so many people are dying from it. I still can't believe this is going to kill me, but sometimes I feel so tired, I believe it could.

Social Security Admin sent a man over yesterday who filled out all the forms for me to get money from them—today the hospital filed for me to get Medi-Cal to pay my medical bills. It's like if you got AIDS you instantly get total disability ✦ the state pays all bills ✦ all you need to do is wait around to die.

Thanks a lot.

John arrived in San Francisco from Milwaukee last night and is very upset about my diagnosis. He's studying the AIDS-virus literature and is dreaming up ways to combat it.

I know this is terrible, especially to write in a diary I hope to publish one day, but it's bothering me a lot since a phone call from ma ✦ Grandmother this afternoon. When I was talking to ma, she assured me that she would be right by my side the whole time I will be deathly sick and she'll hold me in her arms my last moments. But that is not how I want to die—I do not want to be in the clutches of mourners when I take my last breath. So how DO I want to die? In whose arms would I like to be?

I read the obituaries of other gay men dying of AIDS and it really chokes me up with emotion when it says they died in the arms of their lovers. But I haven't a lover, and one who may materialize between now and then may not be close enough to my heart to merit those last moments with me.

How do I want to die?

I would like to die alone. Does that sound crazy? I have always envisioned myself laying on my deathbed and looking back to reassess what I've done on earth. I have always said that, when I'm laying there,

I will be the only one that matters, and I don't want to have to realize that I wasted my life or didn't accomplish what I wanted to. I will be the only one laying there knowing whether I blew it or not, and when I am laying there and knowing I'm ending my time here, I want to be alone and at peace with myself.

How can I make that clear to everyone, that this solitude in death—which everyone fears—is precisely what I want....

In San Francisco this past month (Jan 1987), 93 new cases of AIDS were reported, and I supposed I was counted among these statistics. Good news is I gained 3 lbs.... Well, maybe only 2 because this time I wore my heavy motorcycle boots.

[Dr. Hollander] suggested I take an experimental drug that may possibly retard the spreading of the AIDS virus in my body & brain, called AZT. Have to take every 4 hrs. "indefinitely."

I asked him if I'm going to just keel over one day & die suddenly, or will I be sick & then die ? He smiled & nodded.

Bert's (the guy who was killed with Patrick) brother lives nearby in a houseboat he built, and John contacted him. So yesterday we went on his boat, which is powered by a diesel-engined paddle (like in Mark Twain on the Mississippi), out onto the SF Bay, under the Golden Gate Bridge and down near Alcatraz. A beautiful day & the most fun I've had in a long time.

John introduced me to Ebby (Bert's brother) as his brother Lou. Poor Ebby was so confused. He was certain John's only brother was killed with his only brother, and he looked so confused that I said to him, "The reason you don't remember me is because I had a sex change from a girl. I used to be Sheila." Well, he seemed relieved!

Went to see Brownstein this morning & he kind of pissed me off.

He didn't ask me to undress so he could look at me, but ushered me into his office & said we'd decide whether to do the surgery! I said I definitely wanted it & he said I should ask my UC doc what will happen if I get an infection. Once I get an answer, then we'll schedule the surgery for next week.

He was very concerned about himself—would he get AIDS if he stuck himself with the needle he'd use to sew me up ? And he said a Black nurse who'd be attending agreed to sew me up if he didn't want to. Pisses me off. I asked if this is a common normal occurrence that he's sticking himself with needles. He of course said "no, but...."

That was the whole appointment. We could have done it over the phone. HE should have phoned my UC doc when I gave them the number weeks ago & asked him the questions that concerned him. I think Brownstein just wanted to look at my face to see how sick I looked, or something.

Then this afternoon went to a social services agency that advertised a new support group starting up for transsexuals and transvestites with AIDS! Talk about minority groups. I was very curious to see who'd be there, but I was the only one.

Just the thought of having 2 balls is enough to wake up all my senses, and the reality of my one labia / one testicle is enough to shut down any eroticism I might feel towards myself.

At the last minute I decided to go to the disabled gay men's support group & am glad I did. I'm sitting here trying to say WHY I'm glad I went, but can't put my finger on it. Suffice it to say it was only the 3rd time I've felt tears thinking about how sad my situation is with this fucking AIDS diagnosis. I know I'd rather just keep busy & not think about it, but that doesn't allow me to reach the next stage & "get over it," if there is such a thing as getting over this alive.

Am feeling strong ✦ fine, but there's something wrong with my taste buds, or my saliva. Most dairy products taste sour to me: especially cottage cheese, sour cream, sometimes butter, milk, cheese, cream. Too bad, cuz those are the things I mostly eat. It's been this way since I've gotten sick, but I thought it'd go away.

It's gotten worse.

I go in for my left ball tomorrow and I'm already feeling myself emerging from this fog that has kept me non-sexual and unsocial…and unhappy. It is a miracle to imagine that I will be complete and "regular," that I don't have to be ashamed of my sexual side. I need to learn to love myself, now that I've spent the past 35+ years feeling like a spirit dragging around an outer shell.

I told the moderator of the gay disabled men's group that I feel I never understood the meaning of sex and that I feel that this "important" aspect of life has just passed me by ✦ I've missed out entirely on that supposedly essential part of living. It's true. I mean to quickly remedy that in the however-many years it is I have left.

In fact a new gay men's group is forming for guys with a small dick, or, as the ad read, "hung like hamsters." I sent for their membership application. I have to work fast if I'm ever going to get in touch with the sexual man in me.

Jack-off clubs have become very popular since AIDS, because it's considered "safe sex." I really want to go into these clubs ✦ watch guys play with themselves and each other and being able to go there as one of them, to do what they do and feel how they feel. When I fantasize about this, my mind suddenly because clear and joyous. I feel so brutalized having now to deal with this AIDS disease.

Now, when I finally will be able to undress and feel proud—now my body harbors and transmits a deadly germ. Sexuality will always be a barrier for me, a complication that I must use to communicate with a stranger.

So far so good. About 1:30 yesterday they hooked me up to an intravenous anesthetic and Brownstein put in my left testicular implant. Looks like it's in there for good this time. It's tender but not as painful as the other times. The nurse said Brownstein did sew me up, too. Took a taxi home ✝ John made dinner ✝ waited on me. He was supposed to catch a train back to Milwaukee this morn, but missed it ✝ will try again tomorrow morn.

All's well and I think this implant's going to stay put. I've walked a few blocks, using the cane that Jack left here, mostly to alert others I was slow ✝ shaky.

When I had my chest surgery, it was like I died one night and woke up in heaven with a flat chest. But this crotch surgery has been one long battle that is far from being won.

Everyone, including Steve Dain, has told me to stay in bed.

Just took my first dose of AZT. It's only in experimental use, and, in fact, this evening's newspaper headline says "FDA Approves First AIDS Drug, AZT attacks virus, slowed progress of diseases in 5,000." It says 5,000 is one quarter of all AIDS patients. The worst part of the article says, "Pneumocystic carinii patients," that's what I had, "usually live an average of 40 weeks from the time an infection first appears. The drug extends the number of months between the first and second bout of infection. Few survive their third infection."

40 weeks—less than a year....
This is just too brutal to be real.

The good news is that I weighed in at the doctor's again and I'm 131! That's up 5 lbs in a month! That is wonderful news because the really sick guys are losing weight. I have only 2 pairs of pants that fit my 31" waist now—I've got all 29" waist pants. Seems a shame to buy new pants ✦ only wear 'em 40 weeks HA HA.

Went to visit Kathleen Sunday ✦ she claims she didn't know I have AIDS. She says she doesn't remember mom, Bridget or John visiting, or the whole joke how I've taken the "Sickest Sullivan" title away from her.

T confirmed to me today that the AIDS blood test he took shows that he has not been exposed to the AIDS virus. Pretty strange.

Last Friday I asked the doc for my "T4 helper cell count" which is the supposed crucial number in this immune deficiency, but she said they don't even take that count for people in my condition because knowing the number won't at all change the treatment they're giving me, plus they "already know what's going to happen to people with my condition."

Wednesday night alone in bed was the first time I really broke down ✦ had a boo-hoo-hoo cry. It's now Friday night ✦ I still have a sore throat ✦ stuffed-up nose because of that cry. I feel so helpless ✦ like all I can do is wait to croak.

Any therapy or treatment I take is in vain. I feel pretty good right now, but statistics say I should be dead by November.[27]

I know I have been delaying doing some things just because I don't want to face all this. I guess it's time for me to start admitting this is happening, instead of focusing on how good I feel at the moment and denying the Big Picture. I also need to investigate alternative therapies, even if I am "too far gone."

I guess I just feel that my body has been one big burden throughout my life, and getting this fatal disease…one that can be transmitted to anyone who loves my body…is just the last straw. Just knowing that this is the way I will be until I die is so hard to accept.

I still would like to believe that a few simple carnal pleasures can still be mine.

A student from Univ. of Calif., Berkeley—a Women's Studies major—spent 4 hours going through all the info I've collected on female-to-males for her term paper. She'll return next week. That made me feel really good, too…to provide this resource and have it available. She said she couldn't find much of anything elsewhere. I'm going to be proud to donate all this stuff to The Gay Historical Society after I get killed.

I had a real eye-opening revelation while trying to fall asleep last night. I believe that I was the victim of sexual abuse in my relationship with T. It was always the way HE wanted it & I wasn't to do anything I wanted. So I just "submitted" to him & was glad that he would have anything to do with me.

27 Entry written in April

No wonder I feel paralyzed thinking of sex with someone. I was paralyzed with T. I would feel angry with him, but I went into it with full knowledge—just didn't realize the toll it would take on me.

Am feeling the tightness in my chest more + more, but haven't curtailed my activities. Bought a beautiful expensive rug for my bedroom + am trying to rearrange + equip it for accessibility + ease + comfort.

Last night I had a long dream in which I was trying to slap T, actually punch him, repeatedly, but none of my punches landed. So I spit on him instead. He never flinched, just looked at me with his beautiful eyes.

Today did T's bookkeeping and set up my computer in my bedroom so I can write better, more comfortably, easily.

Everything must be convenient.

I have the urge to make a Mary shrine in my room, like I used to as a kid. I'd used a statue of the Virgin Mary as the center of my shrine in those days, but that would mean nothing to me now. But I can't think of anything that would mean something. I guess I'll just make sure to have fresh flowers in my room like my old shrines.

I never wonder how it would be to have so-and-so make love to me, or how it would be to touch / kiss them. I think of someone else touching them.

Maybe that is why I had to have a sex change—so I could become that someone else, that "other" person in my fantasies—that boy.

Took my motorcycle down to see the fireworks tonight for the 50th Anniversary of the Golden Gate Bridge. Made me think a lot about Jack Garland, who saw the Bridge while it was being constructed, but died about 9 months before it opened.

Yesterday I participated in the AIDS Memorial March. Thousands of mostly gay men walked from Castro & Market Streets, down Market to City Hall, carrying lit candles in honor of the dead & the living.

I ditched out of there as soon as we reached City Hall because the scene there was way too depressing—a lot of people standing around crying, some holding signs with names of their dead friends. So many people put their candles near the City Hall statue that it became a giant bonfire & the Fire Dept had to come with a big hose & it took them pretty long to douse it.

Have had a few dreams that are, I think, premonitions of my impending death. I am able to remember MANY more of my dreams now, since I have to keep waking myself out of a deep sleep to take my AZT.

One dream last week:

My roommate Jim & I were in our living room & suddenly someone was really trying to get in the front door—banging on it, rattling the handle, messing with the lock. Jim started cowering as whoever-it-was was yelling Open-the-door, Let-me-in kind of stuff. I was cool & calm & just comforted Jim saying Don't cry, stop freaking out, he can't get in, the door's locked, etc. A second before the dream ended, I realized the voice at the door was dad's.

I believe I am experiencing my third puberty. My first was when I was actually 12–14 years old; my second puberty was after I first began taking testosterone in 1979–80. My third puberty is happening now, as my genitals heal and awaken with sensual feelings.

I am entering into my body—my mental processes are flowing into and merging with my body.

Great! I made it to 36!

Yesterday I drove my motorcycle about 30 miles to Redwood City down the El Camino Real to see the photograph exhibit.

All 60 close-up facial photos Jim Wigler took of men (and 2 women) diagnosed with AIDS were on display in the San Mateo County Hall of Justice ɤ will be [for another month]. He had black ribbons on 5 of them and it took me a while to realize that meant they were already dead.

I wanted to stand ɤ stare at my photo and read the words over ɤ over, but it seemed like everyone else there (and the place was mobbed) wanted to do the same thing. For sure people lingered looking at my photo, I'm sure because it was the first time they had ever seen a female-to-male, and my quote. There was a big close-up of my face, and beside it my name ɤ age and "I am a female-to-male transsexual living as a gay man. AIDS was the last thing I expected—I haven't had that many contacts. They told me at the gender clinic that I could not live as a gay man, but it looks like I will die as one."

I got the feeling several people "recognized" me, so I didn't want to stand ɤ stare at my own photograph. But my face was so masculine and my eyes truly looked sad.

Pretty nice birthday. Had my first massage ɤ won't be my last. Felt a little nervous before I go there, but this guy had a nice relaxing room with a table ɤ told me to concentrate on breathing ɤ let him do the work ɤ take off my clothes ɤ put them here. So I did.

First laid on my stomach & he rubbed my back, shoulders, arms, butt, legs & feet. Then I laid on my back & he rubbed my scalp, neck & face. At times it felt so good, I felt dizzy! I began feeling really good about my body, as he rubbed certain areas & I felt the shape of my body & it was good, a good shape & a good feeling.

Went out to eat & immediately noticed how GOOD the people looked to me & how GOOD I felt toward them—when usually I'm just the opposite, i.e., I can find fault with everyone. Somehow that massage, someone else touching me in a kind way, made me feel loving towards others in general. So, wow, what a difference it made! I must make it a regular thing.

Then later went to Maryellen's for a birthday party. I jokingly told Cheyney he should make me a Kevin McHale[28] scrapbook from his sports magazines for my birthday & he did! It was really funny. None of the pictures were very flattering, tho. On the airplane en route to Philadelphia. Am getting excited about seeing Bridgie & family & Philly, and I'm real proud that it's ME coming to visit THEM instead of them coming to visit me in the hospital this month, as the doctors forewarned.

As I gaze out the airplane window while we fly above the clouds, I wonder if floating in this spacelessness is similar to the visual of dying.

I must act to place my *Information For The Female-To-Male* in public libraries. Am not sure how to do it, but know it would be the best way to reach those seeking such info. I must also get on with editing my diaries for publication, as I fear it will never be done after I am dead. Stiff enough task for me, let alone one unfamiliar with a phenomenon such as myself.

28   Basketball player who played for the Boston Celtics

I always love returning to San Francisco. It truly is my home.

Had a very productive stay in Milw and without a question the high point was I found Elizabeth.[29] Purely accidental, by Fate it was necessary that it happen.

John and I spent all Thursday ✦ Friday afternoons in the library gathering info on F→Ms in 1883, 1893, 1914. As we were walking out of the library, I saw a woman behind the Check Out desk ✦ it flashed thru my mind: Elizabeth!, but I hesitated because she was so beautiful! So together!

I stopped and looked back, studied the face again, but was so uncertain. That nose! I had to take a chance, so I approached the desk and asked "Elizabeth?" She walked toward me with absolutely no sign of recognition and replied "Yes?" I held out my hand and said "Lou Sullivan." I felt dizzy as we clasped hands ✦ looked into each others' eyes and I felt my heart pounding in my chest as I studied her beautiful face.

John ✦ I arranged to meet her in a restaurant, as she had her own car (Elizabeth! who never had a pot to piss in!) and we had ma's. We three sat a few hours talking and the tranquility in her eyes was so wonderful to see—something Elizabeth never had before.

Just this past November she flew to Colorado ✦ had her complete surgery done by Biber. It made us both feel so good, I know, to finally be sitting there with each other, both of us finally through the whole change.

We've both finally made it over to where we struggled for so long. My heart was in my throat the whole time.

She asked if I would be coming back to Milw again and an intense sadness flowed from her eyes.

29   Elizabeth Marshall

Grandmother laid in bed, being 86, and cried when I first saw her and when I said goodbye. She says she wishes she could die, and she reminded me a lot of Kathleen. She reminisced about The Olden Days and said she remembers Sheila and she remembers Lou, and they are like twin sister + brother—two separate beings.

She never mentioned my illness, but I reassured her that I was feeling well. I hugged + kissed her, and told her I would see her later, and did she want to come along? She looked startled, and asked "Where?" even though she knew what I meant. I answered "Wherever we're going to end up going."

A dream last night: Nanc + Jack were in another room arguing, I was in bed. Then someone starts getting into my bed beside me, I asked in alarm "Who's that?" It was Jack, so I relaxed. He said, "See what I have to put up with?" meaning Nanc. I answered, "What'd'ya mean—you have to put up with! You're out of here! Gone!" He looked surprised + began getting out of the bed, but I took hold of him and quickly asked, "Tell me! What is it like to be dead?"

He whispered "Shhh…" like he couldn't/wouldn't tell me, but then added "Just make sure your room is clean…" and then he was gone.

Well, I finally got my ass into The Academy, the jack-off club that Bruce[30] recommended. I feel so proud of myself. Primed myself by listening to Lou Reed records. Somehow his words have always strengthened me against imagined fears of the outside world.

It cost $5 for a one month membership in this "private sex club," plus $4 entrance fee for the evening. As soon as you walk in, there's a "bar" that doesn't serve liquor, so to buy time I immediately ordered coffee. I wore my leather jacket and a white A-shirt, feeling sexy about my body

30 Sullivan's counselor at Shanti Project

tonight. They had a video screen on the wall with some pretty sexy jack-off/fellatio movie.

I considered just drinking up ✦ leaving, but decided to take a walk ✦ see what was happening. Went upstairs ✦ there's about 4 guys up there, 2 involved in an intense conversation ✦ the other 2 looking half dead. Went downstairs ✦ there's like 5 guys there, 2 short hairy guys making out, 2 others making out ✦ one guy rubbing himself against the wall. When I appear, they all look up in shock because someone else is there! Hey, this is midnight on Friday. Pretty pathetic. I almost had to laugh ✦ left the place.

But I got my one-month pass ✦ will return. At least I know what's there now. Would like a lot more guys there so the spotlight isn't on me as one of the 5 people there. I'd rather fade into the woodwork, get lost in the crowd, be a voyeur, instead of one of the "performers." There were 2 cuties there, both sitting alone, bored. I could have pursued them but felt I'd already dealt with enough challenge just being there.

This step has really helped me. Finally! I feel like a gay man! I'm no longer a fucked-up female. Hallelujah! I'm now a fucked-up male!!

Wow. I'm all spaced out. Finally something FUN happened. Went to the Nob Hill Cinema, gay men's porno. A good one came on with 2 guys fucking in a New York subway car. The movie theater was deserted, except for me. I figured, well, I'll watch this good one ✦ then leave. So I was playing with myself ✦ suddenly I realize there's someone standing up behind me, so I look back ✦ there's a guy TOTALLY BARE! I thought, wow, talk about BOLD.

He's hanging his dick right on my shoulder ✦ I had to think fast. OK…what is safe sex?? I grabbed him with one hand ✦ kept playing with myself with the other. He kept trying to stick himself in my mouth…but I know that's "not safe." Or is it, really? But I just began sucking his balls. He leaned over to explore in my pants ✦ I let him. I thought God! This guy doesn't even care if someone comes in!

He had a Spanish accent & asked "Do you want to?" I answered breathlessly "Yes!" He said "Come on!" and beckoned me toward the aisle. I followed him & he stopped right there in the aisle. I dropped to my knees & he held a small bottle to my nose (poppers, I guess, which I don't particularly like, but I took a whiff, then he took a whiff). Then I did suck him a little. He asked if I wanted to get fucked & I said "Yeah!" He said, "Lean over…" I lowered my pants & he knelt behind me as I stood & played with me a second. I stood & he stood behind me & rubbed his cock between my asscheeks & he pressed me against him, my leather jacket still on & we both laughed in pleasure. No penetration, but I grasped his cock between my legs—isn't that called the Princeton rub?

I asked if he had a rubber, he said no, so I fumbled in my wallet, got one, but couldn't get the goddamn package open. Hermetically sealed! As I struggled he said "Suck my balls!" and I did and he said "I'm coming" and he did. I said "Oh, don't come yet!" still struggling with the hopeless package, but it was too late to get fucked. D A M N !

He hugged me & we caressed & he said "Thank you." I said "thank you" and he smiled & said he "had to go." I collapsed in a seat & wondered, "Who was that unmasked man!" and then realized it was the ticket taker!

Well, the movie was over, the lights went on, I got dressed & went into the lobby. He was behind his counter getting dressed. The front door was locked. Ah-ha. That's why he was so bold. I asked, "Are you gonna let me out, or am I being held prisoner?" He laughed & said just push it open. I said bye & left, my pant leg all wet from his cum. Wow.

It only lasted about 5 mins.

And how did my genitoplasty affect my lovemaking last night? When he reached down to touch me between my legs, I did not have to push him away, when he knelt down I could relax—

A big fear of mine is that I will die before the gender professionals acknowledge that someone like me exists, and then I really won't exist to prove them wrong.

Surely AIDS is one of the only diseases cloaked in all this philosophizing ⚢ moralizing about why it exists. Only because mostly gay men get it do they get away with theorizing that the disease arises from some sort of lifestyle problem.

Last night my roommate Jim ⚢ I rented a video machine ⚢ some fuck movies. I smoked some reefer ⚢ I was feeling amorous ⚢ the phone rings. It's T. He asked if I knew who was calling ⚢ I said "Of course, no one else has such a nice voice…." He was obviously shocked ⚢ flattered ⚢ said, "You think I have a nice voice?" I answered, "Yeah, well, that's not all you have a nice one of…" but I thought enough of that, and asked why he called. He has some typesetting for me to do. But, oh, he just called when I was in a weak ⚢ lonely moment and his sweet little voice just sent me.

Here I sit at Moby Dick's, a "G" bar near Castro, near my home. Contemplating. Reflecting. I've come all this way, gone thru this whole change, crossdressing 14 years, hormone shots for 8 yrs. Finally got all the surgery, or all I'm ever going to get. And now what? Now I sit here the same way I sat before hormones, before surgery. Now what?

My future compressed into a shortened time slot. Most dead in 2 years. Some live for 5. What have I been striving toward? Some erotic ideal that I still cannot reach…or is it only a matter of behavior modification? Is it all in my mind, and not in theirs? The young lean smiling boys here all around me? The mystique so erotic, my fantasies so intriguing. Oh! To be a mere victim of my lust, instead of having orchestrated my desires, my place here.

Is it just too damn bad for us transsexuals? I'll forever be lacking, I'll always have to explain/excuse myself. Yet it's been worth all these years just to be in this bar, here, now, with AIDS, ✦ to be a man among men. To be included, however voyeuristically, however theoretically, in the society of men who can only openly proclaim their ardor for other men—

It may be *the love that dare not speak its name* but it is surely the love that endures, that persists against all condemnation, even through the threat of death, of "AIDS," a love that cannot die; to me, this is the only REAL love.

Just got home from my second visit to The Academy. I felt awake ✦ energetic at 2 am ✦ I felt there would be more men there after the bars closed. I psyched myself up by thinking and believing that all the other guys there were just as "vulnerable ✦ self-conscious" as I am, which kind of adds to the intense sexual atmosphere…thinking of all these sexually needy male bodies.

I finally found the room with all the porn movies. A small room with 3 steps forming a bench-like seating area along 3 walls, the other wall had the video screen. I sat down ✦ opened my pants ✦ just reached into my jockey shorts, watched the fuck films ✦ played with myself. About 5 other men in the room, 3 others of them brought their cocks out ✦ stroked themselves. I tried to make meaningful eye contact with any of them to use as encouragement to go over ✦ touch them, but no go. So I lowered my trousers, pulled my undershirt up to my nipples, exposed my ball through the leg band of my shorts ✦ jerked off. I came 3 times.

I spoke at the Institute for Advanced Study of Human Sexuality again, on their transgender safe-sex panel. When I hear myself tell my story, I feel I deserve more fun times, such as tonight at the Academy.

Looks like this is it for another diary. I feel very lucky to have outlived this one!!!

Am beginning to feel "symptoms" of non-health.

Finally got an answer from Alyson Publications—a fuckin xerox copy of a form letter saying they're all booked up until 1989 and if I want to resubmit my material at that time they'll consider it then. Yeah. I hope the US Postal Service has a box in heaven.

Yesterday went to visit Vince, a 41-yr-old gay man who wrote me in response to my ad in the Small Club. He was average-looking. We sat ✦ talked a while ✦ I became fairly sure that he was attracted to me. He put some gay porn on this television VCR and invited me to lay on his bed. He was extremely talkative. Little by little we both stripped down. The worst was he had a lot of questions. I guess the scar on my left ball surgery is still too visible.

He was also trying to keep some truth from me, as he had a large scar on his stomach ✦ said he had his spleen removed due to immune system problems (which can only mean "AIDS" in this day ✦ age), and he has candida in his mouth (another symptom) but he never came right out ✦ said he had AIDS. He asked me if I "tested positive" and I said yes. He seemed reassured, though, that I "looked healthy."

The best part was when he sucked my dick. No kidding. I never thought anyone would. I felt it was safe, because I wasn't even lubricating ✦ didn't feel he would be exposed to any of my "bodily fluids." He sucked a long time, but too gently. I sucked him, too, but he was very soft ✦ complained that he's had no interest in sex, etc because of his physical deterioration. All in all, he was a rather depressing person.

He also fingered my asshole a bit, which felt very good, but again he was so gentle and careful that I hardly felt anything. After being there 4 hours I left with a giant headache. All that talk. I was so careful not to reveal my transsexuality that I ended up full of tension and wondering if this is a wise approach.

Made me feel like I'm better off going to the jack-off club, or even getting some quick feels in the dirty movies, or cruising the bushes in the parks. I am not particularly interested in "getting to know" someone and even less interested in their "getting to know" me !

I had made a Game Plan before going to this guy's place of speaking as little as possible—remembering Mr. King in *City of Night*. But this guy was so full of questions, I forgot my plan. Anyway, he seemed to want to get together again and I guess we could. I just have to stop trying to be an Honest Joe while lying through my teeth.

Yesterday went for my weekly massage, but this time, while laying on my back, I decided to open my eyes a bit instead of keeping them clamped closed like usual. I didn't really look AT the masseur, but at the ceiling, but could see him moving beside me, touching me so nicely, and tears streamed down my cheeks. I'm not exactly sure why.

Maybe it moved me so to realize I was actually laying there + he was being so nice to me, because when I close my eyes, I'm more fantasizing or visualizing my body instead of really looking at it. I knew he noticed my tears and all I could think to say in explanation was, "It's kinda scary when I open my eyes."

Wow. I think I've found a "fuck buddy." Cory contacted me through the Small-Endowed Guys Club, I phoned him yesterday and we met this evening over at his place. At first he sat in a chair while I sat on the couch. The TV was on as we chatted lightly, then he turned the TV to face me, and sat next to me on the couch. He is quite attractive, blonde, 5'11", 160 lbs. He patted my knees and leaned over to kiss me, and we went on from there. He really does like 'em small!

He removed my pants and went down on me right away. He reached underneath my balls and stuck his finger up my hole. I realized that he obviously assumed it was my asshole, so I let him finger fuck me. He was in my vagina and it felt wonderful! I was unusually relaxed and figured all I had to do was make sure he didn't find two holes down there, and I don't think he ever did.

We hopped into his bed and I was all over him! He was cuddly ＋ kissy ＋ huggy, and laid on his back while I sat on top of him and rubbed my crotch against his. He jerked himself off and at some point he had said to me, "Obviously you know what you're doing!" He screwed his finger up the wrong hole again and I jerked myself off and CAME! I told him it was very unusual for me to come with a partner. We snuggled a long time and then started up again. He finger fucked me again while jerking himself, and I played with myself and came a second time.

Well, he sure liked me and gave me his work phone, too, saying "call anytime" and next time I should come over on the weekend so I can sleep overnight! I have to say that this was my first successful male/male lovemaking experience. Sure, that fun 5 minutes with the dirty movie ticket taker counts, but he hardly saw or touched me and I wasn't satisfied.

But this time, I felt very confident. He just made me feel that way. He never asked any questions about my condition and the lights were very low so I wasn't concerned about my scars.

Today Barbara Grier of Naiad Press calls again. She'd spoken to Sasha Alyson of Alyson Press and he just cannot understand how I got that form letter saying they were all booked up until 1989 and it was a total error and he's very excited about my work, too. Grier said she'll forward the items I sent her to him, but will keep my *Information for the Female-to-Male* for her library. She said I should be hearing from Alyson in 2–3 weeks, and she wants an autographed copy of the book when it's published.

She asked about my health ＋ energy, and wanted to know if I had adequate emotional support from others. She wanted to know what shape my Garland manuscript is in, and I gotta get going and put that baby to bed!

Yesterday Cory phoned & about 8:30 pm I went over to his place again. Wasn't long before we're at it hot and heavy. He said "oh, that juicy pussy," or something like that several times. I don't know what he thinks but he never asks.

I smoked a joint and told him I "needed to be fucked by my daddy."

He can't seem to keep up his hard-on without direct stimulation and it's just a battle trying to get his dick up my ass when he's not even hard and the rubber won't even stay on. But I am as considerate of his shortcomings as he is of mine, and we carry on and enjoy without question or complaint. He is very affectionate and so nice to kiss. It ended with him jerking off and I used my undershirt to wipe it up, and fantasized how I'd wear this cum rag the next day.

Lights went out at 10 pm and we snuggled up to each other off and on throughout the night. I had a hard time falling asleep. This morning we woke to a steady rain and lounged around drinking coffee and I laid on top of him and rubbed against him until he came, while he finger fucked my ass.

It was all very erotic and almost animalistic—I say that because I do not think he is a handsome man. He does have a nice body, but certainly is not "my type." But at this point in my life, "my type" is any homosexual man who will have sex with me without questioning me.

Sunday afternoon I hosted my 4th get-together for female-to-males and good ole Dr. Brownstein spoke to the group on F→M surgery. Had an all-time-record attendance of 16 female-to-males and 5 guests. Afterwards two old-timers came over to my place & we all smoked some reef and shot the shit and laughed.

Then got a call from Cory, thanking me for sending him a Christmas card and inviting me over for the night. YAHOO! Again, had a marvelous time. I did emphasize to him that it wasn't safe for him to be tonguing me between my balls. I said, "You know my hole is down there and that's where my cum comes out, and you know I'm a dribbler not a shooter. I am positive and talked to my doc and he said that's definitely out." He just nodded that, yes, he knew. That was all that was said. He is such an angel for never once asking what the story is with my body.

Even the "experts" disagree on what's safe ✦ what's not. The underground even says oral/genital sex is safe, but the mainstream medical world says no. Anyway I feel I have been upfront with Cory— he has to decide what he feels is safe for him, and I have to decide what I feel is right to do, for me and for him. I won't do several things I would do before: I won't take cum in my mouth, I won't lick a shitty butt, I won't get fucked without a condom. I won't let someone lick my cum hole. Everything else, as far as I'm concerned, is OK.

Saturday night I began hiccuping and at 1 am. Sunday morn I hiccuped non-stop till 2:30 am. None of my usual remedies stopped them—usually if I guzzle water ✦ make myself burp. But nothing helped. I might stop for ½ hour, but then they'll start up again ✦ last an hour. My poor body was just being racked. No way could I sleep. What torture. My headache was overpowering—their medicines didn't do shit.

Sunday night Kathy Stein ✦ I slept together in her bed. She gave me a very relaxing massage and we were both trying to holistically stop the hiccups. I laid on my stomach, she sat on my butt ✦ rubbed my back. She stretched her hands all the way down my arms until our fingertips touched. I felt her energy ✦ loving, and said "Kath, if love can cure anything, this should do it." She answered, "It does cure." And at that moment, my hiccups ceased. She laid on me, neither of us wanting to move, floating on the calm of my released body.

Monday early am the hiccups were back ✦ Maryellen ✦ Kathy took me to the Emergency Room to see if they could stop my hiccups. The doc tickled my back palate til I vomited ✦ the hiccups were gone about 20 mins. Back again. He'd been so proud of his success. Gave me a shot of thorazine in the ass.

HICCUP

I hadn't had a night's sleep in 48 hrs. They gave me ativan and compozene, plus the aspirin/codeine. Stayed in the hospital bed Tuesday. Wednesday they said there was nothing they could do for me there that I couldn't do at home—I went back to Kathy's place. Still hiccuping.

Went for the first time to Stretch and Exercise Class for Persons with AIDS. There were about 7 other guys there, around my age, a couple of cuties, too. While there, again, I swelled with happiness in the realization that I was one of these gay men, I belonged.

How beautiful my flat chest, my muscular arms, my stubbly chin, felt.

Just received Alyson's acceptance letter ＆ publication contract for my Garland biography ＆ I am so overwhelmed, I feel tears welling up.

If I can just last long enough, if I can just live long enough to see this book—I'll be fulfilled! I just want it in libraries all over, so when someone, like I was at age 21, is searching the libraries for a mention of a female-to-male, there Garland will be—proud ＆ beautiful ! I am so lucky!

I am truly actualizing all the dreams I had for myself while young, to be a man, to be a gay man, to be a published writer. That is why I feel at peace with my impending death. It's OK.

Friday evening Cory phoned. We talked a long time about AIDS and safe sex…he said he was so tired of burying his friends and so tired of the whole topic. Said he's never taken "the test" to find out if he's antibody positive but he just assumes he is.

He invited me over and I went.

I just returned from a coin shop where I sold the 1 oz gold Canadian Maple Leaf coin that dad bought for each of us kids in 1980. I used the $455 for which it sold, and added another $300 from the cash I still have left from dad's estate, to prepay my cremation cost with the Neptune Society. I felt very sad and almost like crying when selling the coin. Why? I think because I knew it would have made dad very sad to think I used his gift to pay for my funeral. But now, thinking more about it, I'm trying to think of it rather that I used the coin to pave my way to seeing dad again.

Yesterday morning J left a desperate message on my telephone answering machine, "Call me as soon as you can!" I thought it very presumptuous of him to think I could afford to call Japan, but I did. He was very panicky that I might have died without informing him and said he was planning to fly to San Francisco just to find out what happened to me and had already told his wife he might! So I reassured him I'm fine. He said Al in Milwaukee wanted to come to SF to see me, too. Funny, but I can't remember Al's last name....

IT'S GONE. Mailed my manuscript to Alyson this morning.

I dreamt I was on a building roof and spread out my blankets + pillows to sleep there overnight. The next morning awoke when a large smoke stack nearby started chugging out smoke in my direction. As I gathered up my bedding in order to move, dad appears and says he'll show me a good place to go, and we walked off toward another part of the roof.

I tell ya, I'm beginning to wonder if all this secrecy and fear someone will "find out" is only serving to keep me away from people, rather than helping to make me "just one of the guys...."

And I feel strongly about the benefits of my activism.

So nice to be sitting in the park, the sun shining on my face, the sweet-smelling air and green green grass after last night's rain....

All day yesterday I spent in bed. Felt so exhausted, I just slept the day away. The day before was the presidential election and I felt even more ill when Bush got elected.

Earlier that day I gave my talk on transsexuals and AIDS at the Institute for the Advanced Study of Human Sexuality. After the talk, a very pleasant-looking guy—close to my age and body type, long hair and a mustache—came up ＋ said he'd seen me several years ago giving a talk, and he'd like my phone no. so we could "get together for coffee or something." I was surprised but gave him my number and didn't think much of it.

But then, when I was on my way out, I stopped to read a sign on the wall, and he came up behind me and gave me a big bear hug. Felt so good! and I reached back and squeezed his ass. He said his name was "Jerry Z" so I'd know it was him when he calls.

I was busy the rest of the day so I didn't think about it at all, but that night in bed, I hoped he will call. I sure could use someone to hug me up…someone who knows my story but still wants me.

This past month I've been having "night sweats." That's where, once a night, I wake up and my pajama top is really wet and drenched in sweat. Asked the doc what the mechanics are of these "night sweats"— of course, they don't know.

I met with a female-to-male from New Hampshire who's here to investigate the available bottom surgeries. He knows another female-to-gay-male, Chris, in Tucson. Little by little, I'll find 'em !

I'm pretty well into the Christmas spirit this year. I feel so lucky to still be alive!

I've been off the AZT and all medication for two weeks and feel fine. I even think I have increased energy and stamina—don't get tired and dizzy so fast. I just phoned the doc who said that it's OK for me to be off the AZT for 3–4 weeks. I'm glad she's not urging me to go back on it right away—it's nice taking a break to see what's been me and what's been the medication.

I sure never thought I'd be here for Christmas 1988!!

With each breath, I fill my body with fresh air and thank God I'm alive. What a lucky guy I am !

It's been so cold and raining day after day. When I had that 102° fever, I had the chills and my feet were like ice cubes even though I had three pairs of socks on. It's supposed to rain again tomorrow, but I hope it doesn't. I'd like to go to the grocery store because I ate every little tidbit I had left in the house today—plus I want to get myself a sexy 1989 calendar, and a new diary…which I'm prepared to spend plenty for. There's a gay card shop in the Castro that has some beautiful blank books, but they were plenty expensive. I deserve one! When I started you, diary, I figured you'd be my last book. But the story ain't over yet!

I'm not sure if I had a good time last night or not. A man from Las Vegas who's been writing to me through the Small Hung Guys Club is in San Francisco for some business meeting. He's sent me MANY polaroid photographs of his dick. Anyway he invited me to his hotel room last night, answering the door clad only in a towel, probably in his late 40s, glasses, beer belly but not flabby.

We chatted a while, drank a beer, and eventually I got undressed (left my undershirt, A-shirt, on but pulled it up so it covered my scars. We jerked off and touched each other's crotches.

Anyway he asked if I'd like him to suck me. I said sure, but when he leaned over to do it, I said, "Don't you think we should use condoms?" He looked up quickly and said, "Why? Do you have AIDS?" He was so confrontational that I answered, "As a matter of fact, I do."

Well, he backed off REAL fast and hardly even touched my balls after that. But he jerked off and I jerked myself off while touching him mostly. He wrapped his legs around mine, tangled them up, which was a little gross because I'm sure he shaved his legs, as well as his arms and the rest of his body. Very smooth. But he had nice tits.

Anyway after about 2 hours, he says it's time for him to go to sleep and I should phone him so we can get together again Tuesday evening.

This morning he leaves a message on my telephone answering machine that "something's come up" and he won't be able to see me tonight. So even though he was no bargain himself, he rejected me.

I'm fairly certain it was because of the AIDS thing. He seemed very put off by that.

Pisses me off—because now it seems I've conquered the fear of rejection for being a female, for having female genitals, now that I'm finally gaining self-confidence in my male body, I have to fight rejection because I'm infectious.

Well, I guess Kathleen is going to get better. Jim says she's talking, laughing and can focus her eyes—a long way from the coma state when I saw her a week ago. She was so damned out of it. For all the times she's said to me, "I wish I could die," she still has enough will to live, to come back.

She has a tube down her nose suctioning fluid out of her lungs, so I guess she has some kind of pneumonia.

Jim, her husband, really wants her to continue living. He told me he slept in Kathleen's hospital bed in their living room while she's been in the hospital. Obviously he is not repulsed by her. Kathy Steininger and I will go visit her in the hospital tomorrow.

There is something I've been meaning to write in you, diary—something I recently thought of, but have never told anyone:

I knew from very young that I planned to pass as a man, because I remember when aged 16-19, I was getting a lot of pressure to get my ears pierced—by Bridget and by Kathleen, especially. But I didn't want to pierce my ears, because I knew it was a permanent stamp of "female" on my body—that I wanted my body to look like a boy's.

These past few days I've been typesetting and pasting up the quarterly newsletter of the San Francisco Bay Area Gay and Lesbian Historical Society.

This coming week I'll begin putting together the 7th issue of *FTM*, my female-to-male newsletter. It's getting so good that I'm thinking of charging for it!

My good friend for 16 years, Alyn Hess in Milwaukee, died of AIDS last night. Eldon Murray phoned this morning to tell me. Alyn is the first person who was close to me who has died of AIDS. He had been much sicker than I've been, with brain tumors and all kinds of symptoms. It was from Alyn that I got the phrase "Yours in liberation," the closure I often use when signing off letters. Alyn, as President of

Milwaukee's Gay Peoples Union in 1973, when I first came out, was a gay leader and hero in my eyes. Now, I hope, he has found eternal liberation.

Kathleen died at 6:00 this morning.

I feel deeply saddened, as only death can do. At the same time I feel a sense of relief that she is finally released from her living hell.

When Maryellen and I walked out of the hospital on Sunday, after last seeing Kath, Maryellen said that she had that same feeling as when she and I left the hospital after seeing Dad for the last time. Little did we know how similar it really was.

Her words, "Lou, I care about you very much," relax and comfort me.

She went through the wringer these past four years and endured more than any one human being could bear.

So now she's with Dad and Patrick, and now she knows the answer to Dad's incessant question: "What's it all about?"

Talking with Kathleen's husband Jim this morning and, yes, he will take her ashes to Milwaukee. I told him if I'm not in the hospital that I'd go with him. But it won't be happening soon, so in the immortal words of Jack, we just have to "Hold off!"

He said he went to bed Wednesday night (Kath died Wednesday morning) and suddenly woke up after sleeping only a few hours. He said it was not like a dream, but a vision he described as like energy from a television screen. In a fuzzy apparition, he saw Kath dancing with her hands above her head and she was saying, "I'm free! I'm free! I'm free!"

My chest pains are getting severe…a stabbing pain through the middle of my chest that comes out my back. It's obviously my lungs. I still haven't heard the results of the "Gallium scan" test they gave me last week (the test with the radiation shot). All the docs at The AIDS Clinic have been at a conference. Plus my fever remains between 101°–102.5°. Something is definitely the matter with me and it ain't gettin better. I worry this chest problem will pose a strain to my heart and I'll just have a heart attack and die, without the benefit of being able to lay around sick for a while.

And several times I've just felt overcome by grief about "this Kathleen thing" and had some hard cries, but that just made my chest really hurt bad, but how can one control that sorrow?

Yesterday I held my 9th female-to-male get-together with a record attendance of 21 female-to-males and 14 guests. I get lots of compliments and positive strokes for the wonderful service I'm providing to others by organizing this group.

Finally saw a doctor today. They sent me for ANOTHER chest x-ray and for an EKG. The nurse practitioner said both of them looked normal; she and Dr. Hollander went off to talk in private, then she came back and said they'd continue to do tests to find out what's the matter, but even if they did identify the problem, chances are they won't be able to treat it anyhow and that's "the reality of AIDS." She said I should begin to make preparations for when I can't take care of myself—do I want to get on a waiting list of a hospice, or do I want to go into the hospital, or just stay home and let it happen. She assured me they'd make sure I was "very comfortable" with morphine or whatever, that I wouldn't suffer any pain. But I need to think of how to arrange for when I need 24-hour care, and can I coordinate family and friends to care for me? So that's "the reality of AIDS."

How do I feel about all this? I feel like I should just ignore these symptoms and go about my days as best I can. I'm not so far gone that I can even envision preparing for 24-hour care. I can still take care of myself and I will. I know my main focus needs to be my eating and weight (I'm down to 116 now). Maybe it's time for me to sign up or get on the waiting list for Project Open Hand, a service to AIDS patients where, for free, they'll bring daily meals to your door.

I feel that, if I cannot envision laying down to die, I won't be able to really do it. So I will keep that picture out of my mind.

Saw Lou Reed again tonight. He's 46 years old now and wears glasses, but he's still Mr. Cool. I'd planned to write him a letter, telling him about myself—that I'm "Lou"—but there's just been too much commotion.

Saw the doc today and the CT scan I did on Friday was very revealing.

I'm not going to get too excited about all this again. I've always felt that when doctors come across something they don't know what it is, they call it "cancer."

All I know is my stomach hurts.

Am forming a very close friendship with a female-to-male who just started hormones and who just moved here from Philadelphia. Name's Denis. This weekend he moves into an apartment about 5 blocks from mine. Oh, yes, I forgot to mention—he's also a female-to-gay male.

Anyway, he thinks I'm wonderful and has volunteered to do anything he can for me, especially down the road when I'm too sick to do for myself. He's also been performing "Reiki" on me, which is something like the Laying of Healing Hands and the transfer of vibrations and energy.

My AIDS clinic nurse practitioner is urging me to take a "bone marrow test," where they insert a needle into your hip bone and withdraw fluid to analyze. I understand it's a very painful test and I remember having a spinal tap when I had that hiccuping binge, another needle insertion into my bone, and that was pretty brutal. At this point, I don't feel sick enough to subject my body to this invasive traumatic procedure, and so, for the second time, I cancelled my appointment for the test tomorrow. Maryellen, again, talked sense into me and begged me to "listen to my body" and not let this doc force me to do what I don't feel is good for me. I love her so much. She speaks to my soul.

I've been fixing up my room and have become very relaxed and peaceful therein. Got a 4-drawer file cabinet and sorted my papers, letters, etc. I've bought new blankets for my bed to make it fresh and pleasing.

I don't need to know the name of why I feel so run down.

One hour after they unhooked me from the transfusion, I was in the car with Jerry and am now at a weekend retreat called the "California Men's Gathering." It's a 3-day event at Camp Swig near San Jose. Last night was the welcoming ceremonies and what a rush to hear and be among all these men whooping and groaning and breathing heavy. Lots of bongo drums and swaying back + forth.

There was lots of intense and intoxicating male energy, and I became quite overwhelmed (one of the few times) and I just let the tears fall, thinking of my life, of the journey I've made, how sad and hopeless I was as a young person feeling I could never belong, never be one of the guys.

I've found my place in this world, when before I felt so alienated, a creature from outer space. This "male bonding ritual" just seemed to bring me to the peak of my journey. I've made it! And then the irony, the brick wall, the downward spiral of this disease in my body. But I feel so proud to have really reached my male aspirations, my goals, that to be faced with an end to my life seems not so awful.

They say there are 360 men at this retreat. We chose "support groups" and I went to the one for "HIV and Life Threatening Issues." It was two groups of 7 guys each, and in my group I'm the only one really diagnosed with full-blown AIDS. A few others have ARC, which is a pre-AIDS condition.

So far I feel I am amazingly at ease and comfortable in this group of total strangers. Knowing how I used to be in grade school, high school, even my early adulthood, how withdrawn and afraid of strangers and especially being in crowds I was, this is incredible to experience this sense of ease and belonging. How lucky I am!

First of all, Happy Birthday to Kathleen, even though she's dead. I thought about sending a donation to the Multiple Sclerosis Society in Kath's name, but didn't actually do it. I figured it was the thought that counted.

Saw the nurse practitioner on the 14th and I weigh the same—116 lbs. She had the doctor man come in to feel my swollen gut and he says my liver and my spleen are both "enlarged." Anyway the nurse practitioner gives me the same old rap how they wanted me to take this bone marrow test, but admitted there are no treatments for either of the diseases they suspect (MAI or lymphoma). The nurse told me that, if she were me, she'd do the same thing I am, that she agreed with me but has to play "devil's advocate." Again she offered to "help" me in any way possible to make my transition to the netherworld (not exactly her words) as easy as possible.

So they put me back on AZT because my blood work looked so good and they might put me on a 2-weeks on / 2-weeks-off regimen, if only to keep the virus out of my brain (which AZT does) to prevent what they call "AIDS-related dementia."

Last week I went with a sexologist, Dr. Maggi Rubenstein, and a male-to-female who's just begun the transition to speak to the staff of a Tenderloin city mental health clinic. And among the 15 staff members who assembled to hear about transsexualism was Tom Ossenbeck, the guy who led the gay disabled men's therapy group, which I attended weekly for over a year, but never told them my transsexual past. Well, I really got nervous—my hands even began to shake—but I calmed down in about 5 minutes. I guess I felt "guilty" for having kept it from him, but at that time in my life I wasn't dealing with issues of a transsexual, but issues of a gay man. It was hard to look him in the eye, but when my talk was over, he came up to me. I spoke first and said, "I want you to know that I never lied to you, I just left out a lot of details." He smiled and said he would never have guessed this about me—another great compliment!

I saw Ari Kane from Boston again and he said definitely yes, his "Institute" (or whatever it is) will print the third edition of my *Information for the Female-to-Male*! I am so pleased. I have free license to write it plus I'll do the typesetting and layout, submit camera-ready copy to them and they'll print it for free, plus distribute it, of course, which is also great because I was trying to make sure that the book would continue to be distributed even after I can no longer do it. But I will also get copies of the book from them so I can continue to distribute them myself as long as I want to. So what more can I ask? This is great!

I'm realizing this *Information* book is the most important thing I've done and I want to maintain total control of it so publishers can't hack it up, vis á vis my *Advocate* article and my Jack Garland book.

My weight remains at 116 lbs, but maybe it's all my "huge" spleen and enlarged liver, because I am beginning to get that same look that Kathleen had, i.e., no muscle, and paper-thin skin hanging on my bones. I was in a poorly-lit public restroom the other day and happened to catch sight of myself in the mirror. To my horror, the shadowy lighting accentuated my sunken features and I was staring back at a gaunt, drawn, emaciated face. All I could think was "poor Lou." Something really is happening to me....

I went to the Gay Pride Parade on Saturday and there were tons of people everywhere even before the parade started. I had to crane my neck to see over everyone and within about 15 minutes was exhausted. I sat down on a curb and fifteen people stood in front of me. I had visions of last year's Parade, when I wore myself out trying to peer over the shoulders of giant spectators to catch a glimpse of the Parade, standing the whole time, so that I had no energy left to walk through the Civic Center booths and displays.

So I found out where the Handicapped and Special Needs Seating Area was and asked the guard what I needed to do to prove I had a "Special Need." "I could show you my AZT," I suggested. The guard answered, "I could show you mine." So they had no proof requirement, so I just went in and got this front row seat, no people standing in front of us, met 2 guys there I knew from our Gay Men's Disability Group. It was great!

A volunteer walked around offering us a glass of water. After the Parade, I had plenty of energy to walk through the displays. My friends hung out with me. Last year I just thought, oh, I'm not sick enough to need the Handicapped Area, but this year I thought, yes, I do need it. So glad I used it.

Well, here I am on the plane going to Milwaukee and believe me I had strong doubts up until the very last minute whether I was going to make it. I haven't left my apartment for the past week (except once when Bruce picked me up in his car to go out to eat). I've been so weak, so unsteady on my feet, my heart pounding wildly after just my walking the length of our apartment hallway. I am gasping for air during and after the most mundane activities. My abdomen is so distended, so swollen, that it's tender and sore even after many pain killers. Family and friends have rallied around, bringing + cooking dinners for me, washing the dishes. I must look pretty pathetic because no one hesitates to pick up after me without explanation. I think it scares both me and them to see me this way.

I feel I must make this trip to Milwaukee because I think it will be my last time, and probably the last time I see Grandmother. Oddly enough, I'm eager to see mom, too, and feel a lot of that past resentment and anger toward her diminish. Maybe Kathleen's death has something to do with my new outlook, although I don't know why. Maybe during this really scary decline in my physical state I need some "motherly" comfort—especially from Grandmother.

Steve Dain came over to visit me about 3 hours last Tuesday and made me feel like a very special person. Word is out, I guess, that Lou's on the deep skids, and all the female-to-males who have benefited from my work in the community are coming forward and telling me things like, I'm their hero!

Lots of good news, good vibes, relaxation. Looking back, I think this was the best trip back to Milwaukee I've ever had. I'm so glad ma never asked me to go to Kathleen's grave with her.

I brought Dad's cane to alert others I wasn't at full capacity. Walked several blocks to the health food store, then took the bus to the drugstore and a few blocks walk to the bird food store. Bussed home and was tired by then, I'll admit. But I went to dinner with my Shanti counselor, Bruce, and he drove me to the grocery store so I could stock up on basics.

Today, Thursday, I ate a decent breakfast at home, then returned out with the cane to do more shopping, some banking, to pick up the Thursday free gay newspapers.

I tried starting my motorcycle again this afternoon and it started right up!

So I'm definitely back on the upswing.

I'm feeling MUCH better than even a week ago, no doubt due to the blood transfusions.

John, his girlfriend Annie and her 2 kids drove into town. As usual it was great to see him, and he told Maryellen his purpose in coming was to spend as much time with me as possible. He brought the lamps I'd bought in Milwaukee, and wired and hung my chandelier. I am so pleased with them. My room is slowly becoming a place of beauty. I want it to be a pleasurable and peaceful place, as I hope to die there, as opposed to a hospital room.

We spent a lot of time at Maryellen's and her 2 kids were so cute trying to "help Uncle Lou." Twice Rory took my arm to help me go up the stairs or walk a gravel driveway. I was still using Jack's cane when walking, just because I feel a bit unsteady on my feet—due to whatever…the illness, the drugs, the painkillers?

I am back on the motorcycle. It does take a little bit of effort to hold up, say, at a stoplight, but I just put both feet down instead of just one. I was strapping the cane onto the side of the motorcycle to go where I wanted, but lately don't need it.

Am mostly staying at home. Have plenty to do there—answering mail to the FTM group, writing my 3rd edition of my booklet, doing typesetting for the Gay Historical Society, marking up Alyson's mark-up of my Garland book. Between all this, and going to the doctor every week, and feeding myself—I gained 5 lbs this past week!—I'm busy!

Well, hallelujah! Believe it or not, Alyson has finally accepted the Garland manuscript! I hesitate to say "my" Garland manuscript, because in its present final form, it seems far from the story I began with.

And to really make it wonderfully official, he sent the final two installments of my advance—a check for $1,000!

Brother, now I'm writing this page back to back, and in a few years the ink will soak through and mess up either side.

Tomorrow I go to the doc for my regular AIDS check-up. A new medicine has just been approved for people who can't take AZT called DDI. I'm going to ask for it, but maybe it won't mesh with all this tuberculosis medicine I'm taking for the MAI. I also want to beg my endocrinologist to prescribe the testosterone pills for me as I just can't bear to give myself shots every 2 weeks and, as it's an intramuscular injection, I'm having a hard time finding a muscle on my body due to this wasting syndrome I'm experiencing.

Sunday the 24th I held the eleventh female-to-male Get-Together. Lin Fraser, a psychotherapist specializing in gender treatment, came right from the airport to our meeting to tell us the latest from the Harry Benjamin Gender Dysphoria Association Symposium held in Cleveland. She said there were two significant events: 1. the phalloplasties now being performed are GREAT, look natural and are functional, and 2. it is now officially okay to be a female-to-gay male. She said my taped interview with Ira Pauly was a big hit and everyone clapped after it. I had ended that tape by saying that my motivation for making it was so that future female-to-gay males would not be rejected from the gender clinics as I was. Pauly told Fraser to tell me that my wish has come true.

When I got sick in December '86, there were two things I wanted to accomplish before I died: to publish my Garland book, and to ensure that no other female-to-gay males would be discriminated against by the gender professionals because of their sexual orientation. This week I accomplished them both.

I finally hit on the right moment to attend one of the frequent jack-off parties held on Folsom Street. It was billed as a "Pan International Global Jack Off" or PIGJO, hosted by my acquaintance, Jerry. It was held this afternoon which was perfect, too, as I had a lot more energy to get there. Usually they're held in the evening when I just want to put my jammies on and crawl into bed. Somehow I felt very relaxed and confident about going to this event—possibly all the weekly nude massages I've been getting have helped me feel relaxed about stripping down, and I guess my body is pretty average compared to other men there.

Today there were about 30 men there and the majority were not so attractive either…Of course my dick looks much different than everyone else's, but I figure all dicks look different and I'm confident no one will be mean to me there because I've got a small dick. I also realize that, as out of shape and pathetic as my body is, it will only get more out of shape and pathetic as days go by, and I probably look today better than I ever will, so I better seize the moment. The room was brightly lit, with couches and benches and these guys standing/sitting around playing with themselves while watching each other.

Well, I had a great time, even though I didn't touch anyone and no one touched me. I had two orgasms—was there about an hour.

Well, this is way too much commotion for me! Yesterday there was a major earthquake in San Francisco.[31] They say it's the biggest quake since the one in 1906. I'd feel some camaraderie with Jack Garland's experience in '06, but the destruction from yesterday's quake is nowhere near that of 1906.

I was in my bedroom and took it all in with stride, really, having experienced many lesser quakes. I was trying to catch the things falling off the shelves, but as the quake continued and the violent shaking made cracking noises, I was sure my windows would crack and finally considered my own safety, and took shelter under my doorway. We have some cracked paint but that was all the real damage.

However part of an Oakland freeway collapsed, killing hundreds. I've been listening ever since to my battery-operated radio, as our electricity has been out since the quake. So I felt I've been pretty calm about it, but today my upper lip is sore and I realize I've been unconsciously biting my lip all night.

31   The 1989 Loma Prieta earthquake

That Dave Marshall called me again, and he just bought and moved into a condominium literally one block away from my apartment. NO LIE. He invited me over and I must admit I was very tempted to make up an excuse why I couldn't go. But I reasoned with myself: what am I avoiding? Why don't I want to see him? and I couldn't think of any good answers.

I took a couple of muffins with me ✦ we ate them, talked about the earthquake, AIDS, his move, etc. He's about 28 years old and very good looking in a boy-next-door kind of way. He reached over and put his hand on mine, so I put my arm around him and we began feeling each other up. He then invited me into the bedroom and we both stripped down. I am proud of myself for how relaxed I felt and how natural our exchange was for me.

He played with my dick and balls ✦ I played with his, and we both had orgasms. He let go a fine copious amount of cum, and he thought it was really YUCKY and shuddered dramatically when I scooped it up off his chest with my hand. Just like the man from Las Vegas, Dave commented on how large and tight my testicles are. I disagreed, saying they are as large as his are, but they look bigger because of my small dick and because they're tight in the scrotum and not loose and hanging down. Anyway he seemed to have a good time and I sure did. I even had a bare chest and he never said a word about my chest scars.

I'm sure we'll get together again and it sure is nice he's only one block away and he's very comfortable with the AIDS/safe sex business.

Good for you, Lou!

So here I am, forty-two minutes into 1990, and "thankful" is not really what I am feeling. What I am feeling is amazed, inspired, relieved, amused. Here I am, long after I ever imagined. I remember telling Sasha Alyson that I could not wait to be placed on his publication schedule, because there was no way I would be around in 1989. And now I've left 1989 behind! How funny! I feel such a sense of power and control over the future...that, a word I've hardly dared to utter these past three years.

The nurse at the Univ of Calif. Medical Center's Inhaled Pentamidine Clinic congratulated me on Thursday, telling me that I was among their first thirty patients at the clinic back in 1987.

I am quite proud of all my accomplishments this year. Top of the list, of course, is *From Female to Male: The Life of Jack Bee Garland*. It's done! and will be off the press in four short months. What an accomplishment, and I congratulate myself for living long enough to see the day I will hold the beautiful volume in my hand.

These past two days I read the entire text aloud, while proofreading it, and even now, five years after I began researching the story, it moves me deeply. I can almost feel Garland reaching forth from the netherworld and embracing me. Likewise I am incredibly proud of my educating success in finally making the gender professionals aware of the rightful existence of the female-to-gay male transsexual and the unequivocal acceptance of such condition at the Benjamin Symposium in September.

I have certainly left my mark on all who attended the Symposium and for all female-to-males who present themselves as gay men in gender clinics throughout the world. This past year also included my article about myself in *The Advocate*, the largest gay publication in the US, if not the world. It also showed the continued growth of FTM, my female-to-male support network, now reaching transsexuals and crossdressers across the globe.

But this year also brought sadness. My sweet older sister Kathleen died in a pitiful state, and her sad end haunts me, yet inspires me to make every hour of every day that I survive meaningful to me, alone.

I feel like a sneaking spy, somehow able to observe the daily surroundings I was supposed to have missed. Often I think to myself, "So if I had died like I was supposed to, this…THIS is what I would be missing!" And it makes every little event joyfully amusing to me. So this is what I am supposed to have missed…

Each day is a blessing and a special moment. How lucky I am to be Lou Sullivan!

For about 3 nights in a row last week I had very erotic dreams about T. He sure made an impression on my subconscious.

Last night I attended the 1990 ETVC[32] Cotillion for the 4th year in a row. As usual I escorted Sarah Shaker, a male-to-female who remembers me from ten or more years ago. (We were re-introduced several years ago and she remembers meeting me before either of us embarked on our change.) Attending this drag ball is a kind of yearly milestone for me. I so clearly remember the first one I went to, in December 1986. I felt so delirious and, walking home, I had to rest every block or so and wondered what the matter was with me—I'd only had four rum + cokes...I couldn't be THAT drunk! I found out what the matter was a few weeks later when I was diagnosed with Pneumocystis and AIDS.

So I take special pride in showing up each year at this event and letting my old friends in the male-to-female community know I'm still here. And each year I take Sarah. Last year, when I told her we have a standing date for this year's Cotillion, deep down I really didn't believe I'd still be alive. But, heck, here I am! I find that thoroughly amusing.

It's been a low-key laid-back couple of weeks. I've been sleeping a lot, reading, popping those pain pills (Percocets).

Last week I received a very fancy wall plaque from Rupert Raj, who is the female-to-male activist in Toronto, Ontario, Canada. It's inscribed as follows: "Presented to Lou Sullivan in appreciation for your dedication and outstanding contributions to the F-M TS community—Gender Worker Award 1990."

I have been relishing the extra attention and recognition I'm getting, I'm sure, because people feel sorry for me because I have this terminal

32   Educational Transvestite Chapter

illness, and they're being extra nice to me for that. Still, I do believe I've earned this special recognition, and I'm very proud of my work. I've put the plaque on my bedroom wall but will have to remember to put it away if I ever have someone in my room who "doesn't know" about my transsexual status.

Even though this lazy pace is relaxing, occasionally the thought crosses my mind that "this is how life comes to an end," that I'm simply letting myself slip into this lethargy and it is not all unpleasant.

I heard this remark on television tonight and thought it so appropriate, I wish I'd have thought of it myself back in the olden days, when Dad used to ask me, "What's it all about?" The answer:

You do the hokey-pokey
And you turn yourself around
That's what it's all about…

I've published the 11th issue of my *FTM* newsletter. Took it to T's print shop to make copies and he commented that I looked really bad. I guess I do, at 110 lbs.

Have had several dreams about Kathleen lately. I'm in the bedroom that we shared on Bluemound Rd. and wondering what to do with all her clothes and possessions.

Maryellen and I went to see Paul McCartney (yes! my Paulie) in concert in Berkeley. I felt very emotional during the concert—just remembering back to seeing him with the Beatles in 1964, and now again, here, 26 years later—and all that's happened in my life in the interim.

Although I haven't followed his career in the interim, somehow I see him as the beginning, the awakening of my sexual maturity. I remember so clearly sitting at Bluemound Rd. with Paul's picture in hand, staring and dreaming of him and thinking, "I wish I were you! I wish I was a boy like you!" I also kept thinking of Kathleen and how she would have LOVED to have been at this concert and I kind of dedicated my presence there to her. And like that first concert in 1964, I did quite a bit of crying during this show: "The Long and Winding Road," "Let It Be"…all bring my life full-circle.

This evening I am holding a copy of *From Female to Male: The Life of Jack Bee Garland* in my hand. It is finally a reality—a dream, a vision, now a permanent record, forever, for everyone to feel and learn. Though it is Garland's story, it tells about me…it explains my reality for future generations of female-to-gay males.

Last Friday Eric insisted we go out to dinner TONIGHT, as Sasha Alyson had sent him the money to take me out. Eric had such an urgency about the invitation that I wondered if…if he might have my book. All day I had this pent-up feeling. I wanted to cry, to release it, but what was it? What was there to cry about?? But when I met Eric at A Different Light and he handed me the package with my book inside, the floodgates opened and I cried it all out.

Friday I asked the people at Alyson how I could order a case of books, because I want to fill my bathtub up with copies and get in there and wallow around in them !!

Yesterday I gave a talk on transsexuality at a gay mental health center called 18th Street Services with Kate Bornstein, a MTF lesbian. She offered a second time to be on my list of home care volunteers for when I'm too out of it to take care of myself. That makes: Maryellen, Kathy, Denis, Cuca, Kate B, Kate/Steve Schaetyle, Michael Joseph, Bruce, Michael Sanderson, Eric Garber, Charlie Reitzner, Chris Conley,

Bill Walker...wow...that's quite a list! This is the first time I've really written it down.

A few weeks ago I had several "anticipation of death" dreams. They consisted of my entering a home or a large building or hotel. As I roamed about in the building, I'd enter empty rooms where before there had been furniture and people. I searched around, looking for the people, wondering where I left my coat, etc, but only found empty rooms and desertion.

I made it! I'm really 39 years old! I am so proud of myself and I feel like the luckiest guy. Last year I was sure it was my last birthday, and deep down, I think, now, that this birthday is my last. But who knows? I remember when I was diagnosed, I thought, "I know I'm going to die prematurely, but I'll be satisfied if I can just make it to 40." In my heart I knew that was asking too much, but today I think it's entirely possible. But 39 sounds so masculine!

There must be a hidden meaning to this one: both Maryellen and my roommate Jim gave me the SAME birthday card, purchased separately and in different cities. The card read: "The secret of staying young is to find an age you really like and stick with it." The odds are overwhelming—so this must be true!

Saturday Kathy and I went out with the Oceanic Society on a boat trip to the Farallon Islands, 25 miles off San Francisco. The islands are a nature preserve and I've always wanted to take this trip, especially because it is the breeding grounds for tufted puffins, funny little birds for which I've named my lovebirds.

Well, I guess I should've known better what with the continuously nauseous state of my stomach, but no lie—we were out on the boat maybe 10 minutes, just under the Golden Gate Bridge and onto the Pacific Ocean and I began heaving over the side of the boat. It was horrible. It was an all-day expedition and lasted over 8 hours, and I spent all but about 20 minutes of it below deck, sleeping on a bench. Poor me. I thought of what Jack Bean said about his trip on the army transport to Malina.[33] What misery. I'd puked on myself and couldn't rid myself of the smell for hours. Once we arrived at the Islands, I tried to gather myself and actually did see two puffins (one "horned," the other "tufted") through binoculars, that were swimming like ducks. But that was it. Poor Lou.

Sunday the 24th was the annual Gay Pride Parade down Market Street and I was smart this year, going directly to the "handicapped and special needs" section where it's all arranged for the comfort of people with AIDS and other disabilities. Nothing really new or different at this parade.

This is the 15th one I've attended—all since I moved to SF in 1975.

I got a big compliment yesterday. Kate Bornstein, the male-to-female lesbian who I hope I've mentioned before, phoned to say she was interviewing the world-famous comedienne Lily Tomlin for the gay press. Lily mentioned that she has incorporated several new male impersonations into her act and that she wasn't totally comfortable with her portrayals.

Kate suggested she read *Information for the Female-to-Male* by Lou Sullivan. Lily says, oh, yes, she's heard that name before…that's the female-to-male gay man…but she didn't know I wrote a book and was terribly excited about it and HAD to have a copy! WOW! I mean, where the hell would she have heard of me! Kate says, well, she's got her finger on the pulse of the gay community and would hear about anyone/anything unusual. (Lily's fairly well-known to be a lesbian!)

So this morning I met up with Kate and gave her one of my precious few copies left of my 2nd edition with a nice letter to Lily, a flier for

---

33 "I had had nothing to eat all day, having forgotten about such things in the excitement of getting away, and, growing so weak from seasickness that I could hardly stand, I longed for a place to lie down." - JBG, quoted by Lou on page 121 of *From Female to Male*

the Garland book and a copy of my *FTM* newsletter. Doesn't hurt to let the word out!

But, wow, I really AM famous!

Am sitting in bed, in probably the exact same spot where my bed was when I shared this room with Kathleen in the early 1960s. This house and this city still seem to me to be "home" although I would never want to live here again and nothing draws me here. It is boring and easy and like hiding away. San Francisco is not "home" but it amuses and keeps me in awe and I love living there.

This vacation so far has been relaxing and enjoyable. Doing a lot of eating and napping. Grandmother is the same as she was last year, in bed all the time, but walks to the bathroom and dining room on her own. Her mental faculties are sharp, her voice strong and her sense of humor quick. We still have that special love between us.

In the evenings I usually go off with Flame (John), who took me to Milwaukee's three hip bookstores. As soon as he walked into one of them, the owner announced, "Flame! We just received your brother's book today!" I piped up, "That's me!" They asked me to sign the three copies. But their shop was so disorganized that I feel, once the books are shelved, they'll never be seen again. The second bookstore was better organized but didn't have the book (Flame ✦ I plan to return there Monday to sell them). The third bookstore was closed by the time we got there.

It's true I get very tired very quickly and yearn to be horizontal every few hours. The weather has been cool and breezy and I'm thankful for that.

Saturday afternoon we (mom and I) hosted a Get-Together of female-to-males in the area. Eight female-to-males attended, once driving four hours one-way from Iowa. Mom was very into it, especially as one other FTM's mother came, too. As usual, conversation flowed easily. Everyone (including the moms) crowded into the den to watch the FTM video from New York, though I warned them it was about 25% heavy sex and could be seen as pornographic.

Had a terrible time last night with continuous dreams of T and me breaking up. I don't know what this is all about, as I can't believe I am subconsciously still upset about T. It's gotta have some kind of hidden meaning and I keep thinking if I figure out what it is, I'll be cured and it won't keep haunting me. This is the longest time in my adulthood I haven't been in an intimate relationship…I haven't been "in love." Maybe it's physical deprivity (not depravity) or lack of physical contact. Maybe it's because T and I split just when I got diagnosed, and in a way I feel like my life ended then…that I have no future anymore and am just biding my time until the next stage—whatever that may be. I guess in reality I'm mourning the end of my "future" not of our relationship.

This life-and-death matter just doesn't seem to have answers.

Some good happening: After 3 years of being afraid of the birdie breeding box, my 2 lovebirds have finally figured out what it's for and we now have 3 little birdie eggs in the nest. If all goes right we'll have baby birdies in 3 weeks but I'm not betting on it. I had a lot of dud nests with my zebra finches.

I must get back on my text entry of my diaries as this might be one of those things that I don't finish. And if I don't….

I weigh 88 lbs and can't remember ever feeling worse.

It's 28 minutes into the New Year and it sure is an unexpected surprise to be here. See 1991? No way! I've really been given a gift, and I have to be sure I use this extra time wisely.
I sit here thinking, well, I won't see 1992, but that's what I said in '91.

I phoned Ira Pauly's secretary to cancel my annual trip to his Reno class. I just can't imagine dealing with airports, luggage, etc, when I'm truly having a difficulty going up and down stairs. I don't know...these past few days my legs are so puffy and swollen, and it's creeping up my legs so my knees and thighs are pretty swollen and sore. I've been wearing the compression stockings and sitting in bed with my ankles propped up on pillows, but I don't know if it really helps.

I haven't been out of the apartment in days, but that's OK.

I am just feeling brutally assaulted right now...

This morning answered my front door to face Maryellen, who is sobbing, saying she just can't deal with my impending death and she's been crying all last night and it's so awful. She stayed a few hours while I tried to comfort her with logic and words of wisdom. Yes, I am sorry I am the one to make her so miserable.

Then, this afternoon, just a few minutes ago, I get a phone call from Kathy, also sobbing bitterly, saying she's going to have to break up with her boyfriend because she's so upset about my upcoming death and he is not being sympathetic or supportive to her and she can't handle it. She carried on crying until I was tempted to ask her if she was high on cocaine or what!

And I just feel like, "Hey, I don't need all this guilt that I am causing all this grief for everyone because I'm dying!" Who can *I* talk to about my difficulty of accepting my condition? Bruce just sits there, listening silently, thoroughly detached, so that I even wonder if he's even hearing what I said. And, of course, Nanc is totally useless. Even Charlie, during our last massage session, carried on about how hard it is for him to face my demise. Are these people all just completely selfish? Don't they realize it's ME who needs the support and comforting?

This has been a very traumatic day for me...

I haven't really been out of the apartment at all these past few days—just to get a Sunday newspaper. But this afternoon I had an appointment with Barbara, and for the first time took advantage of Shanti's Transportation Program in which they drive you free to and from your doctor. Well, I was waiting for them outside and tried to step up onto the landing, but couldn't boost myself because my legs are so weak and I sunk down onto my knees and couldn't get back up. I was so horrified and humiliated, I gathered super strength enough to pull myself up. Then the Shanti van came and you had to step up and boost yourself in about two feet high. No way! And this little girl driver had to grab my ass and shove it in. I just have no muscle left in my thighs.

I was quite upset and when I got to the clinic I could barely walk, but could only shuffle along in about 6 inch steps. I hurt so much I began to cry, inching along, and asked the front desk if I could use a wheelchair. They said I'd have to get a referral and fill out a requisition at the Administration Office, blah, blah, blah. I just said oh, forget it, and inch by inch, shuffled to Barbara's office, trying to stifle my tears. Once I got there I had myself a good hard cry. I can't walk anymore.

Kathy came (Barbara called her) to push me in a wheelchair to her car and get me home. Barbara said it's time for me to "let go" and arrange for daily help. I am so bloated and swollen, my abdomen looks like I am 7 months pregnant.

The San Francisco County In-Home Care assessor left a message that he'd be by next week to evaluate my needs, but Barbara said call them back and say I need help NOW—enough with the delays! I'm uncertain what a helper would do for a few hours each day: I guess do my dishes, dust my room…maybe cook once a day, help me get dressed if I'm going out. Maryellen already does my laundry and changes my bed linen during her regular Wednesday morning visits. My biggest need is for transportation, especially to social events I'd love to attend but can't get to, and it's kind of ridiculous to have a taxi take me six or eight blocks.

Details of my daily existence are falling into place naturally, as they usually seem to do. I've thought long and hard about how best to arrange for an "in-home health care assistant." Either the program requires more assistance hours than I need or can use, or it's costly. I have lots of hesitancy about "employing" my roommate Jim to do my chores (although he's already doing most of them, such as washing my dishes and doing household cleaning, taking out the garbage). But he can be so moody and sometimes when I ask him to do things, he seems resentful and "put out." Maybe if I were paying him for his services, that would change. I need to sit down and have an in-depth conversation with him…the more I think of it, he is really the ideal person to do these things. I cancelled my request with the county for their program, which required 2 hours of care.

So today I signed up for a Shanti Practical Support volunteer, who would come 3 times per week for about 2 hours a visit, although it's very flexible and one works it out on a mutually agreed-upon schedule. I have a few weeks before they would begin their service, so I can still cancel that if my arrangements with Jim work out. I can also utilize Denis now that his surgery is complete.

Today I also signed up for the free home delivery food service, where every afternoon they bring me a hot dinner and, once a week, a bag of miscellaneous groceries. I had discontinued because I was out-and-about and not necessarily here to accept their deliveries, but I'm home all the time now, it seems. Plus it's getting hard and harder for me to prepare a decent dinner.

Physically I seem to be on an upswing. My ankles and feet are still very swollen, but my legs are back down to normal size, as are my hands. I'm trying to spend as much time in bed as I can with my feet elevated on a big pillow and that does improve the circulation and reduce the swelling.

Consequently I'm doing a lot of reading, mostly on death and dying, by Elizabeth Kubler-Ross and Stephen Levine. I have learned something from them—most significantly when one said that one of the stages of the dying process is a slow withdrawal from family, friends, society—a turning into oneself and a detachment from the outside world. I've felt that for months now, where I'm irritated when friends call to see how

I am, etc. I just don't feel like socializing, and was feeling guilty about this attitude toward their sincerely good intentions. So knowing it's "normal" makes me able to understand myself.

I did attend a lecture sponsored by the Gay Historical Society last Saturday night, and my friend Eric Garber said I should be receiving my first royalty check from Alyson soon! But I did tell their newsletter editor that this issue was the last I would typeset because it's becoming too exhausting for me to do.

Sunday was our 16th Female-to-Male Get-Together during which I held a "book signing party" for our members of my 3rd edition of my *Information for the Female-to-Male* book. It was a smashing success and a big turn-out of FTMs. And I almost dropped my teeth when, who should appear, but Walter Bockting. So good to see him! I feel so proud of myself for keeping this group going and am more and more confident that it has a life of its own and will continue to happen even after I'm unable to coordinate it.

Still, things aren't all rosy. I'm having increased difficulty walking and climbing stairs. My pulse is quick (100) and I'm taking such shallow breaths that it feels like Pneumocystis lurking in my lungs. My weight is somewhere between 103-108, so that's not too bad.

That's all for now. Maryellen will be here tomorrow morn for her usual Wednesday morning 2-hour visit, then Charlie comes to give me a massage in the afternoon.

P.S. I've purposely been avoiding newspapers and the television to shield myself from all this media propaganda regarding this war in Saudi Arabia. I find the whole thing so repulsive. I don't care who's done what to whom—I just feel all this violence and killing is so disgusting, I don't need any details.

Great compliment: at my routine visit to my nurse practitioner on Friday, I'm laying on the examination table and she says, "Maybe while you're here, I should examine your prostate." I looked at her like, "What?" and then she realized what she said. I burst out laughing and she seemed to be apologizing saying, "Oh, I just naturally think of you as a guy…" I said, "Hey, don't apologize. That's one of the best compliments I've had in a long time."

When Charlie was close to the end of giving me my massage, he commented, "I don't think it's going to take long now," meaning my death. It was very out-of-the-blue, and Chaz is a very sensitive and perceptive man. It didn't disturb me as much as it made me wonder at his premonition. I guess seeing and touching my body so thoroughly every week has allowed him to watch its steady deterioration, and it seems to him I'm closing in on the end. I'm not afraid. I just feel I'll be stepping into a new plane of existence…one that, in all likelihood will be just as interesting, if not more so, than the one I'm in now.

This has been an especially lovely day and I want to record it in some detail. I overslept and was awakened by Kathy, who has been driving me to all my doctor appointments. I hurriedly dressed, but before we left, a delivery man brought a package from Nanc. It was a ring—undoubtedly the most brilliant and beautiful opal I've ever seen. Nanc had it set from an opal that had been part of my great-great-grandmother's wedding ring. It is so incredibly gorgeous that I can't even express it. It will bring such pleasure in my life every day!

It was exhausting and painfully slow getting around and Barbara & I had a long talk about my difficulty relinquishing control and trusting that someone will be there when I need help, that I must learn to give up control—that I must stop trying to control giving up control. I mean, I can't just lay back & believe that, when I can't get out of bed, there *will* be someone there to feed me or assist with my daily maintenance. It's so hard for me to ask for help. I've always been so damned independent.

Jim and I did have a business meeting and he's agreed to do duties for me and I'll pay him $10 per week, which is a LOT cheaper than all this County Social Services deal. I still need to organize my needs so it's understood what I expect from him. So far so good, but he isn't used to caring for others, so seems hesitant to hear my requests. I think eventually we'll both get more comfortable with the arrangement, though.

After the doc, we went to the post office to mail off the last of my *FTM* newsletters, and then to Castro Street for a burger and some ogling the wonderful gay men on the street. Then bought some chocolates and on to A Different Light bookstore where, to my surprise, the book was in their front display window (the Garland book). I need to get my 3rd-edition book in that store, too. (I'm having Jim drop off a few copies of my 3rd edition to the SF Public Library in the neighborhood). Anyway it was a very fruitful day and I think I'm learning to adjust to my new limitations.

It ain't easy,
I assure you…

I am reading Elizabeth Kubler-Ross' *AIDS: The Ultimate Challenge* and just finished the lengthy, detailed description of the death of Peter in chapter 9. What an ordeal! I find it too hard to believe that someone could love me enough to go through that with me…that my dying could have such a significance to someone else. But I have to recall my own feelings when dad and Kathleen were so disabled and needed our love and whatever help we could give. I'd've done anything to ease their transition, and so I must believe that those who love me (Maryellen, Kathy, mom) will be there for me, too.

Saturday night Maryellen came over and we had an intimate relaxing visit. She bustled around, changing my bed, arranging fresh flowers she brought from her garden, lit some candles and we sat on the bed, smoked some reefer and talked. I felt totally loved. She told me that, on his own initiative, out of the blue (they weren't even talking about me), Rusty told her that when I get to the point where I need 24-hour care, that I should come to live with them. That, with this new room addition on their house, I'll have a private room there. I am so thankful, just blown away, by this offer. My worst fears are gone…there will be someone there for me. Maryellen reminded me that she had made this offer many times before, and I had rejected the idea, but I really don't recall that, and I'm now so relieved to know they will take me in. Of course the idea has its drawbacks, what with the three little kids in their house, but Maryellen feels the experience will be a good one for them, to see a family loving and caring for each other in this most crucial of life's experiences. I hope it won't be a long trial, but we must do it as it comes to us. I didn't realize Rusty cared for me so much.

Then, to actualize his sentiments, Rusty came over on Sunday and utilized his carpentry skills to make my daily actions easier. My old-fashioned bed was so high off the ground that I needed a step-stool to get in/out of bed. So he removed the box spring and replaced it with a board, lowering the mattress some 7 inches, eliminating the need for the stool, so I can get in and out of the bed easily.

Next he affixed a hand rail next to the toilet because I was having such difficulty trying to boost myself up off the toilet. My leg muscles are so deteriorated that I can no longer "boost" myself up anywhere!

Well, these two improvements really help me out. Rusty performed them with such care, I am astonished. I know my family ✦ friends are sincerely there for me. I'm really lucky. And my fears are leaving me... that is, my fears of being needy.

A very productive day. I wasn't sure I'd be able to get through it, especially after I fell down while trying to get up the 7-8 stairs in our entrance way. But Charlie drove me to A Different Light bookstore, where I showed the manager my 3rd edition and he eagerly took the ordering information and said he'd send for a supply today.

Next we went to the local branch of the SF Public Library which houses the only special gay/lesbian collection in a library in the world. I donated 2 copies of my 3rd edition and they were glad to get them. So those two acts were high on my "To Do" list, and they're done! I checked some books out on AIDS and dying, too, so I have some reading material while I'm sitting around the apartment.

Unfortunately I did have one bad experience today. While Charlie was giving me my massage, he said he was concerned about touching some dry skin patches and some marks I have on my left, worried he'd catch AIDS from me and then he'd be ejected from his new spiritual group, since their guru is capable of catching it simply by looking at someone with it!

That is so ridiculous, to begin with, but for Charlie to even consider it makes me feel very sad and I wonder how much longer he'll stick with me. Pisses me off that this is the ONLY disease to elicit such prejudice and discrimination, and I'm sure most of it is pure homophobia. Screw all these self-righteous straight people!

Something significant happened to me this morning and I'm still not sure what it was. Awoke at 8:45 am, felt as usual, went back to sleep. At 9:30, Maryellen came over and I was soaked through with sweat and truly "delirious," the only word I can think that described what I felt. I was floating away. Felt I was no longer grounded in this world. I couldn't bring myself back to earth and I really thought, hey, this is it...I'm dying.

Maryellen immediately realized it and called Barbara, telling her I was "weird." Because I didn't want to go into the hospital, they immediately initiated arrangements to get me hospice care. I simply nodded out, seemingly in a dream, unable to move. It was a godsend the way Maryellen, Kathy, and Barbara cared for me. My temperature was 93°. An assessor from Hospice by the Bay came over and signed me up. It sounds like a good deal, very flexible so that whatever and whenever I need ANYTHING I call them and they take care of it. I just laid here all day and gradually collected my brain.

Beginning Tuesday someone will come here shortly after I wake up to get me going for the day—make me a breakfast, help me get dressed, do whatever else I need, spending about 2 hours here. They'll also get me a chair for the shower and a seat to raise the toilet seat so I can get off it easier. Anyway we'll see how it all works out. Jim + Maryellen will continue doing what they have been doing.

Tonight I feel a lot like I have been lately—back to earth. I'm incredibly weak, my feet and legs still very swollen, I can't eat much substantial, my mouth is very dry. I don't know if this is the beginning of the end, or just another bad phase, but it does seem to have been a steady decline since getting out of the hospital in early October. I feel peaceful and accepting and reassured there'll be someone there for me.

Today they delivered a "tub transfer chair" so I can sit in the shower plus a commode for my bedroom (for when I can't make it to the regular bathroom), plus a raised toilet seat for the regular toilet so I can get on/off it easier. I felt pretty perky during the first half of the day, but around 5 pm I was feeding the birds and the task just drained me. My heart was pounding so fast and hard, I couldn't catch my breath and I felt like I need an oxygen tank. Since Barbara's on vacation and that hospice lady on Friday said they can get me anything any time, I called them. Within 45 min she was here. Said my vital signs indicate that my symptoms are the result of very low blood pressure and that oxygen wouldn't help…that I just need to be less active. Nonetheless I'm glad I contacted her because she hadn't arranged for the in-home attendant to come tomorrow and I was expecting them to. So she phoned right then ⁊ there, and someone'll be contacting me tomorrow.

Changes are occurring daily, so quickly that I can hardly keep up with developing adaptations to the obstacles that these deteriorations present in my body. Hospice by the Bay is sending a "personal care attendant" from 11 am to 12:30 pm, who mainly just cooks a breakfast for me. This past Tuesday, one helped me take a shower before Charlie came to give me a massage. He gives me one on Tuesdays and Fridays. Then they get me comfortable in the bed and leave.

Barbara Newlin came to my bedside and acted as though this is really the end. "What are you going to do if you get Pneumocystis again?" she asked. "Go to the hospital?"…"I don't think you want to do that…" She discouraged me from taking anymore aerosol pentamidine treatments, saying at this point they don't help, but I disagree. So they're arranging to come to my place to do the treatments here. I have a fungal rash on my torso and legs and need to have someone apply an antifungal ointment. Denis has helped me with that.

My vital signs are very low—blood pressure 84/52, pulse 68, temperature over the last two weeks 94°. Barbara says my systems are just shutting down. I'm icy cold all the time and am wearing a knit cap, scarf, and gloves in the house. My legs and especially my feet and ankles are very swollen and painful. I'm taking a diuretic that makes me piss often and have begun using a commode in my bedroom because it's difficult to walk down to the bathroom so frequently.

On Sunday Denis and another FTM named Jamie Green came over to discuss my transferring more of the duties of the FTM meetings and newsletter, where I kept the paperwork, etc. I feel much relieved that it'll be in good hands and survive. Then today Bill Walker from the Gay Historical Society came over and we discussed what all I'm bequeathing to them and he promised all my *FTM* donations will be kept together under my name. I'm really glad of that, as this material can so easily get mixed in with all the general transsexual/transvestite and male-to-female and be lost in their volume. So I'm feeling very at peace and re-assured that my work will be preserved. Walker also took on the task of coordinating my friends to, say, come by to assist me in the evenings once a week or so...

I've been scheduled to speak on a panel at the gay writers' conference *Out/Write* on writing as a sexual minority (TV/TS) within a sexual minority (homosexual) this coming Sunday, but I've begged off. It'll just be very hard to get there on Sunday morning (my worst time of the day), plus I haven't anything prepared. But Walker's going to assist me in the wheelchair to be able to attend the keynote address Friday night given by one of my favorite authors, John Rechy. Kathy Steininger took me to the grocery store and I pushed myself up and down every aisle in the chair...it was FUN!

I'm sure there's a lot more I should be writing here, but I'm gonna sign off here now.[34]

---

34   Last entry dated 2/27/91

Glossary

A DIFFERENT LIGHT   Chain of four LGBT bookstores in Los Angeles, New York, San Francisco, and Toronto, named after a gay science fiction novel by Bay Area author Elizabeth Lynn. The first location, in the Silver Lake neighborhood of Los Angeles, was opened in 1979 by George Leigh and Norman Laurila. The Castro location was a community center and gathering place that organized the first two Outwrite conferences and hosted SF Act Up's meetings in its backyard. When it closed in 2011, it was the last LGBT-specific bookstore in San Francisco.

ACADEMY, THE   1980s San Francisco gay sex club. The 5H club, one of San Francisco's two most popular gay jerk-off clubs, met there weekly.

ALYSON BOOKS   Publisher that specializes in LGBTQ books and was for many years the largest independent queer publisher. It was founded as "Alyson Publications" by Sasha Alyson in Boston in 1980, in order to publish Alyson Wonderland, a line of LGBTQ-themed children's books. Alyson was known in its early years for community work including a pen pal service for gay and lesbian teens.

ARMSTRONG, JOHN   Organizer of F2M, an FTM peer-support group that was based in Tenafly, New Jersey. Sullivan received their first "Open Letter," mailed in February 1989. "Even though we want to maintain a low profile, we should not isolate ourselves from our fellow F.M.T/Ss."

AVANT GARDE, THE   An East Milwaukee bar that catered to beatniks and lovers of roots, blues, and folk music. Open from 1962–68, it helped catalyze the local arts scene. Despite rumors to the contrary, a young Bob Dylan never played there.

BENJAMIN, HARRY   A German-American sexologist and the first doctor known to supportively treat transgender patients (beginning in 1948). Publicity surrounding his patient Christine Jorgensen first brought transsexuality to widespread attention. Benjamin maintained lifelong friendships with many patients. He died in 1986 at the age of 101.

BÉRUBÉ, ALLAN   Gay historian who lived in San Francisco. Sullivan learned about Jack Bee Garland from Bérubé's public presentations on the history of FTM crossdressers in San Francisco.

BOCKTING, WALTER   Psychologist and sexuality researcher who works with HIV+ trans people. Directed transgender health services at the Program in Human Sexuality at the University of Minnesota for 20 years. President of World Professional Association for Transgender Health from 2009–11.

BORNSTEIN, KATE   Author, playwright, performance artist, and gender theorist. Bornstein's first book *Gender Outlaw: On Men, Women and the Rest of Us*, first published in 1994, was pathbreaking in reimagining gender systems to be more inclusive of non-binary identities.

BROWNSTEIN, MICHAEL   Bay Area-based surgeon who worked with trans communities for 35 years and performed Sullivan's bottom surgeries. Founded Brownstein & Crane, a surgery clinic that still serves trans people today.

BUSSIAN, RICHARD   Member of The Velvet Whip, known by the band as "The Richard." Whip founder Dan Ball described Bussian as "an experience unto himself." He most embodied the mischevious, countercultural spirit of the band, dancing, playing the tambourine, and wielding the (actual) whip during live shows.

BUZZBY'S   A gay club on Polk Street that was the neighborhood spot for disco and dancing, and one of the first clubs to launch the gay disco movement in San Francisco.

CAPOR, CLAIRE   Therapist who Sullivan saw in the Bay Area while he was considering de-transition. Capor is one of the founders of the Psychotherapy Institute in Berkeley.

CENTER FOR SPECIAL PROBLEMS   Mental health agency that was part of the San Francisco Department of Public Health. Included the Gender Identity Treatment Services program for trans mental health care.

CLUB BATHS   A chain of bathhouses in the United States and Canada that were open from the 1960s–90s. The Toronto location was part of the four-bathhouse raid by Toronto police called Operation Soap on February 5, 1981.

DAIN, STEVE   Dain was fired from his teaching position at Emeryville High School for transitioning in 1976. After a legal battle that made the front page of The New York Times, Dain left teaching to counsel other trans people in the Bay Area and beyond. A pilgrimage to visit Dain was an important step in transition for many, including Sullivan. Dain was the first trans man with whom Sullivan had sustained contact.

FALCES, EDWARD   San Francisco-based plastic and reconstructive surgeon who performed Sullivan's double mastectomy.

FARLEY, ELIZABETH   Born in the early 1940s, Farley lived as a woman for decades without medically transitioning. She was introduced to Sullivan by Eldon Murray in 1973. Though they met only briefly, she made a lasting impression as one of the first people to open Sullivan's eyes to the possibilities of trans life. Nicknamed Betty.

FRASER, LIN   Prominent San Francisco psychotherapist specializing in gender dysphoria, as well as a reference for Sullivan's attempts to obtain gender confirmation surgery. Was president of The WPATH from 2011–13. Dr. Fraser was involved in writing the current Standards of Care for trans patients.

FTM INTERNATIONAL   Longest-running and largest
organization serving the female-to-male trans community, founded
by Sullivan (as the peer support group "FTM") in the Bay Area in
1986. The quarterly newsletter Sullivan launched for the group in
1987 still reaches subscribers all over the world.

FULMER, GEORGE   San Francisco-based endocrinologist who
prescribed Sullivan testosterone.

GARLAND, JACK BEE   Author and nurse who lived as a man,
pursuing social and possibly sexual relationships with other men, in
San Francisco's Tenderloin District at the turn of the 20th Century.
Garland became a minor celebrity in California and was eventually
allowed to crossdress: contemporary newspapers called him "the
trousered enigma." Garland has been shared as an icon by many,
including butch lesbians and gay trans men. Sullivan's biography of
Garland, *From Female To Male: The Life of Jack Bee Garland* was his
most serious endeavor as a queer historian.

GATEWAY, THE   Monthly newsletter for Golden Gate Girls/Guys.
From 1979-80, Sullivan edited *The Gateway*. He professionalized
the design of the newsletter and shifted the content to include
practical tips on trans life and passing that men could receive, even
if they could not attend meetings.

GAY PEOPLES UNION   Group founded at University of
Wisconsin-Milwaukee in 1970. The group quickly split in two, with
the GPU being the moderate wing in contrast to the more radical
Gay Liberation Organization. By 1971, the GPU had left university
affiliation to do important work in the Milwaukee gay community,
founding its first LGBTQ+ community center, health clinic, and
Pride festivities. Sullivan got involved with GPU while working for
UWM's Slavic Languages Department and wrote for their monthly
magazine, *GPU News*.

GIRAFFE, THE   Gay bar on Polk Street. Opened in 1977, when
Polk Street was nicknamed "Polk Strasse" or "Polk Gulch" and
was home to more than 70 gay bars, and closed in 2011, when it

was down to 3. The Giraffe featured pinball machines and was later known as "The Giraffe Video Lounge." As this book goes to press, the Hemlock Tavern, former site of The Giraffe, is about to be demolished to make way for condos.

GOLD COAST   Prominent Chicago leather and BDSM bar that was open from the early 1960s–1987. Opened by Chuck Renslow, who began the International Mr. Leather Contest and the Leather Archives & Museum in Rogers Park, as well as dozens of businesses serving Chicago's gay community.

GOLDEN GATE GIRLS/GUYS   Bay Area social and educational transgender organization, abbreviated "GGG/G". One of the first social groups for trans people that served men as well as women; Sullivan led the charge to have "Guys" added to the group name.

GREEN, JAMISON   Trans-rights leader, educator, and author. Green worked to pass San Francisco's Transgender Protection Ordinance in the early 90s. He helped take over FTM after Sullivan got sick, running the group from 1991–99. His book *Becoming a Visible Man* combines his autobiography with broader advocacy for trans men. President of WPATH from 2013–15.

HARRY BENJAMIN GENDER DYSPHORIA ASSOCIATION SYMPOSIUM   Conference organized by WPATH every two years. Now known as International Symposia, it has been ongoing since 1969.

HARRY BENJAMIN INTERNATIONAL GENDER DYSPHORIA ASSOCIATION   Professional organization founded in 1979 that promotes evidence-based care, education, research, advocacy, public policy, and respect in transgender health. Now known as World Professional Association for Transgender Health (WPATH). HBIGDA was initially funded, as were many early trans organizations and clinics, by a wealthy trans man, Reed Erickson, a patient of Benjamin's.

HESS, ALYN   Early Milwaukee gay activist (b. 1939) whose ground-breaking work in the GPU built community infrastructure such as the GPU STD clinic and GPU Hotline. He was one of the earliest to be an open, out voice for the gay community in Wisconsin when to do so was dangerous. Hess hosted one of the earliest gay radio shows, the weekly *Gay Perspectives*. Later, he organized for the Milwaukee AIDS Project and helped pass Milwaukee's Gay Rights Ordinance. Hess was active intersectionally, as one of the first men to join the National Organization for Women and a national board member of the organization Black and White Men Together (BWMT).

HOLLANDER, HARRY   Infectious disease physician at UCSF. Currently head of the Internal Medicine Residency program; formerly served as medical director of the UCSF HIV clinic.

I-BEAM, THE   San Francisco gay disco that opened in the Haight District in 1977. At that time, the Haight was considered the same district as SF's gay neighborhood, the Castro, and was also a vital part of the city's gay life. The I-Beam had an active bathroom scene and male go-go dancers as late as 1988. It eventually became an important punk and new wave venue and hosted an early weekly hip-hop night. The I-Beam was, in all incarnations, welcoming to all and musically diverse, hosting bands from the Buzzcocks to Sylvester to Duran Duran. It closed in 1994.

INSTITUTE FOR THE ADVANCED STUDY OF HUMAN SEXUALITY   An unaccredited, for-profit, degree-granting institution and resource center in the field of sexology located in San Francisco. Founded in 1976, the Institute has one of the largest collections of sexological and erotic materials in the world, has worked on safe-sex materials and inclusive sexual education, and boasts graduates such as Annie Sprinkle. The Institute has also been critiqued for its lack of accreditation and for-profit orientation, and has been nicknamed "Fuck U" by critics due to its unorthodox course offerings.

JANUS INFORMATION FACILITY, THE   Gender dysphoria support and referral service in San Francisco. Later called J2CP

Information Services. Created resources such as the booklet *Information for the Family of the Transexual and of Children with Gender Identity Disturbances*, published in 1977.

JUNEAU PARK   One of Milwaukee's oldest parks, it became known as a major gay cruising spot in the 1960s. In response, Milwaukee began policing the park heavily. Up to 24 undercover officers patrolled nightly, resulting in many arrests and the death of one man, Elroy Schulz, who was viciously beaten by police. Eventually, pressure to reduce policing costs and LGBTQ activism helped the gay community assert its claim to the park. It hosted the city's "Gay In" in 1973 and Pride was held there from 1991-1994.

KANE, ARI   A crossdresser, activist, and educator. One of the founders of the Fantasia Fair, a week-long conference in Provincetown, MA, that began in 1975 as a support for crossdressers and medical professionals serving the transsexual community. Fantasia Fair now welcomes trans and gender-questioning people.

LAUB, DONALD   Plastic and reconstructive surgeon who made one of the first academic investigations into treating gender dysphoria with surgery and was an innovator in gender-confirmation surgery technique. First director of Stanford University Gender Dysphoria Program. President of HBIGDA from 1981–1983.

LEIBMAN, JACK   Psychologist who worked at the Center for Special Problems. Briefly treated Sullivan while he was in the process of accessing hormones.

MARSHALL, ELIZABETH   Member of the GPU who later worked as a librarian in Milwaukee. Marshall and Sullivan met in 1970 at University of Wisconsin-Milwaukee. They remained friends on and off throughout their lives. Nicknamed Liz.

MILWAUKEE FOURTEEN, THE   Fourteen religiously-inspired peace activists, most associated with the Catholic Worker movement, who burned (with homemade napalm) 10,000 draft files they took from the Milwaukee Selective Service Office to protest the Vietnam War on September 14, 1968. The action shut down conscription in Milwaukee for several months and inspired an even larger action in Chicago, in which 40,000 draft records were burned. All members of the Milwaukee Fourteen served at least a year in prison.

MOBY DICK   Gay bar in San Francisco's Castro district, founded in 1977 by "pantyhose heir" Victor Swedosh as both a bar and a space for gay artists. Moby Dick had its own record imprint in the early 80s that had some success as a gay disco label in California. Still open as a neighborhood bar.

MONEY, JOHN   Psychologist and sexologist who researched gender-role fluidity and the biology of gender. He introduced the terms "gender identity," "gender role," and "sexual orientation," and co-established the Johns Hopkins Gender Identity Clinic (the first in the U.S.) in 1966. Money is today most associated with the controversy over his beliefs about the social construction of gender, which led him to attempt and champion the ultimately unsuccessful gender reassignment of his patient David Reimer from male to female in infancy, after a botched circumcision left Reimer without a penis.

MORRIS, JAN   Celebrated Welsh historian, journalist, travel writer, and author of more than 40 books. Morris detailed her transition in her autobiographal title, *Conundrum* (1974).

MR. BIRD   Pet bird and naming convention. After the first Mr. Bird flew away, Sullivan continued to name his birds Mr. Bird.

MURRAY, ELDON   Eldon Murray was a prominent activist in the Milwaukee LGBTQ community. In addition to his work with the GPU and the Milwaukee AIDS Project, Murray founded SAGE/Milwaukee, the first organization in Wisconsin serving the needs of older queer people through community building and counseling services. In an interview, he mentions that he read that same-sex feelings were normal in adolescence and were outgrown; he then says, "At 17, I decided I didn't want to outgrow homosexuality."

NAIAD PRESS   One of the first publishers dedicated to lesbian literature. Founded by Barbara Grier and Donna McBride, it was the largest lesbian/feminist publisher in the world until it shuttered in 2002. Naiad brought Gertrude Stein back into print and he was first to publish Sarah Schulman. Their early covers were designed by revolutionary lesbian artist Tee Corrine. The Naiad Press Collection resides at the James C. Hormel Gay and Lesbian Center at the SF Public Library.

NATIONAL SEX FORUM, THE   Created by the Institute for Advanced Study of Human Sexuality to develop research methodologies and professional standards around the study of human sexuality.

NOB HILL THEATRE, THE   A San Francisco strip club and theater for gay porn and performance from 1968–2018, with the motto, "Touch Our Junk." The space offered a theater, 20 video booths, a maze area, and private dance and pole-dance rooms. According to the *San Francisco Chronicle*, the front desk sold Tic Tacs, lube, and poppers (discreetly, as "tape head cleaner").

PACIFIC CENTER FOR HUMAN GROWTH, THE   Community center in Berkeley, founded in 1973, offering mental health and wellness services to diverse queer communities, including youth and seniors, as well as training for intern therapists. Sullivan attended their trans-specific peer support groups in the late '70s. Oldest LGBTQ center in the Bay Area and 3rd oldest in the United States.

PALMS, THE   Gay bar on Polk Street that hosted new wave, funk and punk performances in the 1970s. The Palms was one of three gay businesses at the intersection of Polk and Pine.

PAULY, IRA B.   Psychiatrist who spent his career working on trans issues and was supportive of gender-confirming surgery as early as 1961, which was considered a fringe position at the time. He was mentored by and collaborated with Harry Benjamin. In 1965, Pauly authored the first academic study of trans patients. It supported positive outcomes for gender-confirming surgery. He had difficulty publishing it, but received over 1,000 reprint requests from doctors looking for better treatment options for their trans patients. President of HBIGDA from 1985–87. Pauly conducted yearly interviews with Sullivan from 1989–91. A UCLA All-American football player, Pauly was inducted into the Southern California Jewish Sports Hall of Fame.

PIT, THE   South of Market bar, previously known as Cocktails, that was located at 201 N. 9th St. The location is now known as AsiaSF, a restaurant, cabaret, and nightclub that hosts nightly performances by trans women.

POMEROY, WARDELL   American sexologist who began as an interviewer for Alfred C. Kinsey's sex study work as a master's student and became one of Kinsey's closest collaborators and co-author. Pomeroy's two books on sexuality for teens and their families, *Boys and Sex* and *Girls and Sex*, are on the American Library Association's list of most frequently banned books. Sullivan met Pomeroy while he was Director of the National Sex Forum.

PROJECT OPEN HAND   Non-profit organization that provides nutritious meals and groceries to Bay Area seniors and residents with critical illness; over twenty-five hundred meals and two hundred bags of groceries per day. The organization was founded by Ruth Brinker, a retired food-service worker in San Francisco, in 1985. She was responding to the AIDS crisis and to seeing a friend of hers suffering from AIDS-related malnutrition. At first, she hand-prepared and delivered meals to 7 of her neighbors living with HIV.

RAJ, RUPERT   Toronto trans activist. Publisher of *Metamorphosis*, a journal for trans men that ran from 1982–1986, to which Sullivan regularly contributed. Raj was an important source of advice and friendship for Sullivan as he founded his own group, FTM.

RIVER QUEEN, THE   Legendary Milwaukee gay bar open from early 1970s–1980 with a "Storyville bordello theme." Abbreviated "RQ," it was part of a gay nightlife circuit fondly called "the Fruit Loop." Liberace, originally from Milwaukee, stopped by when he was in town, as did Milton Berle and Carol Channing. It was closed by a police-corruption scandal that disclosed the payoffs, gifts, and free drinks the owner had been doling out to officers to avoid police harassment.

RUBENSTEIN, MAGGI   Bisexual activist and sexologist sometimes called "the Godmother of Sex Ed" because of her founding roles in SF institutions such as the Glide Memorial Church's National Sex Forum, the San Francisco Sex Information Hotline, and the Institute for the Advanced Study of Human Sexuality. She was also a founder of COYOTE, a sex workers' rights organization, and the San Francisco Bisexual Center that ran programming from 1973–1984. Rubenstein continues to be a practicing sex therapist.

SAN FRANCISCO EAGLE, THE   Gay bar in San Francisco's South of Market neighborhood that caters to the bear and leather communities, which has been open for over 35 years. According to the *San Francisco Chronicle*, "The Sisters of Perpetual Indulgence blessed [the Eagle] as a 'hallowed queer space,' ashes of some sisters and other AIDS victims were scattered on the back patio, and $50 million for AIDS charities has been raised there."

SHANTI PROJECT, THE   This non-profit organization, founded in 1974 by Charles Garfield in San Francisco, works to improve the health, quality of life, and well-being of people with terminal, life-threatening or disabling illnesses or conditions. The Shanti Project offers a range of emotional and practical services to clients, from navigating medical systems, to in-home care, to time with peer support volunteers. The organization's peer support model, which includes mutual respect, positive regard, empowerment of the client, genuineness, acceptance of differences, and empathy, has been a model for organizations throughout the country.

STANFORD UNIVERSITY GENDER DYSPHORIA
PROGRAM, THE   Full-service transgender health center
that opened in 1968 under the auspices of Stanford University.
The program provided help with legal name changes, counseling,
hormone therapy, and surgical care. The program has been critiqued
for its emphasis (particulary in the '60s and '70s) on passing and
its role in medical gatekeeping for trans care. Donald Laub was
the first director. It left the university in the '80s, when most
university-based programs closed either due to the political climate
or the departure of their founders for private practice. Sometimes
abbreviated "Stanford Dysphoria Program."

STEININGER, CHEYNEY   Nephew.

STEININGER, KATHY   Close friend of the Sullivan family and
lifelong friend of Lou Sullivan's. Mother of Cheyney.

SULLIVAN, BRIDGET THERESE   Younger sister, (b. 1953).

SULLIVAN, JOHN EUGENE, JR.   Older brother, (b. 1949).
Nicknamed Johnney & Flame.

SULLIVAN, JOHN EUGENE, SR.   Father. Nicknamed Jack.
Owned a small hauling and moving company.

SULLIVAN, KATHLEEN MARIE   Oldest sibling, (b. 1948).

SULLIVAN, MARYELLEN   Younger sister, (b. 1955).

SULLIVAN, NANCY LOUISE   Mother. Family manager and sales
clerk in a stationary store.

SULLIVAN, PATRICK RORY   Youngest sibling, (b. 1957).

SUTTER'S MILL   Bar in San Francisco's Financial District that
catered to gay businessmen. Open from 1965–1995. The fact that it
moved five times in 30 years reflects the lease problems that plagued
early gay bars. According to author Ron Williams, it maintained

customer loyalty due to the large number of "ticker tape queens" working in the Financial District, who visited during lunch and cocktail hours.

TIPSIES   Sullivan used the naming convention [first name] + Tipsy for all of his cats (e.g. Mama Tipsy). Abbreviated as "tips" or "tipsies."

VAN MAASDAM, JUDY   Bay Area therapist who specializes in trans care. Coordinated the Gender Dysphoria Program in Palo Alto for 30 years, including the years that it was a part of Stanford University, and corresponded with Sullivan in 1979, when he sought to enter the program.

VELVET WHIP, THE   Improvisational, anarchic Milwaukee rock band with a weekly Thursday night slot at The Avant Garde in the second half of the '60s. Founded by Dan Ball and Henry Steinfort, classically trained musicians who turned to rock. The band's name came from their original singer, a gay man who stayed with the band for only 3 weeks; he suggested the name The Lavender Whip, which the other members loved but could not remember. The band dissolved with the closure of The Avant Garde.

WALKER, PAUL A.   Social psychologist and founding president of HBIGDA, the Harry Benjamin International Gender Dysphoria Association (now known as WPATH). He did research with John Money at the Johns Hopkins Clinic before opening his private practice in the Castro, centered on trans patients. A gay man himself, he also served as director of the Janus Information Facility.

WRECK ROOM, THE   Milwaukee's first cowboy / Levi-leather gay bar. It was open from 1972 until the mid-1990s. Starting in 1973, it was clubhouse to the Silver Star Motorcycle / Leather Social Club. The front end of a T-bird emerged from a wall in a back room of the bar, and in the front was a wooden cart whose yoke was carved to resemble an erect penis. The front of the bar was casual and macho; the back was known for cruising and after-hours sex parties.

Significant Works by Lou Sullivan

"A Transvestite Answers a Feminist." *Gay Peoples Union News*, August 1973.

"Looking Towards Transvestite Liberation." *Gay Peoples Union News*, February/March 1974.

The Gateway, monthly newsletter of Golden Gate Girls/Guys, August 1979–September 1980.

Information for the Female-to-Male Crossdresser and Transsexual, 1st edition, Janus Information Facility, 1980; 2nd edition, self published, 1985; 3rd edition, Ingersoll Press, 1990.

"Sullivan's Travels." *The Advocate*, June 6, 1989.

From Female To Male: The Life of Jack Bee Garland. Alyson Press, 1990.

FTM. Monthly newsletter of FTM, September 1987–February 1991.

Further Reading

Carter, Julian, "Embracing Transition, or Dancing in the Folds of Time," in *The Transgender Studies Reader 2*, edited by Aren Z. Aizura and Susan Stryker. Routledge, 2012.

Feinberg, Leslie. *Transgender Warriors: Making History from Joan of Arc to Dennis Rodman*. Beacon Press, 1997.

Rodemeyer, Lanei M. *Lou Sullivan Diaries (1970–1980) and Theories of Sexual Embodiment: Making Sense of Sensing*. Springer, 2017.

Smith, Brice D. *Lou Sullivan: Daring To Be a Man Among Men*. Transgress Press, 2017.

Stryker, Susan. "Portrait of a Transfag Drag Hag as a Young Man: The Activist Career of Louis G. Sullivan," in *Reclaiming Gender: Transsexual Grammars at the Fin de Siècle*, edited by Kate More and Stephen Whittle. Cassell, 1999.

VINTAGE CLASSICS

Vintage launched in the United Kingdom in 1990, and was originally the paperback home for the Random House Group's literary authors. Now, Vintage is comprised of some of London's oldest and most prestigious literary houses, including Chatto & Windus (1855), Hogarth (1917), Jonathan Cape (1921) and Secker & Warburg (1935), alongside the newer or relaunched hardback and paperback imprints: The Bodley Head, Harvill Secker, Yellow Jersey, Square Peg, Vintage Paperbacks and Vintage Classics.

From Angela Carter, Graham Greene and Aldous Huxley to Toni Morrison, Haruki Murakami and Virginia Woolf, Vintage Classics is renowned for publishing some of the greatest writers and thinkers from around the world and across the ages – all complemented by our beautiful, stylish approach to design. Vintage Classics' authors have won many of the world's most revered literary prizes, including the Nobel, the Man Booker, the Prix Goncourt and the Pulitzer, and through their writing they continue to capture imaginations, inspire new perspectives and incite curiosity.

In 2007 Vintage Classics introduced its distinctive red spine design, and in 2012 Vintage Children's Classics was launched to include the much-loved authors of our childhood. Random House joined forces with the Penguin Group in 2013 to become Penguin Random House, making it the largest trade publisher in the United Kingdom.

@vintagebooks

penguin.co.uk/vintage-classics